William Miller

The Balkans

Roumania, Bulgaria, Servia, and Montenegro

William Miller

The Balkans
Roumania, Bulgaria, Servia, and Montenegro

ISBN/EAN: 9783337239848

Printed in Europe, USA, Canada, Australia, Japan

Cover: Foto ©ninafisch / pixelio.de

More available books at **www.hansebooks.com**

NICHOLAS I.
PRINCE OF MONTENEGRO.

The Story of the Nations

THE BALKANS

ROUMANIA, BULGARIA, SERVIA AND MONTENEGRO

BY

WILLIAM MILLER, M.A. (OXON.)
OF THE INNER TEMPLE, BARRISTER-AT-LAW

NEW YORK
G. P. PUTNAM'S SONS
LONDON : T. FISHER UNWIN
1896

The Knickerbocker Press, New York

PREFACE.

THIS is the first attempt which has been made to present English readers with a concise account of the history of the four Balkan States. Yet the Balkan Peninsula has been in modern times what the Low Countries were in the Middle Ages—the cockpit of Europe. It is there that the eternal Eastern question has its origin; it is there too that the West and the East, the Cross and the Crescent, meet. But it is impossible to understand the great problems, which still await solution in South-eastern Europe and are once more pressing themselves upon the attention of all thoughtful men, without some knowledge of Balkan history. The mutual jealousies of Bulgarian and Serb, the struggle of various races for supremacy in Macedonia, the alternate friendship and enmity of the Russian and the Turk are all facts, which have their root deep down in the past annals of the Balkan lands. Few persons in Western Europe remember what has never been forgotten in the Peninsula, that there was a time when the Servian and Bulgarian Empires were great

Powers, and their respective rulers governed with the proud title of Czar a vast realm, which is still the dream of ardent patriots. Perusal of the following pages will probably convince the reader, that the only true settlement of the mutually conflicting claims of these historic states, which periodically endanger the peace of Europe, is a Balkan Confederation, such as was sketched by the late M. Tricoupis.

Two events seemed to render the publication of the book particularly appropriate in the present year. The Bicentenary of the reigning dynasty of Montenegro and the Hungarian Millenary are both largely concerned with Balkan history, and both occur in 1896.

The facts are taken from all the principal foreign works on the various countries and from my personal knowledge of the Balkan Peninsula. I am specially indebted to H.H. Prince Nicholas of Montenegro for the portrait of himself; to Mr. R. J. Kennedy, C.M.G., British *chargé d'affaires* at Cetinje, for much valuable assistance ; and to Mr. Hagberg Wright, of the London Library.

W. M.

CONTENTS.

PAGE
PREFACE vii

PART I.

ROUMANIA.

I.

DACIA BEFORE THE ROMAN CONQUEST (106 A.D.) 1-18

The Getæ, or Dacians—Their wars with the Macedonian kings—First contact with the Romans—Bœrebistes and Cotiso—Decebalus and Domitian—Trajan's two Dacian campaigns—His column at Rome—Manners and customs of the Dacians.

II.

THE ROMANS IN ROUMANIA (A.D. 106-274) . 19-25

Extent of the new province—Amalgamation of the colonists and natives — Origin of modern Roumanians — Their language derived from Latin—Gothic invasions—Evacuation of the province by the Romans—"Aurelian's Dacia"—Influence of the Roman occupation.

III.

THE BARBARIANS IN ROUMANIA (274–about
1250) 26-34
The barbarian invaders :—the Goths ; the Huns ; the
Gepidæ ; the Lombards and Avars ; the Bulgarians in
Roumania ; the Hungarians ; the Kumani—Origin of the
Wallachs—Final disappearance of the barbarians.

IV.

THE TWO PRINCIPALITIES (1290–1601) . . 35-61
Foundation of Wallachia and Moldavia—Mirtschea the Old—
Wallachia tributary to the Turks —Vlad the Impaler and
Stephen the Great—Moldavia submits—State of society at
this period—John the Terrible and Michael the Brave.

V.

THE PHANARIOTES IN ROUMANIA . . . 62-89
Matthew Bassarab and Basil "the Wolf"—Peter the
Great and the Principalities—The Phanariote governors
—The Russian wars and occupation—Treaty of Kaïnardji
—Loss of Bucovina—Treaties of Jassy and Bucharest—
End of Phanariote rule.

VI.

THE UNION OF THE PRINCIPALITIES (1822–1866) 90-108
Restoration of native *Hospodars*—Growth of Russian
influence — Russian occupation, 1828-34 — The national
movement — Revolution of 1848 — The Crimean War—
Treaty of Paris—The principalities united under Couza—
His deposition—Election of Prince Charles.

VII.

ROUMANIA AN INDEPENDENT KINGDOM . . 109-118
Prince Charles and "Carmen Sylva"—The constitution of
1866—New army organisation—The war of 1877—Siege
of Plevna—The Grivica Redoubt—Exchange of South
Bessarabia for Dobrudża—Roumania a kingdom.

PART II.

BULGARIA.

I.

FROM THE EARLIEST TIMES TO THE CONVERSION
OF THE BULGARIANS (864 A.D.) . . . 119-134

The Thracians—Philip of Macedon—Mœsia, a Roman province—Becomes Dacia Aureliani—Barbarian inroads—The Slavs—The old Bulgarians—Their amalgamation with the Slavs—The Bulgarian princes, Krum and Omortag—Boris I.—Conversion of the Bulgarians to Christianity.

II.

THE FIRST BULGARIAN EMPIRE (893-1018) . 135-158

The zenith of Bulgaria—The Czar Simeon—His vast Empire—Literature of the period—The Czar Peter—First appearance of Russians in Bulgaria—Division of the country: Šišman—The hermits and Bogomiles—Boris II.: his capture and deposition—Downfall of East Bulgaria—The Czar Samuel in West Bulgaria—Basil "the Bulgar-slayer"—Death of Samuel—End of the First Bulgarian Empire.

III.

BULGARIA UNDER THE GREEKS (1018-1186) . 159-166

Administration of Bulgaria under the Greek Emperors—Revolts of Deljan and Bodin—Inroads of barbarians—Persecution of the Bogomiles—First mention of Albanians—Peter and John Asên—A costly slap in the face—Restoration of the Bulgarian Empire.

IV.

THE SECOND BULGARIAN EMPIRE (1186-1398) . 167-193

John Asên I.—Peter—Kalojan—His "union" with Rome—His capture of the Emperor Baldwin—The "slayer of the

xii   CONTENTS.

PAGE

Greeks"—Boril—John Asên II.—Greatness of Bulgaria—
Rapid decline under his successors—The Terterij dynasty
—The Šišmans of Vidin—Battle of Velbužd : the supre-
macy of Servia—John Alexander: his divided realm—
First appearance of the Turks—Capture of Trnovo—The
last of the Czars—Society under the Empire

V.

BULGARIA UNDER THE TURKS (1398-1878)   . 194-214

Organisation of the country—Condition of the Christians—
The *Vojniks*—The church under Greek influence—Spiritual
tyranny of the Phanariotes—Brigandage : Pasvanoglu—
The Russians in Bulgaria : 1810 and 1829—Turkish re-
forms—The first Bulgarian school—The Church question—
The Bulgarian atrocities—The war of 1877—Bulgaria free.

VI.

THE UNION UNDER PRINCE ALEXANDER (1878-
1886)   215-232

The Russian interregnum—The Bulgarian Constitution—
Prince Alexander—The *coup d'état* of 1881—Friction with
Russia—Union of the two Bulgarias—Fury of the Czar—
The Servian War—The Battle of Slivnitza and its results—
Kidnapping of the Prince—His return and abdication.

VII.

PRINCE FERDINAND (1887-1896)   .   .   . 233-248

Kaulbars at Sofia—The Czar's election-agent—Wanted :
a Prince—Election of Prince Ferdinand—The Stambuloff
Ministry—The "Bulgarian Bismarck"—Foreign policy—
The Bulgarian Bishops—The Bourgas and Panitza Plots—
Murder of Beltcheff and Vulković—State of the country—
Stambuloff's fall and assassination—Conclusion.

CONTENTS.   xiii

PART III.
SERVIA.

I.

ORIGIN AND EARLY HISTORY OF THE SERBS
(TO A.D. 1336) 249-271
Origin of the Serbs—Their first appearance in the Balkans
—Their government : Župans and Grand Župans—Their
conversion to Christianity—Conflicts with the Bulgarians—
Nadir of Servia in 924—Voislav the Liberator—Stephen
Nemanja and his descendants—Saint Sava—Overthrow of
Bulgaria by Stephen Uroš.

II.

THE ZENITH OF SERVIA UNDER STEPHEN DUŠAN
(1336-1356) 272-282
Character and conquests of Dušan—Extent and organisation of his Empire—Proclaims himself Emperor—A
Serb Patriarch—War with Hungary—Annexation of
Bosnia—Stephen's code—His march on Constantinople
and death.

III.

THE DECLINE AND FALL OF SERVIA (1356-1459) 283-298
Loss of Bosnia and Albania—Victories of the Turks—
Lazar's campaigns—Battle of Kossovo, 1389—Servia
tributary to the Turks under "despots" of her own—
Stephen Lazarević and George Branković—Temporary
triumph of Servia—Her fall.

IV.

SERVIA UNDER THE TURKS (1459-1804) . . 299-308
Condition of the Serbs under Turkish rule: civil and
religious government of the country—Hungarian Serbs
under "despots" of their own—Attempts to free Servia—
The "Black Legion"—Migration of the Patriarch Arsenius
—The Serbs in Russia—The war of 1788—The Treaty of
Sistova—Revival of national feeling.

V.

THE STRUGGLE FOR INDEPENDENCE (1804-1860) 309-331

Cruelty of the Janissaries: the massacre of 1804—Kara George: the war of 1806-7—Servia practically free—Flight of Black George—The return of the Turks—Milosh Obrenović—Black George's murder—Servia recognised as a Principality in 1830—The Constitutions of 1835 and 1838—Fall of Milosh—Reigns of his sons Milan and Michael—Alexander Karageorgević—Restoration and death of Milosh.

VI.

THE FINAL EMANCIPATION OF SERVIA (1860-1878) 332-346

Restoration of Michael—His domestic reforms—Evacuation of Belgrade by the Turkish garrison—Murder of Michael—The Regency: Constitution of 1869—Milan—War with Turkey in 1876-8—Servia as affected by the treaties of San Stefano and Berlin—Milan proclaimed King.

VII.

THE MODERN KINGDOM OF SERVIA (1882-1896) 347-351

The war with Bulgaria—The Royal divorce—The Constitution of 1888—Abdication of Milan—The Regency—The *coups d'état* of 1893-4—King Alexander I.

PART IV.

MONTENEGRO.

I.

FROM THE EARLIEST TIMES TO THE BATTLE OF KOSSOVO (1389) 353-363

Montenegro: origin of the name—Its early history—The Romans in Illyria—Dioclea—The Serb kings—Montenegro a part of Serb Empire—The battle of Kossovo.

II.

FROM THE BATTLE OF KOSSOVO TO THE LAST OF
THE BLACK PRINCES (1389–1516) . 364-382

The Balshas—Montenegro the refuge of the Serbs—The first Turkish invasion—Stephen Crnoiević—Skanderbeg—Ivan the Black—The first Slavonic printing-press—Cetinje the capital—The story of Stanicha—The influence of Venice—Abdication of the last of the Black Princes.

III.

THE ELECTIVE VLADIKAS (1516–1696) . 383-391

Montenegro ruled by elective Bishops—The civil governors—Troubles with Turks and renegades—Destruction of the Press—The tribute for slippers—State of the country in seventeenth century—A new crusade—Story of Jahja—Cetinje twice captured.

IV.

THE FIRST THREE HEREDITARY PRINCE-BISHOPS
(1696–1782) 392-407

The hereditary *Vladikas*—Danilo I.—The "Montenegrin Vespers"—Expulsion of the renegades—The first connection with Russia—Peter the Great and Montenegro—Turkish invasions—The battle of Tsarevlaz—Sava and Vassili—The Russian indemnity—The story of Stephen the Little—The Perkin Warbeck of the Black Mountain.

V.

PETER I.—THE BONAPARTE OF THE BLACK MOUN-
TAIN (1782–1830) 408-423

Defeat and death of Kara Mahmoud—Formal incorporation of the Berda—Effects of the Treaty of Campo Formio—War with France—Siege of Ragusa—Napoleon's overtures—The "red" mountain—England and Montenegro—Capture of Cattaro; its surrender to Austria—The long peace—Internal reforms—Death and canonisation of the *Vladika*.

VI.

PETER II. AND DANILO II. (1830–1860) . . 424-449

The last of the *Vladikas*—Turkish offer refused—Struggles with the Turks and Austrians—Treachery of Radonić—Abolition of civil governor—A Montenegrin Senate—Peter restores the Press—His poems—The "Billiard-Table"—Danilo II.—Separation of ecclesiastical and temporal power—The "Code Danilo"—The battle of Grahovo—The "Sword of Montenegro"—Assassination of Danilo.

VII.

MONTENEGRO UNDER NICHOLAS I. (1860–1896) 450-468

Character of the new prince—His education—The Turkish War of 1862—Ostrog—Death of Mirko—Military reform—"Constitution" of 1868—The first Montenegrin ministry—The new schools—The Cattaro rising—The Turkish war of 1876—Montenegro after the Berlin Treaty—The Dulcigno demonstration—Albanian feuds—The Prince as road-maker—The New Code—The 400th anniversary of the Press—The Bicentenary of the Dynasty.

INDEX . . . 469

LIST OF ILLUSTRATIONS.

	PAGE
NICHOLAS I., PRINCE OF MONTENEGRO. *Frontispiece*	
DECEBALUS. *From a bust at St. Petersburg*	7
BATTLE OF THE ROMANS AND DACIANS. *From Trajan's Column at Rome*	13
DACIANS SETTING FIRE TO THEIR CAPITAL. *From Trajan's Column at Rome*	14
THE ROUMANIAN ARMS	18
MIRTSCHEA THE GREAT. *From the series of historical MSS. published by the Roumanian Government*	37
STEPHEN THE GREAT OF MOLDAVIA. *From the series of historical MSS. published by the Roumanian Government*	41
MICHAEL THE BRAVE. *From the series of historical MSS. published by the Roumanian Government*	50
MOLDAVIAN COINS. *From the series of historical MSS. published by the Roumanian Government*	59
BASIL "THE WOLF." *From the series of historical MSS. published by the Roumanian Government*	64
MATTHEW BASSARAB. *From the series of historical MSS. published by the Roumanian Government*	65
OLD ROUMANIAN SEAL. *From the series of historical MSS. published by the Roumanian Government*	88

xviii   LIST OF ILLUSTRATIONS.

	PAGE
ROMAN SCULPTURE AT NICOPOLIS. *From Kanitz, "Donau-Bulgarien"*	121
BULGARIAN ATTACK ON CONSTANTINOPLE IN 813. *From Kanitz, "Donau-Bulgarien"*	129
THE FIRST BULGARIAN EMPIRE	138
RUINS OF PRÊSLAV. *From Kanitz, "Donau-Bulgarien"*	140
THE DIKILITAŠ AT JALAR. *From Kanitz, "Donau-Bulgarien"*	153
OLD RELIEF AT VARNA. *From Kanitz, "Donau-Bulgarien"*	165
COINS OF ASÊN. *From Kanitz, "Donau-Bulgarien"*	171
THE BULGARIAN ARMS	176
STATUE OF PAN AT VARNA. *From Kanitz, "Donau-Bulgarien"*	191
OLD BULGARIAN BRIDGE. *From Kanitz, "Donau-Bulgarien"*	207
ROMAN RELIEF AT MADARA. *From Kanitz, "Donau-Bulgarien"*	228
THE SERVIAN ARMS	253
CORONATION CHURCH OF THE OLD SERVIAN CZARS. *From Kanitz, "Serbien"*	265
SERVIA UNDER DUŠAN, c. 1350	274
FORTRESS OF UŽICA. *From Kanitz, "Serbien"*	279
MILOSH OBRENOVIĆ. *From Cunibert, "Essai sur la Serbie"*	317
THE OLDEST CHURCH IN SERVIA. *From Kanitz, "Serbien"*	329
SARCOPHAGUS AT DRMNO. *From Kanitz, "Serbien"*	344
ROSE WINDOW AT KRUŠEVAC. *From Kanitz, "Serbien"*	350
RUINS OF DIOCLEA. *From a photo. by Mr. C. A. Miller*	357

	PAGE
MONTENEGRIN MILITARY INSIGNIA . . 376, 377,	379
A TYPICAL BIT OF MONTENEGRIN SCENERY. *From a photo. by Mr. C. A. Miller* . . .	383
THE "TURKS' TOWER," CETINJE, IN 1848. *From Sir Gardner Wilkinson, " Dalmatia and Montenegro"*	411
THE VLADIKA, PETER II., IN CIVIL DRESS. *From Sir Gardner Wilkinson, " Dalmatia and Montenegro"*	434
THE VLADIKA, PETER II., IN HIS PRIESTLY ROBES. *From Sir Gardner Wilkinson, " Dalmatia and Montenegro"* .	435
MAP OF MONTENEGRO	463
MAP OF THE BALKAN PENINSULA, PRESENT DAY	

Opposite page 1

the Greek colonies on the West Coast of the Black Sea. He calls them "the bravest and most honourable of all the Thracian tribes," and speaks of them as endeavouring to oppose the march of the Persian King Darius. Thucydides alludes to their prowess with the bow and arrow on horseback, and fixes their abode on the shore of the Euxine. At that time however, they had not yet crossed the Danube, but were living in the district south of that river known as the Dobrudža. Here, in the fourth century before our era, they were attacked by Philip of Macedon, who laid siege to one of their towns. The great conqueror was about to give the signal for the assault, when the gates opened and a long line of priests, clad in snow-white robes with lyres in their hands, came forth and approached with song and music the Macedonian camp. Struck with the novelty of the sight, Philip bade spare the citadel and took Meda, daughter of the Getic king, as his wife. From that moment the Getæ became allies of Macedon and aided Philip in his Scythian campaign. But, at the close of his reign, about the year 340 B.C., they crossed the Danube, either from the natural expansion of their numbers, or in order to escape the attacks of some other barbarous tribe. Alexander the Great, in the course of his Thrácian expedition, found himself confronted on the left bank of the Danube by an army of Getic horsemen and footsoldiers, who refused to allow him to land. Nothing daunted, he waited till night came on, crossed the river lower down at daybreak and fell upon the Getæ, whom he defeated and put to flight. But the defeat had no lasting results. The Getæ fled to their forests ; their conqueror contented himself with burning their wooden town. He then returned southwards across the stream, and the Getæ were left unmolested. But some fifty years later they had their revenge. Lysimachus, who succeeded to the Thracian dominions of Alexander, attempted to chastise them for the assistance which they had rendered to the barbarous tribes of Macedonia. But he made the mistake of despising his enemy. Wearied with long marches, and oppressed with thirst in a barren land, his great army was forced to surrender to the Getic king, Dromichaetes. The victor displayed an unwonted generosity towards the vanquished Macedonian. He led him to his capital, a place called Helis, which cannot now be identified, and treated him as his honoured guest. Lysimachus secured his liberty by the payment of a heavy ransom, and half a century ago gold pieces, bearing his name, were found in Roumania and Transylvania, where the natives used them as signet rings and ornaments.

A long period of peace followed this disastrous expedition. The Getæ or Dacians, as they were now more usually called, increased in numbers and received from successive bands of immigrants the rudiments of civilisation. The cunning slaves, who play such an important part in the comedies of Plautus and Terence, were usually of Getic extraction, and, as those authors copied the Greeks, it is evident that there was considerable intercourse between Greece and the country beyond the Danube.

But with the first appearance of the Romans on the confines of Dacia a new era in the history of the nation began. The first conflict between the two peoples took place in 111 B.C., when the Roman legions, already masters of Macedonia, had advanced to the Danube, and found the Dacians assisting the tribesmen of the right bank against them. For some time, no Roman general thought it desirable to enter their territory; and, when at last a commander crossed the Danube, he hesitated to entrust himself to the sombre gorges of the Carpathians, where the Dacian warriors lurked in readiness to surprise the rash invader. If it had not been for the incursions of the Dacians into the Roman provinces, a Roman occupation might have been indefinitely postponed, and the Roumanian race might never have existed.

But under a king called Bœrebistes, a contemporary of Julius Cæsar, these raids became so serious, that Rome was alarmed for her supremacy in the Balkans. Bœrebistes was at the head of a powerful nation, which had gradually absorbed all the minor races up to the frontier of modern Bavaria, and could put two hundred thousand men into the field. His soldiers had been seen as far south as the Balkan slopes, and were threatening Macedonia and the Dalmatian coast. Cæsar himself was meditating a Dacian campaign, and had actually assembled the troops for it, when the dagger of Brutus laid him low. The Dacians would have been no unworthy foemen of the great Roman captain. They were well armed and well led. They knew the use of breast-plates and helmets, and their curved swords were scarcely less deadly than the poisoned arrows, which they fired from horseback. Bœrebistes offered his aid to Octavius in the civil war, which culminated at the battle of Actium, and it was owing to the refusal of his assistance by Cæsar's nephew that the Dacians took sides with Antony at that great conflict which decided the fate of the Roman world. Taught by experience, Augustus conferred upon Bœrebistes' successors the proud title of " friend and ally of the Roman people." But this "friendship" was of short duration. The Dacians again became a terror to the Roman province. Horace makes one of the characters in his " Epistles " ask, " What is the latest news from Dacia?" just as a modern Roman might ask, " What is the latest from Abyssinia?" The exploits of the Dacian king Cotiso are mentioned by contemporary Roman authors, and the gossips of the forum would have it that Augustus intended to marry the daughter of the terrible barbarian, and thus secure peace for the Empire. Whenever the Danube was frozen over, the Dacians crossed on the ice and ravaged the Roman province of Mœsia the present Bulgaria, far and wide. The fortified towns on the Black Sea kept their gates shut night and day for fear of these savage warriors, and the poet Ovid, who spent seven years of exile among them, and acquired such a knowledge of their language that he even composed elegiacs in Getic, wrote with the utmost respect of their martial prowess. The defeat and death of Cotiso, though hailed with enthusiasm at Rome, and followed up by the construction of forts along the right bank of the Danube, were merely temporary checks to the

Dacian power. Augustus boasted that he had subdued the Dacians in their own home and transplanted many of them into Bulgaria ; but the nation was not conquered, much less was its territory occupied. The policy of the early Roman Emperors was to prevent the Dacian bands from crossing the river, not to annex their country to the Empire. When the civil war of 69 A.D. necessitated the withdrawal of the legions from Mœsia, a Dacian invasion of that province at once followed, which was repulsed by orders of Vespasian. Once again, the sole means of pacifying the people was to transplant them over the river. Dacia at this period was little more than a desert, and it looked as if the nation were on the point of disappearing, when a great chief arose and led it to renewed victories. This man was Decebalus whose name, "the strength of the Dacians," is the most appropriate summary of his career. Possessing a scientific as well as a practical knowledge of warfare, he spent the two first years of his reign in making preparations for attacking the Roman possessions south of the Danube. It is said that he even attempted to form an alliance with the Parthians against the common foe. In 86 A.D. he at last crossed the Danube with a disciplined army behind him, and drove the Romans to the Balkans before him. Two Roman generals succumbed to his arms, and the historian Tacitus might well regret the defeat of the Roman legions and the capture of a Roman standard. At the news of this double reverse the Emperor Domitian took the field in person against the Dacian monarch. But he cautiously remained at his headquarters in a small Mœsian town, and entrusted his lieutenant, Julianus, with the task of bearding Decebalus in his own country. Julianus defeated the Dacians at a place called Tapæ, the site of which is uncertain, and besieged, for the first time

DECEBALUS.

in its history, the capital of Sarmizegethusa, the modern Varhely. But the exigencies of Roman policy necessitated a speedy peace, for there were other dangerous tribes besides the Dacians to be subdued. Decebalus had no objection to come to terms with his enemy, and sent his brother as an envoy to the Roman camp. The favourable concessions, which he obtained from Domitian, prove that the Emperor was afraid of driving him to extremities. Decebalus restored the prisoners, whom he had taken, and received in return the title of king; while Domitian added the surname of "the Dacian" to his other designations, and celebrated on his return an empty triumph in honour of his vicarious successes. Slaves, specially hired for the occasion, personified the vanquished in the victor's procession, and the courtly poets, Martial and Statius, praised the Imperial "clemency which had given back to the Dacians their mountain home." A forged letter of Decebalus, imploring the Emperor to spare his country, was read before the credulous senate, but the shrewd commonsense of the people detected the fraud and mocked at the "funeral of the Dacian dead." Domitian had, in fact, bought his scanty laurels by the promise of an annual tribute to Decebalus.

But the accession of Trajan, in 98 A.D., soon put an end to this ignominious arrangement. It is clear that the object of the great Emperor, whose name has ever since been connected with the history of Roumania, was not primarily the conquest of the country, but the removal of this irritating burden. The fullest preparations were made to show the "barbarians," that they were no longer able to insult the majesty of Rome with impunity. Six legions were assembled at the present town of Kostolac in Servia, where they were reviewed by the Emperor. A poet was engaged to celebrate the forthcoming exploits of the Roman arms in an epic, and Trajan himself, like his prototype Cæsar, found time to jot down his impressions of the campaign in a book, now unhappily lost. A more durable monument of the war exists to this day in the Roman road, begun by Domitian and finished by Trajan, along the right bank of the Danube as far as a point opposite Orsova. In some places the road was hewn through the solid rock, in others it consisted of planks fastened over the water along the perpendicular face of the cliff. The traveller may still read on an ancient tablet opposite Gradina a Latin inscription,[1] blackened by the smoke of centuries, which contains the name and titles of Trajan. Crossing the Danube on two bridges of boats at Kostolac and Orsova respectively, the Romans entered Dacia in two divisions, while the two flotillas, which they had for some time been accustomed to keep on the river, supplied them with provisions. No pains were spared to ensure success over a nation which had earned the distinction of being the "most warlike of men." The Dacians themselves recognised that this time they had a man to deal with, and sent a gigantic fungus to the Emperor, upon which was scratched in Roman characters the request that he would leave them alone. So great was the dread, which the expedition inspired, that the messenger, to whom this strange document was entrusted, fell down dead with fright as he delivered it into Trajan's hands.

But the Emperor's march was slow and difficult. No fewer than eighteen months were spent in advancing sixty-five miles to the spot where the two divisions of the army were to meet. The legionaries

[1] When I visited the spot in June, the tablet had just been cleaned.—W. M.

had to grope their way, as it were, in the dark, through a country of which they knew little against an enemy, of whom they could see nothing. The mountains lent themselves to that guerilla warfare, at which the Dacians excelled ; huge boulders of rock were rolled down upon the heads of the soldiers as they entered the narrow ravines ; showers of arrows impeded their progress as they forded the deep streams. At Tapæ, the spot where Decebalus had been defeated fourteen years earlier, they at last met the foe in open combat. The victory of the Romans was hardly bought, and so severe were their losses that the Emperor tore up his own garments to provide bandages for the wounded. The invaders now marched upon the Dacian capital, which, after a desperate engagement, fell into their hands. A great booty, including the standard, which had been captured by the Dacians in the last war, rewarded the Romans for their hardships. Decebalus saw himself deserted by his allies, his sister taken prisoner, his treasures carried off. He bowed his neck to the yoke, resolving to reserve himself for better days. Accompanied by two dignitaries of his court, and followed by a crowd of kneeling warriors, he flung himself at Trajan's feet. The Emperor dictated peace on his own terms. He ordered the king to surrender all his arms, to dismiss the Roman deserters, who had joined his army, to raze his fortresses and abandon all his foreign conquests. Decebalus swore to share the friendships and enmities of the Roman people, and promised never again to receive a Roman into his service. Trajan was contented with what he had accomplished. Leaving a garrison behind him at Sarmizegethusa, he took with him to Rome a Dacian embassy, for the ratification of the treaty, and assumed, with far more reason than Domitian, the title of *Dacicus*, in memory of his triumph. A letter of the younger Pliny tells us how great an impression this " first victory over a hitherto invincible enemy" made upon the Roman populace. Dacia was regarded as finally subdued.

But there was little finality about Trajan's first expedition. Decebalus had only submitted as a temporary expedient, and as soon as his conqueror had gone, he recommenced his forays, and formed a fresh league of tribes against the Roman Empire. Trajan resolved that this time he would finally annex Dacia to his dominions and have done with these troublesome warriors, who had only submitted in order the better to attack him. As a first step towards the annexation of the country, he ordered the construction of a more permanent means of communication than the bridge of boats, which had served to convey his army across the Danube during his former campaign. Opposite the present Roumanian town of Turnu-Severin there may still be seen in the river several piles of the magnificent stone bridge which Apollodorus of Damascus, the most famous architect of that period, erected for the Emperor in 104. The bridge originally consisted of twenty piers, each 163 feet apart, 145 feet high, and 58 feet broad. This done, Trajan declared war against Decebalus, who endeavoured to rid himself of his great enemy by assassination. He had previously seized the commander of the Roman garrison at Sarmizegethusa and refused to give him up, unless the Emperor recompensed him for his losses in the last war. The brave Roman officer took poison in order to relieve Trajan from this dilemma, and the scanty ruins of the mausoleum, which his grateful master raised to his memory, are still to be seen a little to the north of Varhely.

The second Dacian campaign of Trajan was easier than the first. The remembrance of their former defeats made many of the Dacians unwilling to risk further losses. Decebalus offered to make peace. But Trajan replied that he must first lay down his arms. The Dacian monarch preferred to die, and held out with a mere handful of men against the Roman army. No quarter was given on either side; the Roman soldiers cut off the heads of their prisoners and stuck them on pikes; the Dacian women fastened their captives' hands behind their backs and applied blazing torches to their bare bodies. A final battle beneath the walls of the capital ended the war. The Dacians set fire to the town and took poison to avoid falling into the hands of their enemies. Decebalus, tracked by the legionaries to his retreat in the mountains, sank exhausted at the foot of a tree; and when the Romans advanced to seize him, plunged a dagger into his breast. His head was carried to Trajan; Dacia lay at the mercy of the conqueror. By the end of 106 it had become a Roman province. The Emperor, after remaining a short time to arrange for its future administration, returned to celebrate, by what was perhaps the most magnificent spectacle of ancient Rome, his final subjugation of the Dacian people. From every part of the Roman world congratulations were showered upon the victor, and nearly three centuries later the two Dacian expeditions of Trajan, occupying only five years together, constituted his chief claim to apotheosis. To this day, Roumania bears abundant marks of his presence. Walls, plains, and meadows are called by his name, and the modern Roumanians, proud of their Roman

BATTLE OF THE ROMANS AND DACIANS.
(*From Trajan's Column.*)

origin, may say in the language of 'Childe Harold,' " Still we Trajan's name adore."

But the most striking memorial of his Dacian conquest is to be seen at Rome. Trajan's Column is an epitome in marble of his two campaigns against Decebalus, and forms a priceless commentary upon the early history of Roumania. From it we learn, more vividly than from any printed page, the chief events which we have just described. We see the passage of the Roman forces across the Danube on the two bridges of boats, and Trajan, seated on a platform and surrounded by his officers, addressing his army from the Dacian shore. The next relief shows us the obstacles encountered on the march; the sappers and miners are at work; trees are being felled; streams bridged and forts built. Then we

DACIANS SETTING FIRE TO THEIR CAPITAL.
(*From Trajan's Column.*)

have the Dacian envoys, suing in vain for peace, and the figure of the Roman Emperor is seen as he spares the defenceless. The artist next gives us a picture of the Dacian attack; the natives are clad in mantles and tunics with long sleeves, the nobles wearing Phrygian caps of liberty on their heads, such as may be seen to-day in the country districts of

Roumania; the common soldiers bareheaded with no other protection than their flowing locks. We can distinguish the uncouth Dacian standards — long monsters, with the body of a snake and the head of a savage dog, stuck at the end of a pole. Their richly decorated oval shields and curved swords contrast strangely with the weapons of the Romans. Finally, we behold them setting fire to their capital, with a look of desperate determination on their bearded faces, while from a huge vessel filled with poison their chiefs are drinking the fatal draught. On the ground some are writhing in their last agony, and two corpses are being carried away. To crown all, the triumph of Trajan, and the soldiers bearing the head of Decebalus, reminded the Roman world of the Dacian conqueror's success. More fortunate than the bridge over the Danube, the column has survived practically intact, and the 2,500 human figures, which it contains, are the best proof of the skill of Apollodorus, the famous architect. Trajan lies buried beneath it, but the piety of the Popes has replaced his statue, which stood on the summit, by that of St. Peter.

The evidence of the column and the testimony of Latin authors show that the Dacian monarchy had reached a considerable degree of civilisation at the time of its fall. The government of the country, like that of Gaul, was based upon a strongly religious feeling, and the Dacians owed their reputation for bravery to their belief in the immortality of the soul. Herodotus calls them the "Immortals," and tells us that they never spoke of "dying," but always of "rejoining Zalmoxis," their deity. It was this disregard of death which made them such a terror to their enemies. The Dacian knew no fear, either of man or of the forces of nature. He obeyed the orders of his sovereign and the chief pontiff, who was supposed to have inherited the powers of Zalmoxis and to be the deity's vicegerent upon earth. This personage was the chief counsellor of the monarch, and his decisions were received as the voice of a god. His influence may be understood by a single example. When Bœrebistes became king, one of his desires was to stop the drunken habits of his people. He accordingly prohibited the use of wine. But, powerful as he was, he could not make his subjects obey him. He appealed, in despair, to the chief pontiff, who at once ordered every vine in Dacia to be destroyed. The order was executed in a single day, such was the respect which that ecclesiastic inspired. To him Dacia owed its first code of laws and the first germs of physical science. But theocratic as was the Dacian system of government, no temples were found in their land. The simple sanctuaries of their faith were placed on the mountain peaks, far removed from the dwellings of men. The great river, which was their natural bulwark on the south, was for them an object of superstitious reverence, and Roman poets noticed their picturesque custom of drinking the water of the Danube on the eve of a campaign, and vowing that they would never return except as conquerors. The nation was organised on an aristocratic basis. The lower orders, consisting of common soldiers, artisans, and peasants, wore their hair long, as we have seen from Trajan's Column, while the nobles, from whose ranks the king and the chief priest were drawn, were distinguished from the common herd by the bonnets which covered their heads. They formed a privileged class, presided at religious ceremonies, were the leaders of the people in war and peace, acted as judges and teachers, and watched over the preservation of ancient customs. A highly conservative force, we find these "bonneted men," as the Romans called them, in frequent opposition to the king, if he showed any inclination to grant popular reforms. They were, in fact, the predecessors of those Roumanian *boyards*, or landed aristocracy, whom we shall have occasion to mention later on.

Battle and the chase were the most serious business of the Dacians' existence, and Ovid, who knew them well, said that their appearance reminded him of Mars himself. But they had other and more peaceful activities. Agriculture was of such importance even at that early date, that a great official was told off to watch over it. The studs of the Dacian monarchs were deservedly famous, and the country produced large herds of cattle. The gold and silver mines of Transylvania were worked before the Roman occupation, and yielded the precious metals, which were manufactured into ornaments by skilled native artificers. That Dacia carried on a considerable trade with the outside world is proved by the number of foreign coins found there; its situation on the Danube naturally favoured the growth of its commerce. But there were few towns, for the population was scattered. Sarmizegethusa was practically the only city of importance, and the other places mentioned by the Roman historians were nothing but fortified camps, where the country folk sought refuge in time of war, or else military posts on the banks of rivers or at the entrance to mountain passes. The inhabitants dwelt in wooden huts, or even in holes in the ground, which, under the name of *bordei*, were found in Roumania as late as the middle of the present century. In short, Dacia, as it was before the Roman conquest, preserved several characteristics of the country, which has derived its name from the conquering race.

II.

THE ROMANS IN ROUMANIA.

(A.D. 106-274.)

THE Roman province of Dacia, which was constituted upon the ruins of the kingdom of Decebalus, was considerably larger than modern Roumania. For the Dacian realm had included Transylvania and other portions of what is now the Austro-Hungarian Dual Monarchy, and the circumference of the province was thirteen hundred miles. The fact is of more than antiquarian importance, for the so-called "Daco-Roumanian" movement, which has lately given so much trouble to Austrian statesmen, is based upon the racial and historical unity of the Roumanians of Transylvania and the Roumanians of the kingdom.

The ravages of war had decimated the natives, and in order to people so large an area it was necessary to import colonists from the Roman Empire. Trajan summoned to Dacia the veterans of his legions, the landless proletarians of Rome, the venturesome inhabitants of Spain and Gaul. Italy doubtless furnished the bulk of the immigrants, for at the present day the Roumanian language is closely akin to Latin. Some colonists were attracted by glowing reports of the Dacian gold mines, others expected to find their El Dorado in the administration of the new province. Lawyers and doctors were, of course, necessary to the civilisation of the "poor barbarians," and both professions were overcrowded at Rome. It is not necessary to assume, as some writers have done, that the Romans regarded Dacia much as our forefathers regarded Botany Bay, and that the ancestors of the present Roumanians were convicts. We can easily imagine that there would be a general rush for lands in the newly-conquered country, and possibly the first settlers were not drawn from the first families of the Imperial City. The new arrivals intermarried with the survivors of the Dacian race, and the offspring of these Daco-Roman alliances perpetuated the characteristics of both parents. Hence it is that after a period of sixteen centuries, we find the curious phenomenon of a nation speaking a "soft bastard Latin" of its own, and bearing in its life and in its history the traces of its Latin origin, yet separated by hundreds of miles from any other branch of the Latin race.

The peace, which followed the triumph of the Roman arms, assisted the amalgamation of the new and the old elements in the population. Those Dacians, who had left their country rather than live under the foreign yoke, gradually returned, when they saw that their fellow-countrymen were well treated by the conquerors. The famous edict of the Emperor Caracalla, which extended the citizenship of Rome to every inhabitant of the Empire, placed the "barbarian" on an equal footing with the true-born Roman in the eye of the law, and reconciled him to the loss of his independence. Commerce and agriculture flourished, new mines were opened, new towns rose with the rapidity of a western city in America. Palaces, roads, baths, all the usual appendages of Roman life, sprang into existence. Dacia merited the epithet of "blessed," which was ascribed to her on Roman medals; all over Roumania the indelible marks of the Roman occupation can be seen at this day. The Roman monuments in the academy at Bucharest show what a hold Latin civilisation had gained on the country during the 168 years of the Roman occupation. The national religion, which might have been a dangerous obstacle to the progress of Roman ideas, became merged in the elastic creed of the conquerors. The mysterious grotto of Zalmoxis was closed; the solemn banquets of his worshippers ceased; and Jupiter took the place of the Dacian deity in the religious life of the people. All over Dacia the language of the Romans was spoken before a generation had elapsed. It was not the Latin of Cicero or Tacitus, but the homely idiom of the populace and the peasantry, modified by an admixture of Dacian words. Much as in Gaul the Celtic idiom disappeared before the Latin, so in Roumania the conquerors introduced their own speech. A mediæval Pope fourteen hundred years later remarked that the people of Wallachia "even now speak the Roman language;" and the German poet, Martin Opitz, who flourished early in the seventeenth century, describes them as "almost made on the Roman model." Those who are acquainted with Latin or Italian will even nowadays find many familiar phrases in the Roumanian language. *Apa* (water) is practically the same as the Latin *aqua* and Italian *acqua*. *Pane* (bread) is the same in both Italian and Roumanian; *auru* (gold) is the Latin *aurum ;* *portu* (harbour), the Latin *portus ; cina* (supper), the Latin and Italian *cena ; mesa* (table), the Latin *mensa ; vino* (wine), *verde* (green), *strada* (street), and *sera* (evening), appear in precisely the same form in both languages —that of modern Rome and that of modern Roumania. Hundreds of words in daily use at Bucharest display their Latin origin in every letter, or else conceal it beneath the thinnest of disguises. The wonder is that, after such a long lapse of time, the language should have degenerated so little from its prototype.

The Dacians gradually lost, under the influence of Western civilisation, those fierce characteristics which had made them the terror of the provinces beyond the Danube. Occasionally, we hear of disturbances, and in one instance, during the reign of Antoninus Pius, of a serious revolt. But, generally speaking, after about the year 120, when Hadrian meditated the withdrawal of his legions from Dacia and the destruction of Trajan's bridge across the Danube, the Roman occupation was firmly established in the country. Hadrian's scheme of evacuation was due to his desire to keep the barbarians out of Mœsia, and his successors for the next century and a half followed the alternative policy of making Dacia an outpost of the Empire against the attacks of savage hordes. Three great military roads, still visible in many places, united the principal towns of the province ; while a fourth, called by Trajan's name, traversed the depths of the Carpathians and entered Transylvania by the Turnu Rosa or Rothenthurm Pass. Two legions were usually stationed in Dacia, and their headquarters, together with the seat of government, were fixed at Apulum, the modern Karlsburg in Transylvania. On the ruins of the old Dacian capital of Sarmizegethusa rose the stately Roman town of Ulpia Trajana, whose memory is still preserved by a few carved stones and a heap of broken pillars.

With the advent of the third century the incursions of the barbarians became more threatening. Caracalla, about 212, defeated a horde of invaders, and erected as a trophy of victory the town of Karakal, which still preserves his name. The "tower of Severus," Turnu-Severin, on the Danube, marks the defeat of the tribes of Quadi and Marcomanni a few years later. But a more deadly enemy now appeared upon the frontiers. In 247 we hear of the first invasion of the Goths. Some writers, relying on the similarity of the names, have put forward the theory that these Goths were none other than the Getæ or Dacians, the direct lineal descendants of the people, who had withdrawn from Dacia at the time of the Roman conquest. Byron has adopted it in the famous passage, where he calls upon the Goths to avenge the Dacian gladiator, "butchered to make a Roman holiday." The idea is picturesque, and it is in accordance with the requirements of poetic justice that the third and fourth generations of Roman colonists should suffer for their forefathers' deeds at the hands of a Dacian tribe. But there is no real proof of the hypothesis, and the connection between Goths and Getæ rests upon mere theory. From this year the old historians of Roumania date the decline of the province. At first, however, the Goths simply used Dacia as a stepping-stone to Mœsia, on the other side of the Danube, and did not tarry by the way. But they soon found the one province as attractive as the other, and between 247 and 268 there were six invasions, one of which cost a Roman Emperor his life. The shrewdest Romans already regarded their Dacian province as lost, and a Roman pretender attempted for a moment amid the general confusion to claim descent from Decebalus, and revive the Dacian kingdom in his own person. The scheme failed, and the great victory of the Emperor Claudius over the Goths at Naissus, the modern Nisch in Servia, in 269, while it rid Mœsia of their presence, left Dacia still at their mercy. The Roman legions, entrenched in the natural fastnesses of the Carpathians, could protect themselves, but were powerless to save the peaceful inhabitants of the plains. The next Emperor, Aurelian, resolved to evacuate the province, which he could no longer hold, and fall back upon the Danube as his first line of defence. About the year 274 the Roman garrisons withdrew across the river, and took with them all the Daco-Roman colonists who cared to follow them. South of the Danube, in parts of what are now Servia and Bulgaria, a new home preserved under the name of "Aurelian's Dacia," or *Dacia Aureliani*, the memory of the old. Dacia, north of the Danube, had been the last province to be added to the Roman Empire and the first to go. Yet the Roman influence had not ceased with the Roman occupation. Many of the inhabitants preferred to remain behind, dreading, in the phrase of Gibbon, "exile more than a Gothic master." They were no longer a military outpost of the Empire, but they were in a sense the pioneers of Latin culture among their barbarous rulers. For a brief space we shall see Dacia, north of the Danube, once more incorporated with the Empire; but it never entirely lost, even in the darkest ages, the enduring traces of the Latin race.

III.

THE BARBARIANS IN ROUMANIA

(A.D. 274–about 1250.)

FOR the next thousand years from the evacuation of Dacia by the Romans, the history of that country is one long and confused series of barbarian invasions. One horde of savage tribes succeeds to another, sometimes merely marching through the land on its way to the South or West, at other times driving out the occupants and settling in their homes. During the period from the close of the third to the middle of the thirteenth century Roumania presents a number of kaleidoscopic changes, which leave no durable impression upon history. Tribes with names as uncouth as their manners appear and disappear by turn, leaving scarcely a trace behind them. The one permanent feature amidst this world of change was the Daco-Roman element, which had remained in the country after the withdrawal of the Roman officials. The native proverb truly say, "the Roumanian never dies." In that corner of Southeastern Europe, as in Italy, in Spain, in France, the Latin race manifested its enduring vitality. The torrent of barbarian invasion swept over it again and again, but it was not washed away, and when the floods at last subsided, it re-appeared above the waters just as it was before they rose.

The Gothic supremacy, which lasted for a century, was a period of comparative tranquillity. The victors lost much of their ferocity by contact with the vanquished; the natives pursued their agricultural pursuits without interference, and found ample occupation in cultivating the lands which their fellow-countrymen had abandoned when they migrated southwards. Once, for a moment, the exiles returned in the train of the Roman Emperor Constantine, who not only repulsed the attacks of the Goths upon the provinces south of the Danube about 330, but built a bridge across the river, like Trajan, though much lower down, between the present Bulgarian town of Nicopolis and the modern Roumanian village of Turnu-Magurele. The remains of the bridge still mark this second and merely temporary occupation by the Romans. Constantine, indeed, assumed the title of "restorer of Dacia," and boasted that he had repeated the exploit of Trajan. But he contented himself with compelling the Goths to furnish a force of auxiliaries, and soon withdrew from a position which he could not maintain. But his victory had one important effect; it introduced the doctrines of Christianity among the Goths. It is possible that the Daco-Roman colonists had already been converted, for we hear of a Dacian bishop at an early council of the Church. But their Gothic masters now for the first time embraced the new faith. By 360 Dacia was a part of Christendom.

The second batch of barbarian invaders was much more terrible than the first. The Goths were mild and civilised as compared with the savage Huns, who entered Roumania in 375. The "shrill voice, the uncouth gestures and the strange deformity" of the Huns, their meals of wild grass or raw meat, their weird incantations and their pitiless cruelty, filled the inhabitants with horror and alarm. Many of the Goths were allowed by the Romans to settle on the other side of the Danube, while the natives either remained in the plains of Roumania or retreated to the fastnesses of the Carpathians, where they lived for centuries uncontaminated by the wild races which seized their country. The defeat of the Huns by the Roman Emperor Theodosius I. about 378 was only a temporary relief. The whole aspect of the land changed under its new masters; all settled habits of life disappeared, and nomad tribes ravaged the Danubian provinces almost without intermission. Then the "scourge of God," as Attila has been called, fell upon those unhappy regions. Modern Bulgaria, as well as modern Roumania, succumbed to his armies, and the Romans acknowledged him as the ruler of the latter country. But his own allies turned against him at a critical moment. The Gepidæ, a Gothic race, under their King Ardaric, overthrew his dominion in Roumania and established there a new kingdom; Attila perished in 453, and with his death the Huns vanished from the Danube.

The Gepidæ, the third of the barbarian races which occupied Roumania, maintained their hold upon the country for a century, and gave it their own name of Gepidia. They are the most obscure of all these motley bands, and we know little about them beyond the fact of their existence. At one moment they were at war with the Roman Empire, at another they were its allies. At one period, Justinian succeeded in capturing from them several towns, and even re-assumed Constantine's old title of the "restorer of Dacia." But two far more formidable foes appeared about the middle of the sixth century in the persons of the Lombards and Avars, the former coming from the Baltic coast, the latter from the plains of Asia. United by the common desire for plunder, under the leadership of Alboin, these two tribes speedily overthrew the power of the Gepidæ, with such complete success that the vanquished race henceforth disappears. The Lombards did not stay long in the land. Accepting the invitation of the Emperor Justinian to enter his service, they crossed the Danube, leaving Roumania to the Avars. The latter ruled more or less continuously in the country for eighty years, though the seat of their empire was on the site of Attila's ancient capital in the midst of the great Hungarian plain, and not in Roumania itself. But they included it in their dominions until their defeat by the Emperor Heraclius in their campaign against Constantinople in 626. Their influence in the Balkan Peninsula never recovered the effects of that crushing blow, and by the middle of the seventh century Roumania knew them no more. Five different hordes of barbarians had swept over that unfortunate country since the Romans left, and still the descendants of the old Roman colonists remained in their mountain retreat, little affected by the waves which, one after another, had covered their land.

The Emperor had been aided in his victory over the Avars by the Bulgarian chief Kurt, or Kuvrat, a former vassal of the Avar king. The origin and early history of the Bulgarians will be narrated later, and it is therefore only necessary to state in this place their connection with Roumania. Kuvrat and his successors obtained power in the old Dacian province north of the Danube, as well as in what is now known as Bulgaria ; and in the reign of their powerful chieftain Krum, who flourished about the year 810, they occupied a large part of Roumania. During the first Bulgarian Empire, which lasted from 893 to 1018, Roumania was largely in Bulgarian hands. The towns and petty communities, which had been founded by the Daco-Roman inhabitants after the withdrawal of the Avars westward, were more or less dependent upon the Bulgarian Czars, though governed by chiefs of their own. Such was the condition of Roumania when a fresh swarm of invaders descended upon it, and for the first time in Balkan history the name of the Hungarians meets the eye.

This warlike race, which has just been celebrating the thousandth anniversary of the kingdom which it founded, took up its abode in the eastern part of Roumania about 839. The strange habits and fierce disposition of the early Hungarians made them a terror to all their neighbours ; their career of devastation recalled the memory of Attila's campaigns. Their food was the raw flesh of animals; their drink the milk of mares or the blood of their enemies. Fortunately for Roumania they did not remain there long. The Bulgarian monarch, Simeon, then at the zenith of his power, inflicted a severe defeat upon those who had dared to cross the Danube and approach his Balkan capital. During their temporary absence on a western campaign he devastated their settlements in Bessarabia, and, finding their home destroyed, they wandered westward again, and made the present country of Hungary their headquarters. In the eleventh century they annexed Transylvania to the Hungarian kingdom, to which, after various vicissitudes of fortune, it still belongs.

While the Hungarians migrated to the West across the Carpathians, another tribe, called Patzinakitai, had entered the Roumanian land. We know little of this race beyond the fact that its leaders made frequent incursions into Bulgaria, and even dared to defy the majesty of the Byzantine Empire. Powerful in Roumania in the tenth and eleventh centuries, the Patzinakitai are heard of two hundred years later, when they became merged in the Hungarian nation, leaving no traces of their separate existence behind them. Another barbarian tribe, the Kumani, had driven them from their seats on the Danube.

After the First Bulgarian Empire had fallen, the old Dacian province north of the Danube gradually came under the rule of the Kumani, and received from them the name of Kumania. It was an era of comparative peace for the inhabitants of that distressful country.

The barbarian inroads had ceased, and the descendants of the old Daco-Roman colonists could cultivate their farms without disturbance upon paying a tribute to their masters. The commercial importance of Roumania became recognised abroad, and a diploma of 1134 acknowledges the flourishing condition of the region round the town of Berlad, not far from the Pruth, where a sort of democratic commonwealth existed under an elected magistrate. There the products of the Levant were exchanged for the merchandise of Russia, Hungary, and Bohemia, and a brisk business was carried on with the Greek traders of the Black Sea.

During this period the name of the Wallachs first becomes prominent. Treatises without end have been written on the origin of this remarkable race, which gave its own designation to one of the two Danubian principalities, Moldavia and Wallachia, which are united in the modern Roumanian kingdom. The most probable view is that the Wallachs were none other than our old friends the descendants of the Daco-Roman colonists, who in the course of ages reappear under this new name. Some of them remained in Dacia, north of the Danube; others migrated to " Aurelian's Dacia," south of it, and this accounts for the existence of Wallachs in Bulgaria as well as in Roumania. In the Middle Ages the descent of these people from the old Romans, who had colonised Dacia, was generally recognised, and in the next part of this work we shall find a Bulgarian monarch dubbing himself " Emperor of the Bulgarians and Wallachs." This has been interpreted as meaning that he was lord of a part of what is now Roumania, as well as Bulgaria, and a "Wallacho-Bulgarian Empire" has been constructed on this hypothesis. But what the phrase really means is that the "Wallachs," over whom the Bulgarian Czar claimed authority, were not those of Roumania, but those of Bulgaria. In that sense he was "Emperor of the Wallachs," but he was never head of an empire which included the Wallachs north of the Danube, who were at that time subject to the rule of the Kumani. The theory arose at a later period when the only Wallachs whom people knew were the natives of the principality of Wallachia. The Wallachs, who are first mentioned by that name at the beginning of the eleventh century as allies of the Byzantine Emperor Basil, "the Bulgar-slayer," are frequently alluded to after that date, and the descriptions given of them clearly prove that they were of Roman origin.

The long era of barbarian rule in Roumania was drawing at last to a close. The Kumani, who were converted to Christianity in 1227, ceased to be dangerous soon afterwards, and succumbed to the attacks of the Mongol Tartars about 1240. This was the final irruption of savage hordes into the country. The only other foreigners who exercised power there at this period were men of a very different stamp, the Teutonic Knights and the Knights of St. John, who for a score of years at the beginning of the thirteenth century obtained grants of Roumanian land from the King of Hungary. But the stay of these military orders was as short as that of the Tartar hordes. The former soon quarrelled with the King of Hungary and had to leave, the latter, after making the old Dacian province a desert in less than three years, migrated to Russia and troubled the Balkan states no more.

The land had, indeed, rest. For a thousand years, since the Roman legions left, it had been the prey of one set of invaders after another. The lamp of history sheds but little light upon the gloom of this long period. We can see in the dim distance the figures of the barbarians moving in lengthy procession across the scene, but we cannot discern their features or observe their gestures. From this point we are able to see more clearly the leading actors in the drama. With the foundation of the two principalities of Moldavia and Wallachia in the thirteenth century, a new epoch of Roumanian history begins. Then, for the first time, the Roumanian people attempted to establish an independent national existence. True, it was not long before the all-conquering Turks subjected them too to the overlordship of the Sultan. But the national sentiment, which had been awakened, was never wholly extinguished. History possesses few instances of a nation preserving its own individuality so steadfastly and so long. Like those rivers in the Balkan Peninsula, which suddenly disappear beneath the mountains and as suddenly issue forth unpolluted miles away, the Roumanian race pursued for centuries a hidden course only to emerge with undiminished vigour at the end.

IV.

THE TWO PRINCIPALITIES.

(1290—1601.)

AFTER the departure of the Tartar hordes about the middle of the thirteênth century, the Roumanians of the mountains gradually descended into the plains and occupied the lands, which their forefathers had abandoned centuries earlier. For a generation after the last of the barbarians had gone, no settled government seems to have existed in the country, though we hear of petty chiefs, who exercised authority over their immediate neighbours. But in 1290 a Roumanian leader, named Radou Negrou, or Rudolph the Black, came down from the Carpathians and established his sway over Wallachia. A little later, a Roumanian colony, which had made its home in Transylvania, sought to escape from the yoke of the Hungarians, to whom that country belonged, by migrating to Moldavia. A picturesque legend tells us how Dragoche, the leader of this band, halted one day on the banks of a stream, which flowed through a charming region, abounding in game. Here the chief resolved to remain, so he christened the river Moldava, and the land Moldavia after his faithful hound, Molda. Such is the legendary account of the foundation of the two Danubian principalities of Wallachia and Moldavia, which continued to exist in one form or another, until their union under a single ruler in the present century.

The early princes have not left much mark upon history. Radou Negrou and his first five successors, whose reigns together fill about a century, were chiefly occupied in repelling the claims of the kings of Hungary to their newly-constituted state and resisting the efforts of the Popes to convert them to the Roman Catholic faith. But the matrimonial alliances, which they made with the Servian monarchs at a time when Servia was at its zenith, show that they must have been personages of considerable influence. The Moldavian rulers were simultaneously engaged in throwing off the last vestiges of Hungarian authority, and in extending their dominions towards the Black Sea. But in 1386 a strong man arose in Wallachia, who is known in the annals of his country as Mirtschea the Old, or the Great. Like several Balkan rulers, to whom the latter epithet has been applied, Mirtschea obtained the throne by means of a horrible domestic tragedy. It is said that he killed his brother and seized his crown. But such deeds of violence were so common in that age that they attracted little notice, while the appearance of a new and terrible enemy in the country demanded the presence of a vigorous ruler in Wallachia. In 1391 the Turks for the first time crossed the Danube.

MIRTSCHEA THE GREAT.

Already the Roumanians had come in contact with their future masters south of that river. Nearly thirty years earlier a Roumanian contingent had assisted the Serbs in their disastrous attempt to recapture Adrianople from the Mussulmans, and Roumanian soldiers fought by the side of their fellow-Christians on the fatal field of Kossovo, where the Servian Empire fell in 1389. The Sultan Bajazet sent an army across the Danube to punish Mirtschea for this act of hostility. Mirtschea, weakened by the destruction of a large part of his army at Kossovo, was defeated, captured, and sent for a time as a prisoner to Broussa in Asia Minor. He was, however, soon set free on condition of paying an annual tribute to the Turks. On the registers of the Sublime Porte Wallachia is inscribed as a tributary state as far back as 1391. This "first capitulation," as it has been called, provided that "the country should be governed by its own laws, and that its ruler should have the power of making war and peace." But the document proceeds to state that "in return for Our great condescension in having accepted this *rayah* amongst the other subjects of Our Empire, he will be bound to pay into Our Treasury, every year, the sum of six thousand red piastres of the country." But Mirtschea did not long remain the obedient vassal of the Sultan. He made an alliance with his old enemy, the King of Hungary, against the common foe, and the two allies took part in the great battle of Nicopolis in 1396, when the Turks gained a signal victory over the fine flower of the Christian chivalry. Recognising that all was lost, Mirtschea withdrew to his own dominions, where the Turks soon followed him. But this time they were not successful. The Wallachian army routed them with such slaughter that they retired, and the defeat and capture of the Sultan Bajazet by Timour the Tartar at Angora a few years later gave rise to a disputed succession, which was most favourable to the Roumanian cause. Mirtschea, who was not only a good soldier but a clever diplomatist, played off one Turkish pretender against another till the accession of Mohammed I. reunited the scattered forces of the Ottoman Empire and forced him to submit. For the second time Wallachia bowed before a Turkish suzerain, while preserving her local independence. Moldavia, more fortunate because more remote, had hitherto escaped the Ottoman yoke. But she had been forced to acknowledge the overlordship of her Northern neighbour, the King of Poland, who regarded her chief, or *voïvode*, as his vassal.

Mirtschea died in 1418, not long after this second submission to the Turks. Had he been born at a period when they were less powerful, he might have founded a strong kingdom. But, like all the other minor monarchs of his age, he had to yield before the invincible Janissaries. His countrymen cherish his memory, and one of the poets of modern Roumania has sung how

"The aged Mirtschea, firm and undismayed,
With his braves, a handful, meets the furious raid."

The next quarter of a century, in both Wallachia and Moldavia, was marked by civil wars, which distracted the principalities when they ought to have been preparing for a struggle against the Turks. In both of them the law of succession to the throne was the cause of great mischief. There was no fixed system of heredity, but every member of the reigning family had the right to succeed if elected by the nation, represented by an assembly of great nobles and clergy. If the last prince had only one son, all went smoothly; but if he had more than one, the land was honeycombed with intrigues, and there were as many parties as members of the princely family. Nor was that all. When one of the candidates had at last seated himself on the throne, he often found it necessary to secure the support of some stronger power to keep him there. Thus, Moldavia became the shuttlecock of the rival sovereigns of Poland and Hungary. Sometimes the competing candidates for the throne divided the country between them, and thus the confusion was increased. At one period we find three different princes reigning in Moldavia alone, all ready to purchase power, such as it was, at any price. "We cannot defend ourselves," said the advisers of one weak Moldavian ruler about this time, "we must bow our heads before the accursed thing." But in 1456 and 1457 two strong princes ascended the thrones of the principalities; these were Vlad "the Impaler" or "the Devil," in Wallachia, and Stephen the Great in Moldavia.

The hideous surname, which history has bestowed upon this Wallachian prince, was fully deserved. No man, even in that age, was so cruel. Contemporary

STEPHEN THE GREAT OF MOLDAVIA.

writers describe him as a tiger, who thirsted for human blood. In six years he put twenty thousand persons to death by the most horrible tortures—a record which it would be hard to surpass even in the sanguinary annals of the Orient. But Vlad not only craved the blood of his victims; he took a fiendish delight in mocking their agonies when under torture. His cruelty had, at least, the effect of suppressing brigandage and intimidating the disloyal nobles. When the Sultan sent an army against him, not a single man of them dared to desert him, although his brother was on the side of the Turks. Foreign merchants had no fear of travelling with large sums of money through a land where thieves met with such a terrible fate. Vlad chafed under the ignominy to which the puny successors of Mirtschea had submitted, and refused to send the annual tribute of five hundred youths, which Wallachia was expected to furnish for the corps of Janissaries. Mohammed II. headed an army against this audacious ruler, but Vlad, disguised as a Turk, spied out the Turkish camp and utterly routed the invaders, impaling those whom he took prisoners. But he did not long keep his crown. Stephen the Great of Moldavia, whom he had placed on the throne of that country, attacked him in 1462 while he was pursuing the Turks, and forced him to seek refuge in Hungary. Wallachia came under the influence of the sister-principality after his flight, and, though he was afterwards restored, he fell by the hand of an assassin. Moldavia rued ere long the fatal blunder of her prince in dethroning the man, who, in spite of his cruelties, had been a bulwark of the two principalities against the Turks, soon to become masters of both.

Stephen the Great, who owed his crown to Vlad the Impaler, spent most of his long reign of nearly fifty years in constant wars, which he believed to be the best means of keeping up the courage of his people. As he was generally successful, he was very popular, and his physician has given a glowing description of the prosperity of Moldavia under his warlike rule. He acted on the principle of dealing with his enemies singly. Confident in his star, and convinced that sooner or later the Turks would invade his country, he preferred that the struggle should take place during his lifetime. He had incurred their enmity by deposing their puppet, who had followed Vlad on the Wallachian throne, and endeavoured accordingly to form a league of Christian powers against them. At Racova in 1475 the first battle between a Moldavian and a Turkish army was fought. By the device of placing a number of trumpeters in a wood, Stephen made the Turks believe that they had not one but two armies in front of them. The complete victory, which he won, excited the intense admiration of his contemporaries, who addressed him as the "fittest chief of a European coalition against Islam."

The Venetians were so impressed with his importance that they despatched a special envoy to his Court, and the Pope wrote to him as a defender of Christendom. But the next year the Turks had their revenge on a battlefield, which was henceforth called *Valea Alba*, or "the White Valley," from the number of Moldavian soldiers whose bones lay bleaching there. Stephen, nothing daunted, collected a fresh force a few years later, and chased the enemy from the country. The story goes that his mother bade him return to his army, when he was inclined to despair of victory, and a Roumanian poet has represented her as urging him to—

> "Hasten to thy brave ones; for thy country fall;
> Then a mother's love with wreaths shall deck thy pall."

Stephen returned at her bidding, and conquered. But he was wise enough to foresee the ultimate triumph of the Ottomans, and on his deathbed is said to have advised his son Bogdan to make a treaty with the Porte. After this advice he secured the succession by ordering the instant decapitation of the nobles whom he suspected of intriguing against his successor. This last act of a dying man sufficiently shows how little men thought of such crimes in Roumania four centuries ago. The careers of Vlad the Impaler and Stephen the Great are characteristic of their era.

Moldavia now speedily made submission to the Turks. Stephen's father had paid tribute as far back as 1456; Stephen's son, who succeeded in 1504, concluded an arrangement with the Sultan nine years later, in which he promised to pay an annual sum of 11,000 piastres, forty falcons, and forty mares, besides pledging himself to assist his suzerain in time of need. In return, the Sultan guaranteed the integrity of the country, forbade the erection of mosques

and the residence of Turks within it, and granted
the people the right to elect their own princes. But
the subjection of Moldavia remained merely nominal
until another of her rulers, driven out of the country
by dissensions, purchased the aid of the Turks by
further concessions. Not only was the tribute increased,
but a force of five hundred Turkish horsemen
was sent to guard the prince, whose son was detained
at Constantinople as a hostage for his good behaviour.
The degenerate descendants of Mirtschea had done
the same in Wallachia, and the system of buying the
support of the Sultan made that sovereign the arbiter
of Roumania's destinies. One zealous candidate for
the throne even adopted the Mahommedan faith, in
order to curry favour with his patrons. As long as
Hungary preserved her independence, her influence
was usually exerted against that of the Turks; but,
when she too fell before them, they were absolute
masters of the Danubian principalities, and could
make and re-make princes as they chose. The ladies
of the Sultan's harem were won over by the wives of
ambitious Roumanians, and used their insidious influence
with their Imperial master for this or that
party in the principalities. All the artifices of
Oriental diplomacy were employed to win the
favour of those who had crowns to dispose of, and
the vendors showed absolute indifference to the
claims of any save the highest bidder. One of these
purchasers was a Greek adventurer, who had become
a Protestant under the influence of the Reformation
in Germany, and had fought in the armies of the Most
Catholic King of Spain! This remarkable person,

having once obtained the dignity of prince by the most open bribery, set himself to benefit his adopted country, founded an excellent school near Jassy, endeavoured to check divorce, even then a fashionable Roumanian foible, and built a Lutheran church, the first of its kind in Moldavia. By far the most beautiful religious edifice of Roumania, the celebrated Cathedral of Courtea d'Ardges, on the slopes of the Carpathians, dates from this period. Erected by Neagoe Bassarab, who was prince of Wallachia about 1520, and one of the few peace-loving and artistic rulers of his day, this splendid monument may compare with some of the finest efforts of ecclesiastical architecture. The story runs that the founder, while a prisoner at Constantinople, was employed by the Sultan to design a mosque. But the materials proved to be more than sufficient, and the architect obtained leave to transport those which were not required to his native country. Out of these he built the cathedral, as a tablet outside it informs the traveller. But the work seemed as though it would never be finished. Neagoe ordered his assistant architect, Manole, to complete it without delay, and the latter, fearing for his life, resolved to build a live woman into the foundations, in accordance with a horrible custom. He summoned his men to decide upon the victim, and they agreed that the woman who first appeared with their food next day should be doomed to this terrible fate. In order to make the chances equal, none of them was to tell his wife what might be in store for her on the morrow. Manole alone kept his promise, and, in consequence, his wife, unconscious of her fate, came first on the following day.

A Roumanian poem tells how he carried out the agreement, and with his own hand built his wife Utza into the wall, and from that time the cathedral fell no more, for " Utza within the wall upholds it." But the guilty masons met with a frightful punishment. So loud were their boasts, when the cathedral was at last finished, that Neagoe had the scaffolding removed and left them to die of hunger on the roof. In their despair, they tried to leap down, only to meet with certain death on the stones below. Last of all, Manole approached the parapet and prepared to jump. But as he came near, he heard the cries of his wife, and fell senseless on the rocks. A fountain, called by his name, commemorates his fall. The cathedral, restored in the seventeenth century, is a striking proof of the taste of the prince who founded and the prince who renovated it. It shows that even at a period when Wallachia had sunk politically low, she was not without refinements of art, while the philosophical writings of Neagoe, couched in the form of precepts addressed to his son, are among the earliest literary productions of Roumania.

The state of society during this period was based upon the feudal system. The nobles, or *boyards*, as they were called, were a privileged class, and did what was right in their own eyes. They made and unmade princes, promoted civil wars and oppressed the peasantry, as they chose. All the great offices of the principalities were in their hands. One of their number was *logothete*, or Lord High Chancellor, and kept the great seal ; another was Groom of the Bedchamber ; a third was Minister of Finance. Lesser nobles held the posts of Chief Cook, Master of the Horse, and Head Janitor. The *boyards* paid no direct taxes, and in the beginning of the present century were granted complete exemption from all taxation whatsoever. They were entitled to make the peasants work on their lands and exact a tithe of the poor man's crop. But in the earlier days of the principalities, the peasant was not a serf, tied to the soil, but could migrate as he pleased, and was permitted to hold property of his own. Agriculture was the chief occupation of the people, horses and cattle were the greatest source of wealth. Genoese merchants drove a good trade in velvets and silks with the luxurious nobles, who were always noted for their love of fine clothes, and the Roumanian town of Giurgevo derived its name from San Giorgio, the patron saint of Genoa. The prince always reserved to himself the right of pre-emption, and in this, as in all other respects, he was autocratic. The sole check upon his power was the fear of a rival, supported by a faction of the nobles. He enjoyed supreme judicial power, his will was law ; he could order off an innocent person to instant execution without a murmur being heard. Violence was the characteristic of the epoch, and human life was accounted cheap. Hence the population did not increase. There were few towns of any size, and in Roumania, as in Servia, there was no fixed capital. At different periods there were four capitals of Wallachia and two of Moldavia. Cimpulung, Courtea d'Ardges, Tirgovischtea, and Bucharest were selected one after the other as the seat of the Wallachian Government, while Jassy succeeded Suceava as the Moldavian metropolis. With the final choice of Bucharest and Jassy as capitals, the nobles abandoned country life and gravitated towards those cities. Their main employment came to be appointments at Court, and they regarded their stay on their estates as little short of exile. The nobles, who held no State office, were gradually looked upon as a separate class with the special name of *mazili*, and ultimately became so impoverished, that they were hardly distinguishable from the peasants. The one civilising force at this period was the Church. Favoured by the princes and respected by the people, the clergy exercised considerable political influence, while they had a monopoly of such science as existed. Enormous gifts were made to the monasteries of both principalities, and some idea of their wealth may be gained from the fact that, when their property was secularised in 1863, the State received an annual revenue of £1,000,000 by the transaction, not including the vast tracts of forest which belonged to them. By means of their religious authority, the Roumanian clergy acquired a larger share of wealth than any other class, and the wildest of Roumanian princes acknowledged the favourite maxim of the priesthood, "the sabre does not cut off the bowed-down head."

Towards the end of the sixteenth century two princes revived the old spirit of resistance to the Turks. John the Terrible of Moldavia and Michael the Brave of Wallachia, stand out from among their contemporaries like Stephen the Great and Mirtschea the Old in earlier times. John obtained the throne by starting as a diamond merchant at

Constantinople, and thus securing the patronage of high Turkish officials. Thanks to their support, he

MICHAEL THE BRAVE.

became prince of Moldavia in 1572, whereupon he turned round upon his supporters and summoned his people to follow him against the Mussulman host, which threatened him with deposition. Hated by the nobles the "terrible" prince found that his appeal excited the utmost enthusiasm among the masses. Strongly backed by them, he routed the Turkish armies even without the assistance of the nobility. But one of their number, who had remained with him and had been rewarded with an important command, sold him to the enemy. Faithful to his faithful peasants, he refused to surrender till the last gasp. At length the Turks overpowered him, and their cruel commander ordered his body to be quartered.

The career of Michael the Brave is perhaps the most striking episode in Roumanian history. His brief but brilliant reign illuminated for a moment the darkness which had fallen over Wallachia, and he is regarded by the Roumanians of to-day, who have erected an equestrian statue in his honour at Bucharest, as one of their national heroes. His revolt against the Turkish yoke was the last attempt of the people to recover their independence. Michael ascended the throne of Wallachia in 1593 by the usual means—intrigues at Constantinople, which cost him a fortune. It was the importunity of the Turkish usurers, from whom he had borrowed, which drove him to extremities. These gentry besieged him in his palace and filled the adjoining streets with their constant altercations. At last the prince could tolerate their complaints no longer. He summoned them all to the palace under pretext of dividing a sum of money between them. No sooner were they all inside than he gave the signal to his soldiers to set fire to the building. Not a single Turk escaped; account-books and creditors alike perished in the flames. The Wallachs imitated the example of their prince; everywhere the Turks were ruthlessly massacred. These "Wallachian Vespers" were at once followed by war. The Turks, finding that all attempts to seize Michael by treachery failed, sent an army of forty thousand men into Wallachia with orders to depose him. Three successive Roumanian victories freed the country from the invaders, and when they rallied their beaten forces and renewed the attack, Michael crossed the Danube on the ice, and utterly routed them. Aided by the Moldavian prince, Aaron, he made himself master of both banks of the Danube and ravaged the Turkish provinces as far as the walls of Adrianople. The booty, which he took back to his own country, was immense. Roumania was for the moment lost to the Turks, and Constantinople and other Turkish towns, which largely depended upon the principalities for their supplies of meat, were almost starved. At the Turkish capital the confusion, caused by Michael's triumph, was increased by the fact that the Sultan did not know whom to send against him.

Finding, however, that none of their other plans could be carried out until Wallachia was subdued, the Turks resolved upon another campaign against Michael. The latter, anxious not to fight alone, recognised the nominal authority of Sigismund Bathori, Prince of Transylvania, and consented to act as his lieutenant. In theory he now became the vassal of Sigismund, pledged himself to execute no treaties without the latter's approval, and accepted the decisions of the Transylvanian Diet, in which twelve Wallachian nobles were henceforth to sit as deputies. But although Sigismund actually deposed Aaron of Moldavia, and assumed the high-sounding title of "Prince of Transylvania, Moldavia, and Wallachia," his suzerainty over Michael was merely nominal. It had the desired effect of ensuring his active co-operation against the Turks. In a narrow defile, the Thermopylæ of Roumania, between Giurgevo and Bucharest, Michael awaited the advance of the enemy with a tiny band of followers. The Grand Vizier unfurled the standard of the Prophet at a critical moment of the battle, and Michael at the head of his men performed prodigies of valour. The victory remained with the Roumanians, and three Pashas were among the victims of that day. The Grand Vizier with difficulty escaped death in the marshes which bordered the road. Upon the news of this success, won on August 13, 1595, Sigismund marched to the aid of his vassal with a large force, and the allied armies completed the rout of the invaders. One place after another fell into their hands, and the Turks fled before the "dog" Michael, as they contemptuously called their deadly enemy. Now was the time to carry the war into their country and deal a decisive blow at the Ottoman Empire in its own provinces. The Bulgarians had sent to Michael, promising to rise against their Turkish masters, if he would only come over and help them. But the indolence of Sigismund deprived Michael of his most valuable ally, and in 1596 he made peace with the Sultan, who sent a splendid embassage to the prince whom he had been unable to conquer. Michael was assured of the pardon and favour of the august ruler, whose armies he had scattered before him. It is interesting to note that he availed himself of the good offices of the English Ambassador at Constantinople in his negotiations with the Sultan.

Michael had accomplished his great object of freeing his land from the Turkish yoke. He now set to work to realise the grand idea of uniting the whole Roumanian people in one nation by annexing not only Moldavia but Transylvania to his own principality. For a moment he succeeded in making the dream of a Daco-Roman realm an accomplished fact, and his success, temporary though it was, has not been without influence on the Roumanians of our own time, who look upon him as "the representative of the national unity." He first attacked Transylvania, where Sigismund had been succeeded by his cousin, Cardinal Andrew Bathori, who was ready to become the vassal of the Sultan. A single battle placed that country, the "citadel of ancient Dacia," in his power. This decisive blow was struck at Schellenberg in 1599. The cardinal fought at the head of his troops and hurled the bitterest reproaches at the enemy, who had so treacherously attacked him. As he fled from the field, some shepherds fell upon him and slew him, and Michael entered the Transylvanian capital as a conqueror. His entry was long remembered for the kingly pomp which he displayed. His richly-ornamented scimitar, his costly mantle of silk and gold, his band of gipsy musicians, and the roar of his cannon proved to his new subjects that the victor was no ordinary man. By his conquest of Transylvania, a country reputed almost impregnable by reason of its mountain fastnesses, Michael won for himself a front rank among the warriors of his age. But the German Emperor, who regarded Transylvania as a fief, became suspicious of the ulterior motives of the prince, who pretended to be acting in his name, but had been welcomed as a deliverer by the Roumanian peasantry of the conquered land. For the moment, however, Michael was unmolested. The common people were devoted to him because he was of their own blood; the Hungarian nobles, who formed the dominant class in Transylvania, concealed from fear the hate which they felt for him.

Master of Transylvania, Michael next turned his attention to Moldavia. He assembled a large army, under the audacious pretext of putting an end to the Ottoman Empire, and then suddenly entered Moldavia in 1600, "in the name of the German Emperor," who was greatly opposed to the scheme. The campaign was as short as that in Transylvania. One victory sufficed to crush all resistance, and Michael was lord of the whole Roumanian race. All its three divisions were united under his sway, and he proudly styled himself, "Prince of all Wallachia, Transylvania, and Moldavia." But this union was of short duration. Michael's "big Roumania" collapsed almost as soon as it had been built up.

Michael had committed a tactical blunder in Transylvania by the severity with which he repressed the revolt of the Roumanian peasants against their

Hungarian masters. He thus alienated the sympathies of the class which was devoted to him without gaining those of the nobles, who regarded him as an alien, and only awaited a favourable opportunity to overthrow him. The Emperor had grown more and more suspicious; the Hungarian malcontents worked on his fears; his emissaries invited them to rise against Michael. Surrounded by traitors on every side, Michael's one chance would have been to encourage the peasants to attack their superiors. But it was too late. The mercenaries in his army had preyed upon the wretched country folk and thus completed what Michael himself had begun. The Roumanians of Transylvania were less eager than ever to take up arms in defence of a prince who, although a fellow-countrymen, punished their misdeeds with severity and allowed his troops to plunder their homes. The feeling of a common nationality was not strong enough to counteract grievances so practical as these. Meanwhile the nobles, aided by the Imperial General Basta, raised the standard of revolt. Michael threatened the Emperor with the terrors of a Turkish alliance, pointing out that the Sultan would willingly grant him undisturbed possession of all Roumania as the price of his support. But he hesitated to carry out his threat, and while he hesitated, Basta hastened to attack him. The battle took place near the village of Mirischlau in the autumn of 1600. The wily "Italian hound," as Michael termed his adversary, pretended to retreat. Michael fell into the trap, was taken at a disadvantage during the pursuit, and defeated. When he saw that all was lost, he bade his officers bring him the flag, a raven with a red cross in its beak upon a field of green. Hiding it in his breast, he rode at full speed from the field, pursued by the enemy. He came to a river where there was no ford, and it looked as if he would certainly be taken prisoner. But his trusty steed swam the stream, and Michael was saved. He now betook himself to the Carpathians, where the Hungarian nobles sought him high and low. A price was put upon his body, alive or dead, and most of his followers forsook him. Moldavia revolted; Transylvania he had lost; even Wallachia was taken from him. In his despair, he took the bold step of throwing himself at the feet of the German Emperor. He presented himself at the Imperial Court at Vienna early in 1601, and after a somewhat cold reception, recovered the favour of that sovereign. The fact was that, since his defeat, the Transylvanian nobles had restored their old prince, Sigismund Bathori, and the Emperor preferred even Michael to him. Besides, Transylvania was the bulwark of the Empire against the Turks, and a strong arm was needed to defend it. Accordingly, Michael was appointed Viceroy of that country, and commissioned with an army for the purpose of deposing Sigismund. In conjunction with his old enemy, Basta, Michael made short work of that prince. But the jealousy of the two allies soon provoked a catastrophe. Basta hated Michael, and Michael despised Basta, while each regarded the other as a rival. The Italian resolved at last to "remove" the Roumanian from out of his path. At a moment, when his enemy was off his guard, he ordered a body of mercenaries to arrest him as a traitor. When the captain of the band summoned him to yield, he sprang up from the bed on which he was lying in his tent, and vowed that he would sooner die. But before he could reach his sword, he fell, pierced through the body. Not content with his death, the assassins cut off his head with his own weapon. His few faithful followers dispersed, and Basta had nothing more to fear from them. But the Emperor refused to reward the murderer of a man who, with all his faults, was the greatest Roumanian of them all.

No other Roumanian hero achieved so much in so short a space of time as Michael the Brave. His whole reign was only eight years long, for he died in 1601, yet he had compressed into it the events of a generation. The results of his policy were quickly obtained, and as quickly lost. He made his unfortunate people pay heavily for the glory of his conquests. Having to maintain a large army of mercenaries, and receiving scant subsidies from the Emperor, he had to raise funds on his own account. He could not safely extort money from the Wallachian *boyards*, because he relied upon their loyalty while he was absent on his campaigns. He did not consider it politic to increase the burdens of the conquered countries, and actually lowered the taxes of Moldavia, so that he was driven to oppress the poor peasants of Wallachia, who were too humble to resist. In order to meet his demands, many of them gave up their little farms, and sold themselves and their children as serfs for cash down. Villages, which could not pay

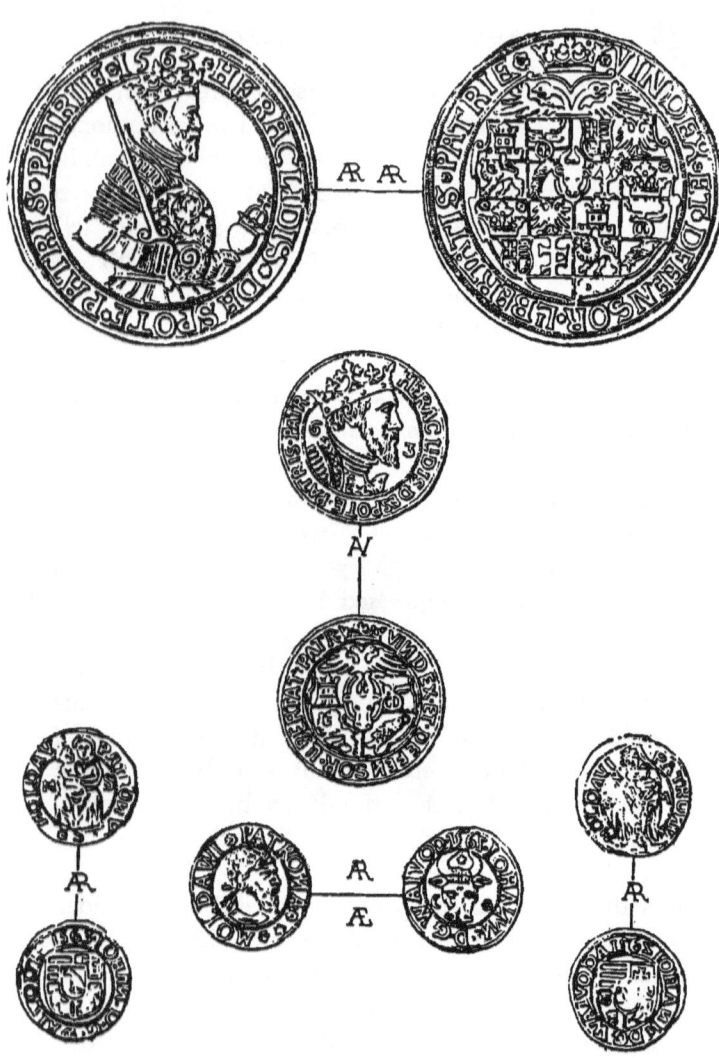

MOLDAVIAN COINS.

the taxes, were sometimes confiscated by the prince, and the inhabitants chained to the soil. In short, he found political support among the nobles, rather than the people, and accordingly favoured the former at the expense of the latter. He would have succeeded better had he "taken the people into partnership," instead of treating them as food for powder or taxpaying machines. His policy was thus the exact opposite of that of John the Terrible in Moldavia, who relied upon the peasantry and was hated by the nobles. It was, more than anything else, the lack of popular support, which rendered the work of Michael the Brave so ephemeral. He endeavoured to make up for the want of it by diplomatic devices, playing off one great power against another, now leaning towards the Emperor, now appearing to incline towards his old enemies the Turks. While he averted the political decline of his country for a short space of time, he accelerated its economic ruin by the legal sanction of serfdom. The condition of the peasantry became visibly worse from his time onwards, and an oligarchy of privileged nobles tended more and more to concentrate power in its own hands. Instead of combining with other Christian princes in a league for the permanent emancipation of their lands from the Turkish yoke, he frittered away his resources on other, though less important, schemes of conquest. He is said to have meditated an even larger extension of his dominions. But no Roumanian kingdom could have stood, so long as the Turks were to be feared.

With Michael the heroic age of Roumanian history

closes, and the Ottoman ascendency becomes more marked. Hitherto, attempts had been made to shake it off, but now resistance seemed useless. True, the Turks never converted the principalities into a Pashalik like Bulgaria and Servia; they professed to rule the lands beyond the Danube by deputy. Hitherto, that deputy had been a native. But in the next period we shall find a new influence, that of the Greeks, making its way into Roumania, and gradually overpowering the old native families, until at last Greek governors take their place.

V.

THE PHANARIOTES IN ROUMANIA.

UPON the death of Michael the Brave the principalities fell more and more under the influence of foreigners. The Greeks had long occupied prominent positions in the Roumanian hierarchy, a common form of religion holding the two races together. But they now began to take a more active part in the political life of the people. Radou Mihnea, one of the early successors of Michael, was the first prince who favoured the Greek element at the expense of the native aristocracy. Educated on Mount Athos, this ruler arrived in Wallachia with a whole army of Greek adventurers, whose speedy advancement soon raised the anger of the *boyards*. A bloody revolution was the result, in which the latter prevailed. Meanwhile, the Turks had become harder masters than ever. They made and unmade princes, or transferred them from one principality to the other with such frequency that in seventeen years there were six reigns in Wallachia and ten in Moldavia. These transactions were conducted by the Greeks of Constantinople, who had constituted themselves the Turks' men of business, and were adepts at the sale of such profitable property as the Wallachian and Moldavian crowns. Fresh revolts of the *boyards* followed, and the poorer inhabitants were almost ruined by the exactions of their rulers. In Moldavia the ravages of the Poles were an additional grievance, and the servile prince consented to pay a tribute to the King of Poland as well as to the Sultan. The peasants had therefore to provide the funds to satisfy two simultaneous demands. No wonder that, in the words of a Venetian diplomatist, the " land sweated blood." Yet so eager was the competition for the Moldavian throne, that we find one candidate going as far as England, in order to obtain the good offices of King James I. with the Sultan. As soon as a prince was elected, he at once realised the truth of the saying that every appointment causes twenty disappointments. Office at Court had become the great object of the nobles, and as the number of offices was limited, all those who found themselves excluded naturally joined the opposition, and intrigued against the ruler whom they had just helped to the throne. The one cry which united all the *boyards* in the early years of the seventeenth century was that of " Roumania for the Roumanians." Against the Greeks they were solid ; otherwise, each man fought and intrigued for his own hand ; no one cared one jot for the welfare of the people. But their efforts to keep out the foreigner failed, and the Sultan showed his disregard for the national sentiment by sending an Italian to govern Moldavia in 1619. The independence of the Roumanian nation had, indeed, almost disappeared. The one oasis in

BASIL "THE WOLF."

MATTHEW BASSARAB.

this desert of corruption is the vigorous administration of Matthew Bassarab and Basil "the Wolf" in their respective principalities.

These two remarkable princes were contemporaries. Bassarab ruled over Wallachia from 1633 to 1654, Basil governed Moldavia from 1634 to 1653. Both owed their elevation to the throne to a wave of indignation against the growing influence of the Greeks; both represented the national party at the outset, but both found that they could not dispense with the aid of the foreigners, who held the key of the situation at Constantinople. To keep on good terms with the Sultan, it was necessary to pacify his Greek advisers; to pacify the latter, it was necessary to be gracious to their fellow-countrymen in Roumania. While Bassarab temporised between the two parties, Basil, once on the throne, threw in his lot with the Greeks, to the disgust of the natives.

The reigns of these two princes are noteworthy as the era of law reform and general culture in Roumania. The first systematic attempt to give the principalities a code of law was due to them. Hitherto custom had taken the place of written paragraphs, and judicial proceedings had been rough and ready. There are, indeed, traces of an institution found there at a very early date analogous to our trial by jury; but the prince had been regarded as the chief arbiter between litigants, and he could decide as he chose. Now, however, a change was introduced. The criminal code of Basil, savage as it is, constituted a great advance upon any previous method of jurisprudence. Draco himself was hardly more severe than the Moldavian lawgiver. The leading principle of his judicial system was "an eye for an eye and a tooth for a tooth." The man, who set a house on fire, was burnt alive; the serf, who was guilty of rape, met with the same horrible fate; the children of a poisoner were degraded, to show the ruler's detestation of that very common form of murder; the Roumanian, who had two wives, was put naked on a donkey's back, and whipped through the streets; the seducer was sentenced to have boiling lead poured down his throat. Theft was pardoned, however, if it was committed to avert starvation, or if the thief had stolen from the public enemy. One curious trait in this legislation is the resolute attempt to suppress sorcery and put down quacks of all kinds, whose evidence is not accepted. The torture of the innocent, in order to gain information, is expressly forbidden. But there is no conception of equality before the law. The *boyard* and his children might not be hung or impaled, or sent to work in the salt mines or the galleys. In Moldavia beheading was considered to be the appropriate end of a noble criminal, while banishment was the punishment of his lesser misdemeanours. The serf met with little consideration in the eyes of the law; to harbour him, if he fled from his lord and master, was a crime; to ill-treat him was no offence. Bassarab drew up a similar code for the sister principality, and incorporated with it a number of civil ordinances for the distribution of property after death, the appointment of guardians, and several other enactments, borrowed from the Roman law.

To him belongs the credit of establishing the first printing-press at Bucharest. The first book printed in the Roumanian language on Roumanian soil was his collection of canon law, which appeared in 1640. Hitherto, while the Roumanian had been the vernacular, Slav had been the language of literature. But henceforth books were issued in a tongue which the people could understand. Basil soon followed the example of his rival, and the printing-press of the monastery at Jassy produced a volume of sermons in 1643. Beginning with legal and religious treatises, the printers soon widened the area of their labours, and Roumanian began to be the language not only of the peasants and nobles, but of the printed books, which the more cultivated of them began to read. Basil founded a school at Jassy, where instruction was given in the mother-tongue, and the growth of Greek culture and the spread of the Greek idiom could not stifle it.

Unfortunately, Bassarab and Basil did not seek to rival one another in the arts of peace alone. From the first, they were deadly enemies. Bassarab sought the aid of the Emperor at Vienna; Basil denounced his foe to the Sultan at Constantinople, and invaded his territory. Defeated by the Wallachian prince, and coldly treated by the Turks, he applied to the Poles for support, and again attacked Bassarab. But this second venture was more disastrous than the first. Not only was he routed in battle, but driven from the throne by a rising of his subjects, who were weary of his anti-national policy. The year after his flight, his rival died, and with their removal from the scene, the principalities relapsed into their previous unfortunate condition. The fratricidal conflict of these two rulers, harmful though it proved, was more than counterbalanced by the great advances in culture and legality, which Roumania had made under their auspices.

Their work was continued after an interval of a quarter of a century by Scherban Cantacuzene, who ascended the Wallachian throne in 1679. This enlightened ruler, whose restoration of the cathedral of Courtea d'Ardges has been already mentioned, diminished the burdens of the peasantry, fostered the growth of education, and brought out a Roumanian version of the Bible. Forced against his will to assist the Turks in their famous siege of Vienna in 1683, he turned against them at a critical moment, and when ordered to bombard the city, loaded his cannon with balls of hay. After the defeat of the Ottoman besiegers, he contemplated proclaiming the independence of Wallachia, and entered into negotiations with the Emperor Leopold, who offered him his protection. At one moment, it looked as if a general rising of the Christian subjects of Turkey might have ensued, and Scherban dreamed of leading a new crusade against the Sultan and transplanting his own throne from the banks of the Danube to the shores of the Bosphorus. But his worst foes were those of his own household. His brothers and nephew opposed his schemes, and he was poisoned at their instigation. Wallachia was too small a state to liberate herself unaided, and with Moldavia was rarely at one. Those who desired to emancipate her from the Turk looked abroad for aid. Vienna was the place, from which many of them had expected help; but they now saw in the rising power of the "Colossus of the North" an alternative means of safety. The star of Russia had appeared in the firmament, and they sought guidance from its light.

The Russians, whose close connection with the history of Roumania now begins, had for some time been on friendly terms with its rulers. As far back as the end of the fifteenth century a prince of Moldavia had married his daughter to a son of the Czar. But the personal relations thus formed had had no political influence until a much later date. In 1674, however, the two principalities made overtures to Russia through the mediation of a monk, who was sent to implore the Czar to throw his protection over the Danubian Christians. The offer was favourably received. Alexis, who then sat on the Russian throne, suggested that a number of Roumanian notables should be sent to arrange terms, and promised that, as soon as the "sovereigns" of Moldavia and Wallachia had taken the oath of allegiance to him, he would "grant them subsidies and defend them against the enemies of the Cross." Nothing, however, came of this proposal at the time, but in 1688 the Prince of Wallachia, wearied with the exactions of the Turks, again applied to Russia for aid. Peter the Great, who was then Czar, made the same response; but it was not till 1711 that the Russians and Roumanians formed an alliance for the first time. At this period Constantine Brancovano was prince of Wallachia and Demetrius Cantemir of

Moldavia. The former promised to provide Peter with thirty thousand soldiers and ample provisions, for which he received a large sum of money from Russia; the latter concluded a secret treaty with the Czar, by which the Russians bound themselves to defray the expenses of maintaining a standing army in Moldavia, guaranteed the safety of the Moldavian throne, and undertook neither to marry nor acquire land in the principality. The object of Peter the Great was clear. Devoted to naval affairs, he was resolved to be master of the Black Sea, and convert it, if possible, into a Russian lake. To attain this object, he was glad to avail himself of those religious ties which were a bond of union between the Christian subjects of the Porte and himself. Long before, a Venetian diplomatist had said that "the Sultan feared the Muscovite ruler, because he belonged to the same faith as the peoples of Bulgaria, Servia, and Bosnia, who would always be ready to take up arms on his side and submit to his authority, in order to throw off the Turkish yoke." Peter himself laid stress upon the religious character of his enterprise. He started as if for a crusade. His banner bore the ancient device "By this sign thou shalt conquer"; his soldiers set out "in the name of the Saviour and Christianity." Had his expedition proved successful, one or both of the principalities would have become part of the Russian Empire, and his boundary might have stretched to the Danube.

The treaty, humiliating though it may seem, was generally popular in Moldavia. The nobles told Cantemir that he had "done well"; the people echoed their sentiments. When the great Czar arrived at Jassy, all the principal inhabitants went out to welcome him as a deliverer; the cathedral bells were rung in his honour; the clergy rejoiced at the advent of a Christian Emperor. There was, it is true, a national party still left, which suspected the motives of the liberator, and it was noticed that when the Russian guests lay down to rest with their generous hosts after the state banquet, the gold-laced boots of the *boyards*, their costly pistols, and their rich ornaments were not forthcoming in the morning. But the enthusiasm of Peter's reception did not compensate him for the inefficiency of his Moldavian allies. Cantemir himself, who wrote a history of the Ottoman Empire, and was a man of great learning, lamented the riotous habits of his subjects, who "spent their pay in the taverns, and preferred plunder and pillage to military service." Brancovano, less zealous than Cantemir, suspended relations with Russia, and Peter, instead of securing a brilliant victory, only escaped capture through the corruption of the Turkish commander. So ended the first campaign of the Russians in Roumania. Cantemir withdrew to Russia with many of his *boyards*, where he received a grant of lands and became a prince of the Empire; Brancovano died a violent death. The Sultan, convinced of his complicity with Peter, and unappeased by his subsequent conduct, ordered his arrest. The emissary entrusted with this command, forced his way into the prince's audience chamber with his Janissaries, threw a black shawl over Brancovano's shoulders, and proclaimed his deposition. Not a hand was raised in the prince's defence. Carried off to Constantinople, he was beheaded in the presence of the Sultan. One member of his family was spared, and the name still exists in Roumania. But his vast possessions, including the crown of the principality, were confiscated by the Turks; the son of the man who had revealed his intrigues with Russia to the Porte was appointed as his successor on the Wallachian throne. But Stephen Cantacuzene, as he was called, did not long enjoy the dubious honour. He shared, two years later, the fate of Brancovano, and, both thrones being vacant, the Sultan resolved to appoint no more native rulers. In the Greeks of Constantinople, who from the " Phanar," or district of the city where they resided, had obtained the name of " Phanariotes," he thought that he would find more pliable instruments of his policy. Nicholas Mavrocordato, whose father had risen from the position of a common labourer to the office of dragoman to the Porte, was accordingly appointed governor of Wallachia in 1716.

The rule of the Phanariote governors of Moldavia and Wallachia, which lasted from 1716 to 1822, was, with some notable exceptions, distinguished by the corruption and maladministration which mark the decline of the Ottoman Empire. The Greek rulers of the two Danubian principalities had to pay heavily for their appointment, and took good care to make their unfortunate subjects make up to them more than they had expended. At their accession they were expected to hand over some sixty thousand pounds sterling to the Sultan, whose interest it naturally was to appoint fresh governors at as frequent intervals as possible. Thus in a period of 106 years there were no fewer than thirty-three different governors of Moldavia, and thirty-five of Wallachia. Having, on an average, only about three years in which to recoup themselves for their initial expenditure, the Phanariote rulers increased the burdens of the natives as much as they could. No sooner had one governor retired than another came to squeeze the unhappy people, and thus there was no limit to the extortions to which the Roumanians had to submit. Besides, the ceremonial which was kept up was most expensive, and for that, of course, the poor provincials had to pay. An English writer, who was Consul at Bucharest towards the end of the Phanariote period, has given a graphic account of their accession to the throne. A *berat*, or patent, signed by the Sultan, was a necessary preliminary, and that, of course, was a costly item. Then, while the newly-appointed governor was engaged in the tedious formalities which were essential to his departure from Constantinople—swearing allegiance to the Sultan and assuming the *kukka*, or military crest, and the grand robe of office—a messenger was despatched before him to prepare his subjects for his arrival. As an interval of about two months generally elapsed before the governor arrived at Bucharest or Jassy, this courier acted as his deputy, not without profit to himself. When at last the great man appeared, he did not come alone. Swarms of needy retainers were in his train, ready to fill all the fat offices which awaited them in the promised land. For every new *Hospodar*, as the governors were called, at once changed all the officials, thinking that the spoils belonged to the new-comer. It can well be understood how badly a country was managed whose civil servants were foreigners, and foreigners, too, who were turned out of their places just when they had begun to grasp the details of administration. While in power, the governor had to expend money judiciously at Constantinople, in order to counteract intrigues against himself. We have from the pen of one of their Court physicians early in the present century a graphic account of their mode of life. Bucharest and Jassy became centres of Asiatic luxury. The *Hospodar* out-ottomaned the Ottomans in his determination to avoid even the slightest form of exertion. His bread was cut up into small pieces, so that his noble fingers need not be compelled to break it, his cupbearer held his goblet of crystal ready at his elbow, his afternoon sleep was ensured by the complete cessation of all business in the city. No bell might ring, no noise of men's voices be heard before his palace while he slept, and it is even said that some of these rulers were lifted by their footmen, so as to save them the trouble of walking from table to bed. Their consorts were as extravagant and extortionate as themselves. The dresses of one princess cost her nearly £2,300, which meant more in the last century than now. Another of these amiable ladies, unable to afford a costume which would " kill " all rivals, persuaded her husband to banish a nobleman's wife who was better dressed than herself. When the princely exchequer was full, and the princess so resplendent with clothes and jewels that she feared no comparison, she invited the disgraced lady to Court and gratified her spite by the spectacle of her enemy's discomfiture.

The Roumanian nobles were contaminated by the example of their Phanariote governors. Naturally fond of luxury and display, they beggared themselves in the foolish attempt to keep up appearances. The main idea of the men was to obtain favour by toadying to the authorities; the chief desire of the women to make good matches. Divorce became frequent; the sons and daughters of noble families saw in a rich marriage the only chance of restoring their fallen fortunes, and the natural result was infidelity or indifference. Even now divorce statistics are high in Roumania as compared with many other countries. As for the clergy, they too became the victims of extortion, and were at last compelled to extort money from their flocks. Society was rotten to the core. The condition of the people was deplorable. Upon them the whole burden of supporting this system of government ultimately fell. If they ventured to murmur, they were put in prison, and the result was that many of them, driven desperate by these exactions, became brigands and took to the mountains. If caught, they were condemned to a lingering death in the salt mines; if fortunate enough to evade the soldiers of the governor, they often acquired great wealth at the expense of their country. Sometimes, however, the scandals of the administration were so notorious that the Sultan felt bound to interfere. In that case, the *Hospodar* had a very short shrift, for his enemies at Constantinople took care that he should not escape.

Thus one of these governors was strangled, and others exiled. Finally, to complete the misery of the people, the currency was debased and huge monopolies interrupted the ordinary course of commerce.

Bad as the Phanariotes were according to the unanimous testimony of their contemporaries, they were not all black. Nicholas Mavrocordato, for example, the first of them who ruled in Wallachia, showed himself the friend of the peasants by abolishing the bands of retainers which the *boyards* kept at their beck and call. This blow at the feudal system was followed by the establishment of law and order throughout the principality. Another Wallachian governor, Constantine Mavrocordato, further weakened the power of the native nobles by transferring their serfs to the new Greek aristocracy which had grown up under the protection of the Phanariote rulers. The change was of doubtful advantage to the peasantry, but it was a source of great strength to the Government. Other governors left their mark on the principalities by erecting fine public buildings and founding large charitable institutions, and occasionally the alien ruler proved a better patriot than the native nobility, the "sleeping dogs," as the people called them.

The chief political events of the Phanariote period were the Russo-Turkish wars, by which the two principalities were deeply affected. The abortive campaign of Peter the Great in 1711 had only served to stimulate the desire of his successors for the development of their Empire. But it was not till 1736 that the Russians made a second attempt to acquire the two principalities. Before declaring war, the Empress Anne, who then ruled the Russian dominions, demanded from the Porte the recognition of Moldavia and Wallachia as independent principalities under a Russian protectorate. This would have been the first step towards a Russian advance into the Balkan Peninsula, for, from their geographical position, the principalities effectually barred the way to any attempt at bringing the Bulgarian and Servian population under Russian influence. Naturally, the Porte refused to accept these terms. The war was less disastrous to the Empress than to her Austrian allies. The Russian Field-Marshal Münich entered Moldavia in 1739, and met with such success that Gregory Ghika, the *Hospodar*, retired with his courtiers, leaving a deputy in his place. Accompanied by the two sons of the former native prince, Cantemir, Münich entered Jassy in state, and received the keys of the Moldavian capital from the head of the Church. But the Field-Marshal was no diplomatist. He treated the country as that of an enemy; he came, not as a liberator, but as a conqueror. In fact, he made the same mistake in Moldavia which in our own time General Kaulbars made in Bulgaria. When the Metropolitan offered him the cross, he declined to kiss it; when the prelate began to pray, he burst out laughing. His conditions, which included a nice annuity for himself, and free quarters for his men, could not have been more oppressive if he had been dealing with Turks instead of co-religionists—and yet their common religion was the favourite plea of the Russians for their intervention. " The people saw," quaintly writes the old Moldavian chronicler, "what a costly honour it was to receive Münich as a guest; sweet wine became vinegar, laughter tears, joy terror, and riches poverty." The eyes of the people were opened; they saw that a Muscovite "liberator" might be as harsh as a Greek governor, and from that moment dates the rise of a strong anti-Russian party in the principalities. The peace of Belgrade in 1739 restored Moldavia to the Turkish Empire, and, as far as their Roumanian projects were concerned, the Russians were no better off at the close of this second war than at the end of the first.

The third attempt was much more successful. Catherine II. began, soon after her accession, the task of preparing the Roumanian people for a Russian occupation. Her secret agents fomented the discontent of the peasantry and played upon the feelings of the native nobles, who saw themselves being gradually displaced by the scum of the Phanar. The declaration of war in 1768 found the Turks at a disadvantage, and a great Russian victory on the river Dniester placed the principalities in the power of the victors. Moldavia hastened to proffer its homage to the Russian commander, Galitzin. In the cathedral of Jassy the congregation took the oath of allegiance to "the too compassionate Empress Catherine," and swore to "consider the enemies of the Russian army as those of Moldavia, and to behave in all things as the good and faithful slaves of Her Majesty." Nothing short of complete annexation was intended. Wallachia next acknowledged the authority of the great Empress. Gregory Ghika, the Wallachian *Hospodar*, turned traitor, and was received at the Russian Court with the utmost honours. Epistles, drawn up by the clergy in the most servile terms, were despatched to Catherine by both principalities, and from 1770 to 1774, they experienced a Russian occupation.

Catherine had promised the native deputations that their countries should enjoy their ancient customs and have complete management of their internal affairs. Moldavia desired to be governed by twelve *boyards*, elected for three years. Wallachia professed to wish for complete incorporation with the Russian Empire. But the people groaned under the necessity of providing quarters and provisions for the Russian army during the war, and discovered that their protectors were as difficult to satisfy as the Turks. The Empress was not able to annex the principalities definitely to her dominions. Austria had become restive at the great expansion of Russia and the jealousy between the two great Powers had already begun to show itself in their dealings with the Christians of Turkey. It was solely in order to pacify Austrian fears that Russia, by the famous treaty of Kutchuk-Kaïnardji in 1774, restored Moldavia and Wallachia to the Sultan on conditions which were very favourable to the inhabitants. The Sultan pledged himself to grant an amnesty to all who had taken sides against him in the late war; to allow full religious liberty; to restore the lands of the monasteries; to levy no taxes for two years, in consideration of the ravages of the contending armies; to impose moderate and regular taxes at the close of that period; and to receive two Greek Christians as the accredited agents of the principalities at Constantinople. Most important of all, a pregnant clause of the treaty granted the Russian Ambassador there the right of "speaking in behalf of the principalities as circumstances may require." This informal Russian protectorate was fatal in the long run to the suzerainty of the Sultan.

But if Austria had been the means of saving the Roumanians from a permanent Russian annexation, she soon showed that she had designs of her own upon their territory. She obtained from the Sultan in 1777 the cession of Bucovina, which then formed the northeastern part of Moldavia and contained Suceava, the ancient capital of the principality, and the venerable convent of Putna, where the remains of the princes were laid. Gregory Ghika, who had been placed by Russian influence on the throne after the war, refused to sign the deed, which deprived him of the most fertile part of his country. His action was interpreted by the Sultan as a further proof of his sympathies with Russia. The order for his "removal" was issued, and he fell beneath the yataghans of some Turkish emissaries in his own capital.

Catherine II. had not abandoned her schemes for the extension of Russian influence in the principalities. In 1782 she obtained from the Porte permission to have Russian consuls at both Bucharest and Jassy, who naturally became the centres of Russian intrigues in their respective spheres. The cost of their maintenance was defrayed by the Moldavian and Wallachian treasuries, and they used their influence to undermine the authority of the Sultan. Their appointment, however unpalatable to the Turks, was the logical outcome of the treaty of Kaïnardji. But Catherine soon took a further step in the pursuit of her grand idea. She met Joseph II. of Austria, and arranged with him a scheme for the partition of the Ottoman Empire—the first of many such proposals, which have seen the light. According to this plan, as neither of the two great Powers would consent to give up the two Danubian principalities unreservedly to the other, they were to be united under Prince Potemkin, the favourite minister of Catherine, as an independent state, which would undoubtedly have been speedily converted into a Russian province. Russia not only invaded the Crimea, then part of the Turkish dominions, but advanced on the Caucasus, and the Sultan replied by declaring war in 1787; a few months later Austria joined in the attack upon the Turks. The Prussian minister Herzberg strongly advised the Sultan to separate his two enemies by handing over the principalities to Russia. "What advantage," he said, "do you Turks gain from the possession of those provinces, whose only use is to enrich a few wretched Greeks and to nourish a few Tartar hordes?" But the Turks thought otherwise, and ordered Nicholas Mavroghéni, who was at that time governor of Wallachia, to raise an army against their enemies. Mavroghéni summoned the *boyards*, and bade them take up arms for the cause of their suzerain. The nobles refused to obey the orders of the Greek viceroy, who did not know a single word of their own language. Mavroghéni, indignant at their conduct, told his groom to lead all the horses in his stables into the courtyard. When the steeds were ready, he again called upon his nobles to mount. Not one of them showed signs of obedience, and the Greek, resolved to show his scorn for these great officials of state, who remained idle at his call, conferred upon his horses the high-sounding titles, of which the *boyards* were unworthy. "Degenerate descendants of Mirtschea, Vlad, and Michael the Brave," he cried, "I banish you from my presence; henceforth my horses shall hold your offices and enjoy your honours." Some of the nobles were so moved by his reproaches that they mounted and followed him, while the rest slunk away and sought an ignominious exile. But Mavroghéni's efforts were futile. The Russians entered the principalities and took up their quarters at the two capitals, and the Greek governor, who had served the Sultan with such rare fidelity, was rewarded by his ungrateful master with degradation and death. His head was cut off, as if he had been a traitor, and his successors were thus effectually discouraged from following his example. But the death of Joseph II. and the outbreak of the French Revolution diverted the attention of Austrian statesmen from the East. Austria made peace with Turkey, and in 1792 Russia concluded the treaty of Jassy with the Porte, by which the former treaty of Kaïnardji was confirmed. The principalities remained in the hands of the Sultan, on condition that the exactions of his Phanariote governors should be checked, while Russia retained her right of intervention. The position of Moldavia and Wallachia after this war, from which so much had been expected by the enemies of Turkey, was almost precisely the same as it had been eighteen years earlier.

The promised reforms of the Phanariote system of government remained a dead letter. A Turkish edict of 1784 had prohibited the removal of the governors except for felony; but this too was disregarded. All the evils of the system continued undiminished. Plague and famine afflicted the land, which had once been the granary of the Turkish Empire. Brigand chiefs, like the notorious Pasvanoglu, of whom we shall hear again in the history of Bulgaria, made repeated inroads into the principalities. The Turkish soldiers, who were sent to suppress him, fraternised with his robber-band; Wallachia cried aloud to be defended from her defenders. The Greek governor and the *boyards* fled at the mere rumour of the terrible brigand's approach, as if a new horde of barbarians were upon them. Such was the condition of the present kingdom of Roumania a century ago.

But in 1802 the dawn of a new era began. The fear of Bonaparte had thrown the Sultan into the arms of Russia. The Czar obtained a provision to the effect that henceforth the governors of Moldavia and Wallachia should be appointed for seven years, and should not be removed during their term of office except for good reason, and even then only with the permission of the Russian ambassador at Constantinople. Thus the vague right of intervention, which Russia had obtained by the treaties of Kainardji and Jassy, was converted into a definite understanding. Another event of much benefit to the Roumanians was the appointment of a British consul at Bucharest, while Russia secured the nomination of two puppets of hers to the Moldavian and Wallachian thrones. These rulers not only pursued an anti-Turkish policy in their own dominions, but privately supported the Serbs, who had just risen under Black George against the Turks. Their consequent deposition by the Sultan in 1806, three years before their term of office had expired, was regarded by Russia and England as so serious a breach of faith, that a bombardment of Constantinople was threatened. The princes were restored, but the Czar, anxious for an excuse for intervention, demanded further securities for the Roumanian people, against the raids of the brigands under Pasvanoglu. Russian troops entered the principalities and war began. But, as long as she feared Napoleon, Russia could make no headway against the Sultan. It was not until the peace of Tilsit in 1807 had relieved her from the necessity of opposing him, that she could devote her undivided attention to the Danubian principalities. The French Emperor was now willing to see her annex Bessarabia, Moldavia, Wallachia, and Bulgaria as far as the Balkans. But, even though liberated for the moment from the fear of Napoleon, the "Colossus of the North" made little progress in Roumania. The treaty of Bucharest in 1812 at last ended this protracted struggle. The delta of the Danube, and the part of Moldavia between the rivers Dniester and Pruth were ceded to the Czar, and the latter instead of the former stream was now the boundary of the Russian and Turkish Empires. The whole of Bessarabia thus passed into the hands of Russia. So disgusted was the Sultan with the conduct of his plenipotentiaries, that he ordered them to be beheaded. The Roumanians, on their part, had gained nothing by the war. Their country had suffered terribly from the presence of the hostile armies, and the inhabitants had sought refuge with all their worldly possessions in the churches in order to escape pillage. The requisitions of the army of occupation were a heavy tax upon the peasants, and the five years during which they had to support their "liberators," were long remembered in the land. To crown all, just as Austria had dismembered Moldavia by taking Bucovina in 1777, so Russia disintegrated the principalities by annexing Bessarabia. A contemporary historian has left us a pitiful account of the heartrending scenes, which took place on the banks of the Pruth, when the moment arrived for the formal cession of the well-loved land. For weeks beforehand, the people went to and fro, bidding farewell to the friends and relatives, from whom they were soon to be separated. From that moment the Pruth became in the language of the peasants, the "accursed river." Thus the century of Russo-Turkish wars from 1711 to 1812, through which they had passed, had been fatal to the Roumanians; instead of recovering their independence, they had lost one part of their ancient territory to Austria, and another to Russia; in the place of Greek and Turkish exactions, they had had Russian armies to maintain. They had learnt one political maxim from these five Russian interventions, that their safety lay in the mutual jealousies of the two great Christian Powers on either side of them.

The Phanariote rule continued for ten years more. But the Greek War of Independence, which broke out in 1821, was destined to give the final blow to the system. The movement in favour of a free Greece was strongly supported in Moldavia by Alexander Ypsilanti, son of a former governor of Wallachia, who set up the standard of revolt at Jassy, and was followed by the reigning *Hospodar* of Moldavia, Michael Soutzo. But the Roumanians had no desire to throw off the Turkish yoke merely to strengthen the influence of the Greeks, whose oppression they had borne so impatiently for more than a century. They refused to take up arms for the Greek cause, more particularly as they saw that Russia was indisposed to assist it openly. They knew that, if it proved successful, they would not be benefited, while, if it were unsuccessful and they were found to have assisted it, the Turks would take a terrible revenge upon them. In Wallachia, a revolution broke out under the leadership of Toudor Vladimirescou, a noble of popular sympathies, whose primary object was to deliver the peasants from the grinding tyranny of the aristocracy, but whose efforts were ultimately directed against the Greeks. Thus the whole Roumanian people was in a ferment ; while one principality was agitated by the rising of Ypsilanti on behalf of Greece, the other was stirred to its foundations by the bold attacks of Vladimirescou against Greek supremacy. A collision between the two revolutionary leaders was inevitable. Ypsilanti, to rid himself of so dangerous a rival, ordered one of his underlings to seize the nationalist chief and bring him before him. A mock trial followed, and the brave Roumanian was murdered by Ypsilanti's cut-throats. The national movement subsided, and

Roumania was given over to the struggles of the Greeks against the Turks. Ypsilanti retired before the advance of the Turkish army, the Greek flotilla was destroyed on the Danube, the Greek leader was routed; fleeing across the Carpathians, he was arrested by order of the Austrian Government, and died in prison, bequeathing to his brother Demetrius the duty of avenging him upon the Turks.

OLD ROUMANIAN SEAL.

But the rising of Vladimirescou had not been altogether in vain. The loyalty of the Roumanians, contrasting as it did so forcibly with the faithlessness of the Phanariote governors, had at last opened the eyes of the Sultan to the real state of things in the two principalities. His interest, no less than theirs, demanded a change, and the most indolent of Turkish officials recognised that it was unsafe to entrust two important governorships to men whose natural sympathies must inevitably be with the Greek insurgents. It has always been the plan of the Turks to maintain their influence by the mutual jealousies of the rival Christian nationalities under their sway. The demands of the Roumanians for governors of their own race were therefore heard at last; and, unwilling to have a discontented Roumania as well as a rebellious Greece, the Porte yielded in 1822. The Phanariote rule was formally ended, and two native *boyards*, Jonitza Stourza and Gregory Ghika were appointed respectively *Hospodars* of Moldavia and Wallachia. For the first time for years the nomination was secured without bribery, and the best men were chosen. The national spirit had revived, and with it the desire for liberty had manifested itself among the people.

VI.

THE UNION OF THE PRINCIPALITIES.

(1822—1866.)

THE influence of the Greeks over the Roumanians was shattered; the ascendency of the Turks was on the wane; the problem, which faced the principalities after the restoration of their native princes, was how to maintain their independence against Russia. The period, which began in 1822, supplies the answer to that question and closes with the picture of a free, autonomous, and prosperous Roumania.

The newly-appointed *Hospodars* found their subjects in a deplorable condition. War, corruption in high places, and universal discontent had marked the Phanariote rule, and there hung over the twin lands the dark shadow of Russia. The masses began to demand a share in the government; the nobles were resolved not to abate one jot of their ancient privileges, and denounced any prince, who showed popular tendencies, as a traitor to his caste. In Moldavia, the *boyards*, supported by the Czar, wrung from the reluctant ruler a "golden bull," by which they were exempted from all taxation; in Wallachia, they tried in vain to overthrow the Government. Such was the state of the principalities when Russia concluded the convention of Akermann with the Sultan in 1826, which gave her greater power over the destinies of the Roumanian people than she could have secured by a successful war. By this arrangement it was provided that the princes of Moldavia and Wallachia should be elected by the general assembly of the nobles for the term of seven years, and that this election should be subject to the approval of the Porte, which could neither refuse its consent nor order their deposition without consulting the Czar. A further clause made it incumbent upon the two princes to "take into their consideration the representations of the Russian ministers and consuls on the subject of the privileges enjoyed by the principalities." The Autocrat of all the Russias thus became the "predominant partner" in Roumania; the Sultan's name came first in the deed of partnership, but the Czar was the active member of the firm.

When the Russo-Turkish war of 1828 broke out, the Imperial troops at once invaded the principalities, which had for the sixth time to experience a Russian occupation. The Turks offered little opposition to the invaders, who dictated peace to the Sultan at Adrianople in 1829. By this treaty, Moldavia and Wallachia were restored to the Turks, but only on condition that the *Hospodars* should be elected for life. All the fortified places, hitherto occupied in Wallachia by Turkish troops, were to be given up, complete internal independence was guaranteed, and nothing but a fixed money tribute was to be exacted in future by the Porte. But the most important point of all was reserved to the last. The Sultan undertook to ratify all the administrative regulations, which had been drawn up during the Russian occupation. Under another article, the Russians were entitled to keep a garrison in the principalities until the full payment of the war indemnity by the Turkish Government. Thus the occupation was prolonged till 1834, and lasted, in all, some six years. All the time the utmost efforts were made to establish the influence of the Czar upon a permanent basis. A constitution was devised which is known as the *règlement organique*, with the express object of strengthening the power of Russia. The Russian Minister Nesselrode wrote complacently that "the conquest of Wallachia and Moldavia was superfluous, for Russia was already their master, without having to keep a permanent force of soldiers in those countries." For the phantom of Turkish suzerainty, the Roumanians had received in exchange the stern reality of a Russian protectorate. The *reglement organique*, the work of the Muscovite administrators, Pahlen and Kisselef, who managed the affairs of the principalities during the Russian occupation, was based upon extreme oligarchical principles. It separated the nation into two sharply divided classes, the nobles and the people; and, while it conceded the greatest latitude to the former, it treated the latter like pariahs. The power of making the laws, the election of the prince, all political offices, all military appointments—these were the peculiar right of the *boyards ;* the less pleasant task of paying all the taxes—that was the exclusive privilege of the peasants and the small tradesmen. In a word, according to the Russian constitution, the Roumanian people had no rights, the Roumanian nobles no duties. At the same time, true to the principle, which afterwards found its fullest expression in the constitution, drawn up for Bulgaria in 1879, the prince and the *boyards* were made to act as a check upon each other. With the bulk of the nation disfranchised, with a puppet on the throne and a privileged aristocracy to keep him in order, there was little fear, so it seemed, of a national awakening against the influence of the great Czar. But, in spite of this reactionary method of government, introduced at a time when Western Europe was in the throes of constitutional reform, there were practical benefits derived from the Russian occupation. For the first time, Roumanian law recognised the principle that some limit must be set to litigation ; magistrates were made irremovable, sanitation was enforced, new tribunals were created, and justice was brought to every man's door by the establishment of a petty court in every village. These were practical improvements, which compensated in some measure for the refusal of political rights.

Meanwhile, however, a national spirit had been slowly developing. The Roumanians began to feel proud of their ancient origin, their native language, and their past history. Young men of promise, who were sent to study abroad, returned home with a grander conception of their country's destiny than could be fulfilled by a Turkish suzerainty or a Russian protectorate. More particularly, the contact with France and French ideas, which now began and has never since ceased, reminded them that they too were members of the Latin race. A society for the promotion of a national literature had been founded in 1826 by two gifted Roumanians—Constantine Golescou and John Heliade Radoulescou ; and a national theatre was projected. Radoulescou wrote treatises upon almost every subject in the vernacular. He was the poet, grammarian, historian, and dramatist of his country. A ruined monastery served him as a lecture-hall, and every winter his pupils braved cold and wet for the pleasure of listening to his instruction. The war of 1828 somewhat checked the educational movement, but the Russians were not opposed to culture up to a certain point, and the year 1829 witnessed the issue of the first Roumanian newspaper. Schools, where the pupils were taught in their mother tongue, were opened in larger numbers, and the service of the Church was conducted in the same language. A national society arose for the study of art, and it became the fashion to join it. Books became more common, and a curiosity of the period was a " Manual of Patriotism," published at Jassy. After the Russian occupation, the national movement advanced apace, until the Czar thought that it had gone too far. Authors had dared to attack him and to manifest a dangerous love of independence. The more retrograde of the nobles made themselves the instruments of the reactionary policy. Higher education was suppressed, and in Moldavia the prince declared that, as the offices of state were open to the *boyards* alone, it was absurd to give to the rest of the nation the same instruction as to them. But it was easier to deal with the schools than with the men of letters. A great poet bade the Roumanian people "awake from the sleep of death," and his verses, set to music, became the national anthem of the patriotic party.

Political, as well as literary events, were rapidly leading up to the great revolution of 1848, which, sweeping over Europe, took the Danubian principalities in its course. In 1842 the Czar, finding that the prince of Wallachia was not sufficiently docile, induced the Porte to depose him. No fewer than thirty-seven candidates came forward for the vacant throne, but the choice of the *boyards* finally fell upon George Bibescou, who appeared before his people in the costume of Michael the Brave. He became involved in a dispute with the national assembly over some mining concessions, and prevailed upon the Sultan to suspend that refractory body for the remainder of its term. This aroused against him the intense animosity of the great nobles, who were always jealous of any one of their number who had ascended the princely throne over the heads of his fellows. The lesser nobility, on the other hand, embraced his cause, and, when the Revolution broke out, it was directed not against him, but against the influence of Russia. The spark was kindled in Paris in February 1848, and the flames rapidly spread eastward. In Hungary the Roumanians of Transylvania rose against the tyranny of the Magyars; in the two principalities the people were animated by the desire to throw off the protectorate of Russia and so terminate the reactionary system of government which she had introduced. The masses were led by men of distinction, two of whom, Constantine Rosetti and John Bratiano, were destined to play an important part in the later history of their country. The leaders proposed to the prince that he should put himself at the head of the movement. But Bibescou did not share the views of the revolutionists. Convinced that Russia could crush them in a moment, he told them that he did not consider the season propitious for such an enterprise. Another attempt to persuade him proved futile, and on the 9th of June the revolution broke out at Bucharest. Bibescou ordered the arrest of several members of the revolutionary committee; their supporters fired at him as he drove through the streets. An immense crowd gathered in front of his palace, and forced him to sign the scheme for a new constitution and appoint a ministry from among the popular leaders. Bibescou upon this abdicated, leaving the revolutionists in possession of the field. Not a single drop of blood had been shed.

The aim of the more moderate reformers was not the formal independence of their country from the suzerainty of the Sultan, to whom they addressed a letter expressive of their devotion, but the practical freedom of the nation from Russian interference, coupled with full political equality. All the usual watchwords of 1848—"freedom of the Press and of public meeting," "ministerial responsibility," and "civil liberty for all"—were re-echoed on the banks of the Danube. But there was a more advanced section which advocated the proclamation of Roumanian independence and a war, if need be, against Sultan and Czar alike. Some even dreamed of a big Roumania, which should include the Transylvanian brothers within its ample frontiers, and the "lost provinces" of Bessarabia and Bucovina. Meanwhile, another revolution had taken place in Moldavia. There Michael Stourza, who had had the wisdom to make considerable reforms, had no difficulty whatever in suppressing the movement without Russian aid. But the Czar thought that the time had come to make his power felt, and urged upon the Sultan the necessity for intervention. A Turkish commissioner was despatched to Bucharest, who requested the dissolution of the provisional government which had been formed on the flight of Bibescou, and the substitution in its place of a Lieutenancy under Turkish suzerainty. His request was obeyed, and a Lieutenancy of three persons established. The Turkish commissioner expressed his satisfaction, and all seemed well. But this did not suit the autocrat of Russia. A Russian army occupied Moldavia on the pretext of "protecting" the Roumanians, and thence marched to Bucharest. The revolutionary leaders fled to Western Europe, the Roumanian Revolution was at an end. Russia and Turkey concluded in 1849 the Convention of Balta-Liman, which limited the reigns of the *Hospodars* to seven years, suppressed all national assemblies, and replaced them by councils or *divans*, nominated by the prince in each principality. In order to destroy the last vestige of independence, the princes were to be no longer elected by the great nobles, but were nominated by the Sultan as suzerain, and the Czar as protector. Russia contrived to secure the appointment of men in both principalities, who were likely to serve her interests rather than those of the Turks.

But the "doctrine of nationalities" was spreading all over Europe, and the Roumanians had become imbued with it. The chiefs of the Revolution disseminated their country's grievances wherever they were scattered. In France and England they found ready listeners. Lord Palmerston raised the Roumanian question in the House of Commons; Ubicini, whose pen has done so much for Roumanian history, constantly reminded the French nation that there existed another branch of the Latin race under foreign rule. John Heliade published in Paris a defence of the Revolution; and Constantine Rosetti appealed from exile to all parties in his native land to unite against alien domination. Western Europe woke up to the historical fact of a Roumanian nationality, which had aspirations for freedom and independence. A few shrewd diplomatists discovered that the Danubian principalities were not intended by their geographical position to be vassals of either Russia or Turkey, but might form a powerful buffer-state between the two great rivals. Even in the principalities themselves the new *Hospodars*, Barbe Stirbeiu and Gregory Ghika, appointed though they were by Russia and Turkey, encouraged the national movement by restoring Roumanian as the language of instruction. Then came the Crimean war, which led to the ultimate emancipation of both countries and their union under one sovereign.

It is not necessary in this place to retell the oft-told tale of that great struggle between Russia and the Western Powers. It is sufficient to notice the war only as far as it affected the Danubian principalities. The Czar Nicholas I., in his ultimatum to the Sultan, threatened to invade them unless his demands were granted, and, as an unfavourable reply was despatched, lost no time in carrying out his threat. On July 3, 1853, General Gortschakoff crossed the Pruth, and for the eighth time a Russian army of occupation held Moldavia and Wallachia in its clutches. The two princes were informed that they might keep their thrones on condition of breaking off relations with the Porte. The latter ordered them to hold no communication with Russia, but pay their accustomed tribute to their lawful suzerain as heretofore. Thus placed between the Russians and the Turks, the princes thought it prudent to flee, and left the supreme authority over their respective states in the hands of the Russian generals. On this occasion, however, the "liberators" had learned by experience. Efforts were made to win over the *boyards*, and offices were bestowed upon some of their number. Meanwhile, Turkey demanded the withdrawal of the Imperial troops, and followed the demand by a declaration of war. Omar Pasha crossed the Danube at Vidin, and it looked as if the theatre of the war would, as so often before, be the unhappy principalities. Moving eastward to Oltenitza, a small place on the Roumanian bank of the river about forty miles from Bucharest, he repulsed the Russians in a three days' battle, and then retired across the river into Bulgaria. In the following spring the Russians in vain attempted the capture of Silistria and received another blow in Wallachia near Kalafat. But the intervention of the Western Powers in February 1854, and the threatening attitude of Austria compelled Nicholas to remove his forces. France and England insisted upon the evacuation of the Danubian states; Austria massed troops on the Transylvanian frontier and held herself in readiness to enforce the British and French ultimatum. The attacks of the allies upon the Crimea made it imperative upon the Czar to defend that part of his dominions, and in July, after another defeat at Giurgevo, his army marched out of the principalities. The two Powers at once returned, and an Austrian army with them. For more than two years these new protectors remained in the country in accordance with an arrangement made with the Porte. The Roumanians had good reason for desiring to be defended from their defenders.

The remaining operations of the war were conducted outside the principalities; but they reaped full benefit from the victories of the allies when the Treaty of Paris was signed in 1856. The southern part of Bessarabia was joined to Moldavia in order to keep Russia away from the Danube, and the delta of that river, which had been taken by the Russians in 1812, was restored to Turkey for the same object. The Russian protectorate over the principalities was abolished, the course of the Danube placed under the control of an European commission, and the armed intervention of any one Power without the consent of the others expressly prohibited. The Sultan still retained his suzerainty, but promised to grant an "independent and national administration." At the Congress the representatives of France and England desired to go one step further and unite Moldavia and Wallachia in one Roumanian state, which would thus, as they pointed out, become a powerful barrier against Russian aggression in the Balkan Peninsula. But Austria and Turkey strongly opposed the idea, maintaining that the inhabitants were not in favour of a scheme which would mean the loss of their local customs. But public opinion in the two principalities was favourable to the union. Ever since the poet Vacarescou had apostrophised in indignant verse the "powerless rivulet," which "dared to keep the brothers apart," there had been an increasing desire for amalgamation. History had proved that the two states had had a common fate; science showed them to be peopled by a common race; practical experience demonstrated that they had common interests and a common foe. The Russians themselves had admitted in the regulations which they drew up in 1834, that "secondary and fortuitous circumstances alone had been responsible for the division," and they would have been prepared to support a union even then, provided that the united principalities could have been placed under a member of the Imperial family. Bibescou had contributed greatly to their political fusion by abolishing all customs-dues between them, and thus in Roumania as in Germany, a customs' union was the forerunner of national unity. The revolutionary leaders of 1848 had been inspired with the same idea, and their cause had gained the ardent support of Napoleon III., with whom the "doctrine of nationalities" was a passion. England was, however, won over to the Austrian view, and a compromise was the result. It was decided that the wishes of the inhabitants should be consulted on the subject.

The elections, held under the auspices of Turkey, could only be an utter farce, for that Power was the principal opponent of the Unionist idea. Every effort was made by the adversaries of the scheme to gain the support of Moldavia, for that principality being the smaller of the two had most to lose by the proposed change, which would inevitably relegate Jassy to the position of a second-rate town. The Porte and its "Lieutenants," who carried on a provisional government in the principalities, left no stone unturned to secure the election of anti-unionist bodies; Unionist journals were suppressed; Unionist meetings prohibited. The register of electors was carefully "revised" in the interests of the Separatist party, and the Turkish authorities showed a marvellous appreciation of the causes which govern elections by arranging that Moldavia should vote first, and so exercise an unfavourable influence upon the Unionists of Wallachia. But the officials had not reckoned upon the wave of feeling which swept over the people. France aided the Roumanian cause, and threatened to break off relations with the Sultan, unless the opinions of the inhabitants were fairly and freely consulted. The sham elections were declared void; a second appeal to the Moldavian people, this time unaccompanied by official intimidation or interference, resulted in an overwhelming majority for the Union. Only two deputies out of eighty-five were opposed to it. The two constituent assemblies, or *divans ad hoc*, as they were called, met in the separate principalities and decided in favour of the Union of Wallachia and Moldavia in a single state, under the same government. This government was to consist of a foreign prince, a member of some reigning family, who was to be hereditary on condition that his heirs embraced the national religion. Bibescou, Stirbeiu, and Ghika all patriotically sacrificed themselves to the interests of their country. By the side of the prince there was to be an assembly, elected on a wide franchise, which would represent the general interests of the people, and not those of the nobles alone. These decisions were communicated to the Powers, and the Convention of Paris in 1858 devised a scheme which was neither Union nor Separation. According to this diplomatic arrangement there were to be two princes, two national assemblies, and two governments, but one central committee to devise common laws for the "united principalities of Moldavia and Wallachia," as they were officially designated. But the diplomatists had not provided for the case of both principalities electing the same person. This was what now happened. When, in the early days of 1859, the election of the new Princes came on, Moldavia chose Colonel Alexander Couza, and Wallachia followed its example. Cleverly and quite unexpectedly the Roumanians had solved the problem which had baffled the collective wisdom of Europe. Just as in 1885 the union of the two Bulgarias, expressly prohibited in the Treaty of Berlin, was achieved by a popular movement which placed Alexander of Battenberg over both, so in 1859 the union of the two Roumanian principalities, so hotly contested at the Congress of Paris, was quietly accomplished by the double election of Alexander Couza. Roumania had attained her long-sought unity. Austria, just entering upon the Italian war, had no time to intervene ; two years later the Sultan, at the suggestion of the Powers, gave his formal consent to the arrangement. Union had been won, independence remained to be achieved. The united principalities had received on the 9th of November, 1859, the name of " Roumania," but their position towards their suzerain remained the same. To him tribute was still paid, from his hands the prince received his investiture.

The new " Prince of Roumania," who styled himself Alexander John I., but was invariably known by his family name of Couza, sprang from an old Moldavian family and had served his country, first in the army and then in the civil service. By his marriage with a daughter of a distinguished house he became connected with all the highest nobles in the land, and his career from that moment was assured. His dismissal from his post of Prefect of Galatz at the instigation of the Turkish authorities a couple of years earlier had won him great renown as a patriot and a subsequent appointment as Minister of War. He was, with that exception, little known, and this fact was an advantage in the eyes of the deputies. Much was expected from him, while the abilities of other candidates had already been accurately gauged.

But Couza sadly disappointed these great expectations. A series of ministerial crises, followed by perpetual dissolutions of the legislature, created a feeling of unrest which was increased by the financial blunders of the new government. Roumania was not really ripe for a very elaborate constitution such as she had received, and she naturally made mistakes at the outset of her career. Couza's measures were at the same moment ultra-democratic and despotic. His motto was that of Rabagas in Sardou's play, that "the happiness of the people could only be established by a *coup d'état*." He alienated the clergy by the confiscation of the property of the Roumanian monasteries, which was declared invalid by the Powers, unless pecuniary compensation were paid. He abolished the feudal obligations of the peasantry which had long been the curse of Roumania, and by a stroke of the pen created a class of peasant-proprietors, who were allotted the lands of the *boyards* at low prices fixed by the Government. These two measures estranged the sympathies of the nobles and the priests, who were accordingly brought under control by being made officials of the State. A *coup d'état* in May, 1864, rid him of the National Assembly, and called a Senate into existence on the basis of universal suffrage. But Couza's popularity with the masses was undermined by the tobacco monopoly which he introduced, for in Roumania every one smokes. He became more and more autocratic, and attempted to govern without a Budget. His avarice was notorious; his morals, or the want of them, were the common talk of Bucharest. People forgot his public services and remembered only his private vices. He had founded a University at Jassy, introduced the telegraph into the country, improved the coinage, embellished and increased the towns, and gave any person a plot of ground in the suburbs of the capital free of cost, on condition that he would promise in writing to erect a suitable dwelling-house on it within three years' time. But the *boyards* had long been discontented with their old colleague and now that the masses were against him, they had no difficulty in compassing his fall. The story of his forced abdication is doubly interesting, because it formed the precedent which was afterwards followed by the Bulgarians who deposed Prince Alexander. On February 23, 1866, a body of forty conspirators, under the command of General Golescou, entered the palace, forced open the door of the Prince's bedroom, and discovered him there with one of his mistresses half undressed. Couza, cowed at the sight of their loaded revolvers, asked feebly what they wanted. They replied that they wanted his abdication. Pen and ink were provided, and one of the conspirators knelt down with his back to the Prince and offered his bent shoulders as an impromptu writing-desk. There was no alternative but to sign the deed of abdication, and the Prince yielded. He was allowed to dress, and then driven away from the palace. Not a hand was raised in his defence, not a voice pleaded his cause. He was permitted to withdraw with the spoils of office to Paris, the haven of Balkan princes in retirement, and Roumania concerned herself with him no more. A provisional government was formed with Golescou at the head, and a proclamation issued calling upon the nation to proceed to the election of a foreign prince as its chief, and deploring the "anarchy and corruption" which had marked the seven years of Couza's reign. By an almost unanimous vote the two Chambers of the united principalities elected the Count of Flanders, younger brother of the King of Belgium, as Prince of Roumania. But the Sultan protested against the recent action of the people, and convened a Conference of the Great Powers in Paris to consider the situation; a Turkish army corps was mobilised in Bulgaria, and the threatening secession in Moldavia completed the dangers which awaited the new ruler. The Count of Flanders declined the proffered honour, and a new candidate, Prince Charles of Hohenzollern-Sigmaringen, a connection of the Prussian reigning house, was put up in his stead. The Prince was unanimously elected by a plebiscite of the whole people and proclaimed on the 20th of April. The Paris Conference declared his election null and void;

but Prince Charles, acting on the instigation of Bismarck, resolved to set its decisions at defiance. The great Prussian statesman sent for the young officer of dragoons, as thirteen years afterwards he sent for Prince Alexander of Battenberg, and advised him to go straight to Bucharest, adding in a phrase, which he repeated on that occasion: "If you fail, you will at any rate have a pleasant reminiscence for the rest of your life." On the 22nd of May, the Prince, who had travelled through Austria in disguise, arrived at his capital and was received with the utmost enthusiasm by his people. The Sultan protested, and demanded from the Conference permission to occupy the country with an army. The Conference refused, but war seemed certain. The Sultan appointed the redoubtable Omar Pasha to the command of the troops on one bank of the Danube; the Roumanians were massed to resist him on the other. But the success of the Prussian arms over Austria at the battle of Königgrätz and the Cretan insurrection diverted the attention of both Austria and Turkey from Roumanian affairs. The Conference of the Powers relented, the Sultan yielded, and both gave their sanction to the election of the new Prince. The Roumanian crisis was at an end.

VII.

ROUMANIA AN INDEPENDENT KINGDOM.

PRINCE CHARLES was proclaimed ruler of Roumania on his twenty-seventh birthday. His father was head of the non-reigning branch of the great Hohenzollern family, and had acted for a short time as Prussian Premier; his grandmother had been connected with the house of Bonaparte. He was thus on the best of terms with the two great Powers which dominated the West of Europe in 1866. His training had been that of an officer in a crack Prussian regiment, and stood him in good stead at a critical period of his career. But he was much more than a mere soldier. He was liberal in his ideas for a Hohenzollern, and filled with that deep sense of duty which has always been a marked characteristic of that powerful race. He at once made it his business to study the requirements of the nation which had summoned him to preside over its destinies. He soon acquired great personal knowledge of the land and its inhabitants, and found ample scope for his favourite hobby of forestry in the woods of the Carpathians. By his marriage with Princess Pauline Elizabeth of

Wied, he gained a consort who gracefully seconded his efforts to identify the foreign dynasty with the interests of its adopted country. The Queen of Roumania is known all over Europe, under the pseudonym of "Carmen Sylva," as a royal authoress, who, even if she had not had the advantages of rank, would still have made a name in literature. Her poems and stories, the collection of Roumanian folk-lore which she has published, and the encouragement which she has given to the national idea by her preference for the Roumanian dress and her patronage of the old Roumanian customs, have won her general esteem. "Carmen Sylva" has bidden a poetic farewell "for ever" to her father's castle on the Rhine, and has made her home on the slopes of the Carpathians and on the banks of the Danube. Her own writings and her husband's soldierly qualities have made the name of Roumania familiar to the world. The difficulties which beset the new Government at the outset have gradually disappeared, and the sovereign, who at one time thought of resigning in consequence of the bitterness of party spirit and the opposition of the politicians to his methods, has just celebrated, amidst universal rejoicings, the thirtieth anniversary of his reign. The intrigues of the revolutionary party, which professed to desire a Republic, the extreme licence of the press, and the perpetual changes of ministry, which characterised his three first years in Roumania, have given place to a general recognition of his services to a country, which, after centuries of misgovernment, has at last found repose.

The first act of the new Prince was to sign the

Constitution, which had been drawn up by a Constituent Assembly directly after his accession. The Constitution of 1866 gave the Roumanians a free press and free compulsory education, and guaranteed freedom of conscience and public meeting. But the religious toleration thus enjoined has not prevented bitter attacks upon the Jews, whose commercial supremacy aroused the jealousy of the less enterprising natives. Roumania has had her *Judenhetze* no less than Russia and Germany, and the free press has stimulated the agitation, which has been at last suppressed by force. Besides the Prince, a Senate and an indirectly-elected Chamber of Deputies composed the Government. This constitution, with modifications introduced in 1879 and 1884, has existed ever since, and has, on the whole, worked well. The Roumanians, like other branches of the Latin race, import a large amount of vehement speaking into political life, and are apt to be easily excited. But their country has been fortunate in the possession of statesmen such as M. Constantine Rosetti and M. John Bratiano, who would have made their mark in any assembly, and the experiment of parliamentary government has succeeded there better than in either Servia or Bulgaria.

The military training of Prince Charles had convinced him of the necessity of a strong and disciplined army for a country situated like Roumania, between the twin fires of Russia and Turkey. At his accession to the throne he found in existence a small military force, full of enthusiasm, but sadly deficient in organisation and arms. Couza had, under French auspices, increased it from 8,400 to 25,000; his successor obtained permission from his suzerain, blissfully unconscious of the use to which the troops would soon be put, to raise the number to 30,000. He then bought a large supply of the Prussian breechloaders, which had just done such signal service against the Austrians, and borrowed Prussian instructors to train his raw levies on the most approved model. The Roumanian army soon became an important factor in the politics of the Balkan Peninsula; and, before its creator had been many years on the throne, it had proved, beneath the walls of Plevna, that it was capable, under proper guidance, of great military achievements. The assistance of Roumania has become an object of considerable value in any war in the East; and, in addition to her very efficient army, she now, alone of the Balkan States, possesses the nucleus of a navy. Even the great military Powers of the Triple Alliance would not disdain the aid of a nation at once so well armed and so opportunely placed.

The *Eastern Question, which became acute in 1876, naturally affected the interests of Roumania in the most vital manner. Under the rule of Prince Charles, she had accustomed herself to consider the suzerainty of the Sultan as a mere form; and accordingly when Midhat's abortive constitution proclaimed the unity and indivisibility of the Turkish Empire, including the privileged provinces, and gave the name of Ottomans to the Sultan's subjects and vassals of every race and creed, the indignation at Bucharest knew no bounds. Roumania, which had taken no part whatever in the war between Turkey and Servia and Montenegro, was aghast at the idea of being treated as a Turkish province, and resolved to put an end for ever to the semblance of authority which the Sultan still possessed over her. On April 16, 1877, a secret convention was signed with Russia, which placed a free passage through Roumania at the disposal of the Czar's troops, without, however, promising the active co-operation of the Roumanian army. The Porte denounced this convention as a violation of the Treaty of Paris, but in vain. The Sultan then took the matter into his own hands. He issued an Irade, deposing Prince Charles, and ordered the Turkish monitors on the Danube to bombard Kalafat. The reply was the declaration of war by Roumania and the proclamation of her independence on May 21st. Nearly five hundred years had passed away since Mirtschea the Old had first acknowledged the overlordship of the Sultan. At last the long period of dependence was over. Roumania was free.

For the first three months after the declaration of war the Roumanian troops took comparatively little part in the active hostilities between the Russian and Turkish armies. The railways, hospitals, and every other advantage which the principality possessed were placed at the disposal of the Imperial forces, and the Prince devoted himself to improving the defences of his country along the Danube. So long as the Russians were successful, Roumania pursued the policy of protecting her own frontier. But when the armies of the Czar were checked at Plevna and at Erzeroum, when the balance of victory was on the side of the Turks, then Prince Charles hesitated no longer. Crossing the Danube at the head of twenty-eight thousand infantry and four thousand cavalry, he soon made himself so invaluable to his allies, that he was appointed Commander-in-chief of the Russian and Roumanian forces before Plevna. The Roumanians had already shown, during the bombardment of Kalafat, that, if they lacked experience, they were not wanting in courage; and the Russian veterans soon recognised that the soldiers of Prince Charles were not the unskilled amateurs whom they had at first imagined them to be.

The post of danger in front of the famous Grivica redoubt, the strongest of all the fortifications which defended Plevna, was entrusted to the Roumanian army. Onlookers of the operations believed the task of taking this redoubt absolutely impossible, even if the besiegers "bombarded it for a week and sacrificed a brigade of infantry in the attempt." The fact that the position was allotted to the Roumanians, who were numerically much weaker than their Muscovite allies, was regarded as a proof that nothing more than a "demonstration" was intended. But the Roumanian gunners soon showed that they meant business, and picked off the Turkish artillerymen with unerring aim. On September 11th a grand attack was made on the "indomitable redoubt" by the allies. But the Russians arrived, by an accident, half an hour too late, and at first the battalions of Prince Charles were repulsed. Three hours later a second assault proved more successful. The redoubt was captured, and the Turks driven back. But a fog came on, and the Roumanian reserves, who had been ordered up to occupy the position so lately won, lost their way, and thus allowed the enemy to recapture the works. But it was not for long. A third attack, later in the evening, utterly routed the brave defenders of the redoubt. No further attempt was made to recover it; and when the sun rose next morning, it revealed to the astonished hosts the spectacle of the Roumanian colours proudly floating from the summit of the terrible outworks of Grivica. But the thrice-fought struggle for the redoubt had been dearly bought. An eye-witness, who visited the place a few hours after the last assault, found the whole of the interior choked with heaps of dead and wounded, Turks and Roumanians, lying in inextricable confusion, uncared for and unheeded. No doctor was at hand to ease the sufferings of the injured, no comrade was there to soothe the last moments of the dying. Amid the horrors of the siege, there was no time to think of the victims which it claimed.

A second redoubt, scarcely less formidable than the first, was next attacked. For a week the Roumanians tried in vain to capture it, and then, finding their efforts unsuccessful, set to work to dig trenches, so as to approach the hostile lines. Impartial critics could not help contrasting their perseverance with the apathy of the Russians, who remained quietly waiting for reinforcements, while their allies were slowly but surely advancing. Outside the lines of Plevna, at Rahova, on the Bulgarian bank of the Danube, they gained fresh laurels by the occupation of that town ; and when, on December 10th, Plevna at last fell, and Osman Pasha, its brave defender, surrendered, every one admitted that no small share of the credit for its capture was due to the soldiers of Prince Charles. The independence of Roumania had been won on the Grivica redoubt.

But a long and bitter experience of former Russo-Turkish wars had taught the Roumanians that there is little gratitude in politics. From the first there had been considerable opposition to the alliance with Russia among those who remembered her past conduct towards their country. The fall of Plevna for the moment, however, had united all parties in general rejoicings, and when the "Czar liberator" arrived at Bucharest on his way back from the seat of war, he was greeted with enthusiasm. But the Treaty of San Stefano, signed on March 3, 1878, justified the suspicions of the Roumanian people. While, on the one hand, the Porte formally recognised the independence of Roumania ; Russia, on the other, acquired from Turkey the district between the Danube and the Black Sea, known as the Dobrudža, with the express object of exchanging it for the southern part of Bessarabia, which had been taken from the Czar and given to Roumania after the Crimean war. The subsequent Treaty of Berlin, which in so many ways amended the arrangements made at San Stefano, confirmed this exchange, with the slight modification that a rather larger strip of territory was given to Roumania. But Russia had by far the best of the bargain. The extra piece of land awarded to Roumania was taken not from her, but from Bulgaria.

The Czar's dominions were once more bounded by the Pruth, and once more the Roumanians had cause to hate the name of the "accursed stream," which, after an interval of twenty-two years, again separated them from their kinsfolk in Bessarabia. At the end of 1878 the exchange was effected, to the great grief of the Roumanians, who felt that their heroic sacrifices at Plevna should not have been thus rewarded. Bessarabia had been part of the old Moldavian principality; its name enshrined the memory of a once famous Roumanian family; its loss in 1812 had been bitterly lamented and only partially compensated for by the surrender of a portion of it in 1856. Now it was all gone again. On the other hand, the Dobrudža was of less value, and inhabited by a mixed population, which comprised many Bulgarians and Turks as well as Roumanians. But the greatest point of all had been gained—the formal recognition of Roumania as a sovereign state. As the Prince expressed it, there was an end to those "ill-defined ties, which were known at Constantinople as suzerainty, at Bucharest as vassalage." But for a ruler who controlled the destinies of so proud and ancient a race, and whose dominions covered nearly fifty thousand square miles, the title seemed inadequate. On March 26, 1881, Roumania proclaimed herself a kingdom, and the Prince styled himself King Carol I. As an appropriate sign that Roumania, like Germany, had won her position among the nations "not by the decrees of majorities, but by blood and iron," the crown of her first king was made from the Turkish cannon which he had captured at Plevna.

From that time onwards Roumania has belonged to that fortunate class of countries which have no history. She has gone on increasing in prosperity and strength; the succession to the throne has been made doubly sure by the marriage of her Crown Prince with a granddaughter of Queen Victoria ; the capacity of her people for self-government has been tried. If some ardent patriots still cherish the dream of a big Roumania, which shall embrace the Roumanians of Transylvania and Bessarabia, no less than those of the kingdom, all moderate men are content with what has been won, and none regret the bygone days of Turkish suzerainty.

PART II.

BULGARIA.

"The glory of the Bulgarians was confined to a narrow scope both of time and place."—GIBBON.

"The Bulgarian is not devoid of those unobtrusive household virtues, which enrich the state, and keep at a distance the vice and the pauperism which are the cancers of the more crowded communities of Europe."—A. A. PATON, *The Bulgarian, the Turk, and the German.*

I.

FROM THE EARLIEST TIMES TO THE CONVERSION OF THE BULGARIANS.

(864 A.D.)

THE early history of Bulgaria is shrouded in mystery. The discovery of ancient tombs near Trnovo and Philippopolis points to the existence of a primitive civilisation in that part of the Balkan Peninsula. But of this no other traces remain, and when we first hear of the country it was inhabited by wild Thracian and Illyrian tribes, of whom Herodotus said that " if they were only ruled by one man and could only agree among themselves, they would be the greatest of all nations." For a moment some chieftain, stronger than his fellows, might succeed in bringing about a temporary union. But the tribes lived, as a rule, in perpetual feud with each other, until the strong hand of Philip of Macedon subjected them all to his authority. Philip is the first great name in the history of the land ; a name perpetuated in that of the picturesque capital of South Bulgaria ; and the union of Bulgaria and Macedonia under his sceptre is still regarded with admiration by many Bulgarian politicians. But the Macedonian supremacy was short-lived ; upon the death of Alexander the Great, the Thracians, who had composed so large a part of his armies, returned to the congenial business of flying at each other's throats. Other barbarous tribes joined in their quarrels, until, during the second Punic War, the Romans made their first appearance in Bulgaria. The Thracian and Illyrian warriors now combined in self-defence ; the struggle lasted for a century and a half ; the conquerors at first permitted the native princes of Thrace proper, south of the Balkans, to retain their thrones on payment of a tribute, and then reduced their country, like the region between the Balkans and the Danube, to a province. *Mœsia*, as the latter was called, was conquered by Crassus and brought under the immediate sway of Rome in 29 B.C. ; *Thracia*, as the former was officially designated, became a part of the Roman Empire in the reign of Tiberius in 26 A.D. The name of *Mœsia* was retained until the evacuation of Dacia by Aurelian, described in the first part of the book, when it was changed to that of *Dacia Aureliani*. Considerable remains of this Roman occupation exist at the present day. The marble pillars brought from Nikopul by one of the Bulgarian Czars to adorn the famous "Church of the Forty Martyrs" at Trnovo are perhaps the best known

ROMAN SCULPTURE AT NICOPOLIS.

of these relics. But the Roman influence was not permanent in Bulgaria as it has been in Roumania. For a time the Latin language made headway in the country, and the land, where the exiled Ovid had once complained that none could understand him, produced Latin authors of its own. But the local dialect was soon formed, and the flood of barbarian invasion finally swept the traces of Western culture away. To this day the Bulgarians are less refined, less luxurious, and less European than their neighbours across the Danube.

As early as the time of Constantine, who included what is now Bulgaria among his provinces, hordes of uncouth warriors had begun to pour into the country. At first the new and the old elements appear to have combined harmoniously. An author of the fourth century describes the territory south of the Danube as inhabited by a dense population, half Roman, half barbarian, which united the fresh energies of the new-comers to the civilisation of the Western race. But this state of things was not of long duration. Other and fiercer tribes swooped down upon the promised lands. The Goths ravaged the country in their terrible march of destruction from the Bosphorus to the Alps. The Huns, who followed them, exacted a tribute as well. On the death of Attila, their ruler, a number of smaller tribes, who had accepted his sway, flooded the province. In some parts the entire population is said to have perished by their swords. At this period the country resembled a kaleidoscope, in which a series of apparitions is presented, each more horrible than the last. One race stands out pre-eminent above the others in this grim transformation scene. It is now that we hear for the first time in Bulgarian history of the Slavs.

The precise date, at which this remarkable tribe first made its appearance south of the Danube, is doubtful. According to one theory, indeed, the Slavs were the original inhabitants, children of the soil, of whom no one knew whence they came. This opinion, however gratifying it may be to the pride of a great race, is disproved by the best Bulgarian historian, who regards them as foreigners, like the Goths and Huns. But whether they first entered Bulgaria in the third century, or considerably later, is uncertain. At any rate, by the seventh century they are found settled there. From them and the other tribes who subsequently mixed with them, the modern Bulgarians are descended, and derive their language, customs, and habits of thought. The Slavs drove the survivors of the old Thracian and Illyrian population before them to the mountains and occupied their lands in the plains. But they were not permitted to perpetuate their dominion. In the second half of the seventh century the *Bulgari* crossed the Danube and entered the territory which has ever since borne their name.

The origin of these Bulgarian invaders has been much disputed. The best authorities, arguing from the obvious difference between their mode of life and that of the Slav races as well as from the Oriental names of their ancient rulers, have decided that the Bulgarians were an Asiatic tribe, totally unconnected with the Slavs. Some regard them as of Finnish stock, others as a Tartar people, and others again as of Turkish blood. It seems probable, however, that their former home was on the banks of the Volga, a river from which some have derived their name. But it is much more likely that the men gave their name to the river, rather than the river to the men. Their history, previous to their arrival in what is now

Bulgaria, borders on the marvellous. We read of primitive Bulgarian princes, whose ages rivalled that of Methuselah, and whose reigns averaged a century apiece. An ancient chronicler even purports to give a complete list of these patriarchal rulers. One of them, Kurt or Kuvrat, was sufficiently important to be accepted as an ally by the Emperor Heraclius, and defeated the Avars who had besieged Constantinople, and brought the Bulgarians under their yoke. Upon his death, his five sons, according to a picturesque story, divided his substance and set out in different directions, each accompanied by a band of followers, in search of fame and fortune. It is probable, however, that this division of the Bulgarian stock had taken place much earlier. We read of battles with the Bulgarians in the reign of Theodoric, and they had doubtless made earlier incursions into the Balkan Peninsula. But it was not till the year 679, when Isparich, Kuvrat's son, was their chief, that they crossed from Bessarabia and established themselves in the region south of the Danube. At first they were concentrated on the shore of the Black Sea, in the Dobrudža, and at Silistria, all places where the Turkish element has ever since been the strongest. Gradually their influence extended, but while they conquered the country they were all the time being quietly vanquished by the conquered. They slowly adopted the customs and language of the Slavs, who absorbed them, just as the Saxons absorbed their Norman conquerors in England. By a curious compensation, the Bulgarians kept their name but lost their language, while the Slavs kept their language but lost their name. The old Bulgarian tongue of the invaders has left no mark upon the modern speech of the people ; for such words in the Bulgarian language of to-day as are not of Slav origin, may be traced to the old Thracian and Illyrian settlers. But the Bulgarians succeeded in imposing their name upon the combined mass of people, who dwelt in the land, henceforth called Bulgaria. Two and a half centuries were required to complete the amalgamation of the two races. The present inhabitants of the principality are therefore descended from two separate stocks—the Slavs and the old Bulgarians —which were welded together between the seventh and the ninth centuries. The Slav element predominated, and of the old Bulgarians little now remains but the name.

The primitive customs of these old Bulgarians were in many respects the opposite of those of the Slavs. In war the Bulgarians fought mostly on horseback, the Slavs chiefly on foot; the former had usually several wives, the latter generally only one ; the institutions of the former were aristocratic, those of the latter democratic. The wide trousers, worn by the Bulgarians of both sexes, the veils of the women, the turbans of the men, betrayed their Asiatic origin. The principal Bulgarian food was meat, and the number of fast-days was a great obstacle to their conversion to Christianity. The Slavs, on the other hand, lived on bread, fruit, and vegetables, as well as flesh. The Bulgarians were as cruel to their prisoners as the Slavs were lenient, and in time of peace the punishments which they inflicted were severe. Their chief, called *khan*, was surrounded by an elaborate system of Oriental etiquette, while the Slavs never submitted to the rule of one man. In short, the two races, at the moment when they met, were the antitheses of each other.

While the Bulgarians have given their name to the country, the Slav language has supplied the designations of most of its towns. Jablanica is christened by the Slav name for an apple, Bukovica by the Slav term for the beech. The fort or *grad*, which was always built in Slav communities, has supplied the suffix to countless names of towns. It is no wonder, then, that the Russians have regarded the modern Bulgarians as their "little brothers," and that many of the latter have looked for protection to the head of the great Slav community.

The two centuries, which intervened between the settlement of the Bulgarians on the right bank of the Danube and their conversion to Christianity, were chiefly occupied in sanguinary campaigns with the Eastern Empire.

The power of the new-comers was speedily recognised by the feeble emperors, who were the unworthy successors of the ancient Romans. True to their policy of buying the aid of one barbarous nation to repel the assaults of another, they consented to pay tribute to the Bulgarian prince and to give up their own claims to the ancient province of Mœsia, in order that Thrace might be spared. Justinian II., however, refused to continue this payment to Isperich, and a war followed, in which the Emperor, at first successful, finally escaped with difficulty from the hands of his enemy. Isperich's successor, Tervel, was the means of restoring the banished tyrant to his throne. When Justinian, after several years' exile, landed in a tiny skiff at the mouths of the Danube, he found the Bulgarian prince ready to forget his past animosity and assist his future enterprise. Bribed by the promise of the Emperor's daughter and a fair share of the Imperial treasure, Tervel, whose dominions extended to the borders of Thrace, besieged Constantinople and restored its master. Justinian rewarded his benefactor with a heap of gold, which the Bulgarian "measured with his whip," and bestowed upon him the title of Cæsar. But the benefits which he had received soon rankled in his mind. He again declared war on the Bulgarians, only to be defeated by them once more. A few years later we find Tervel concluding a treaty of peace with the Empire, and relieving Constantinople from the attacks of the Arabs. The last act of his reign was an attempt to foist another emperor upon the Byzantines. These facts show that very soon after their establishment in their new home, the Bulgarians became a powerful people, whose influence reached to the Bosphorus. Kormisoš, the next of their princes, of whom history has anything to record, was, after the monks, the chief object of Constantine V.'s aversion. This Emperor undertook no fewer than eight campaigns against the Bulgarians, and erected new fortifications in Thrace for the express purpose of keeping them in order. Kormisoš at one moment had almost reached Constantinople; at another he was forced to sue for peace. But he soon recovered from his humiliation, and inflicted a severe defeat on the Emperor near Varna. But internal discord marred the effects of this victory. Many Slavs migrated from Bulgaria to Asia Minor; civil wars raged in the land; the old line of Bulgarian princes disappeared, and a youth named Telec was chosen ruler. This was Constantine's opportunity; he utterly routed the Bulgarian army; the captives were carried off to grace his triumph at Constantinople and butchered before the Golden Gate; Telec himself fell beneath the blows of his own infuriated subjects. Complete confusion followed; the Bulgarians, divided into rival camps, seemed to the Emperor an easy prey. He marched once more into their country and laid many of their villages in ashes. But the advent of Cerig, a strong and crafty prince, prevented the incorporation of Bulgaria with the Empire. By a cunning trick, he obtained from Constantine the name of every traitor in the land, and at once put them all to death. His successor extorted an annual tribute from the Empress Irene and restored the influence of his race.

A still more powerful prince now mounted the throne. The name of Krum was long remembered as that of the strongest and most bloodthirsty of these old Bulgarian chiefs; for, in the phrase of Gibbon, he "could boast an honour, which had hitherto been appropriated to the Goths, that of slaying in battle one of the successors of Augustus and Constantine." It was Krum's capture of Sofia, the present capital of Bulgaria, from the Eastern Empire in 809, which led to this memorable event.

At first, as we have seen, the Bulgarians had gathered round Varna and the mouths of the Danube, but under Krum they had occupied a large part of what is now Roumania and were spreading westward towards modern Servia. Nicephorus, the Greek Emperor, was resolved to avenge this audacious act.

BULGARIAN ATTACK ON CONSTANTINOPLE IN 813.

He assembled a huge army, burnt Krum's wooden palace to the ground, and devastated the country with fire and sword. But his crafty enemy blocked the Balkan passes in his rear; the Emperor saw that he was caught, and exclaimed in his despair, "unless we had the wings of birds, we could not escape." A fierce battle ensued; the whole Imperial army was annihilated; no quarter was given, and the cruel Bulgarian prince, following the custom of his race, ordered the head of his adversary to be cut off, and used the skull as a goblet at his feasts. Krum then marched into Thrace, routed the successor of Nicephorus, who tried in vain to resist his march, and encamped before the walls of Constantinople. The barbarian is said to have begun the siege with the most elaborate ceremonies. Human sacrifices were offered up before the Golden Gate, the chief washed his feet in the waves of the Bosphorus and sprinkled his people with its water, while his wives did obeisance to him in the sight of the defenders on the walls. In order to save his capital, the Emperor agreed to give him a yearly tribute, a quantity of fine clothing, and a fixed number of maidens. During the negotiations, however, Krum himself was nearly slain, and in his rage at this treachery, he laid waste the outskirts of the city and then retired with a host of captives, among them the future Emperor, Basil I. On a second expedition against Constantinople, Krum was seized with apoplexy and died. Omortag, the next Bulgarian prince, of whom anything is known, made a long peace with the Eastern Empire, and devoted his attention to the Franks, who had become his neighbours on the west. But his expedition up the river Drave and his occupation of the territory between that stream and the Save had merely temporary results. He is now chiefly remembered for the remarkable inscription, discovered forty years ago on a pillar in the "Church of the Forty

Martyrs" at Trnovo, which tells of a great house which he built, and for his persecution of the Christians. But the efforts of this Bulgarian Diocletian were powerless to prevent the adoption of Christianity by his people.

Even before the coming of the Bulgarians, the Church had made considerable headway among the Slavs. The wars between Krum and the Greek Emperors were indirectly the means of spreading the gospel, owing to the great numbers of Christians, whom the Bulgarian conqueror led captive to his own country. The prisoners, many of them priests and some even bishops, did not hide their faith from their gaolers, and so successful was their preaching, that Omortag became alarmed. His execution of four bishops and several hundred other Christians only increased the zeal of the missionaries. Converts were made in high places, and a brother of Omortag's successor, in whose reign we hear of the first war between Serbs and Bulgarians, died a martyr to the new religion. The next prince, Boris I., adopted the creed which his predecessor had proscribed, and from his conversion in 864 the formal recognition of Christianity in Bulgaria dates. Throughout the history of the country religion has played a most important part, and to this day Bulgarian politics are coloured by the decision of Boris a thousand years ago. The motives which prompted the Prince to become a Christian were political rather than religious. Two pretty stories have, indeed, been circulated. According to one, his sister, who had been carried off a captive by the Greeks, convinced her brother on her return of the beauties of the religion, which she had learnt in prison. According to the other, a Greek named Methodius terrified the conscience-stricken Bulgarian by the fiery picture which he drew of the Last Judgment. But the story is due to a confusion of names. The apostles of Bulgaria were two brothers, Constantine and Methodius, the latter of whom has been mistaken for the painter. These brothers, born at Salonica, of which their father was a high military official, early devoted themselves to missionary work. They had an intimate acquaintance with the Slav language, and Constantine is said to have invented the written character which is still called "Cyrillic" after his adopted name of Cyril. Partly by preaching, partly by their Slav translations of the Bible, they acquired great influence in Moravia and the regions bordering on Bulgaria, and Boris at last found that he was becoming isolated by the conversion of his neighbours. He saw that it would be to his advantage to make profession of the new faith. The opportunity soon offered itself. A war with the Greek Emperor Michael III. brought him into contact with the Eastern Church. On the spot, where the treaty of peace was signed, the Bulgarian prince was baptised under the name of Michael, out of compliment to the Emperor, who had acted as his godfather. Many of his nobles followed his example, and the cession of territory by the Greeks confirmed them in their belief. But the Bulgarian aristocracy was by no means unanimous in its zeal for Christianity. Boris had to suppress a rising, which aimed at the substitution of a pagan ruler for himself. The heathen element among the nobles was exterminated with ferocious cruelty, and Bulgaria received from her prince a baptism of blood.

Boris hesitated long between the Greek and the Roman Church. Even before his acceptance of Christianity from Byzantium, he had dallied with Rome. Here again the political character of his theology is apparent. Anxious for the ecclesiastical independence of his country, and unable to obtain a Bulgarian Patriarch from the Greek Church, he sent an embassy to Pope Nicholas I. in 866 with a most remarkable document. The Pope was expected to answer no fewer than one hundred and six questions upon the Christian life, some of which must have caused him to smile, while others touched upon the gravest themes. Thus, we find one question asking what punishment is to be meted out to idolaters, while another requests the Pope to decide whether the Bulgarians may continue to wear trousers. The morality of dowries, and minute points of Court etiquette were submitted in the same breath as the treatment of fugitives and the desirability of sorcery. The countrymen of the late M. Stambuloff might with advantage have remembered the old Papal warning that "a man, who cannot be allowed to leave his country, is not a free man." But to the most important question of all, the right of Bulgaria to an archbishop of her own, no definite answer was given. The Pope avoided the question, but promised to send two bishops to study the state of the country. The bishops came and brought Bibles with them, but it was not till the time of the next Pope that an arch-

134　THE CONVERSION OF THE BULGARIANS.

bishop was sent, and then Boris refused to receive him. Meanwhile the accession of the Emperor Basil I., who had been as a boy a Bulgarian prisoner, led Boris to turn once more to Constantinople. The famous Council of 869 decided that Bulgaria belonged to the Eastern and not to the Western Church, and the decision has never been revoked. The Roman clergy left the country, which was now placed under the spiritual care of the Archbishop Joseph and ten bishops, sent from Constantinople. Successive Popes in vain endeavoured to prevail upon Bulgaria to return to the Western fold. The Bulgarian Archbishop was awarded the next place to the Greek Patriarch on great occasions at Constantinople; the closest relations began between the Bulgarians and the Greeks. The oscillation of Boris between the Eastern and the Western Churches has in our own time been exactly paralleled by one of his name. This very year another Boris of Bulgaria has been the unconscious object of fierce competition between the Greek Church and that of Rome. Baby Boris, like his ancestor, has been won over to the Greek ritual.

Boris, weary of the throne, retired in 888 to a monastery, hoping to pass the rest of his days in peace. But his eldest son Vladimir, who succeeded him, was so rash a ruler that he emerged from his cloister, and appointed his younger son Simeon to rule in his stead. He then returned to his cell, and died in 907. His name lives still in the memory of the Bulgarian people, and he ranks as the first of their national heroes.

II.

THE FIRST BULGARIAN EMPIRE.

(893—1018.)

THE historian of the "Decline and Fall" has remarked in a famous passage, that "the glory of the Bulgarians was confined to a narrow scope both of time and place," but he admits that in the reign of Simeon "Bulgaria assumed a rank among the civilised powers of the earth." The era of this monarch was, indeed, the golden age of Bulgaria. Neither before nor since has the Bulgarian name been so feared and so respected, and to-day the nation looks back with pride to the thirty-four years of Simeon's rule as the period when the country reached its zenith.

The remarkable man, to whom the rise of Bulgaria was chiefly due, had been educated by his father's desire at Constantinople. The lad studied the masterpieces of ancient eloquence and philosophy with so much zeal, that his comrades called him half a Greek. But his acquaintance with Greek literature did not dispose him to look with favour upon the Greek Empire. His object was to found upon the ruins of the Byzantine dominion a new Greco-Slav realm, of which he himself would be the head.

He lost no time in setting about his plan. The thirty years' peace between Bulgaria and the Greeks now came to an end. Simeon found a convenient pretext for war in a commercial question, which shows that in those days the trade of Bulgaria was considerable. The Emperor Leo the Philosopher had granted a monopoly of the Bulgarian markets to two Greek merchants, who levied heavy dues upon all the native industries. Simeon, unable to obtain redress, declared war. The feeble Leo was taken at a disadvantage. Simeon routed his armies, and contemptuously restored the Greek prisoners to their sovereign with their noses cut off. The Emperor now summoned to his aid the Magyars, who had become near neighbours of the Bulgarians since their entry into the eastern part of what is now Roumania. These fierce auxiliaries under their leader Árpád crossed the Danube, which had hitherto divided them from the Bulgarians, and forced Simeon to retire to Silistria, while they ravaged the country as far as his residence at Prêslav on the northern slopes of the Balkans. On their return march, however, the Bulgarian prince fell upon them and defeated them. In order to prevent further Magyar invasions, he took advantage of their absence on a Western campaign to carry off or butcher their wives and little ones, whom they had left behind. Finding their Bessarabian home desolate, the Magyars wandered once more westward to found the kingdom of Hungary.

Simeon by a timely victory secured peace with

Leo. But upon the death of that Emperor, an insult to the Bulgarian envoys aroused the anger of their sovereign, who vowed that he would never rest till every Byzantine town in Europe was his. The Bulgarians again appeared at the gates of Constantinople; Adrianople fell before them. The Greeks attempted to divert their enemy's attention from the Imperial city by an expedition against his own coast. But a great Bulgarian victory at the mouth of the river Achelöus near Mesembria annihilated the Greek forces. Simeon renewed his attack on Constantinople with a vast army, and endeavoured to obtain a fleet from the Arabs of Tunis. Romanus Lecapenus, the associate of Constantine Porphyrogenitus on the throne, was forced to beg for peace from the proud Bulgarian, who held the fortunes of the Greek Empire in the hollow of his hand. Simeon, fearing that the tribes of the north might assail him in the rear, consented to spare the Imperial capital. Riches were offered to the victors; free trade—the original bone of contention—was granted, and the chief places at festivals were reserved for the Bulgarians and their friends. Further hostilities with the Greeks were prevented by the death of their dreaded foe.

Meanwhile Simeon had extended his dominions in other directions. He deposed two princes of Servia, and drove a third to seek refuge among the Croats, while a Bulgarian army ravaged his country with fire and sword. Under Simeon's sway the Bulgarian frontier ran from Mesembria on the shore of the Black Sea past Adrianople to Mount Rhodope, and then right across the peninsula from Mount Olympus to the

Albanian coast opposite Corfu. Albania, with the exception of a few ports, was Bulgarian as far as the river Drin, while nearly the whole of the present kingdom of Servia, including the important town of Nisch and Belgrade itself, belonged to Simeon. Even across the Danube his power was felt. Before the Magyar invasion he seems to have included part

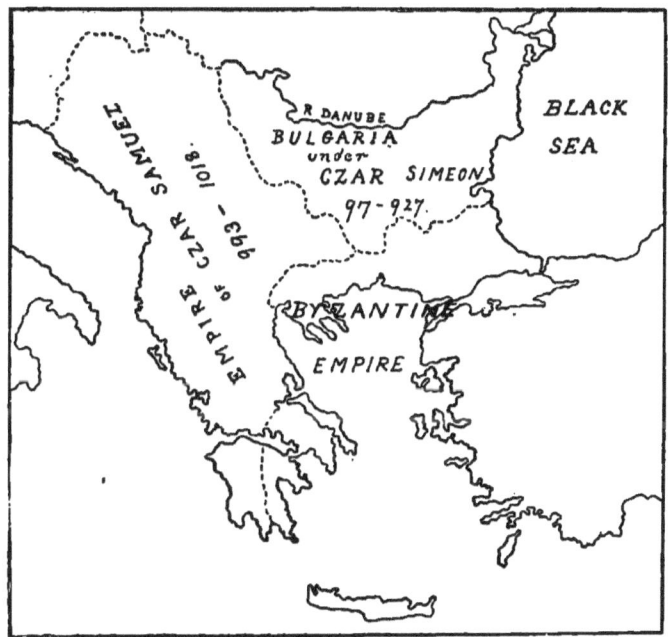

THE FIRST BULGARIAN EMPIRE.

of Roumania in his dominions, and it is possible that portions of Hungary and Transylvania owned his sceptre. At his death he was meditating the addition of Croatia to his possessions. Bulgaria, under his auspices, was—what she has never been again, but what she still aspires to be—the dominant state of the Balkan Peninsula. Indeed, there was little room left for any one else. Not even the "big Bulgaria," projected by the treaty of San Stefano in 1878, would have been so large as the Bulgaria of the first three decades of the tenth century.

It was hardly to be expected that the lord of such a vast expanse of territory would remain content with the simple title of *knez*, or prince. Simeon sought the name as well as the dominions of an Emperor, and obtained from Rome the title which he desired. He styled himself "Czar of the Bulgarians and Autocrat of the Greeks," and his successors called themselves "Czars" after him. Thus, five centuries before there were Czars of Russia, Bulgaria had adopted that proud designation for her rulers. But without a Patriarch the Empire of a Czar was incomplete. Boris had never succeeded in obtaining for his chief ecclesiastic any higher title than that of Archbishop. But his son was more fortunate, and a Patriarch was installed at his capital at Prêslav.

We may judge of Simeon's power, not merely from the extent of his Empire, but from the splendour of his palace. The Bulgarians had rivalled the pomp of the Greeks at the siege of Constantinople, and they now erected a capital worthy of their huge realm. Prêslav, better known under its Turkish name of Eski-Stambul, is now a wretched village, but a thousand years ago its splendour excited universal admiration. A personal friend of Simeon, John the Exarch, has given an interesting description of the Bulgarian Czar's residence. "If a stranger coming from afar enters the outer-court of the princely dwelling, he will be amazed, and ask many a question as he walks up to the gates. And if he goes within, he will see on either side buildings decorated with stone and wainscoted with wood of various colours. And if he goes yet further into the courtyard he will behold lofty palaces and churches, bedecked with countless stones and wood and frescoes without, and with marble and copper and silver and gold within. Such grandeur he has never seen before, for in his own land there

RUINS OF PRÊSLAV.

are only miserable huts of straw. Beside himself with astonishment, he will scarce believe his eyes. But if he perchance espy the prince sitting in his robe covered with pearls, with a chain of coins round his neck and bracelets on his wrists, girt about with a purple girdle and a sword of gold at his side, while on either hand his nobles are seated with golden chains, girdles, and bracelets upon them; then will he answer when one asks him on his return home what he has seen: 'I know not how to describe it; only thine own eyes could comprehend such splendour.'"
In the seventeenth century there was still existing near Prêslav a huge wall, dating from pre-Turkish

times, which enclosed a larger space than the area of Constantinople itself. Nowadays a few fragments of stone alone remain to mark the spot.

The reign of Simeon was long remembered as the golden age of old Bulgarian literature. The Czar, like several other Balkan princes, was a patron of letters, and dabbled in them himself. It is uncertain whether the Slav translation of St. Chrysostom's best speeches was from his pen, but it was at his instigation that the selection was made. Before his time there were already the germs of a national literature. The oldest known specimen is the catalogue of ancient Bulgarian princes, referred to in the last chapter. At first, it seems probable that the Greek alphabet was used, but after the invention of the Cyrillic character it was discarded. The first Slavonic books were mainly religious works, translations of the Bible and ecclesiastical books executed by Constantine, Methodius, and their pupils, who were collectively known as the "seven saints." With the accession of Simeon, the bulk of the national literature increased. John the Exarch, from whom we have already quoted, wrote and dedicated to the Czar a work called Šestodnev, a descriptive account of the Creation, compiled from a variety of sources. Another priest, named Constantine, translated by the Czar's orders four orations of Athanasius—a further proof of Simeon's rhetorical taste—and made a collection of homilies for every Sunday in the year. We now hear for the first time of a historical work, a translation of the chronicle of John Malalas together with a sketch of Old Testament history and a life of

Alexander the Great—the whole undertaken by a monk named Gregory at the express desire of Simeon. Philology, too, found a Bulgarian votary in the monk Chrabr, who composed a treatise on the invention of the Slavonic alphabet. An encyclopædia of contemporary learning translated from Greek authors was the work of this reign, and bears the name of "Simeon's *Sbornik*," but its authors are unknown. It will be seen that the literature of the period was entirely in monkish hands, and Simeon himself owed his literary accomplishments to his training as a monk. But works of originality were sadly lacking; no great Bulgarian poet arose to kindle the feelings of the people by his songs. Oral tradition had accumulated legends, proverbs, and fables, but there was no Bulgarian Homer or Virgil to weave them into a national epic. Simeon compared his literary associates with the learned men who had gathered at the court of the Ptolemies. His death threw a shadow over the culture which he had done so much to foster, just as it checked his conquests. He died in 927, and Peter, his eldest son by his second marriage, whom he had made his heir to the exclusion of Michael, his son by his first wife, reigned in his stead.

The new Czar was a very different man from his father. Simeon had sought the diadem of an Emperor, Peter desired the halo of a saint; Simeon had led his people to the gates of Constantinople, Peter could scarcely defend his country from the Greeks Alike at home and abroad, in politics and religion, dissension and weakness were the characteristics of this long reign, with which the decline of the first Bulgarian Empire began.

Peter had hardly mounted the throne when his neighbours prepared to take advantage of his youth and inexperience to attack his dominions. The Greeks were the first in the field, but a peace was arranged through the efforts of the young Czar's uncle and guardian, Sursubul, and cemented by a marriage between Peter and the grand-daughter of the Emperor Romanus Lecapenus. This Byzantine union had an evil influence upon the future of Bulgaria. For the close relations between Constantinople and Bulgaria which date from the marriage of Peter, brought the sturdy warriors of the Balkans under the spell of the Byzantine Court. The Bulgarian Czar, who had derived his diadem from Rome, now drew near to Constantinople. The Greeks recognised the validity of his title, and allowed the dignity of a Patriarch to the Archbishop of Silistria. The Bulgarian Church thus became independent, and the aspirations of Boris I. were fulfilled. Moreover, the Greek Emperor still paid a yearly tribute to the Bulgarian Czar. But the party of action in the country was not satisfied with this Greek alliance. Simeon's old generals despised the enemies whom they had so often put to rout, and in Peter's younger brother John they found a leader. But John was defeated, and Michael, Peter's disinterested half-brother, fared no better. But the connection with the Eastern Empire was severed by the Greeks themselves. With the accession of the Emperor Nicephorus Phocas a series of energetic rulers began, and Bulgaria was not long in feeling the effects of the new order of things. Nicephorus, flushed with his conquest of Crete and Cyprus, determined to subdue the Bulgarians and avenge the victories of Simeon. The incursions of the Magyars, who five times ravaged Bulgaria under Peter's weak rule and then strayed over the border into the Byzantine provinces, furnished him with an excuse. He demanded satisfaction from the Bulgarians, and when they retaliated by asking him for tribute, he beat their envoys and occupied their frontier. But, warned by the fate of his predecessors, he resolved to take no further steps until he had secured a powerful ally. He accordingly begged Sviatoslav, chief of the Russians, to assist him.

The first appearance of the Russians in Bulgaria was a most important event, which affects Bulgarian politics to this hour. From that memorable day of August, 967, when the Russian fleet arrived with ten thousand men at the mouth of the Danube, we may trace the first interference of Russia in the affairs of the Southern Slavs. Sviatoslav, a hardy warrior, whose food was horseflesh, whose couch was a bear skin laid upon the ground, made short work of such resistance as the feeble Peter offered to his arms. Silistria, the great Bulgarian stronghold, fell, and so rapid was the progress of the Russians, that Nicephorus began to fear for the safety of his own capital. He hastened to make peace with the Bulgarian Czar, and promised to drive the terrible Northmen from his land. A double marriage was to be a token of this new alliance.

While Bulgaria had thus been menaced by Greeks and Russians, Servia, enslaved by Simeon, had regained her independence. Under the leadership of Česlav she severed herself from Bulgarian domination and owned no superior save the Emperor at Constantinople. The Patzinakitai, a savage tribe occupying the southern part of Roumania, crossed the Danube and made repeated incursions into Bulgaria on the north, and to add to these external troubles, a schism arose at home which rent the Empire of Simeon in twain. Disgusted at the weakness of Peter, a Bulgarian noble, named Šišman, a native of Trnovo resolved to found a dynasty of his own. Unable to subject the whole country to his sway, he contented himself with the western half. He soon extended his influence in Macedonia and Albania, and from 963 there were thus two separate Bulgarian Empires, one in the west, the other in the east. Šišman had himself proclaimed Czar, and his descendants held their own for half a century after the other half of the Empire had fallen beneath the Byzantine yoke.

The decadence of Bulgaria was as marked in the domain of literature and theology as in the arts of war. To the zealous preachers and teachers, whose lives and writings had illuminated the reigns of Boris I. and his still greater son, there succeeded a race of gloomy hermits, who preferred the seclusion of the forests to the task of instructing the people. We find in the fiery speeches of Kosmas, who lived a little later, vigorous denunciations of these monkish ascetics, who sacrificed useful studies to the mortification of their own bodies, while the nation, which they ought to have taught, was wholly devoted to gaming and drinking, the music of the *guzla*, and the singing of "devilish songs." The kind of life led by the spiritual leaders of that period may be judged from the career of the most famous of them all, John of Ryl, who was afterwards chosen as the patron saint of Bulgaria. Born in a village, of humble parents, he spent his youth in tending a flock of sheep. On his parents' death he entered a cloister; but, desiring absolute solitude, soon retired to the remote but beautiful Ryl mountains. Here he spent twenty-seven solitary years, first in a dark cavern, then in the hollow of an old oak, and finally on an inaccessible crag, which now overshadows the fine monastery erected to his memory. Here the Czar Peter once visited him in his retirement, and perhaps may have wished that he could follow his example. But the lonely hermit did not lack imitators. Three other "dwellers in the wilderness" are mentioned in the history of the period, and commemorated by similar monastic foundations, which served during the long period of Turkish domination to keep alive the torch of Slavonic learning.

While literature had thus fled from the land, a strange doctrine of theology had insinuated itself into the minds of the people. The heresy of the Bogomiles has played a great part in the history of the Balkan Peninsula. In Bosnia it defied all the efforts of the Popes to suppress it; it made its way into Italy, and even France; but it was in Bulgaria that it first attained importance. During the early part of

Peter's reign, there appeared in his country a priest named Bogomil, the " Beloved of God," the author of several mystical works, strongly imbued with Oriental ideas. Bogomil's teaching was peculiarly appreciated by a Slavonic race, such as the Bulgarians had by this time become. His cardinal doctrine of a good and an evil deity found its counterpart in the old Slavonic myth of good and evil spirits, called *bogy* and *bésy*. Upon this dualism his whole system was based; by means of it he built up a complete theory of the universe. The good deity, according to the Bogomiles, was the creator of what is heavenly, unseen, and perfect. It is to the bad deity, the Satan of the Scriptures, that we owe everything that is visible and tangible, the world and all that dwell therein. In Platonic language, they describe how in the soul of man both elements are combined, how everywhere exists the antithesis between mind and matter, between what is temporal and what is eternal. For all the misfortunes which befell mankind in the Old Testament they make the evil deity responsible —for the murder of Abel, the Flood, the Tower of Babel, the destruction of Sodom. The Virgin Mary was, in their view, not the mother of our Lord, but an angel; the death of Christ upon the Cross was not a reality. For the emblems of Christianity as practised by the monks they had nothing but contempt. They blasphemed against the crucifix; they regarded pictures and statues as idolatrous. They rejected the mass, set orthodox bishops at defiance, and called themselves "the salt of the earth," " the lilies of the field," and " the light of the world."

Adults were alone admitted into their community, and fasting and prayer, followed by the laying of the Gospel according to St. John on the head of the proselyte, took the place of baptism. There were two grades among the faithful, one of "simple believers," the other of "perfect" men and women. Any member of the latter grade might preach, and the elders of the Church were elected by the congregation. There was no regular service of prayer, and no churches were needed for the simple worship of the Bogomiles. Like the ancient Slavs, they addressed their supplications to God under the canopy of heaven or in their straw-thatched huts. A "perfect" Bogomile might not marry; to eat meat was a crime, to kill any animal but a snake a deadly sin. This horror of bloodshed made them prohibit warfare and capital punishment, for these they regarded as works of the evil spirit. The "perfect" Bogomile was, in fact, a hermit, for he was compelled by his creed to avoid everything that savoured of the world. It was easy to recognise him, as he rode through a village, by the prayers which he murmured as he went. But only a chosen few arrived at so high a grade of self-denial. An ordinary member of the sect lived externally much like other men. He married a wife, and could divorce her at his will; he went to the wars, and engaged in commerce. But on his death-bed he was always received into the community of the "perfect." Such was the Bogomile heresy. Its influence upon the people was very great: in spite, or because, of persecution, it spread far and wide. A mass of legends and fables sprang from the mystical teachings of the Bogomiles, and this curious lore was disseminated from Bulgaria through Russia and the Balkan lands. But the political results of the heresy were even more serious. It added yet another to the thorny theological questions which divided the Christians of South-eastern Europe against each other. Two new parties were thus formed, and at a later period, when nothing but unity could have saved the Balkan nationalities from the victorious march of Islâm, they were separated and split asunder by their own religious differences.

Boris II., who succeeded his father Peter upon the death of the latter in 969, found himself surrounded by difficulties. The Russians, under their redoubtable chief, Sviatoslav, having once tasted the delights of a warmer climate, were not likely to remain in their capital of Kieff. David, son of Šišman, who now styled himself Czar of West Bulgaria, seized the opportunity of Boris's absence in Constantinople to attack the eastern half of the country. With a promptitude worthy of Simeon, Boris hurried back and repulsed the usurper David. But the threatened Russian invasion was much more serious. This time Sviatoslav came with the intention of staying. He told his mother Olga that he had resolved to move his throne from Kieff to Prêslavec, on the Danube, where he had pitched his winter quarters on his former expedition. The site of Prêslavec, which must not be confounded with Simeon's capital of Prêslav on the northern slopes of the Balkans, is now lost; but it must have seemed to the hardy Northmen a veritable paradise. Sviatoslav described to his mother the advantages of its situation. " At Prêslavec," he said, " the riches of the whole world are to be found. Thither Greece sends her silk, her wines, and her fruits ; Bohemia and Hungary their steeds ; Russia her furs and her wax, her honey and her slaves." Prêslavec, as well as Prêslav, fell before the lances of the Russians, Boris himself was captured by the invaders ; a Russian army for the first time crossed the Balkans, and, after a desperate struggle for Philippopolis, appeared on the Greek frontier and threatened Constantinople. But the warlike Armenian, John Zimisces, who had just succeeded to the Byzantine throne, came to the assistance of the Bulgarian Czar. Traversing the Balkans, he suddenly appeared before Prêslav, where Sviatoslav's trusty lieutenant had been left in charge of the booty and the Bulgarian monarch. The skill of the Greeks in sieges soon told. After a desperate assault, the city was captured, but the palace of the Bulgarian Czars perished in the flames. Boris and his family were rescued, and the handful of Russians who escaped retreated to Silistria. With the fall of that last refuge, peace was concluded. Sviatoslav renounced all hostile designs upon Bulgaria, and was allowed to go free. But near the rapids of the Dnieper he was attacked by the fierce tribe of Patzinakitai ; his head was cut off and converted into a goblet, in accordance with that savage custom of which Bulgarian history has already furnished us with one notable example.

Bulgaria had been freed from the Russians, but she found that she had merely exchanged one servitude for another. The crafty Armenian had not released Boris from pure compassion for his fate, and the kindness with which the rescued Czar was treated was merely the prelude to his final deposition. It had long been the desire of the Byzantine Emperors to add Bulgaria to their dominions, and chance had at last given them an opportunity of accomplishing it. Master as he was of the country, Zimisces destroyed the Empire of Simeon without a blow. Boris II. and the Patriarch Damian were deposed, the diadem of the Bulgarian Czars was offered up as a trophy in the Church of St. Sophia at Constantinople, the fallen sovereign was stripped of his purple mantle and his scarlet shoes, while he received in return for the loss of his dominions the sorry dignity of an Imperial magnate. To make the downfall of his dynasty doubly sure, his younger brother, sole survivor of Omortag's line, was emasculated by order of the conqueror. Thus, in 971, three centuries after Isperich had led his Bulgarians across the Danube, the Empire of Simeon ingloriously fell. Only in the western portion of the country—in Macedonia and Albania—the new dynasty, which Šišman had founded, still survived to maintain the name and fame of the Bulgarian Czars. Five years after the fall of the East Bulgarian throne, a man arose in the West whose exploits threw a final lustre upon the last years of the First Bulgarian Empire. This man was Stephen Samuel, fourth son of Šišman, who has left a great mark upon the history of his country.

The circumstances under which Samuel received the crown are somewhat obscure. His eldest brother,

David, is known to have been murdered by a band of wandering Wallachs in the mountains. Moses, the second brother, fell in battle. Aaron, the third of the family, was put to death by Samuel's orders because of his sympathies with the Greeks. A story was long current to the effect that Samuel had put his father's eyes out and then strangled him, in order to secure the throne. But this is probably an invention. Samuel was a cruel ruler, but it is not necessary to accuse him of parricide. The fact is certain that in 976 he became Czar, and for nearly forty years the fortunes of Bulgaria were in his hands.

The empire to which Samuel succeeded was Macedonian rather than Bulgarian. At first, indeed, he fixed his residence at Sofia, the present capital; but he soon moved to Macedonia, and established himself in a rocky and beautifully-wooded island in the lovely lake of Prespa. The travellers who have seen the place have still been able to trace the ruins of his castle, or *Grad*, from which the island derives its present name. Amid the clusters of the vine and the fiery glow of the pomegranate, the columns of four churches still rise in silent grandeur; while a second island, called *Mali Grad*, or "the little castle," testifies alike by its title and the carved stones upon it to the past glories of the Bulgarian Czar. Yet nearer the Adriatic did Samuel penetrate, for above the lake of Ochrida two ruined fortresses still remind the natives of their ancient lord. Further westward the Albanian town of Berat owned his sway, while in the south Joannina, the present Albanian capital, and the coast opposite Corfu were parts of his empire.

THE DIKILITAŠ AT JALAR.

In the north his dominions included Nisch and Belgrade; in the east he held most of the towns on the Struma and the Vardar, and thus connected Macedonia with Sofia and the east of Bulgaria. Opposed as he was to the Emperor at Constantinople, he naturally looked to Rome for his crown, like Simeon and Peter; but he was statesman enough to see that it was only by a strict neutrality in the theological disputes of his subjects that he could keep it. The parties of the Roman Catholics, the Orthodox Greek Church, and the Bogomiles were so evenly divided in his domains, that no other course was open to him.

The confusion, which followed the death of the Emperor Zimisces, induced the people of Eastern Bulgaria to revolt against their Byzantine masters. In Samuel they found a leader, and in a short time all the Bulgarian towns on the Danube opened their gates to him. Meanwhile the captive Czar, Boris II., and his brother had escaped from Constantinople. But the unhappy Boris, on his way home, was killed by one of his former subjects, who imagined from his garb that he was a Greek. His brother escaped to Samuel's court, where he was received with favour and entrusted with an important post. Having Bulgaria at his feet the Czar marched southwards into Thessaly, then inhabited by a considerable Slavonic population, and by the capture of Larissa provided himself with a Greek wife.

But in Basil II., the new Emperor, the Bulgarian Czar found a foeman worthy of his steel. From his early years this heartless ascetic seemed to have but one desire, the complete subjugation of the Bulgarian race. It took him forty years to accomplish his task, but at last he succeeded, and is now chiefly known by the epithet of the "Bulgar-slayer," which his cruelties and his victories won him. His first campaign against Samuel in 981 was a complete failure, and it was with the utmost difficulty that he escaped with his life. Warlike operations elsewhere prevented the Emperor from renewing his attack for fifteen years, and in the meanwhile Samuel extended his sway in all directions. The Czar occupied Durazzo and the Adriatic seaboard as far north as Ragusa, and attacked John Vladimir, the Serb ruler of the district known as the Zeta, which was the germ of the present principality of Montenegro. Vladimir retreated into those inaccessible mountain fastnesses which no enemy has ever been able to capture, and received as a token of the conqueror's esteem the hand of his daughter and North Albania as his vassal. This was the zenith of Samuel's rule; from that moment his power began to decline. In his second war against Basil he sustained his first crushing defeat. On his way back from a campaign in the Morea he was attacked by night on the banks of the river Helláda not far from the famous pass of Thermopylæ. A terrible slaughter ensued, and Samuel fled for refuge to his rocky island home in Lake Prespa. From that moment his fortune turned. Durazzo was lost to him, and the loss was all the more bitter because his own daughter helped her Armenian husband to betray the place. East Bulgaria, with the old capital of Prêslav, acknowledged once more the Byzantine sway; Vidin surrendered after an eight months' siege.

Basil marched through the land destroying fortress after fortress as he went. The four campaigns of this second Bulgarian and Byzantine war left Samuel nothing but West Macedonia, Albania, and the mountainous districts of Vitoš and Ryl. Fresh distractions in Asia alone prevented Basil from giving the final blow to the First Bulgarian Empire. A third war, which broke out in 1014, was even more disastrous for the Czar. Fifteen thousand of his subjects were taken prisoners in a great battle near Bélasica, a mountain in Macedonia, which looms large in Bulgarian ballads. With a refinement of cruelty unparalleled even in the annals of that barbarous age, Basil had their eyes put out, allowing every hundredth man to retain one eye, in order that he might be able to guide his comrades to the headquarters of their sovereign. In spite of his own fierce disposition and deeds of bloodshed, Samuel was overpowered at the spectacle as a long line of blind warriors entered the gates of his camp. He fell to the ground in a swoon ; for a moment he seemed tő recover, but his heart was broken, and he died ten days later on September 15, 1014. With him perished the last hope of Bulgaria. It was his strong arm and resolute will which had so long kept the Greek Emperor at bay, and though his son Gabriel Roman or Radomir, who succeeded him, had the courage and more than the stature of his father, he could not stay the downfall of his country. An evil fate seemed to dog the House of Šišman ; the blood which Samuel had shed was upon the head of his son. For a time the Czar Gabriel, who had stood at his father's right hand in many a battle, made a stand against the inveterate enemy of his race. Basil, flushed with his success, refused all offers of peace, and pressed on into Macedonia. But the Bulgarians, fired by Gabriel's example, disputed every position with the Greeks, and Basil had to resort to treachery to accomplish his ends. Samuel's murdered brother Aaron had left a son, John Vladislav, who was as devoted as his father before him to the Greek cause. Forgetful of the fact that his own life had been spared by Samuel at the request of his cousin Gabriel, Vladislav assassinated the Czar at the instigation of the Greek Emperor. Not content with one victim, Vladislav gave orders for the murder of Gabriel's wife, blinded her eldest boy, and slew Vladimir prince of the Zeta who had married Gabriel's daughter. Thus was Samuel's fratricide avenged fivefold.

Vladislav was unable to reap the fruits of his treachery by handing over Bulgaria to the Greeks. The Bulgarian *boljars* or nobles, who had always been the mainstay of the Czars, forced him to continue the struggle for national independence. Under the patriotic Ivac the aristocracy showed that the spirit of Simeon and Samuel was not dead. Basil's career of plunder and cruelty was momentarily stopped, and Vladislav himself seems to have changed his mind and done his best for his country. But he fell before the walls of Durazzo in 1018, Bulgaria was left without a Czar, and the nobles themselves became convinced that further resistance was useless. A few, however, still held out; the majority surrendered to the Greek Emperor. Basil marched in triumphal progress to Ochrida, where the widow of Vladislav and the survivors of the House of Šišman received him in the former residence of Samuel. An immense treasure and the crown of the dead Czar fell into the victor's hands, and it did not cost him much to confirm the privileges of the Bulgarian nobles, and confer a few Byzantine titles upon their chiefs. The mountains of Albania still sheltered the dauntless few, among them three sons of Vladislav. But Ivac, who had been the soul of the struggle for freedom, was cunningly entrapped and blinded. Deprived of their leader, the remaining *boljars* yielded, and in 1018, after forty years of stratagems and battles, Basil the "Bulgar-slayer" realised the dream of his youth. Bulgaria, West as well as East, the Empire of Samuel no less than the Empire of Boris, was a dependency of Constantinople. The Serbs and Croats were dragged down in its fall, and the Balkan Peninsula obeyed the commands of a Byzantine Emperor.

III.

BULGARIA UNDER THE GREEKS.

(1018—1186.)

THE period of one hundred and seventy years which intervened between the First and Second Bulgarian Empires is almost a blank in the national history. The Greek supremacy stifled the patriotic feelings of the people. The country had been devastated by the long struggle between Samuel and Basil, thousands of its inhabitants had fallen in war, many had migrated to Asia. The nobles, the natural leaders of the masses in an aristocratic state such as Bulgaria, were occupying subordinate positions at the court of the conqueror; even Samuel's daughter was a lady-in-waiting to some Imperial Highness at Constantinople. Bulgaria, though its ancient boundaries were nominally preserved, was for all practical purposes an integral part of the Greek Empire. The Emperor announced, indeed, in one of his proclamations that, although he had conquered the country, he intended to maintain its rights. But he divided the dominions of the Czars into *themata*, or provinces, like the rest of the Empire, each under the control of a *strategos* or governor, who combined in his person both military and civil powers and usually held office for little more than a year. During this time his chief object was to make as much out of the unfortunate provincials as he could, and scarcely had one official been satiated than another hungry placeman appeared in his stead. From the testimony of Greek writers themselves we learn that their countrymen behaved like "robbers" to the helpless Bulgarians entrusted to their care. Above the *strategi*, who resided in the chief towns such as Ochrida, Prespa, and Durazzo, there was a Governor-general whose seat was at Skopje in Macedonia. Beneath them there were two inferior grades of military officers, so that there was a complete hierarchy of Imperial functionaries. In fact, under the Greek rule the Bulgarians had a foretaste of the coming Turkish domination. The men were different, the methods very much the same.

One national institution was allowed to retain much of its former independence. The Bulgarian Church had always been closely connected with the life of the people. Basil spared the religious susceptibilities of the conquered nation from political motives. He permitted the Bulgarian ecclesiastics to govern themselves without interference; but he substituted the title of Archbishop for that of Patriarch; and after the first appointment took care that the occupant of the post should be a Greek. Ochrida, the seat of the Archbishop, thus became the centre of Greek influence in Bulgarian lands. Nominated by the Emperor at Constantinople the head of the the Church was his willing tool, and the former residence of the Czars was converted into the headquarters of Greek culture. But the Bogomile heresy continued to make headway, and the hair-splitting of Greek theologians rather increased than hindered the growth of the schism. The Emperor Alexius I. persecuted the heretics with fire and sword, with the result that they threw themselves into the arms of his barbarous enemies, preferring a pagan ally to a Christian foe. The territorial jurisdiction of the Church was, however, the same as under the old Bulgarian Czars. The "golden bulls" of the Emperor Basil enumerated no fewer than thirty bishoprics of the Bulgarian community with six hundred and eighty-five priests in their respective dioceses, which included all Macedonia, parts of Albania and Thessaly, Sofia, Vidin, Prisrend, and even Belgrade, between them. In short, the network of the Bulgarian hierarchy was, even under the Greek Emperors, fully as widespread as the temporal dominion of Simeon or Samuel had been. The National Church was practically free, but it was a free Church in an enslaved state.

The anarchy which ensued all over the Byzantine Empire on the death of Basil II., was favourable to the Bulgarian cause. Vladislav's widow and son were suspected of intriguing against their masters, and the latter was deprived of his sight. Peter Deljan, a son of the hapless Czar Gabriel, appeared in 1040 in his father's country and was received with acclamations as its ruler. The natives, ground down by the exactions of the Greek governors, flocked to his standard, and town after town welcomed him as a deliverer. But a rival Czar was proclaimed, and, as Deljan said, the land could not support two monarchs. He therefore offered to withdraw if the people wished it. "We will have no Czar but Deljan," was the enthusiastic reply. His rival was stoned, and for a time fortune favoured the arms of the united Bulgarians. The Byzantine tax-gatherers were hewn in pieces, the Emperor himself was forced to flee, his treasure fell into the hands of the enemy, and Salonica was only saved by a miracle. It seemed for a moment as if the Bulgarian Empire had been restored. But a fresh quarrel divided the Bulgarian ranks. Vladislav's younger brother had sought refuge with his cousin at the outbreak of the rebellion, and shared with him the glory of the campaign. With the hereditary treachery of his race he invited Deljan to his table, and blinded his guest when the latter was in his cups. Fate seemed to dog the steps of Šišman's House, and the crime of Samuel who had slain his brother was literally being visited upon the third and fourth generation. The traitor was richly rewarded by the Greek Emperor, and Bulgaria, once more without a leader, succumbed to the oppressor. Only in the impregnable fastnesses of Montenegro did Voislav, a prince connected by marriage with Samuel's line, defy the armies of the invaders, whose bones bleached on the cold grey limestone rocks. But the Bulgarians were still not without hopes of freedom. They were ready to follow the lead of any one who shared their religious views. Thus we find them offering the title of Czar to the grandson of the redoubtable Voislav, Constantine Bodin in 1073, on condition that he would free them from the Greeks. Bodin consented, was proclaimed Czar under the name of Peter, but speedily collapsed. The only result of this abortive rising was the destruction of the palace of the Czars upon the lake of Prespa by mercenaries. Thus perished the most interesting monument of the old Bulgarian Empire. When, however, Robert Guiscard and his Normans landed in Albania and occupied a large part of Macedonia, the orthodox Bulgarians refused to make common cause with the "heretics." But the Bogomiles did not scruple to form military and even matrimonial alliances with barbarous chiefs who would assist them against their Greek persecutors.

For these native insurrections were not the only disturbances during the Greek occupation. Two fierce tribes from beyond the Danube made repeated incursions into Bulgaria, which the successors of Basil II. were too weak to prevent. The Patzinakitai were crushed by the Greek commanders, but the conquerors committed the blunder of allowing their barbarous prisoners to settle on the plains round Sofia and Nisch. To the unfortunate Bulgarian peasantry the new colonists were most unwelcome neighbours, for they invited their kinsmen from over the river to join them in plundering the natives. The Kumani, a wild gipsy race, speaking a language somewhat resembling Turkish, appeared in Bulgaria for the first time about the middle of the eleventh century. United with the Patzinakitai, they proved invincible; but at last their allies were utterly routed, and henceforth disappear from the Balkan Peninsula. Another people, perhaps the oldest in the Balkans, is now first mentioned in history. The Albanians, or Skipetar, as they prefer to call themselves, are still a riddle to philologists. Their language is almost unintelligible; their country is to this day less known than many parts of Central Africa. Their utter disregard of human life and complacent indifference to their present Ottoman masters make any study of their customs well-nigh impossible. The blood feud and constant border warfare permit few of them to die a natural death. Their obedience to their own chiefs and their natural aptitude for fighting—none of them ever stirs abroad without his belt of cartridges and his weapons—might have formed the basis of an Albanian Empire. But they have no national history; even their great hero, Skanderbeg, was not an Albanian by birth. Their literature consists mainly of terse proverbs, which show them to be shrewd observers, and in Montenegro they have become, under a firm government, industrious citizens. In their own country they exhibit a lawlessness which makes them the Kurds of Europe.

The last sixty years of the Greek rule in Bulgaria were comparatively undisturbed. The barbarian inroads had almost ceased, the natives had sunk into despair. But in 1186 an event occurred which roused them to fury and led to the final overthrow of the Greek supremacy. There were living about that time in Trnovo two brothers, Peter and John Asên, who traced their descent from the Imperial race of

Šišman. Anxious to push their fortunes or seeking a pretext for revolt, the brothers betook themselves to the Greek headquarters and asked for commissions in the army and a grant of lands on the Balkans. Their petitions were refused, and John Asên received for his importunity a slap on the cheek from the highest official of the Court. The affront was never forgiven. Asên was a fiery adventurer, of the stuff

OLD RELIEF AT VARNA.

of which revolutionary leaders are made. Eager for revenge, he hastened home to Trnovo, and there the two brothers called a public meeting in the Church of St. Demetrius, which they had founded. They had no difficulty in working upon the feelings of the people. The Greek Emperor, Isaac Angelus, in order to defray the cost of his nuptials with the daughter of the Hungarian king, had extorted the last farthing from his Bulgarian subjects, whose flocks and herds had been seized by his rapacious officials. To this material injury was added the popular belief that the day; appointed by God Himself for the restoration of their ancient freedom, had arrived. The holy Demetrius, it was said, had abandoned his desolate church at Salonica and come to the birthplace of Šišman to succour his faithful Bulgarians. Nobles and peasants flew to arms. All that was wanted was a leader, and John Asên was at once recognised as the man. He was at once crowned " Czar of the Bulgarians and Greeks," and a new archbishop was appointed, who did not derive his title from Constantinople. After the lapse of one hundred and sixty-eight years Bulgaria was once again an independent state.

IV.

THE SECOND BULGARIAN EMPIRE.

(1186–1398.)

THE Bulgarian Empire was not re-established without a struggle. The Greeks lost no time in sending an army against the insurgents, and the temporary success which they gained led them to believe that the movement was no more serious than those of Deljan and Bodin. But the assistance of the great Servian Prince Nemanja, the Wallachs and the warlike Kumani, and still more the dissensions of his enemies enabled John Asên to hold his own. The Byzantine system was rotten to the core. Commanders, instead of attacking the foe, intrigued for the crown; the Byzantine armies, largely composed of mercenaries and aliens, were devoid of patriotism when their pay was in arrear; the masses had lost their faith in the Church ; the Church had lost touch with the world. Upon the throne of the Cæsars sat a luxurious and indolent monarch, who proved himself such a contemptible opponent that the Bulgarians sarcastically wished him a long life and reign. Asên scornfully told his countrymen that all the Greeks were of the same character as their effeminate ruler. " Behold my lance," he cried, " and the long streamers that float in the wind. They differ only in colour ; they are formed of the same silk and fashioned by the same workman; nor has the stripe, that is stained in purple, any superior price or value above its fellows." Bulgaria, from the Danube to the Balkans, was soon freed from the Greeks, and a guerilla warfare began in Thrace. At this style of combat the Bulgarians greatly excelled. When the Greeks advanced, they retired ; when the Greeks retired, they advanced. At one moment, the capture of Asên's wife in an ambush placed them at a disadvantage, but they more than made up for this by an overwhelming defeat of the Byzantine army in a narrow defile, where, heedless of his predecessor's experiences, the Emperor Isaac had foolishly ventured. The Bulgarians, in the language of a Greek historian who took part in these campaigns, "ran like stags or goats" upon the steep crags, whence they hurled huge blocks of rock and fired showers of arrows upon their helpless foes. Isaac's army was annihilated, and the Emperor with difficulty escaped alive. The Bulgarians now grew bolder. They abandoned their guerilla warfare, and laid siege to fortified towns. Varna, Nisch, and Sofia fell before them, and Asên rescued and carried off from the present to the old Bulgarian capital the relics of St. John of Ryl, the patron saint of his country. We find him even promising to assist the Emperor Frederick Barbarossa, who was then engaged upon the third crusade, provided that he would confer the diadem of the Greek Empire upon the Bulgarian Czars, and recognise their present title. But nothing came of this daring proposition. Alexius III., the feeble successor of Isaac on the Byzantine throne, made overtures of peace to Asên, who indignantly refused them, and the latter might have rivalled the exploits of Simeon, and appeared before the gates of the Imperial capital, had he not fallen a victim, in the midst of his career of conquest, to the sword of an assassin. Among his trusty comrades was a noble Bulgarian named Ivanko, a man of giant stature and fierce passions. The Czar suspected him of an intrigue with the Czarina's sister, and summoned him to his presence to explain his conduct. Ivanko came with his sword concealed beneath his clothes, and, when Asên, mad with fury, rose to smite him, he drew the weapon and plunged it into his sovereign's heart. Thus perished in 1196, after barely ten years of power, the energetic founder of the Second Bulgarian Empire. The name of Asên is still honoured by the people; distinguished men love to call their sons after him, and, though much of his career is obscure and his work has perished, the memory of his race is cherished in Bulgaria.

Ivanko, although he had slain the Czar, was unable to seize the diadem. Asên's second brother, Peter, who had already governed a part of the country, at once made himself master of Trnovo, and associated his younger brother, Kalojan or Johannitz, with him in the throne. But Peter's mild and peaceful disposition displeased the warlike Bulgarians. Like his eldest brother, he, too, fell by the hand of an assassin, and in 1197 Kalojan reigned alone. From his earliest days he had imbibed an intense hatred of the Greeks. Sent as a hostage to Constantinople during the war, he had learned to despise the effeminate Byzantines, who in their turn nicknamed him *Skylojoannes*, or "Dog-John." Cruel and ferocious in character, he resembled his eldest brother Asên, and his victories completed what Asên had begun. Connected by ties alike of policy and of blood with the Kumani—for his wife was one of that savage race—he speedily became such a terror to the Greeks that they made peace with him, and formally gave up the territory which he had captured. At the close of the twelfth century, the newly-established Second Empire of Bulgaria accordingly included a wide extent of country. Belgrade, Nisch, and all the present kingdoms of Servia east of the Morava were Bulgarian, and the Czar's dominions stretched from the mouth of the Danube to the Struma and the Vardar. In Macedonia, too, a Bulgarian noble, named Strêz, established himself as an independent prince upon a towering rock, where he held his own "like a spider or a scorpion," for many years against all comers.

Kalojan had now the substance of Imperial power; but, like other Bulgarian rulers, he wanted recognition of his title. Following the example of the old Czars, who turned to Rome when baffled at Constantinople, he sent repeated embassies to the Pope, which were, however, intercepted by his enemies on the way. At last there arrived at Trnovo in 1199 a Greek priest as an emissary from Innocent III. with a Papal letter in his hand. The Pope made flattering allusion to the reputed origin of the Bulgarian monarch from a Roman stock, and called upon him to show his devotion to the Holy See by deeds as well as words. Kalojan acknowledged the compliment and replied in a grandiloquent Latin epistle, in which he described himself as "Emperor of the Bulgarians and Wallachs." He begged the Pope to receive him into the Catholic faith, and besought an Imperial crown at his hands. But he soon found that Innocent wanted something more than empty phrases. Political considerations made it imperative to obtain Papal recognition with-

COIN OF ASÊN.

out further delay. Accordingly, he signed a Golden Bull, in which he acknowledged the supremacy of the Papacy for himself and his heirs for ever. The Pope then despatched a Cardinal to Trnovo with a royal, not an Imperial, crown, for in Papal documents of the period we always find the title of king, not that of emperor, bestowed upon the Bulgarian monarch. On the 8th of November, 1204, Kalojan was crowned by the Cardinal with great ceremony, and received at his hands a sceptre and a banner with the picture of St. Peter emblazoned upon it. Permission was also accorded him to issue coins bearing his own image and superscription. On the previous day the Papal envoy had consecrated a Bulgarian primate, two metropolitans and four bishops. Kalojan still continued to style himself Czar and the primate called himself Patriarch. He had, in fact, obtained the best of the bargain. Orthodox writers have censured him severely for his "alliance" with Rome, and have stigmatised him as an apostate from the faith of his fathers. But his object, like that of Boris I., in accepting Christianity was political; and the union with Rome had little or no effect upon the ritual or dogma of the Bulgarian Church.

The celebrated phrase, in which Kalojan had dubbed himself " Emperor of the Bulgarians and Wallachs," has led some writers to suppose that he was lord of a part of Roumania as well as of Bulgaria. It is not, however, necessary to infer from his words that he ruled over a "Wallacho-Bulgarian Empire." The Wallachs, whose emperor he claimed to be, were to be found scattered over Bulgaria, while in Wallachia proper the Kumani were then settled. Nor is there any evidence for the assertion that Kalojan and his brothers were of Roumanian or Wallachian descent. The Papal compliment is the only authority for the statement, and the title of " Emperor of the Bulgarians and Wallachs " never once occurs in Slavonic documents.

Kalojan had been frightened into seeking the patronage of the Pope by an event which had much influence upon the history of the Balkan Peninsula— the capture of Constantinople by the Crusaders under the blind Doge Dandolo and the election of Count Baldwin of Flanders to the Imperial throne. Kalojan, like Asên, had sought an alliance and a crown from the Franks and offered to assist them with an army in their crusade. But Baldwin contemptuously told him that he regarded the Bulgarian ruler as a slave, whose possessions were legally part of the Byzantine Empire. The haughty Frank lived to repent his taunt. The Greeks, in their hatred of their new masters, turned to Kalojan for aid. A great battle took place near Adrianople on the 15th of April, 1205, between the Czar, assisted by his Greek allies, and a savage contingent of Kumani on the one side, and the Franks on the other. Kalojan gained an overwhelming victory, and Baldwin fell into his hands. The fate of the Frank Emperor is one of those historical mysteries which research has failed to solve. It is known that he was imprisoned, and a ruined castle on the ramparts of Trnovo retains the name of "Baldwin's Tower" to this day. According to one version, Kalojan is said to have treated his prisoner with kindness, though he refused to release him even at the request of the Pope. According to another, he cut off his hands and feet and then had him thrown into a ditch to die; while a third account ascribes his end to the injured feelings of Kalojan's Kumanian wife, who had in vain endeavoured to attract the comely Frank. Twenty years later, a false Baldwin appeared in a forest of Flanders; but, though he found a large following, there can be no doubt that the real Emperor had long ere that perished. Kalojan himself met with a violent death. The overthrow of Baldwin had dissolved the alliance of the Greeks and Bulgarians, and the Czar slaughtered the hereditary enemies of his country wherever he found them, boasting that, as Basil had been called the " Bulgar-slayer," he would be remembered as the " slayer of the Greeks." For a time he carried all before him. Boniface, Marquis of Montferrat, who had been made king of Macedonia, fell in a Bulgarian ambuscade, and his head was brought to his barbarous conqueror. But Kalojan's cruel spouse was his worst foe. At her suggestion, one of his Kumanian generals stabbed him with a lance as he slept in his tent before Salonica. The Czar died of the wound, but not before he had accused his murderer of the crime. The assassin declared that it was not himself but his double who had appeared to the victim in the night. The legend soon spread that it was none other than St. Demetrius, the patron-saint of Salonica, who had dealt the blow.

Upon the death of Kalojan in 1207 his throne was seized by his nephew Boril, while the rightful heir, John Asên, son of the founder of the Second Empire, was forced to flee to Russia. Boril has been described by his contemporary, King Stephen of Servia, as a man " whose soul found a sweet pleasure in shedding the blood of his countrymen," and all that we know of his career bears out the statement of the royal biographer. Either from natural ferocity or theological zeal, he persecuted the Bogomiles, although they had always been on the side of Bulgarian freedom. No previous Czar had established a tribunal of priests and nobles for the trial of heretics; yet it is by this synod and the marriage of his daughter with the Frank Emperor Henry, that his name is chiefly remembered. Together with this new ally he undertook a fruitless campaign against the growing power of Servia, but neither at home nor abroad was his leadership successful. Powerful nobles began to declare themselves independent, and the restored Bulgarian Empire might have crumbled to pieces had not young John Asên driven him from the throne. With the accession of that monarch in 1218 the glories of Bulgaria were revived. Just as the first Bulgarian Empire reached its zenith under Simeon, so the second culminated under John Asên II.

Of all the Bulgarian Czars John Asên II. is the pleasantest figure. A great ruler in the best sense of the word, he has left behind him a name undefiled by the barbarities of which so many of his most powerful predecessors were guilty. A contemporary wrote of him that he had "neither drawn his sword against his own countrymen, nor disgraced himself by the murder of Greeks. So not only the Bulgarians, but Greeks and other nations loved him." He seldom engaged in war, and the generation during which he sat on the throne witnessed a great development of trade, the independence of the Church, and the erection of fine and costly buildings. Under him Bulgaria, as the first state of the Balkan Peninsula, was one of the great Powers of Europe, and he nearly accomplished the dream of his race, and united the crown of the Cæsars to that of the Czars.

His Empire reached the Black Sea, the Ægean, and the Adriatic. Bulgaria proper, a part of Servia, including Belgrade, all Macedonia, all Albania as far as Durazzo, obeyed his commands. He routed and captured Theodore, the despot of Epirus, and reduced

Constantinople to such extremities that the young Emperor Baldwin II. went as far as England in quest of help. There was even talk of appointing him Regent of the Byzantine Empire, which needed a firmer hand than that of its Latin sovereign. John Asên was willing to accept the task, and a marriage was arranged between Baldwin and his daughter. But the jealousy which then, as in our own time, Bulgaria has inspired among other nationalities, prevented the realisation of the project. His efforts to

THE BULGARIAN ARMS.

secure the support of the Pope for his candidature were equally fruitless. But we will let Asên speak for himself. An inscription on a pillar in the church of the Forty Martyrs at Trnovo, gives, in his own words, the brief chronicle of his conquests. "In the year 1230, I, John Asên, Czar and Autocrat of the Bulgarians, obedient to God in Christ, son of the old Asên, have built this most worthy church from its foundations, and completely decked it with paintings in honour of the Forty holy Martyrs, by whose help, in the 12th year of my reign, when the Church had just been painted, I set out to Romania to the war and smote the Greek army and took captive the Czar Theodore Komnenus with all his nobles. And all lands have I conquered from Adrianople to Durazzo, the Greek, the Albanian, and the Servian land. Only the towns round Constantinople and that city itself did the Franks hold ; but these too bowed themselves beneath the hand of my sovereignty, for they had no other Czar but me, and prolonged their days according to my will, as God had so ordained. For without him no word or work is accomplished. To him be honour for ever. Amen."

His comparatively peaceful reign was very beneficial to the trade of his country. Under the earlier Czars we have heard of commercial treaties between Bulgaria and other states, but it was reserved for Asên II. to secure for his subjects by his wise concessions constant communications with the merchants of Ragusa, whose city was the western outlet for the whole inland trade of the Peninsula. An ancient charter of Asên allowed them free access to all his dominions as "the truest and dearest guests of his Majesty." When, in the reign of his son Michael, the Ragusans gave Bulgaria what we should now call the "most-favoured-nation clause" in their treaties, they mentioned "the genuine friendship of the famous Czar John Asên," and granted the Bulgarians free entry to their city "by gate, bridge, or ford," and permission to buy or sell everything within ; grain alone it was forbidden them to export without a special order. Both Venice and Genoa had their Consuls in Bulgaria, and the legal rights of foreign traders were carefully defined.

Trnovo, his capital, rivalled and even surpassed the splendours of Prêslav under the earlier Empire. Even to-day, after all the changes of centuries, the ancient residence of the Asenide dynasty cannot fail to attract the tourist, alike by its quaint position and its historic ruins. But the modern Trnovo is but a shadow of what it was in the golden age of the second Asên. The "queen of cities, the famous burgh," as patriotic writers loved to call it, seemed to Asên's contemporaries scarcely inferior to Constantinople. No other town in Bulgaria is so intimately associated with the most stirring events of the national history. "Built by the hands of giants"—so ran the legend of its foundation—it had witnessed the rise of Šišman and his doughty line. Within its walls the first Asên had received the crown from the hands of the people; and in its modest inn first saw the light the ablest of modern Bulgarian statesmen, the ill-starred Stambuloff. Here were the Palace of the Czars and the residence of the head of the Bulgarian Church; here, too, was the great cathedral, long since gone. But the Church of the Forty Martyrs still remains to tell of Asên's power and compensate us for the loss of the ancient coronation church of the Bulgarian Czars. Within its vaults was their last resting-place, on its walls are still visible many an inscription of their epoch. The glory has departed from Trnovo; a new and modern capital has taken the place which it once occupied in the history of Bulgaria. But in the thirteenth and fourteenth centuries the "citadel of thorns," from which Trnovo took its name, looked down upon all that was splendid and all that was noblest in the land.

Asên's peaceful activity extended itself over the Bulgarian hierarchy. He was not only a builder of churches, but he refounded the National Church. Kalojan's "union" with Rome had only lasted as long as he had something to gain from the Pope or something to fear from the Franks. Asên threw off even the pretence of devotion to the Papacy; the head of the Catholic Church hurled at him the terrors of excommunication, and, when that failed, hounded on the King of Hungary against him. But this crusade proved a failure, and the threat of excommunication fell flat. Asên declared the Church of Trnovo independent, alike of Rome and Constantinople, and in the presence of Greek and Bulgarian bishops the Primate of Bulgaria was solemnly raised to the dignity of Patriarch. But Asên had broad sympathies. One of the chief complaints made against him by the Pope was his protection of the Bogomiles; but lovers of toleration will reckon as not the least of his glories the generous permission, which he extended to Catholics, Orthodox Greeks, and "heretics" alike, to worship in their own way without hindrance from him. No Czar was more beneficent towards the monks. The great monastery of Ryl was richly endowed, and the "holy mountain" of Athos enriched by his donations. No wonder that a Bulgarian priest wrote of him that "he had exalted the Empire of the Czars to the glory of God above all his forbears; for he built monasteries and adorned them with gold and pearls and stones of great price; every grade of the hierarchy did he honour, bishops, priests, and deacons alike, and at last restored the Bulgarian Patriarch." When he died in 1241, the two boys, who followed him in rapid succession on the throne, had neither the experience nor the strength to avert the decline of the state. The history of the Balkan Peninsula proves that the welfare of a Slav nation is almost invariably bound up with one man, and when he falls the nation falls with him.

Within three months half of Asên's empire was gone. His eldest son, Kaliman I., a boy of nine, was helpless, and his half-brother, Michael Asên, struggled valiantly but in vain to recover the lost provinces. The Venetians attacked him on the Black Sea, and the whole of his father's Thracian and Macedonian possessions remained in the enemy's hands. Kaliman II., his cousin, who rose upon his murdered body to the throne, died a violent death, and, in default of a direct lineal descendant of Asên, the nobles and clergy met at Trnovo and elected Constantine, a Serb, as their Czar. The new sovereign endeavoured to strengthen his position by taking the honoured name of Asên and marrying the granddaughter of John II., but his reign was spent in barren wars with the King of Hungary and the restored Greek Empire. The former threatened the Bulgarian capital, and boastfully styled himself " King of Bulgaria "—an incident which is interesting as the first appearance of the Hungarian monarchy as a claimant of the Balkan lands. The alliance of Constantine Asên with the King of Naples against the Greek Emperor is a proof of the importance attached to Bulgaria in Italy at that date, and it is curious to find the Neapolitan archives full of Bulgarian names, and a part of that city called after these strange allies. But the greatest mistake of Constantine's reign was his second marriage with a Greek princess. We have seen before that these unions were usually disastrous for Bulgaria. Indeed, as a rule, the wives of the Bulgarian Czars have left an evil record behind them. But Constantine's Greek consort was the worst of them all. She made her husband's severe illness an excuse for seizing supreme power for herself in the name of her boy Michael. By intrigues, more worthy of the Byzantine than the rough Bulgarian Court, she "removed," under the most solemn protestations of affection, all the most dangerous of the nobles. Meanwhile the empire lay open to the attacks of the Tartars, who, after overrunning Roumania, had begun to cross the Danube. In this extremity, with a disabled Czar and a designing woman on the throne, Bulgaria threw itself into the arms of a restless adventurer, named Ivajlo, who had abandoned the profession of a shepherd for the more congenial one of a brigand. Ivajlo's career reads like a romance. He told the people how the holy saints had appeared to him in a dream and bade him prepare himself for the great destiny which lay before him. Numbers flocked to his standard; his success over the Tartars brought the whole country to his side; Constantine lost his life and his throne, and the Greek Emperor himself began to fear that another Simeon or Samuel had arisen. Constantine's crafty widow became the wife of the conqueror; but a new pretender of the stock of old Asên, supported by Byzantine troops, arrived with an army at Trnovo. The inhabitants, believing that Ivajlo had died in the act of repelling a fresh Tartar invasion, acknowledged their assailant as John Asên III., thankful to be rid of the cunning Greek woman who had brought so much harm upon them. When the holy office was chanted in the Bulgarian churches to the memory of the departed consorts of the Czars, her name was alone omitted from the list.

The glory of Bulgaria had fallen low. A generation had barely elapsed since the death of the second Asên, yet his empire had been shorn of all his conquests; a nominee of the Greek Emperor sat upon the throne of the Czars; a Tartar chief was commander of the Bulgarian armies; dissension and the lack of authority were bringing the country to destruction. At this moment Ivajlo suddenly reappeared, as if from the dead. The magic of his name made the Greekling tremble in his palace at Trnovo, and the Greek armies sent to assist him were easily defeated. To rid Bulgaria of her feeble ruler was easy, but Ivajlo found that there was another rival in the field. This man, the founder of the fourth Bulgarian dynasty, sprang from an old Kumanian family called Terterij, which was allied with the noblest of the land. His aristocratic connections and personal bravery led the Bulgarians to prefer him to the humble shepherd, who had led their armies against the Tartars, and in 1280 George Terterij I. was proclaimed Czar. His peasant foe fled to the court of Nogaj, Chan of the Golden Horde of Tartars, at that time the terror of the Balkan Peninsula, who cut his throat in a drunken fit. But several years later a false Ivajlo could still find a following among the Bulgarian hinds.

Terterij I. was unable to stem the tide of Tartar invasion either by force or diplomacy. The dreaded Nogaj, accustomed to play the part of king-maker, married his son Čoki to the daughter of the Czar, and then deposed him, setting up a Bulgarian noble as a puppet in his place. For the first time the proud Bulgarian Empire had become a mere Tartar fief. But the Tartars soon sought to be masters in name as well as in fact. Čoki marched into Bulgaria and claimed the crown, but the country found a liberator in Svętslav, son of Terterij, who made an end of the Tartar chief and was hailed by a thankful people as their Czar. For a time the days of the second Asên seemed to have returned. Svętslav put down all his rivals, won back territory from the Greeks, and gave his subjects for many years the unwonted blessings of peace. But with his son and successor, Terterij II., his race became extinct, and, in order to prevent the Empire from falling to pieces, the nobles had to select a new dynasty, the fifth and last of old Bulgarian history. For more than a generation Vidin and the country near it had been formed into an independent principality under the House of Šišman—a family distinct from the old Šišman clan of Trnovo, but connected with the Kumanian aristocracy. It was upon his son Michael that the choice of the Bulgarians now fell, and in 1323 he became their Czar.

At first his policy was a complete success. By playing off one Byzantine faction against another, he nearly realised the dream of Simeon and Asên by adding Constantinople to his dominions. But by a complete turn of fortune's wheel, the same monarch, who was within an ace of capturing the capital, fell, and involved his country in his fall, before the growing might of Servia.

It had long been evident that sooner or later the Serbs and Bulgarians would fight for the hegemony of the Balkans, and the domestic differences, which sprang up between the two courts owing to Michael's shameful treatment of his Serb consort, were the occasion rather than the cause of the collision. Michael formed a league of Greeks, Roumanians, and Bulgarians against the Serb King Stephen Uroš III., and boasted that he would set up his throne in his rival's land. But the Serbs fell upon his army unawares at Velbužd, the present Köstendil, on June 28, 1330, a day still remembered with sorrow by patriotic Bulgarians; Michael's forces were routed, and the Czar fell from his horse and was slain on the spot. When next morning the nobles were shown by the victor the corpse of their sovereign, they burst into tears. And well they might; for the might of the Bulgarian Empire had fallen for ever. The Serb monarch abstained, indeed, from annexing the country; but Dušan, his successor, who had shared the victory with him, reduced the Bulgarian government to complete dependence. For sixty years more, Bulgaria continued to retain her Czars of Šišman's stock, but from the battle of Velbužd to the death of Dušan in 1356 they were content to follow the policy of Servia, with whose ruler they were closely connected by ties of marriage. Dušan even added the title of "Czar of the Bulgarians" to his other attributes, and when the war broke out between

Servia and Bulgaria in 1885, the people in the streets of Belgrade invoked his name.

During his reign of a quarter of a century, Bulgaria was secure from the Greeks in the south and the Hungarians in the north. The close alliance of the two adjoining Balkan states under two able rulers formed an impenetrable barrier to foreign invasion, which might teach a lesson to the Balkan statesmen of to-day. John Alexander, Dušan's brother-in-law, who was contemporary with him on the Bulgarian throne, was a man of considerable energy and an assiduous patron of literature. He was the last of the old Bulgarian monarchs, who extended the frontiers of his country at the expense of the Byzantine Empire; but his conquests were soon to be taken away by a far more formidable foe. It is now for the first time that we hear of the Turks in Bulgaria. About the middle of the fourteenth century they began to harry the Bulgarian territory south of the Balkans. The natives fully recognised the gravity of this new danger. As the Czar rode through the streets of his capital, the people cried aloud that he should make a league with the Greeks against the common foe. But the foreign policy of Bulgaria was then wholly guided by that of Servia, and it did not suit the latter that her neighbour should enter into close relations with the Greek Empire. The story goes that the Emperor sent a message to both the Servian and Bulgarian rulers, telling them that they would rue the day on which they had refused to help him. Dušan and John Alexander are said to have scornfully replied that when the Turks came near them, they would know how to defend themselves. The Greek Emperor's words came true; and nothing assisted the advance of the Ottoman power in Europe so much as the jealousies of the Balkan peoples. To the same cause it owes in no small measure its maintenance to this day. The first serious blow which the Turks dealt at the Bulgarian Empire was the capture of Eski Zagora and Philippopolis in 1362. From that moment dates the establishment of a Turkish governor in Roumelia and the formation of the celebrated Turkish corps of *vojnik* or "warriors," composed of Bulgarian Christians, who were exempt from taxes in return for military service to their Ottoman masters. The national legends have preserved the memory of princes and nobles who "fought like heroes against the paynim, and shed their blood for the true faith of Christ." Yet at this moment of all others, we find them raising Turkish mercenaries for a final attack on the Greek Empire! John Šišman III., the last of the long line of Bulgarian Czars, who came to the throne in 1365, actually seized the Greek Emperor, John Paleologus, when he came to implore his aid against the Turks, and only released him at the armed intervention of the Count of Savoy.

Theological quarrels yet further weakened the tottering Bulgarian realm. To the Bogomiles, whose schism had so long divided the people against itself, were now added other fanatical sects, whose votaries ran about the streets with no other clothing than a hollow gourd, or revived the last lingering traces of pagan worship. Councils were held in vain, the punishments of the Church were useless. The second marriage of the Czar John Alexander with a lovely Jewish maiden was a fresh source of discord. The sons of the first and second union divided their father's empire between them; Šišman III. reigned at Trnovo, Sracimir at Vidin, while a third independent prince, Dobrotić, established himself in the low-lying region of the Drobrudža, which still bears his name. Thus contemporary writers speak of "three Bulgarias." The one pleasant feature of this gloomy era was the revival of learning. At the instigation of John Alexander, Greek chronicles and works of theology were translated into the Slavonic tongue. No other period is so rich in manuscripts, some of them exquisitely illuminated. Theodosius of Trnovo and still more his pupil, the Patriarch Euthemius enriched the national literature with their theological and biographical works. But their successors were mere rhetoricians, whose bombastic writings were the last expiring efforts of the dying empire.

The Turks advanced apace when the death of Dušan had removed the last Balkan ruler who had the power to resist them. The Bulgarian Czar Šišman III. became their vassal in 1366, and pledged himself to aid them. Suspicious of his sincerity, the conquerors demanded his sister as a hostage. An old chronicler tells of "the great lady who was given to the mighty Sultan Murad for the Bulgarian people, and, although his wife, kept the Christian faith and saved her country." The "fair Bulgarian," so the story goes, was offered a mosque full of silver candelabra as the reward of apostasy; but she replied with pride, "Dear is my religion to me, a Turkish woman will I never be." A few years later Sofia was captured by a trick, and Šišman forced to fall down on his knees with his wife and family and implore the Sultan's mercy. For a brief space he was allowed, on payment of a tribute, to keep his throne. But, when the Serb kingdom fell on the plain of Kossovo, Bulgaria was doomed. The ancient capital of the Czars surrendered after a three months' siege in 1393. Palaces and churches perished in the flames, the cathedral became a mosque, the relics of the saints were destroyed. Amid the general convulsion one noble figure stands out in solemn grandeur. The learned Patriarch Euthemius went fearlessly forth from the city to soften the fury of the conqueror. His persuasions prevailed with the Sultan's son, who commanded the besieging force. But the governor, who was appointed on his departure, resolved by one sanguinary deed to crush the Bulgarian chivalry for ever. He summoned the nobles and principal citizens together in one of the few remaining churches under pretext of a debate, and then ordered his soldiers to cut them down. Euthemius, stripped of his holy garb, was ordered to be beheaded on the walls in the sight of his flock. But a miracle from heaven arrested, so says his biographer, the headsman's hand, and the victim was set free. At the command of the Sultan, the survivors of this horrible carnage were driven forth as exiles from their native land, and in the heart of Asia Minor found a grave. Turkish colonists occupied their places, and the famous hill of the Czars received a Turkish name.

Šišman had not been at Trnovo when the city was besieged; but he did not long survive its capture. His end is obscured in uncertainty; most authorities state that he died in prison or on the scaffold. But the patriotic fancy of the national bards has depicted the last of the Czars as dying in battle for his country. Hard by the sources of the Marica, according to this legend, was he wounded seven times, where seven springs of water may still be seen. So fierce was the fight, that the river ran red with blood, and the plain is called the "field of bones" to this day. The ruins of a neighbouring castle preserve the name of Šišman, and even the Turks respected his grave. His half-brother Sracimir still remained in Vidin, but in 1398 was expelled by the Sultan; the attempt of King Sigismund of Hungary and Mirtschea of Wallachia to rescue Bulgaria from its conquerors collapsed on the battlefield of Nicopolis; the whole land owned the supremacy of the Turk.

Thus fell, after the lapse of two centuries, the Second Bulgarian Empire. The causes of its fall are not difficult to perceive. The old Bulgarian system was concentrated in an aristocracy which, except under the iron hand of a strong Czar, was rarely united. The masses, degraded to the level of serfs and chained to the soil, had no common interests with their lords. The clergy, instead of striving to raise and influence the people, wasted their energies in hairsplitting or passed their lives in monkish seclusion. Their intolerance drove the Bogomiles in Bulgaria as in Bosnia, into the arms of the Turks, who seemed to the persecuted heretics more generous than their Christian oppressors. Morally, Bulgaria was slowly but surely undermined by its intercourse with the Byzantine Empire. The nobles and the priesthood were most affected by this sinister influence, and it is noticeable that in the old as in the new Bulgaria the ablest men have usually sprung from the virgin soil of the peasantry. Now and again a great ruler, a Simeon, a Samuel, or an Asên II., raised the Bulgarian state to a commanding position. But the power of these princes died with them, and their empire soon dwindled away.

The social condition of the people under the rule of the Czars was much the same as in other parts of Europe during the Middle Ages. When the Czar made a progress through his land, nobles and monks, townsmen and peasants had to accompany him and provide food and lodging for him and his own retinue at their own expense. This *priselica*, as it was called, became a grievous burden, and it was not the only one which the peasantry were forced to bear. The Czar's subjects were obliged to work on his estates, look after his vineyards, and reap his crops. Only the dependents of the monasteries were exempt from this forced labour. In the towns the burghers had to build the castle and guard the gaol; in the country the peasant was a serf, who was permitted to hold land and money of his own, but could not quit his property if he would. It was hoped that in this way the depopulation, caused by the constant wars, might be checked. Then, as now, agriculture was the favourite pursuit of the Bulgarian race. Horse breeding was a great source of wealth, and sheep and pigs were abundant. But trade, as we have seen, expanded at a very early date all over the country, and caravans laden with Italian wares might be seen slowly wending their way through the moun-

STATUE OF PAN AT VARNA.

tain passes or along the great highway from Sofia to Philippopolis. The customs dues were no insignificant part of the revenue, and the number of gold, silver, and copper coins, which date from this period, shows that there must have been a large demand for a medium of exchange. Under the old Czars, however, the taxes were paid in kind, until the Greeks introduced the system of cash payment.

War was, of course, the favourite pursuit of the Bulgarian monarchs, although they sometimes contented themselves for long periods with the mimic warfare of the chase. The love of fighting, now much less conspicuous in Bulgaria, was before the long Turkish domination, the chief characteristic of the people. We find Bulgarian mercenaries in many lands during this period, but they were of little use in sieges; in guerilla warfare among mountains they were pre-eminent. Their love of booty became proverbial, but they spared the lives of their Christian prisoners. Yet in time of peace there was profound respect for those ancient customs, which took the place of any regular code of law. The ancient Slavonic practice of making the whole village responsible for the offences of any of its inhabitants, in case the culprit had escaped punishment, existed in Bulgaria. The "Golden Bulls" of the Czars were very elaborate documents, and the ordinances of the Church are often mentioned. Traces of representative institutions are to be seen in the assemblies of the two classes of nobles or *boljars*, great and small, and the various grades of clergy. These gatherings were held for two purposes, the election of a Czar, when there was no lineal descendant of the last ruler, and the punishment of heretics. Three of the Czars owed their throne to this method of election. The masses had no voice in the proceedings, for old

Bulgaria, unlike the "Peasant state" of to-day, was essentially aristocratic. All the court offices, of which there were many, were filled by the nobles, and it was from their ranks that the Czar's Council of State was chosen. In fact, the monarch himself was often merely *primus inter pares*. Gorgeous court ceremonies and princely hospitality lent splendour to the Bulgarian Empire, but the lot of the people, even in the golden age of the nation, cannot have been ideal.

V.

BULGARIA UNDER THE TURKS.

(1398–1878.)

THE Turkish supremacy in Bulgaria, which lasted from the end of the fourteenth century down to our own time, is the gloomiest epoch in the national annals. One after the other every Christian state in the Balkan Peninsula, with the sole exception of Montenegro, fell beneath the power of the Ottoman invaders, whose armies reached the gates of Vienna. Freedom vanished, literature languished, and even the memories of Bulgaria's glorious past under Czars of her own were obliterated as far as possible by her Turkish masters. The very character of her once warlike sons changed under the steady influence of an alien domination. Without intellectual or practical leaders, the Bulgarian people bowed down for nearly five centuries beneath the yoke of the Sultans. At last there came a time when Western Europe had almost forgotten the existence of a nation which had once taken a prominent rank among the great Powers.

The conquerors lost no time in organising the

government of the country after their own fashion. The whole of the Balkan Peninsula, with the exception of Bosnia, was called Rumili, a corruption of the Byzantine form Romania, and placed under the authority of an official known as a *Beglerbeg*. Bulgaria was included in his province, and he fixed his residence at Sofia, which seemed marked out by its central position as the capital of the Peninsula. Rumili was further subdivided into twenty-six *sandjaks*, or districts, several of which were included in Bulgaria. The officials were not always Turks, for the apostasy of the noble Bulgarian families was usually rewarded with place and power. At the close of the sixteenth century we find a Bulgarian occupying the proud position of Grand Vizier, and Bulgarian Mussulmans exist to-day, under the name of *Pomaks*, in several parts of the country, especially in the north-east corner, as well as in Macedonia. The Turkish practice of carrying off the flower of the Bulgarian youth every five years to serve in the corps of Janissaries was not only a terrible grievance to the people, but introduced a dangerous Slav element into the Turkish army. The position of the Christians in the conquered provinces was indeed miserable, especially after the Turkish rule had begun to decline. During the best days of the Ottoman Empire large sums of money were spent on roads, trade flourished, the rights of citizens were respected, and the churches of the Christian communities remained unviolated. But the decay of the Turkish power affected the whole Empire. The people of Ragusa, the "South Slavonic Athens," as it was called, had always been specially favoured by the rulers of Bulgaria, and the Turks continued their privileges. But gradually commerce fell off, foreign trades were hampered by absurd regulations; the highways were neglected, the *khans* and caravanserais allowed to fall into ruins. The Christian *rayahs* were forbidden to build churches or possess bells; their dress was to be of one cut, their daughters were seized to grace the harems of their masters. Taxes became enormous, tax-collectors extortionate. Every Christian above the age of fourteen had to pay a poll-tax or *haratch* of a ducat, a tax for every head of cattle and the tithe of the products of the field. In addition to this, he was forced to labour, as in the old days, on the land of his feudal lord, who was often one of his own countrymen converted to Islâm. These regular payments were augmented by the irregular extortions of corrupt officials, who, having gained their posts by bribes, had to recoup themselves for their outlay at the expense of their subjects. One fortunate class of Christians escaped all these annoyances. We have already alluded to the *vojnik*, warriors who placed their swords at the disposal of the Turks on condition of exemption from taxation and feudal burdens. Whole village communities, forming a privileged caste, were thus to be found side by side with the downtrodden Christians, who did not care to fight the battles of the Ottoman. The traveller could tell the *vojnik* by his parti-coloured garments, his martial gait, and his prosperous appearance. He received, it is true, no pay; but that was an advantage, for it could not fall into arrear, while his positive gains were very great. But his privileges gradually ceased, though the name survived down to the present century.

The Church had always been an important factor in the life of the Balkan states. But under the Turkish domination it ceased to be a national institution in Bulgaria. For while the country became politically a part of the Ottoman Empire, its church passed into the hands of the Greeks. As early as 1394 the see of Trnovo was subordinated to the Patriarch of Constantinople, and Greek bishops and Bibles entered Bulgaria, displacing the native priesthood and the vernacular scriptures. In Bulgaria, as in Roumania, the Phanariotes obtained a fatal influence; but while in the latter country they gained political power, in the former their sphere was ecclesiastical. The lowest as well as the highest offices in the Church were bought and sold, and the purchasers were often men of the lowest class. We even hear of barbers becoming bishops and coffee-sellers priests. No fewer than 140 patriarchs are mentioned in 390 years, and it is therefore clear that the Phanariotes, who had paid highly for their brief period of office, must have lost no time in recovering their expenses. "The art of extortion," says a Prussian diplomatist of the last century, "has been reduced by them to a system," so that between Greek ecclesiastics and Turkish governors the lot of the poor Bulgarian peasant was hard to bear. When the last independent Slavonic churches of Ipek and Ochrida were sacrificed to Phanariote zeal, the sole remaining obstacle to their scheme for making the Greek language and liturgy supreme throughout the Peninsula was removed. In the early days of Turkish rule books in the vernacular were still printed at Sofia. But the Phanariotes made short work of them. By their orders the old library of the patriarchs of Trnovo was committed to the flames. Ancient Bulgarian manuscripts, which had survived the ravages of war, were wantonly destroyed. No wonder that records of the Turkish period are scarce, for the Greek clergy ended what the Turks began. The Cyrillic character itself was forgotten, the language of the people proscribed. The Bulgarians learnt off their prayers in a tongue which they could not understand. Greek schools, the Greek alphabet, and Greek books were the dominant features of the Bulgarian's intellectual life at the dawn of the present century. A man considered it a disgrace to be called a Bulgarian. "No," he would reply, "I am a Greek." The spiritual tyranny of the Phanariotes was even worse than the political tyranny of the Turks. For the Turks were not bigots, the Phanariotes were.

Slowly a national movement against both these forms of oppression began. For long years the Bulgarians lay helpless and hopeless beneath the power of their twin masters. At the very outset, it is true, there were faint attempts to drive out the Turks. Thus the sons of the last two Czars of Vidin and Trnovo, Sracimir and Šišman, raised the standard of revolt in 1405, and the Hungarians, who had in the old days laid claim to the Bulgarian crown, twice endeavoured to conquer the country. But these efforts were futile, and the decisive defeat of the heroic John Hunyad and the death of the Hungarian King Vladislav on the fatal field of Varna in 1444 put an end to the aspirations of Bulgaria for more than a century. Once again, in 1595, we hear of an abortive rising instigated by a Ragusan agent. This man, who had lived many years among the people, strongly urged the Prince of Transylvania, at that time engaged in war with the Turks in Roumania, to call the Bulgarians to arms. He told the Prince that they were discontented owing to the increased extortions of the officials and the brutality of the troops. They were only waiting the arrival of Christian allies to rise as one man. The Prince was quite ready for the enterprise, and the Ragusan stirred up disturbances in Varna and other places. But the insurrection failed, and we read of no further organised revolts until the present century.

In the dearth of national leaders the patriotic movement fell into the hands of the brigand chiefs. These popular heroes of the Balkans appear in Servia under the name of *Haiduks*, in Bulgaria under that of *Haidutin*, and in Greece under that of *Klefts*. Like Robin Hood in our own ballads, they are represented as the protectors of the poor, and the weak, the friends of Christians, and the ruthless scourge of the Mohammedan oppressor. Thousands of legends and songs are connected with their exploits; their ranks were recruited from all those who had insults to avenge or nothing but their lives to lose. If a Bulgarian once joined them his only chance of safety was to stick loyally to his fellows, for he had put himself beyond the pale. The hand of every Turk was against him and his hand was against every Turk. The villagers, groaning beneath the exactions of their lords, welcomed the *Haidutin* as a deliverer. Women were sacred in the eyes of these chivalrous cut-throats, for they firmly believed that whoever touched a helpless damsel would die in a Turkish gaol. They even included the fair sex in their ranks. We hear of Bulgarian Amazons, who stormed Turkish caravans, sabre in hand, with the skill and courage of men. A hundred years ago one of the most desperate of these bands was commanded by a woman, who performed such prodigies of valour that she actually passed for a man. When caught no mercy was shown to them; after death their heads adorned the town-walls, their bodies being impaled alive before the gates. In winter the lack of cover on the Balkans drove them to seek an honest livelihood, and they would bury their arms ready for the next summer beneath the trees. To this day the bark of many an ancient oak bears the secret sign by which they marked the spot.

The *Haidutin* despised mere thieves as "poultry-stealers," and regarded himself as a patriot and a benefactor of his race. In the regard which they showed for their own countrymen they differed from the notorious *Krdžaligen*, who devasted Bulgaria between 1792 and 1804. The Turks were powerless against these desperadoes. The soldiers sent to subdue them as often as not sided with them, and at the end of every fresh campaign in the Peninsula numbers of discharged troopers flocked to the mountain camps. One of their chiefs, known as "the cunning leader," became quite a hero of romance. But most of them were bloodthirsty ruffians, who spared neither woman nor child, and made no distinction between Turk and Bulgarian. Their most celebrated patron, Osman Pasvanoglu, who established himself as Pasha of Vidin in defiance of the Porte, levied taxes and coined money on his own account. He had a large army at his disposal, which enabled him to laugh at the regular forces of the Sultan. Repeated sieges of Vidin proved a complete failure, and the Pasha meditated a descent on Constantinople in return. Upon the suppression of the *Krdžaligen*, the survivors augmented his following. But he died shortly afterwards, and they entered the service of the Government, quartering themselves on the villages and demanding " tooth money " or *Dyščhak* for the wear and tear of their teeth on the hard bread of the peasants. Terrible was the destruction which they had caused. A Frenchman, who travelled through Bulgaria at this period disguised as a Tartar, has left a grim description of the condition of the country. A stillness, as of the grave, reigned over the deserted fields, corpses and smouldering cottages marked the spot where the brigands had been, the peasants had either fled or had fallen a prey to the wild beasts and still wilder men who roamed the land.

The hopes of the Bulgarians had been temporarily raised by the Austrian victories over the Turks at the end of the seventeenth and beginning of the eighteenth century. But after the disastrous Peace of Belgrade in 1739 it was to Russia rather than Austria that they looked for aid. At Tilsit Napoleon actually drew up a scheme of partition, by which Bulgaria and the two Danubian Principalities were to be assigned to the Russians. The latter actually overran the country in 1810, and captured Plevna and other strong places. But Napoleon's march to Moscow forced them to retire. One advantage accrued to the natives from this Russo-Turkish war : the cession of Bessarabia to Russia at the Peace of Bucharest provided the victims of Turkish oppression with a place of refuge, where they were kindly treated by a paternal governor. But even there, as afterwards in their own country, they soon learnt that Russian protection might be as onerous as Turkish tyranny. But when the Russians marched through Bulgaria in 1829 they found a warmer welcome than before. Many brigands enlisted with them just as they had joined the Greeks during the Greek War of Independence, and a certain Mamarcov attempted to unfold the banner of Bulgarian freedom on the ruins of Trnovo. His countrymen were ready to respond to his appeal ; but the Russians arrested him and the peace of Adrianople put an end to the movement. A few years later he organised a conspiracy on his own account which was betrayed to the Turks, and he died in exile, meditating on the ingratitude of the Russian Government. It is remarkable that an Englishman, who was travelling through Bulgaria during this Russian occupation, had prophesied to the natives that England would sympathise with them in their struggle to be free and that an independent Bulgaria would be a wall between Russia and Turkey. The result of the Crimean War diminished their hopes of Russian aid, and they began to look to those Western

Powers, who had shown disgust at the "Bulgarian atrocities" of 1841, and had wrung from the Sultan the famous promise of civil and religious equality in 1856. Both Abdul Medjid and his predecessor Mahmoud II. were really anxious to improve the condition of their Bulgarian subjects; the former had taken the unusual step of personally visiting his Balkan lands; the latter established provincial councils, on which Christians sat. But the best and ablest of all Turkish governors was Midhat Pasha, whose four years' administration of the newly-created *vilayet*, or province of the Danube, which included Bulgaria and had its centre at Rustchuk, did more for the material improvement of the country than any number of paper reforms. In spite of the havoc caused by the migration of a horde of Tartars from the Crimea and nearly half a million Circassians from the Caucasus, Bulgaria became under Midhat a model to the rest of the Turkish Empire. If he had remained there longer, he might have made it what Bosnia is to-day.

Men of letters are apt to exaggerate the influence of literature upon politics; but there is no reason to doubt that the literary revival in Bulgaria was a very powerful factor in bringing about the national independence. It began with the publication of Paysij's "Bulgarian History" in 1762—a work with no pretensions to scientific accuracy, but which aroused the dormant patriotism of the people where a coldly critical and impartial narrative would have failed. Paysij's pupil, Sofranij, who has given us a graphic picture of his own times, laboured hard to interest the masses, who had been, by virtue of their ignorance, far less tainted than their superiors with cosmopolitan ideas, in the glorious past of their country. These isolated efforts were followed early in the present century by the Bulgarian colony at Bucharest, whose aim was the establishment of a national literature and system of education. An enthusiastic admirer of Bulgaria, a Russian named Venelin, whose devotion to learning under the greatest hardships is most affecting, gave expression to their ideas in his "Old and New Bulgarians" which indirectly led to the foundation of the first Bulgarian school in the principality. It was at Gabrovo in 1835 that this important event took place, and the founder, Apriloff, had been inspired by the perusal of Venelin's book. Keen as the Bulgarians have always shown themselves to be for instruction, they eagerly embraced the opportunity of learning the elements in their own language. Other schools quickly followed, and in the brief space of ten years fifty-three were founded. The Turks, governed at that time by a reforming Sultan, did not interfere, and the Greeks, though viewing this new policy with dislike, were not actively hostile. Yet it is to the influence of these institutions that we may trace the growth of national feeling and the desire for political and spiritual independence. The national schools of Bulgaria and Robert College, the American foundation at Constantinople, were the nurseries of many a Bulgarian patriot and not a few Bulgarian statesmen. For the first time the native writers extended their sphere beyond the dry bones of theological or scholastic controversy. Collections of popular songs were made; Karaveloff, the uncle of the well-known politician, wrote novels and plays, while another politician, Dragan Zankoff, issued a German and a Bulgarian grammar. To "teach school," in Bulgaria no less than the United States, was the most usual training of the men who afterwards rose to power.

To rid themselves of the Phanariote bishops and revive the National Church, became the chief aim of the patriots. A regular *Culturkampf* raged for nearly twenty years, in which the Turkish officials were far less adverse than the Greek clergy to the Bulgarian demands. An eminent Turkish statesman even went so far as to express the opinion that to separate the Greek and Bulgarian Christians was the true policy of the Porte. The newspapers and periodicals, the earliest of which dates from 1844 and was published at Smyrna, greatly encouraged the agitation. The Greeks exhausted every device to frustrate the aims of their fellow-Christians. When the Porte insisted at last upon the appointment of a Bulgarian as bishop, the Greek Patriarch nominated him *in partibus infidelium*. After a tedious struggle, a Bulgarian Exarchate was created by a firman of 1870. Two years later the first Exarch, to be resident at Constantinople, was elected by the Bulgarians and confirmed by the Sultan. The Greek Patriarch promptly excommunicated him and all his followers, but the power of the Phanariote clergy was broken for ever.

Such was the state of Bulgaria when the whole Eastern question was reopened by the outbreak of the insurrection in the Herzegovina in 1875. Thanks to the reforms of Midhat, the concessions of the Porte in ecclesiastical questions, and the stubborn character of the Bulgarian race, the country was in a superior condition to that of most parts of the Turkish Empire at the period just previous to its liberation. Indeed, the Russian officers, who visited Bulgaria during the war of 1877, thought that the "little brothers," whom they had come to free, were materially better off under the Turkish yoke than many of their own *moujiks* under the benevolent despotism of the Czar. An impartial eye-witness has declared that to exchange their lot for that of the Bulgarians "would have been no bad bargain for the Russian peasants." But the cruelty and stupidity of the Turkish soldiers destroyed at one fell blow any good that Midhat had done, and outraged Europe regarded the Bulgarians as Christian martyrs.

The peasants of the Balkan slopes, less political in their tastes than the Greeks or Serbs, and less warlike than the Roumanians or Montenegrins, had been little affected by the struggles of their neighbours for freedom. * A central revolutionary committee had existed for some years at Bucharest with sub-committees in Bulgaria. But the execution of Vassili Levsky, the most active of these revolutionists in 1873, had damped the ardour of the exiles. "Apostles," as they were called, of whom Stambuloff was the most energetic, continued to make futile efforts to raise their countrymen against the Turks, without, however, arousing any general enthusiasm. But the universal ferment of the Slavonic elements in the Turkish Empire during 1875 extended to the usually stolid and unemotional peasants of Bulgaria. In the spring of the following year, a slight rebellion took place under the leadership of schoolmasters and priests, some of whom had imbibed with their Russian education the Panslavist ideas then in vogue at St. Petersburg. At first the rising attracted little notice, and even the British Ambassador at Constantinople

OLD BULGARIAN BRIDGE.

treated it lightly. But the cruelty with which it was suppressed aroused the indignation of Europe. The massacres of Batak have even now, after the lapse of twenty years, remained impressed upon the mind of every one who is old enough to remember them. The energy of an English newspaper correspondent first gave to the world the tale of horror; an official inquiry, conducted on the spot by Mr. Baring, fully confirmed the story of the journalist. The village of Batak, which lies in the mountains about eight hours' journey from Tatar Bazardjik, had been preparing for some days past to join in the insurrection, when a force of Bashi-Bazouks under the command of Achmet Agha of Dospat, and his colleague Mohammed Agha of Dorkovo, arrived at the place. After a desultory struggle the villagers surrendered, Achmet giving his word of honour that "not a hair of their head should be touched." On the 9th of May the massacre began. The defenceless inhabitants, who had surrendered their arms, were butchered like sheep. Some took refuge in the church, only to find that the sanctuary was turned into a shambles. The roof was torn off by the Turkish soldiers, who flung burning pieces of wood and rags dipped in petroleum down upon the poor wretches within. One old woman was the only survivor whom Mr. Baring could discover, and when he visited the spot more than two months later, the stench of the still unburied corpses was overpowering. Skulls with grey hair still attached to them, dark tresses which had once adorned the head of a maiden, the mutilated trunks of men, the rotting limbs of children—such was the sight which met the eyes of the British Commissioner and his Turkish companion. Torture had been applied to those who escaped death in order that they might reveal where their treasures were hidden. "To Achmet Agha and his men," wrote Mr. Baring, "belongs the distinction of having committed perhaps the most heinous crime that has stained the history of the present century." The Turkish Government showed its sense of propriety and at the same time set a precedent, which has recently been followed in the case of the massacres at Sassun, by decorating the butcher of Batak. The Ottoman High Commissioner sent to inquire into the outrages formed, however, a truer estimate of what had been done. Addressing one of the authors of the massacre he asked him how much Russia had paid him for a deed which, as he phrased it, would be "the beginning of the end of the Ottoman Empire."

Batak was not an isolated example of Turkish ferocity. Mr. Baring estimated the total number of Christians slaughtered in Bulgaria during the month of May at about 12,000. At Batak 5,000 persons out of a population of 7,000 had fallen; at a small hamlet near Yamboli, all the male inhabitants were shot without trial; M. Zankoff, the subsequent minister, only owed his escape on this occasion to the timely intervention of the station-master. The indignation of the civilised world at the news of these horrors knew no bounds. Mr. Gladstone by both pen and voice contributed to swell the torrent which threatened to sweep the whole system of Turkish administration in Bulgaria away. His famous pamphlet on the "Bulgarian Atrocities" speedily went through many editions; and Lord Derby telegraphed on behalf of the British Government, that "any renewal of the outrages would be more fatal to the Porte than the loss of a battle." His words were literally true. For all unconsciously the wretched victims of Batak had done more for their country by their pitiful death than if they had perished sword in hand on the field. For from this moment Bulgaria, hitherto well-nigh forgotten by Western Europe, became a household word, and its liberation became the object of practical statesmen no less than philanthropists. Russia, above all, had been provided with an excellent handle against the Sultan, and could go to war with the cause of the Balkan Christians as a watchword.

In the war itself the Bulgarians played a much less important part than the Roumanians. Bulgaria, disorganised by nearly five centuries of Turkish rule, which had sapped the martial spirit of the people, could do little but provide a theatre for the war. It was upon Bulgarian soil that the chief struggle took place, and the siege of Plevna and the occupation of the Shipka Pass attracted the eyes of the whole world to this remote corner of the map of Europe. To the best of their abilities the peasants helped the Russian forces; wherever the Czar's legions went the natives welcomed them, not because they wished to exchange the Turkish for the Muscovite domination, but because they regarded them as instruments for the liberation of the country. Their local knowledge was placed at the disposal of the invaders, Bulgarian guides directed the Russian army through the mazes of the mountains, Bulgarian boys carried water to the Russian soldiers in battle at the risk of their lives. Volunteer corps were formed to fight by the side of the Russian and Roumanian regulars, five thousand Bulgarians accompanied General Gourko in his operations in the Balkans, and won the praise of their allies by their gallant defence of the Shipka Pass, and their conspicuous bravery at Eski Zagora, where four-fifths of the Bulgarian combatants were left dead upon the field. But lack of military training, the terror inspired by the massacres of the previous year, and the fear of reprisals in case the war went against their liberators, hindered them from displaying those high military qualities which eight years later won them renown at Slivnitza. One grievous blot marred their struggle for freedom. On the approach of the Russians the maddened peasantry gave way to its thirst for revenge. Mindful of the atrocities to which their countrymen had been subjected by the Bashi-Bazouks, the Bulgarians descended from the mountains whither they had fled, and slew the Turks without mercy.

The Treaty of San Stefano, which the conquerors endeavoured to impose upon the conquered, would have created a " Big Bulgaria " almost beyond the dreams of the most fervent patriots. In a single moment, from the position of a Turkish province the country would have risen to the rank of an independent state with boundaries almost as extended as those of the Empire under Simeon or Samuel. The Bulgaria of the San Stefano Treaty would have cut the European territories of Turkey in two, and thus effectually dismembered the Ottoman Empire. In addition to a coast line on the Black Sea extending a little farther north, and considerably farther south than that which she at present possesses, Bulgaria would have had a frontage on the Ægean. But it was in Macedonia, the " land for which Samuel and Basil had once striven so stoutly," that she would have acquired the greatest accession of territory. The lakes of Ochrida and Prespa, ancient homes of her Czars, would have once more owned her sway; the Vardar and the Struma would have been from source to mouth

Bulgarian streams. No wonder that Bulgarian eyes still look with longing upon the "promised land." Prince Alexander told a friend of the writer, who had remarked that Sofia was not sufficiently central to be the capital of Bulgaria, that the annexation of Macedonia would make it the heart of the country. Prince Ferdinand is known to cherish similar aspirations, and nowhere was the Macedonian agitation of last year more popular than in Sofia. The Bulgarians can never forget that a large part of the Macedonian population speaks the same language and belongs to the same race as themselves. But Greece and Servia would have been indignant at the loss of a country which contains many of their own fellow-countrymen as well. Over this big Bulgaria a Christian government was to be appointed, and a complete union was decreed between North Bulgaria and the part south of the Balkans, to which the diplomatic title of "Eastern Roumelia" had been given. But the Western Powers, and more especially England, anticipated that the new and autonomous state thus created by the Czar would become a mere appanage of the Russian Crown. It must be confessed that such a prospect seemed at that time only too probable, for no one suspected the sturdy independence of the emancipated Bulgarians, or expected the subsequent treatment by which their liberators alienated their affections. The history of Roumania, indeed, might have proved that any diplomatic attempt to sever North and South Bulgaria from one another would be as futile as the similar scheme for the separation of the two

Danubian principalities twenty years earlier. But the dominant sentiment was the fear that Bulgaria would be a Russian outpost, a convenient resting-place on the way from St. Petersburg to Constantinople. So the Treaty of San Stefano was torn up, and that of Berlin substituted in its place.

By this memorable instrument, upon which the international position of the country still depends, Bulgaria was created an "autonomous and tributary principality under the suzerainty of His Imperial Majesty the Sultan"; its limits were defined to be the Balkans on the south, Eastern Roumelia being thus excluded from it, the Danube on the north, the Black Sea from just south of Mangalia to near Cape Eminch on the east, and Servia on the west, from the point where the river Timok joins the Danube to the place where the two principalities and Macedonia meet. Thus not only were the Bulgarians in Eastern Roumelia and Macedonia separated from their kinsmen in the new principality, but the Bulgarian-speaking district of Pirot was handed over to Servia. Here were the germs of future troubles, and the wording of the famous article which regulated the election of the Prince, has since caused great inconvenience. The article provided that the Prince should be "freely elected by the population, and confirmed by the Sublime Porte, with the assent of the Powers. No member of the reigning dynasties of the great European Powers may be elected Prince." The words "with the assent of the Powers" have been interpreted to mean that if one of the signatory Powers object, no valid election can be made. Thus, after a reign of nine years as Prince *de facto*, the present ruler of Bulgaria has only just become Prince *de jure*. The Treaty then went on to proclaim complete civil and religious liberty in the new principality, provided for the payment of an annual tribute to the Porte, and made Bulgaria responsible for a portion of the Ottoman debt. Temporary arrangements were drawn up for the administration of the country under an Imperial Russian Commissary aided by a similar Turkish official and the consuls of the other Powers for nine months, the period which was fixed for the occupation of both Bulgaria and Eastern Roumelia by a Russian army of fifty thousand men. As for the latter district it was to " remain under the direct political and military authority " of the Sultan, and to be administered by " a Christian Governor-General, nominated by the Sublime Porte with the assent of the Powers for a term of five years." But facts were soon to prove stronger than the artificial arrangements of diplomacy.

Thus, after nearly five centuries of Turkish bondage, Bulgaria was once more free. For the third time in her long history she was a practically independent state. More fortunate than Servia and Montenegro, she had not had to fight for her freedom but owed it to the swords, and perhaps no less to the pens, of foreigners. It remained for her to emancipate herself from the tutelage of Russia and bid her brothers beyond the Balkans join her in one united Bulgarian principality.

VI.

THE UNION UNDER PRINCE ALEXANDER.

(1878—1886.)

BULGARIA, to use a phrase of Prince Bismarck, had thus been "put in the saddle," but she had not yet "learnt to ride." Under the long rule of the Turks there had been no opportunity for acquiring the elements of political education. The old Bulgarian Empire had been based upon serfdom, and maintained by an aristocracy. But the Bulgarian state which suddenly came into existence in 1878, was essentially democratic. Its people were mainly peasants with little knowledge of the art of government. Naturally the Russians were the practical rulers of the country. Prince Dondukoff-Korsakoff the Imperial Commissary, during the interregnum which intervened between the Berlin Treaty and the election of the first Prince of Bulgaria, made progresses through the land just as if it were a Russian province. All the administrative posts were filled by Russians, and no care was taken to spare the feelings of the natives. Of all races in the Peninsula, the Bulgarians are the most suspicious of foreigners, and the most economical. Yet, the Russian Government not only monopolised every office in the principality, but sent as officials to Bulgaria men who had proved either failures or firebrands wherever they had been employed, and who spent money—the peasants' money —right and left. Prince Dondukoff was personally popular, and he began his career when all the memories of the Turkish captivity and the Russian liberation were fresh in the minds of the people. But the Bulgarians are practical persons with whom gratitude is chiefly a sense of favours to come. When the first flush of excitement was over many of them began to doubt whether they had not exchanged the rule of King Log for that of King Stork. During the first two years of its independence Bulgaria was materially less prosperous than in the four fat years of Midhat.

In order to make Russia's hold upon the country doubly secure, Prince Dondukoff drew up a constitution, which might have been framed by a pupil of Machiavelli. A more inconsistent document was never devised by a statesman, but there was a method in its author's inconsistency. The Commissary had to plan an elaborate system of checks and balances. If the Prince of Bulgaria, when elected, should prove a willing tool of Russia, that was an excellent reason for granting him almost autocratic power over his people; but, on the other hand, he might become refractory, therefore his people must be provided with the means of checkmating him. In either event Russia would rule, whether Prince or people governed, and a constitution at once very autocratic and very democratic was accordingly created to suit either emergency. The calculations of the wily constitution-monger were, however, vitiated by one defect: he never considered the possibility of Prince and people both uniting against Russia. Yet that was what actually came to pass, thanks to the tactless conduct of the Russian officials.

An Assembly of Notables, in accordance with the provisions of the Berlin Treaty, met at Trnovo early in 1879 and passed the Constitution. Of the two hundred and thirteen Bulgarians, mostly peasants, whose signatures attested this curious instrument few had any conception of its meaning. Except to those who had travelled in the West of Europe, parliamentary institutions were a profound mystery. Yet, without any previous training, they were suddenly presented with a system of representation, outwardly far more democratic than that of England or America. The Parliament, or ordinary *Sobranje*, was to consist of a single chamber, elected by manhood suffrage, to which any citizen of thirty years of age, who could read and write, was eligible. Payment of members and equal electoral districts are both " points " in this Bulgarian charter. On the other hand, the ministers are absolutely independent of the chamber. They are nominated by, and responsible to, the Prince; no parliamentary majority can upset them; they are not necessarily members of Parliament. As head of the army, the Prince can dismiss and appoint every officer; he may dissolve the *Sobranje* when he chooses, and if the country should decide against him, he need not give way. Care was taken by the framer of the constitution that there should be no way out of a deadlock, which might arise between Prince and Parliament. The princely dignity was made hereditary in the male line, and the civil list fixed at £24,000. Absolute freedom of the press was guaranteed, and Bulgarian journalists avail themselves of it to the utmost. Freedom of election exists in theory alone, for Bulgarian statesmen are adepts at the art of "managing" voters, and the number of votes recorded often bears no proportion to the actual number of voters. A Ministry, by means of its hold upon the local authorities, can generally contrive to keep in power, and the peasant statesmen have learnt the cynical maxim of Prince Dondukoff himself: "*Les constitutions, c'est comme les jolies femmes, elles ne demandent qu'à être violées!*" Conscription and elementary education are compulsory, and the democratic spirit of the people was gratified by the prohibition of all titles of nobility.

Although Bulgaria has no second chamber, the constitution provided for the creation of a Grand *Sobranje*, which meets, not at Sofia, like the ordinary Parliament, but at Trnovo, to consider the election of a Prince, the nomination of Regents, the extension of territory, or the revision of the Constitution. This body is elected by the same constituencies as the other, but consists of twice as many members, and ceases to exist as soon as the specific business for which it was chosen has been discharged. Thus Bulgaria, a state without statesmen, a nation devoid of a governing class, without experience, without traditions, was equipped in a few months with a brand-new paper constitution. It is highly creditable to the common-sense of the people, that the machinery of government has worked so well.

The constituent assembly, having passed the constitution, proceeded to the election of a Prince. The choice of the deputies fell upon Prince Alexander of Battenberg, son of Prince Alexander of Hesse, and, as nephew of the Czar Alexander II., presumably a person acceptable to the Russian Government. The first Prince of Bulgaria was, at the time of his election, twenty-two years of age, and living in the humble quarters of a Prussian officer at Potsdam. It is said that he hesitated at first to accept the doubtful honour thrust upon him; but a throne was too tempting to be refused. He consulted Prince Bismarck, who, thirteen years earlier, had advised another German Prince to accept a Balkan throne, and received a reply that at any rate a reign in Bulgaria would be a "pleasant reminiscence." Prince Alexander made a preliminary tour of the European Courts, and, amidst great enthusiasm took the oath to the constitution at Trnovo on the 9th of July. A week later the Russian army of occupation evacuated Bulgaria.

The first Prince of Bulgaria is one of the most romantic figures in the history of our time. His career borders on the marvellous, his character had something of the heroic about it. His frank and open bearing, his social charms, and his military prowess on behalf of his adopted country on the field of Slivnitza, endeared him to the cold hearts of a people which is seldom enthusiastic. He was essentially a soldier, and was the best possible ruler of a country like Bulgaria in time of war. But he was lamentably deficient in the arts of a statesman. A diplomatist, who knew him intimately, has described to the writer the "obstinacy" and "singular incapacity" which he showed in matters of business, while he committed indiscretions of speech which proved that he had, like some other sovereigns, never mastered that aphorism of Metternich, that "a monarch should not talk." He had a singular knack of quarrelling with his advisers, which once drew down upon him a sharp rebuke from the Czar. He was not a great administrator or a clever politician; but if he had had an old and experienced statesman to guide him, he might have succeeded. Unfortunately, he estranged first the Liberals, who included all the ablest men in Bulgaria, and then the Russians, and when the latter desired his fall, he fell. For the first two years of his reign, down to the death of the Czar Alexander II. in 1881, his position was comparatively easy. His Imperial patron had a personal liking for him, and fear of their sovereign's displeasure checked the arrogance of the Russian officers who were sent to Bulgaria. Having ascended the throne as a Russian nominee, the Prince naturally chose his early advisers from the Conservative, or Russophil party, and openly described the Liberal or national party as "Nihilists." But as the first Bulgarian Parliament was elected without Government pressure, the Liberals obtained an enormous majority, and a deadlock at once ensued. The Prince gave way, and Dragan Zankoff, the Liberal leader, and at that period Russia's principal antagonist, became

Prime Minister. This man has in his time played many parts; he has professed all political and most theological creeds; he has been alternately the sworn foe and the salaried agent of Russia, and his one guiding principle has been his own advancement. When he fell from office in 1880, he made a remark, which has become historical, that he wanted "neither Russia's honey nor her sting." Prince Alexander had been convinced by this brief experience of constitutional government, that he could not work with his Parliament. Accordingly, on the 27th of April, 1881, he executed a *coup d'état*, suspended the Constitution, made a Russian General Ernroth his Premier, and demanded irresponsible power for seven years, threatening to resign unless he obtained it. A packed Assembly granted him his demands, and in July the Prince, under the auspices of Russia, was absolute master of the country. Two more Russian generals were sent from St. Petersburg to "uphold his prestige," and representative institutions were only preserved by "a small Assembly," which had no function save that of voting the budget.

But the Prince soon found that he was not master in his own house. His Russian ministers plainly told him that they took their orders from the Czar, and Alexander III. had the greatest dislike for his cousin. Bulgaria after the *coup d'état* was as much a province of Russia as if she had been annexed to the country. The President of the Council, the Minister of War, the Chief of Police, the Governor of Sofia, and three hundred superior officers in the army were all Russians. The Russian Agent, M. Hitrovo, cleverly worked upon the national dread of Austria, and tried to play the part of a British political Resident at the court of an Indian prince. But both Prince and people grew restive under this alien bondage. The native officers became impatient of Russian control in the army; the sovereign chafed under the impertinences of his Russian ministers. The Prince restored the Constitution in 1883, his Russian advisers resigned, and the Liberals, under Zankoff, ruled in their stead. The discovery of a plot to kidnap the Prince widened the breach with Russia. In the dead of night, Generals Soboleff and Kaulbars arrived at the Palace and demanded an audience of the sovereign. The sentry refused admittance; and, when they attempted to force it, drew his sword and threatened to cut them down. A search revealed the presence of a carriage at the gates, in which the Prince was to have been privily conveyed to the Danube. Proclamations, announcing Alexander's expulsion and the formation of a provisional government under the two leading conspirators, proved conclusively the complicity of Russia. For the moment, however, the plot had failed.

Meanwhile, in Eastern Roumelia, the bitter disappointment caused by the separation of the two Bulgarias in the Treaty of Berlin, had increased. The Bulgarian, Aleko Pasha, who had been appointed first Governor-General after the departure of the Russians in 1879, had looked with some favour upon the national aspirations of the people, and so far incurred the hostility of the Russian party, that he was superseded by Gavril Pasha, a Slav, in 1884. Early in the reign of Prince Alexander, deputations from Eastern Roumelia had come to Sofia, begging for a union, and offering to support it by force of arms. In the summer of 1885 the Liberals of Eastern Roumelia felt that now was the moment to strike the blow. On the morning of September 18th, as Gavril Pasha was quietly sipping his coffee in the *Konak* at Philippopolis, Major Nikolajeff and several officers entered his room and informed him that he was their prisoner. The Pasha yielded to superior force, and, under the guard of a schoolmistress with a sword in her hand, was driven round the town amidst the jeers of his late subjects. The army fraternised with the insurgents, and without a drop of blood the capital of Eastern Roumelia was theirs. Nikolajeff at once proclaimed the union of the two Bulgarias under Prince Alexander. The Prince hesitated to accept the honour. He consulted Stambuloff, at that time Speaker of the *Sobranje*, who pointedly told him that he stood at the crossroads of his career. " The one road," he said, " leads to Philippopolis, and as far further as God may lead, the other to the Danube and Darmstadt." Alexander chose the former, and on September 20th issued a proclamation as " Prince of North and South Bulgaria." He soothed the feelings of his Mussulman subjects by visiting the chief mosque at Philippopolis, and the care, which he had always taken to prevent outrages against Mahommedans in Bulgaria, gained him the confidence of their co-religionists in Eastern Roumelia.

But every one expected international complications. It seemed incredible that Turkey would acquiesce in the Union without a struggle; it was known that the aggrandisement of Bulgaria would excite the wildest jealousies of both Greeks and Serbs. But the Sultan, from fear of assassination, dared not strip his capital of the necessary troops; Greece was kept in order by a naval demonstration of the Powers, and Servia alone entered the field. At the Conferences, which were held at Constantinople, Sir William White, the British Ambassador, strongly supported the Bulgarian cause, while the Russians, who seven years earlier had advocated the Union of the two Bulgarias at San Stefano, now counselled the Sultan to occupy Eastern Roumelia by force. Thus England and Russia had exchanged parts in the "Great" Bulgarian drama. To mark yet more clearly his displeasure at what he regarded as "ingratitude," the Czar struck Prince Alexander's name out of the Russian army list, and recalled every Russian officer from Bulgaria. But the blow recoiled on its author. From that instant Prince Alexander became in the eyes of his people a national hero, whom they would follow to the death. Then for the first time was heard the ominous phrase, "We would rather be Turkish than Russian."

While Bulgaria was thus suddenly thrown upon her own resources, Servia suddenly declared war. About a year before the Union there had been boundary disputes with Servia, which had been jealous of Bulgaria ever since the Berlin Treaty. King Milan thought the moment favourable for that territorial extension which his people desired. His neighbours had just seen their army denuded of its

Russian officers; their Prince was under the ban of the Powers; their frontier was open to invasion. There could, he thought — and most onlookers thought too — be only one result of a war undertaken under such conditions. So, on November 13, 1885, his Premier, M. Garashinine, telegraphed to Sofia that hostilities would begin next morning. The people of Belgrade toasted their sovereign as "King of Servia and Macedonia," and the troops invoked the name of Stephen Dušan as they marched through the streets. But the statesmen of Servia had not reckoned with the enthusiasm of their adversaries. Prince Alexander again reaped the reward of his toleration towards his Mussulman subjects, for six thousand of them at once volunteered for the war. The Bulgarians of Macedonia formed a "brigand brigade" of three thousand more, and in a few days the Prince found himself at the head of ninety thousand men. At the first intelligence of the war he had hurried back from Philippopolis to Sofia, and the evening of the 16th found his headquarters established in a wretched little *khan* at Slivnitza, a town on the direct route from Servia to Sofia.

The three days' battle of Slivnitza revealed the Bulgarians to Europe in a new light. The courage of the Prince, who exposed himself to the enemy's fire with the most reckless disregard of danger, inspired his soldiers to the utmost efforts. Early on the morning of the third day a rumour reached headquarters that the enemy was marching by the south on Sofia, and a panic broke out in the capital. The Russophil party, under Zankoff, was preparing for a

'Provisional Government," the national exchequer had been sent for safety to Plevna, when the news came that the alarm was false. At Slivnitza the Bulgarians had triumphed, everywhere the Serbs had been driven back. King Milan sent a letter, asking for an armistice, which was refused, and the victors crossed the frontier and occupied Pirot. Belgrade seemed in danger, for its defenders had only one round of ammunition left; but Count Khevenhüller, the Austrian Minister to Servia, arrived in the Bulgarian headquarters, and told Prince Alexander that, if he advanced further, Austria would join Servia in resisting his march. The Prince yielded to superior force, and in March, 1886, a treaty of peace was signed at Bucharest. Servia did not cede a single yard of territory; she did not even pay a war indemnity, which ought, according to the Bulgarian statesmen, to have consisted of two million pigs, the commodity of which the Serbs had most to spare. But if Bulgaria had not gained land or cash from Servia, the Union with Eastern Roumelia was secured •by the war. The Sultan made a treaty with Prince Alexander early in 1886, and named him Governor-General of the country, which was henceforth known as South Bulgaria. The war had not been in vain; Slivnitza was found by the politicians to have its literal meaning of "that which unites"; for the blood of the soldiers who died there cemented the union of the two Bulgarias.

Prince Alexander had driven back the Serbs, and returned in triumph to his capital as the "hero of Slivnitza"; but the vengeance of Russia dogged his footsteps. Baffled by his success, enraged at his growing spirit of independence, the Russian agents in Bulgaria were keener than ever to overthrow him. Peace had scarcely been signed, when a conspiracy was discovered at Bourgas to carry off, or, if necessary, kill, the Prince. Foiled in this second attempt against his person, the Russophil party used every means to poison public opinion against him. There were officers in the army, like Bendereff and Dimitrieff, who were ready to avenge real or imaginary slights received from their sovereign. The rumour that the Serbs were about to renew hostilities had the double effect of stripping the capital of loyal troops and of causing much discontent among the peaceful and thrifty Bulgarians. Russophil prints described the Prince as a monster of vice, a creature who fattened upon the hard-won earnings of the poor. A regiment upon which the conspirators could rely was quietly marched into Sofia, and all was ready for the final blow. As Bendereff was acting Minister for War, and Grueff head of the Military Academy, the gang held all the trump cards. To crown all, the Church, in the person of the Metropolitan, Clement, a sworn friend of Russia and a born intriguer, pronounced its blessing on the enterprise.

At two in the morning of the 21st of August, 1886, the Prince was aroused from his slumbers by one of his guards, who rushed into his bedroom, thrust a revolver into his hand, and told him that the palace was surrounded by a band of conspirators. Escape was hopeless, repeated volleys and cries of *Dolu, dolu!* "Down with him, down with him!" rent the air,

Hurrying on his clothes, the Prince went into the hall, where a crowd of officers, led by Major Grueff, called on him to "abdicate," emphasing their demands by pointing their loaded pistols at his head. Captain Dimitrieff tore a page out of the visitors' book, which lay in the hall, and sat down to draw up the deed of abdication. Drink and excitement prevented him from scrawling more than a few unintelligible words on the paper, and a young cadet took the pen from

ROMAN RELIEF AT MADARA.

him and finished the document. Grueff, presenting his revolver full in the Prince's face, cried out, "Sign, or I'll shoot!" To resist would have been fatal; the Prince wrote the words in German, "God protect Bulgaria—Alexander," and the deed was done.

From the Palace the conspirators took him to the War Office, where every humiliation was put upon him. Bendereff, with a terrible oath, asked him why he had not made him a major; Dimitrieff grinned, as he munched an apple in his sovereign's face. Grueff alone felt some pangs of conscience; for when the Prince said reproachfully, "So you are also with them," he turned away and made no reply. At five in the morning the captive was driven, with an armed escort of military cadets, to the monastery of Etropol, in the mountains, about seventeen miles from Sofia. After a night spent in one of the cells, the Prince was conducted to the Danube, where his yacht was waiting. At the last moment, a chance of escape was offered him by the captain of an Austrian tug, which was lying alongside the yacht with full steam up. But the Prince's guards were too much on the alert for their prisoner to evade them. He was conveyed on board the yacht, and on the morning of the 23rd landed on Russian soil.

Meanwhile, consternation prevailed among the loyal Bulgarians. The Metropolitan Clement and the Russian Agent received the fulsome adoration of Zankoff and his partisans at the Russian Agency, and a new Ministry was formed, which assured the people by a proclamation that Bulgaria might count upon the protection of the Czar. But it had scarcely been launched, when a counter proclamation, signed by Stambuloff, as Speaker of the *Sobranje*, and Lieutenant-Colonel Mutkuroff, who was in command at Philippopolis, declared Clement and his colleagues to be outlaws, and appealed to the Bulgarians to defend the throne. It was at once clear that the country was with the loyalists. Stambuloff had no difficulty in dissolving the Provisional Government; and he and two other persons constituted themselves a

Regency until the Prince could be found. To discover the vanished sovereign was no easy matter; but after telegraphing all over Europe, it was ascertained that the Russian authorities had set him at liberty at Lemberg. Stambuloff at once telegraphed to him to return and resume his sway. The Prince accepted the offer, and, before a Russian Commissioner could forestall him, he had landed once more in Bulgaria.

The conspiracy, conceived and carried out on almost exactly similar lines to the Roumania mutiny against Prince Couza in 1866, had succeeded at first, only to be frustrated by the promptitude of the man who was for the next eight years to play the leading part in Balkan politics. The most extraordinary series of accidents had enabled the conspirators to execute their plans; a letter, which he had neglected, had warned the Prince of his fate, and at the last moment the yacht, which bore him a prisoner down the Danube, narrowly escaped the Bulgarian and Roumanian fire from the opposite banks. Thanks chiefly to Stambuloff, he had regained his crown. Thanks to his own weakness, he now voluntarily renounced it.

Among those who had assembled to meet the Prince on his landing at Rustchuk was M. Shatokhin, the Russian Consul. Without consulting his friends Prince Alexander despatched to the Czar, at this man's suggestion, a telegram, in which he thanked that monarch for sending a Russian High Commissioner to Bulgaria, and for the recognition which his Majesty's representative at Rustchuk had shown him.

The message ended with the servile phrase, "Russia gave me my crown; I am ready to return it into the hands of her sovereign." This telegram was the Prince's ruin. The Czar at once replied, "Cannot approve your return to Bulgaria. I shall refrain from all interference with the sad state to which Bulgaria has been brought as long as you remain there." The Prince saw that the game was up; by one foolish move he had lost, and had no furthur choice but to go. In vain Stambuloff urged him to remain, and, when arguments failed, threatened to keep him on the throne against his will. At last it was agreed that he should go, provided that Russia permitted the Bulgarians to elect some one in his stead. The Russian Agent consented. On September 7th Prince Alexander publicly announced his abdication, and appointed Stambuloff, Mutkûroff, and Karaveloff as Regents. Next day, sadly and sorrowfully the Prince bade farewell to Bulgaria for ever. He summoned the chief men of Sofia to the palace, told them how the welfare of his adopted country had been his sole desire, and confessed that he had failed because of the great opposition which he had met. And then he set out with Stambuloff, amidst the tears of his subjects, sorry to leave them, yet glad to be freed from the responsibilities of a Balkan throne.

His memory lived, and still lives after his death, among the people of his adoption. Under the name of Count Hartenau, happily yet humbly married, he tried to bury the prince in the simple Austrian officer. But long after his departure there were men in Bulgaria who hoped for his return. His faults—

and they were many—were forgotten; it was remembered that in seven brief years he had created an army, led a nation to victory, and united the two Bulgarias together. And when he died in 1893, many a peasant in his humble cottage mourned for the soldier prince, the "hero of Slivnitza."

VII.

PRINCE FERDINAND.

(1887—1896.)

THE abdication of Prince Alexander made it desirable to select a suitable candidate for the vacant throne without delay, in order that law and order might be restored as soon as possible. With the avowed object of "assisting" the Bulgarians in their difficulties, the Czar sent them Major-General Kaulbars, Russian military attaché at Vienna and brother of the General Kaulbars who had acted as Bulgarian war minister five years before. To the action of this man more than to any other cause may be attributed the antipathy to Russia which has grown up in the country which she helped to liberate. For General Kaulbars, as a Bulgarian statesman once said, "came with a knout in his hand." His methods were unparalleled in the history of diplomacy. Instead of expressing his views in official interviews with the usual diplomatic forms, he took the mob into his confidence and stumped the country as the election agent of the Czar. His "twelve commandments" to the Russian consuls and vice-consuls in Bulgaria aroused the utmost indignation. His great desire was to postpone the elections to the Grand *Sobranje*, which were prescribed by the constitution to take place within a month, in order that the new prince might be chosen at once. As the regents insisted on holding these elections, he started on an electoral tour through the towns and villages of Bulgaria. His speeches were interrupted by cries and groans; when he discoursed on what he was pleased to call his "three points"—the raising of the prevailing state of siege, the liberation of the officers involved in the late conspiracy, and the postponement of the elections—he was greeted with shouts of " Impossible." At two places alone did he succeed in persuading the electors to abstain from voting. Stambuloff and the national party obtained an immense majority, and General Kaulbars had to fall back upon the allegation that the elections were invalid, a convenient theory, which his agents endeavoured to substantiate by their violence and the riots, which they incited. A second plot at Bourgas and the presence of two Russian men-of-war at Varna failed to frighten the Bulgarians into submission, and finally, disgusted and disappointed, General Kaulbars and all the Russian consular agents shook the dust of Bulgaria off their feet and returned to their own country.

The Grand *Sobranje* met at Trnovo and elected Prince Waldemar of Denmark, brother of the Princess of Wales and the Dowager Empress of Russia, as Prince Alexander's successor. It was thought that the Czar would approve of so near a kinsman; but he would not consent, so Prince Waldemar declined the proffered crown. To the candidature of the Prince of Mingrelia, a Caucasian potentate, who was put forward by Turkey and was considered to be acceptable to Russia, the Bulgarians would not listen. The best of all choices would have been the King of Roumania, to whom the throne was actually offered. Had King Carol accepted, he might have formed the strongest of all Balkan states, which would have realised the ancient idea of a "Wallacho-Bulgarian Empire," and might have even proved to be the "nucleus of a Balkan confederation." But the King was afraid of arousing the jealousy of the Powers, and once more the welfare of the Peninsula was sacrificed to the exigencies of its great neighbours.

Meanwhile, the position of the Regents was becoming dangerous; plot succeeded plot in rapid succession, Russia had been mortally offended, and it was imperative that a prince should be found. Three delegates were accordingly sent out on a tour of inspection among the royal cadets of Europe. One evening a member of the deputation was drinking his glass of beer at Ronacher's Circus in Vienna, when a friend introduced him to a gentleman, who professed to know the very man for the post. The delighted delegate told his colleagues, and next day all three waited upon Prince Ferdinand of Saxe-Coburg-Gotha, and offered him the throne. In order to meet the prince's objections, the Grand *Sobranje* promptly elected him. At first, he made his acceptance conditional on the approval of the Powers. But his scruples were overcome, and on August 14, 1887, he took the oath before the Grand *Sobranje* in the ancient capital of the Bulgarian Czars, to whom he alluded in his opening proclamation.

At the time of his accession Prince Ferdinand was twenty-six years of age. The younger son of a distinguished family, his father was a nobleman possessing large estates in Austria, his mother, Princess Clementine, was the granddaughter of King Louis Philippe. Well connected and with ample means, he had two indispensable qualifications for the throne. But he was wholly ignorant of the language and customs of his subjects, to whom he came, like Alexander, as a foreigner, but without Alexander's Russian introductions and dashing manners. Accident made Prince Ferdinand a sovereign, nature intended him for a student. He is never so happy as when rambling through the mountains in search of choice botanical specimens, and his tastes are not those of soldiers and sportsmen. The Bulgarians, as he has himself admitted, are not enthusiastic Royalists. They have adopted monarchical principles, because that was the only means of making their independence acceptable to the Powers. No one could, therefore, have expected them to display intense loyalty to a young sovereign, of whom few of them had ever heard, and who seemed deficient in those qualities which had endeared Alexander to the hearts of his people.

The Regents resigned upon Prince Ferdinand's accession, and retired into private life. But for M. Stambuloff, to whom more than any other man Bulgaria owed the maintenance of her independence and Prince Ferdinand his throne, there was little rest. On September 1, 1887, the Prince requested him to accept the post of Prime Minister, which he occupied without intermission till his fall on the last day of May, 1894. For the greater portion of these seven years, the history of Bulgaria is little else but the story of his career.

Stepan Stambuloff was undoubtedly the ablest statesman whom the Balkan states have produced since their regeneration. Born at Trnovo in 1854, the son of an innkeeper, this remarkable man had acquired a European reputation at an age when most budding British premiers have been undersecretaries at the most. But youth is too common an attribute of Bulgarian politicians to attract any special notice. What gained Stambuloff the respect and admiration of foreign nations was the extraordinary skill and firmness which he displayed under most trying circumstances. He was always counted as one of the two or three really "strong men" of Europe. His friends called him the "Bulgarian Bismarck"; even hostile critics admitted that he was *un géant dans un entresol*. No doubt he had great faults. He believed that the end justified the means, and never hesitated to employ force if he considered it indispensable to the success of his plans. Like every other minister who has governed in Bulgaria, he manipulated the elections for his own purposes, but those purposes were also the nation's; for he was a true patriot, whose whole public life was given up to Bulgaria. As a young man, he had been mixed up in frequent conspiracies for the emancipation of his fellow-countrymen. Under Prince Alexander, he had chiefly devoted his time to his practice as a lawyer, but when the country was in danger he came forward as its saviour. Arbitrary he undoubtedly was, but for sheer ability and force of character he stood unrivalled among Balkan statesmen. If he had shown more tact towards his sovereign and more polish in his dealings with his sovereign's consort, he might have kept his place and his life for years. But the Bulgarian peasant was strong within him; he was the very opposite of a courtier, while his Prince attached an exaggerated amount of importance to the pomp and circumstance of royalty. It was inevitable that sooner or later the two men should disagree, and at the very first the minister thought that he could never get on with his master. But as long as Prince Ferdinand was a comparative stranger to the manners and customs of Bulgaria, there was peace between them, for the minister, from his superior knowledge, was necessarily supreme. It was only when the Prince had begun to feel himself capable of judging and acting for himself, that the two fell out. Stambuloff. treated the Prince like a puppet, and had not the tact to rule his sovereign without showing that he ruled.

The first difficulty which beset the new Prince and his minister was the hostile attitude of Russia. By the Treaty of Berlin it was necessary that the ruler of Bulgaria should be elected by the Grand *Sobranje* with the consent of the Powers. This consent Russia, as one of the Powers, refused, basing her refusal upon the alleged invalidity of the elections to the Grand

Sobranje. Bulgaria was, therefore, socially boycotted by the Powers. From the Prince's point of view the formal recognition of his position was most desirable; but the question was of much less interest to his people, who, being practical persons, did not care to fight for mere forms when they had obtained the solid substance. Indirectly, the non-recognition of Prince Ferdinand had this advantage, that there was no Russian Agent accredited to his court, and consequently no Russian agency always at work to undermine his throne. At first Russia did, indeed, protest openly, on her own behalf and through the medium of the Porte, against the Prince's position, and even proposed at one time to eject him and put General Ernroth, who had been Minister of War at Sofia in 1882, as governor in his place. But the friendly policy of England towards the young state and the firm resolve of the Bulgarian Government to resist such a proposal by force deterred Russia from the attempt, and from 1888 to the present time she has taken no open steps to oust Prince Ferdinand. This year he has at last secured recognition.

Having checkmated the designs of Bulgaria's former liberators, Stambuloff proceeded to establish friendly relations with his country's ancient master. Since the war Turkey had made no attempt to interfere with the practical independence of her old province, and she was quite ready to meet the Bulgarian Premier's overtures. Stambuloff's policy was as successful as it was statesmanlike. Thanks to this good understanding with the Sultan, he was able to obtain in 1890 Turkish *berats* for the appointment of two

Bulgarian bishops to the sees of Ochrida and Uskub in Macedonia, which had been abolished by the Porte after the war. This important concession was followed four years later by the nomination of two more Bulgarian bishops in Macedonia, while the Bulgarian schools in that part of the Turkish Empire were granted the same rights as the Greek, and forty Bulgarian communes were formally recognised. These successes were hailed with the greatest enthusiasm in Bulgaria, but aroused much jealousy at Athens and Belgrade, and were regarded by Europe generally as a signal blow to Russia, which had formerly asked on behalf of Bulgaria, and been refused a similar favour. Stambuloff visited Constantinople and was received by the Sultan, and his foreign policy seemed to have been fully justified. Bulgaria rose in the estimation of Western Europe, and fell more than ever under the displeasure of the Czar.

But it was not to be expected that a country, which for so many years had been honeycombed with conspiracies, would become suddenly free from these subterranean movements. If Russia had ceased to trouble Bulgaria, there were not wanting Russophils, who were ready to stir up the people to revolt. The Prince had been barely four months on the throne when two plots were discovered at Eski Zagra and Bourgas, the scene of two former insurrections against his predecessor. Nabôkoff, the author of the Bourgas rising, had already been implicated in a similar attempt at the same spot. Followed by a band of Montenegrins, whom he had collected with the assistance of Zankoff at Constantinople, he landed in the harbour, and, after a brief encounter with the authorities, was shot by the peasants. A much more serious movement was crushed in 1890. Major Panitza, the leader of this conspiracy, was a well-known officer in the army, who had been a friend and fellow-comrade of Prince Alexander. Disappointed of his colonelcy and annoyed at the failure of a negotiation for the purchase of rifles by the War Office, in which he was pecuniarily interested, he resolved to dethrone Prince Ferdinand, as Bendereff had dethroned Prince Alexander. He found considerable support for his plans, and three-fourths of the garrison of Sofia were on his side. Stambuloff, who had been informed of Panitza's intentions, lost no time in striking. With sardonic humour he ordered two officers, whom he knew to be Panitza's accomplices, to arrest their leader, and ordered a detachment of men, upon whom he could rely, to see that they did their work. Panitza was arrested and put on his trial by court-martial. Confident of the power of Russia to protect him from the consequences of acts undertaken, as the documentary evidence proved, with her approval, he showed no fear of the result. But Stambuloff vowed that, at all hazards, the sentence of the court should be carried out. That sentence was death, and Panitza was shot without ceremony as a traitor.

A year later the Premier himself narrowly escaped assassination. One evening, as he was walking home with M. Beltcheff, the Minister of Finance from a café, where the ministers were wont to adjourn after Cabinet Councils, a bullet suddenly whistled past their ears. With a cry to his companion to "run,"

Stambuloff set him the example and made for the nearest guard-house on the road. Two more shots followed, and the cry, " Stambuloff is killed," convinced him that it was at himself and not at his unoffending colleague that they had been aimed. Returning with the guards, he found the unfortunate Beltcheff lying dead in the public garden, whither he had fled, with a shot through his heart. The crime aroused the most intense indignation. Stambuloff, although he felt from that day that his doom was certain, followed up the assassins with relentless zeal. Torture was applied to extort a confession from one of the prisoners, and the utmost rigour of the law was put forth against every suspicious person in the country. Terrified by the violence of these measures, the conspirators fled from Bulgaria and chose their next victim abroad. This was Dr. Vulković, the Bulgarian agent at Constantinople. While walking through the streets he was stabbed in the back by one of the same gang, which had been guilty of Beltcheff's murder. This double crime made it clear, that, though brigandage had been suppressed in Bulgaria, the time-honoured Oriental plan of "removing" political opponents still prevailed. But the worst example of this horrible practice was yet to come.

The possibility of the Prince's untimely death by the hand of an assassin made it all the more desirable that he should found a dynasty as soon as possible. Accordingly, in the spring of 1893 he married Princess Marie Louise of Parma, a member of the Bourbon family, gifted with more than the usual abilities of her race. Later in the year, the death of

Prince Alexander made Prince Ferdinand indispensable to his people. To the last some had hoped against hope for the return of their first ruler, and would have no Prince but Alexander. These now loyally rallied to his successor. The birth of an heir in the following January, who received the name of the ancient Czar Boris, gave for the first time a national character to the Prince's rule. The greatest enthusiasm greeted the event, and the dynasty was further strengthened by the birth of a second son, Cyril, last winter. Over the head of the tiny Boris there has raged, however, a most unseemly theological controversy. The Duke of Parma had consented to his daughter's marriage on condition that her children should be brought up in the Catholic religion. The Bulgarian constitution provided that the heir to the throne should belong to the Orthodox Greek Church, which is the creed of the vast majority of his future subjects. Stambuloff, anxious for the marriage, was ready even at the risk of his personal popularity, to procure the revision of this article of the constitution, and Boris was baptised a Catholic. But Prince Ferdinand, desirous to please Russia, and rightly believing that the conversion of Boris to the Greek faith would be the means of obtaining his own recognition by the Czar, endeavoured, without success, to obtain the Pope's consent to this step. Policy certainly dictates that the future Prince of Bulgaria should profess the same form of religion as his people, and, without the consent of the Holy See, Boris has been formally converted. Thus, in our own day, the old struggle between the Greek and Roman

Churches for supremacy in Bulgaria, which we saw in the times of the present Czars, has been once more apparent.

Prince Ferdinand's marriage and the birth of an heir strengthened the dynasty but weakened its great minister. From that date, the sovereign became increasingly impatient of control, until at last on the 31st of May, 1894, the world learnt with surprise that he had dismissed the "Bismarck of Bulgaria" from his counsels. His alliance with a Bourbon princess had greatly increased his desire for recognition, and he regarded his minister as the chief obstacle in the way. There were intriguers at the Prince's elbow, old colleagues whom Stambuloff's growing arrogance had alienated, who poisoned their sovereign's mind against the Premier. Relations between the two men became worse; conversations at the palace were faithfully reported to the minister, who was not backward in telling his master to his face what he thought of his conduct. Stambuloff twice offered to resign, the Prince declined to accept his resignation, fearing that the great popularity, which his minister had just gained by the appointment of the second batch of Bulgarian bishops in Macedonia, would make him even more dangerous in opposition than in office. A domestic scandal, in which one of Stambuloff's most trusted colleagues was involved, gave the Prince his opportunity. He pressed for the nomination of a favourite of his own to the vacant portfolio, and carried his point by threatening to abdicate rather than yield. The presence of an enemy within his Cabinet embarrassed the Premier and emboldened the Prince and the opposition to further attacks. In a moment of anger, Stambuloff sat down and wrote a hasty letter to his sovereign, in which he informed him of his resignation, and expressed the hope that his successor in the premiership would not be such a "common fellow"—the epithet which the Prince had conferred upon him. On May 31, 1894, M. Stoiloff, an able lawyer, who had been private secretary to Prince Alexander and had left Stambuloff in disgust, became President of the Council. The people of Sofia, for whom the fallen statesman had done so much, now proved the truth of the maxim that there is no gratitude in politics. He, who had been but yesterday the idol of the populace, was spat on in the streets and greeted with shouts of "Down with the tyrant!" when he took his walks abroad with his faithful servant. His house was besieged by the mob, and the Government took no steps to protect him from the violence of his enemies. Only one thing was needed to complete the parallel between the "Bulgarian Bismarck" and his great prototype, and that was not lacking long. Following the bad example of the great ex-chancellor, Stambuloff unbosomed himself to a sympathetic journalist, who published in a German newspaper a violent diatribe against Prince Ferdinand. For this indiscretion Stambuloff was never forgiven. From that moment the buttons were off the foils, and it was war to the death between the rivals. The Prince instituted legal proceedings against him for defamation; the new Cabinet dismissed his adherents from every official post. If Stambuloff had chastised the electors with whips, Stoiloff chastised them with scorpions. In one night the newly-elected *Sobranje* passed thirty-two laws, one of them consisting of some three hundred sections. A law was enacted "for the prosecution of government officials, who appear to possess more wealth than they ought"; another abolished the existing pension system, and thus reduced the families of ex-Ministers to beggary. Stambuloff's property was sequestrated; bands of peasants felled the timber on his estates; he was almost ruined, and had to borrow money to avoid an execution on his furniture; he applied for a passport, in order to recruit his shattered health at a foreign spa, and his application was refused. But he had not to endure these insults much longer. On the evening of July 15, 1895, as he was driving home from the Union Club with an old friend, three men leapt into the street, with yataghans and a revolver in their hands. Before Stambuloff's old servant had had time to fire, the assassins had cut his master down and were hacking his prostrate body with their knives as it lay on the roadway. At the first shot, the three murderers fled, and the police, who were present, made no attempt to arrest them. Their unfortunate victim was taken home to die. Death came as a relief, for both his arms had been cut to pieces, one eye had been half gouged out, and his forehead bore the marks of fifteen wounds. Three days later the ablest of Bulgaria's sons breathed his last. But his enemies did not spare him even when dead. The scene at his funeral was scandalous, and showed that seventeen years of modern civilisation had not entirely effaced the savage characteristics of the ancient Bulgarians.

Since that date Bulgaria has been in disgrace in the eyes of Europe. This is not the place to discuss the truth of the charges which have been levelled at the head of Prince Ferdinand by the murdered statesman's friends, who have not hesitated to accuse the sovereign of complicity in the crime. But the neglect of the Government to bring the assassins to justice has excited general indignation, and Bulgaria, so long the admiration of Western Europe, has fallen under the ban.

It would be unfair, however, to judge the Bulgarian nation by the misdeeds of some of its members or by the passing temper of the moment. With all their faults, and in spite of all their trials and temptations, the peasant statesmen have achieved great triumphs during the comparatively brief period of their country's existence as a practically independent state. Roads have been improved; railways constructed; bridges built. The capital has been remodelled, until the traveller can scarcely recognise in the stuccoed Sofia of to-day the squalid Turkish village of twenty years ago. The old feeling of hatred towards the Turks has all but died away; and, though we still hear of occasional outrages upon Mohammedans, the "Bulgarian atrocities" of 1876, and the subsequent reprisals during the war have left no traces behind. The migration of the Mussulman inhabitants is deplored by the Government, because it deprives the country of a source of prosperity, and at the last census, out of a total population of considerably over three millions, scarcely more than half a million were Turks. But it is upon the Bulgarians themselves that the future of the nation depends. Sir Frank Lascelles told them when he was British representative at Sofia that they possessed more common-sense than any other people whom he knew. Sternly practical, thrifty, and without wild ideals, they may not be the most attractive of the Balkan races; but they possess qualities which must tell in the long run, and which should one day secure them, under proper Government, the foremost place in the history of the Peninsula.

PART III.

SERVIA.

> "On Kossovo lay the headless body;
> But the eagles touched it not, nor ravens,
> Nor the foot of man, nor hoof of courser."
> BOWRING, *Servian Popular Poetry*.

> "Of all the Balkan peoples, the most important and the most powerful were the Serbs: they seemed to have a great destiny before them; but this brave, poetic, careless, frivolous race never attempted to assimilate the remains of ancient culture, and incurred the hatred of the Catholic West and the penalty of isolation."—DE LA JONQUIÈRE, *Histoire de l'Empire Ottoman*.

I.

ORIGIN AND EARLY HISTORY OF THE SERBS.
(TO A.D. 1336.)

THE people known as Serbs did not always inhabit the country which now bears their name. The ancient Greek geographer, Ptolemy, mentions them as living on the banks of the river Don, to the north-east of the Sea of Azov. Other authorities believe that their primitive home is to be found in the regions adjoining the Carpathians, where we hear of Serbs at the period just previous to their immigration into the Balkan lands. It is probable that in the second and third centuries of the Christian era small, scattered colonies of Serbs settled in the Peninsula; some of the colonists may have come from choice, others may have been brought there as prisoners of war. But it was not till the middle of the sixth century that they appeared in South-Eastern Europe in large numbers, plundering and ravaging the country south of the Danube in all directions. The Greek Emperors of Constantinople, who at that time held the whole Peninsula as far as that river beneath their sway, were at first too much occupied with wars and invasions in other parts of their dominions to pay much heed to this new invasion of strangers. In fact, the Emperor Heraclius about the year 620 actually encouraged the Serbs to cross the Danube and settle on the right bank, in order that they might serve as a buffer against the assaults of a much more dangerous race, the Avars, who in the seventh century were the fiercest of all the Empire's barbarous foes. The Serbs were accordingly permitted to occupy a large tract of territory in the western part of the Peninsula. They displaced the old Illyrian inhabitants of the Adriatic coast, made the present city of Ragusa their capital, and stretched as far south as Macedonia, including what is now Montenegro in their settlements. Belgrade, the present Servian capital, belonged to them, but was not regarded as a place of much importance. Thus, by about 650 A.D., the Serbs had set their mark upon a considerable portion of the Balkan lands. Recognising the more or less nominal authority of the Greek Emperor, to whom they paid tribute, they lived under a government of their own, obeying their own chiefs and following their own customs. A Greek historian of the period expressly mentions that they "had the right of choosing their rulers, who governed them in patriarchal fashion." The names of these early chieftains have not been preserved. We are not told who headed the first great migration of the Serbs into the Peninsula, or who presided over their fortunes during the first two centuries after their coming. It is not till 830 that we hear of a prince or Grand *Župan*, of Servia, known as Voislav.

The constitution of the Serbs at this period seems to have closely resembled that of all the Slavonic nations. The Serbs have "the defects of their qualities," and the strong spirit of independence, which they have always shown, has caused a singular disinclination to unite under the sceptre of a monarch. Throughout Servian history we may trace the misfortunes of the race to this lack of union, just as its greatest glories are due to its love of freedom. At the dawn of their history their government was framed upon this idea. The people, instead of forming a compact nation under the guidance of one man, consisted of a number of tribes; at the head of each was a chief called by the name of *Župan*, derived from the word *župa*, which means a "district." These various *Župans* used to meet together in an assembly known as the *Skupchtina*, from a verb meaning "to assemble," for the purpose of choosing one of their number as Grand *Župan*, or prince. Thus we have a loose confederation of tribes, each ruled by a chieftain of its own, presided over by that chieftain who seemed to his colleagues the strongest and most capable, and who, in his turn, was nominally the vassal of the Greek Emperor at Constantinople. Each of the *Župans* enjoyed full independence in his own province, and in early times the authority of the Grand *Župan* over the rest of his fellows—for they hardly regarded him as their superior—was never very strict. In short, down to the accession of Stephen Nemanja in 1143, the Serbs formed a sort of aristocratic republic, a kind of government which exactly suited the national character.

Religion is inseparably intermingled with the political life of every Eastern nation, and no event was of such great importance for the Serbs as their conversion to Christianity. We have shown in the last part of this book how the Bulgarians were converted by the efforts of Constantine and Methodius, the two apostles of the Balkans. The same two eloquent preachers spread the tidings of the gospel among the idolatrous Serbs. Radoslav, who held the office of Grand *Župan* about the middle of the ninth century, adopted the new faith, his successor followed his example, and the people imitated the lead of its chiefs. Civilisation came with the Christian missionaries, and the savage customs which the Serbs had brought from their ancient home gradually disappeared. But the religion of peace did not make them forget those warlike pursuits to which they had been always addicted. It was at this period that we hear of the first war between the Serbs and their Bulgarian neighbours.

Just as in our own time the mutual jealousies of these two kindred races have helped to maintain the

Ottoman Power over a large part of the Peninsula, so a thousand years ago the same motives were fully appreciated by the Greek Emperors, who occupied the position which the Sultan now holds at Constantinople. From the latter part of the ninth century, when Vlastimir was head of the Servian Confederation, dates the long series of hostilities between the two countries, which, with varying fortune and con-

THE SERVIAN ARMS.

siderable intervals of peace, continued down to the subjugation of both races by the Turks, only to survive at the close of the nineteenth century after both had been emancipated. It was Presjam, predecessor of the Bulgarian hero, Boris, who began the attack which lasted for three years without any material advantage to either side. The river Timok, then, as now, the boundary between the two states, was presumably the principal theatre of the war, and the Serbs seem, on the whole, to have held their own in this first trial of strength. But Boris resolved to avenge this national defeat. He selected a moment when the Serbs were more than usually divided, owing to the partition of Vlastimir's power between his three sons, to fall upon them. But the three disputants sank their differences and defeated the invader, whose son was taken prisoner. Boris sued for peace, and subsequently assisted Muntimir, the eldest of the three Servian brothers, to secure the supremacy in his own land. For a considerable period the Serbs remained unmolested by their neighbours and at peace among themselves. The power of the Grand Župans was gradually consolidating, and two principles of government became noticeable—one, that, in order to avoid competition, a near relative of the last chief should be made head of the Confederation whenever a vacancy occurred; the other, that the residence of this ruler should be at Desnica.

The accession of Simeon to the Bulgarian throne was followed by disastrous results for the Servian race. The Grand Župan, Peter, had offended the mighty Bulgarian Czar by assisting his enemy, the Greek Emperor, against him. Egged on by one of the Confederate Servian chiefs, who was Peter's bitterest foe, the Bulgarian monarch despatched a large army against his neighbour. By means of a deceitful stratagem, the Bulgarian generals induced the unsuspecting Peter to visit their camp. No sooner had he arrived, than they put him under arrest and carried him off as a prisoner to their own land, where he died by the hand of an assassin about 917. In his place the conquerors set over the Servian people Paul Branković, a nephew of the former Servian prince Muntimir, whe had spent his life in banishment in Bulgaria, and had accompanied the Bulgarian army on its victorious march. But Paul did not prove to be a mere puppet. He took the earliest opportunity of showing his independence of Bulgarian dictation as well as of the Greek Emperor, his nominal suzerain. Unfortunately for him, a pretender appeared upon the scene in the person of Muntimir's grandson, Zacharia, whose claims were naturally supported by the indignant Greeks and Bulgarians. Paul easily defeated the former, but against the latter he was powerless. The Bulgarian Czar deposed his creature as easily as he had set him up, and Zacharia was speedily installed as ruler of the Servian stock, the chiefs accepting as law the will of the Bulgarian sovereign in their choice of a prince. But Simeon once more learnt that it was one thing to put a puppet on the throne and quite another to keep him subservient. Zacharia, like his predecessor, soon set Bulgarian tutelage at defiance. At first, his efforts were successful; the Bulgarian generals fell into his hands, and he sent their heads to his ally, the Greek Emperor, as a proof alike of his triumph and his allegiance. But Simeon took a terrible revenge. He was soon able to turn his individual attention to Servia, and in a single battle overthrew the power of Zacharia. The defeated ruler fled for ever from his country, which was ravaged as it had never been ravaged before. All the towns became the booty of the victorious army. Many of the inhabitants fled, like their prince, to Croatia; their land, to use the phrase of an old writer, "had become one vast, gloomy, uninhabited forest." Travellers who visited the country about this period could discover "no more than fifty vagrants, without women or children, who extracted a precarious subsistence from the chase." While the first Bulgarian Empire was at its zenith, Servia was almost blotted out from the map. It was the first instance of that historical see-saw between the two adjoining Balkan states which has lasted ever since: when one is up, the other is down; what one gains is usually at the expense of the other.

To Česlav, the son of Paul Branković, whom the Bulgarians had carried away into captivity, belongs the honour of restoring the might of the Servian name. When Simeon died, and the power of his Empire began to wane, Česlav made his escape from his confinement and sought the aid of the Greek Emperor against their mutual foe. Following his traditional policy of playing off one Balkan race against another, the Emperor consented, and Česlav returned to Servia sure of his support. The scattered Serbs flocked to his side, and Česlav was elected as their head. He speedily drove out the Bulgarians, while he had the tact to show himself the grateful and devoted vassal of the Greek Empire, whose nominal authority he was not strong enough to throw off. From this period, about 950, down to the early years of the eleventh century, there is a complete gap in the Servian records. We hear of a certain "just, pacific, and virtuous prince," John Vladimir, who, although defeated by the great Bulgarian Czar Samuel, was fortunate enough to win his conqueror's friendship and the hand of his daughter. But he was brutally murdered by John Vladislav, the last of the early Bulgarian Czars in 1015, and his name is still cherished in Albania as that of a saint. But the Bulgarians did not hold Servia for long. Three years later their supremacy succumbed to the

Greek Emperor, and with them the Serbs too became the subjects of the same ruler. It is not till 1040 that we find Servia once more free. The author of its freedom was a certain Stephen Voislav or Dobroslav, a chief of the sainted Vladimir's race, who escaped from his prison at Constantinople and fled to his native fastnesses among the rocks of Montenegro. From this mountain eyrie he swooped down upon the rich argosies of Constantinople, which passed to and fro along the Adriatic, while he annihilated an army which was sent against him in the narrow defiles of the limestone rocks. A simultaneous rising of the Bulgarians against their Greek masters strengthened his hands, and even when Bulgaria once more fell beneath the imperial sway, the Serbs maintained their hard-won independence. So great were the disasters which befell the Emperor's troops, that Byzantine writers could only explain them by the appearance of a comet. The earliest Servian composition extant, a chronicle by an anonymous priest of Dioclea in Montenegro, dwells with pardonable pride and Oriental exaggeration upon these victories of the national arms. What became of Dobroslav, we are not told; but about 1050 his son, Michael Voislavić, succeeded him, and reigned uninterruptedly for thirty years. His reign is remarkable for the first evidence of political and ecclesiastical relations between the Serbs and the Italians. We find Pope Gregory VII. addressing Michael by the title of "king," and sending him a consecrated banner. Fear of the Normans prompted the Servian prince to seek the protection of the Holy See, and political reasons had quite as much to do with his conversion from the Greek to the Roman faith as religious scruples. But the union with Rome was not lasting, and any hopes which Gregory may have had of bringing the Serb race permanently under the papal authority were doomed to failure. With the Greek Emperor there was peace during a great part of Michael's reign, and that prince was content to hold certain honorary posts in the official hierarchy of Constantinople. But later on he abetted the Bulgarians in an abortive revolt, which aimed at placing his son Bodin on the Bulgarian throne, and captured the important harbour of Durazzo on the Adriatic from the Greeks. His son extended his conquests, and at the beginning of the twelfth century the power of the Serbs had made itself felt. But it was with the accession of Stephen Nemanja, which is variously fixed at 1143 or 1159, that the greatness of mediæval Servia really began. This able man descended from a princely family of Dioclea, where the Servian rulers had taken up their residence, founded a new dynasty which was called after his name. He could truly boast that he was "no less a man than his forefathers," for he governed all the territory that they had ever possessed, and more besides. He united Bosnia to Servia in 1169, and humbled all the chieftains beneath him, founded many churches and monasteries, and persecuted those who did not follow the tenets of the orthodox Greek Church. But it was long before he succeeded in making much headway against the Greek Emperor, who was still the suzerain of Servia. While Manuel Comnenus sat upon the throne of Constantinople, rebellion was useless. After twice attempting to throw off his allegiance, the Servian prince came to the Emperor's camp with bare feet and arms, a halter round his neck, and his drawn sword pointed to the earth, in token of submission. He became the ally of his liege lord against the Venetians, and received as a reward the district of Rascia, the modern Novibazar, which separates Servia from Montenegro. But when Manuel died in 1180, Nemanja at once availed himself of the weakness of the Empire to extend his power. Pristina became his capital, Nisch was added to his dominions, which were now double of what they had been at his accession. He refused to pay tribute any longer, and in 1185 proclaimed his complete independence and assumed the title of "King of Servia," but was never crowned. The attempts of the Emperor to reduce him to his former position of a vassal failed, and the Greeks were compelled to sue for peace. Nemanja now treated the Emperor as an equal, and the marriage of his son with the daughter of his former suzerain showed that Servia was no longer a subordinate state. It is curious to see the desire which he showed for a closer friendship with the German Emperor, Frederick Barbarossa, who was then setting out on the third crusade. Nemanja despatched a Servian embassy to Germany and offered Barbarossa a free passage through his dominions and his best town to rest in by the way. An ancient writer has expressed the utter astonishment which this offer created in Germany, where the very name of Servia was at that time unknown; in fact, the common opinion was that it was situated between Russia and Hungary! Barbarossa, however, came to Belgrade, where Nemanja met him, and the two monarchs held numerous friendly conversations. Tired of the world and satiated with his conquests, Nemanja resolved to devote the evening of his days to the exercises of religion. In 1195 he abdicated in favour of his eldest son, who, like all the Servian kings, bore the name of Stephen, which, from its literal meaning of a "crown," had come to mean "the man who is crowned." This done, Nemanja retired to the monastery of Chilander, which he had founded on Mount Athos. He died five years later under the name of Simeon, which he had adopted when he became a monk. His youngest son, who had already retired to a cloister on the Holy Mount, is known as the first Archbishop of Servia, and was canonised as St. Sava. He played a very important part in the history of his time and exercised a great influence upon the Servian people. It was owing to his efforts that the Greek patriarch of Constantinople allowed the Serbs to elect an archbishop from among the members of their own priesthood, and he cast a halo over the Servian crown which made the nation respect it as they had never respected it before. Sava crowned his eldest brother Stephen with his own hands in the midst of a great assembly, and cried aloud, "Long live the first-crowned king and autocrat of Servia, Stephen." And all the people cried "Amen," and repeated the Creed after the fashion of the Eastern Church. From that moment Stephen Uroš bore the title of "the first-crowned," for he was the first of his race who was solemnly anointed king. From that moment, too, the supremacy of the Eastern Church was established in Servia. Pope Innocent III. made strenuous efforts to induce Stephen to enter the Catholic fold. But his arguments were in vain, and Servia remained attached to the Eastern communion.

The reign of Stephen Uroš was of great benefit to the Servian nation. Essentially a pacific ruler, the sovereign devoted his whole attention to the consolidation of the dominions which his father had conquered. He never once voluntarily drew the sword during the quarter of a century for which he sat on the throne, but founded monasteries and strengthened the internal organisation of the country. The earliest Servian coins date from this period and bear his superscription. By means of alliances with the Bulgarians and the Greek Emperor, he greatly raised the position of Servia abroad, and when the Latin conquest of Constantinople placed the Emperor Baldwin on the throne, one of his first acts was to recognise Stephen Uroš as "independent king of Servia, Dalmatia, Bosnia," and other adjoining districts.

But this union of Bosnia and Dalmatia with the Servian crown brought down upon the peace-loving Stephen the enmity of Andrew II., King of Hungary. Hitherto Servia and Hungary had been separated from one another, except at one point, by a "buffer state," consisting of Bosnia, the Herzegovina and Dalmatia. But when these territories were merged in the new Servian kingdom, the two rivals were brought face to face. Andrew II. stirred up Stephen's second brother, Vouk, against him, promising to make him an independent prince. But St. Sava once more appeared on the scene as the good angel of Servia, and reconciled the two brothers. The Hungarian monarch's attempt failed, and the reign of Stephen Uroš ended peacefully in 1224. His two sons, Stephen III. and Ladislas, who succeeded him at brief intervals upon the throne, left comparatively little mark on the history of their country. The elder of the two rounded off his dominions to the east and west by the capture of the important town of Vidin from the Bulgarian Czars—a place which has always been an object of discord between the two nations—and by the addition of Syrmia, the district between the Save and the Danube, which was ceded to Servia by the King of Hungary. But Stephen III. was compelled by a mental malady to resign, and his younger brother, Ladislas, abandoned the Bulgarian conquest on his marriage with the daughter of Asên, the great Czar. Peace, however, was established by means of this matrimonial alliance between the rival nationalities, to the great advantage of both. Ladislas availed himself of the opportunity to improve the education of his people, to make laws and encourage commerce. The Servian mines, of which much has lately been written, date from his reign. Ladislas, like Milosh six hundred years later, sent to Germany for mining experts to report on the mineral wealth of Servia, and the roads and excavations which are found at the present day show that at an early period attempts were made to develop the natural resources of the country.

A third brother of the last two sovereigns followed them on the throne in 1237, under the title of Stephen IV., surnamed "the Great." Stephen IV. was a wise and prudent monarch, a lover of peace like his father, and a patron of schools and such learning as there was. Ably seconded by his French wife, Helena, a niece of the first Latin Emperor of Constantinople, he laboured hard for the civilisation of his warlike people. But he could not escape the terrible inroads of the Mongols, which threatened the kingdom of Hungary with destruction, and were a grave source of danger to Servia as well. Stephen gave the Hungarian king a refuge in his domains, and thus called down upon himself the vengeance of the barbarian hordes. In a great battle the Serbs and Dalmatians drove them back to Spalato, but on their way home bands of stragglers traversed Servia and levied blackmail upon its unfortunate inhabitants. Freed from these marauders, Stephen found a greater source of trouble in the rebellious spirit of his eldest son. Not content to wait until his father's crown descended to him, the heir-apparent intrigued with the ungrateful King of Hungary, whose daughter he had married. The old King Stephen refused to resign, whereupon his son marched into Servia at the head of a Hungarian army, deposed his father and put the crown on his own head, assuming the title of Stephen V. The aged monarch, abandoned by his retainers and naturally a man of peace, accepted his fate, and lived, till his death in 1272, as a subject of his treacherous son. But the young king did not long enjoy his ill-gotten title. Stung by remorse, and believing himself to be the object of divine vengeance, he abdicated in 1275, and his brother took his place under the style of Stephen VI. With him begins what may be called the "great century" of the Servian kingdom, when Servia became the dominant factor in Balkan politics and enjoyed an influence such as she has never possessed either before or since. The events of the long reign of Stephen VI. led up to the culmination of Servia's power under the greatest of all her monarchs, Stephen Dušan.

The first gains of Servia were made at the expense of the Greek Empire, which the Serbs were now strong enough to despise. During the war between the Emperor Michael Paleologus and the Bulgarians in 1278, the Byzantine troops violated the territory of the Servian monarch. Stephen VI. was not the man to suffer such an insult without a protest, and when he found that his protests were unavailing he sent an army to protect his frontiers. The Greek Emperor swore that he would "sweep him off the face of the earth," and as soon as he had made peace with the Bulgarians, set out in 1282 to carry out his vow of vengeance. His sister had been affianced at his desire to the Servian king, at a time when he was not yet on the throne. But the Byzantine princess, accustomed to the luxury of Constantinople, took such a dislike to the monotony and simplicity of life at the Servian Court of Pristina, that she refused to marry its future master. The Emperor laid the whole blame of his sister's refusal upon Stephen, who, however, was a Lothario rather than an ascetic. The tales which are told of his private life certainly do not accord with the patriarchal manners and primitive virtues which usually prevailed in the Royal family of mediæval Servia. But, whatever were the motives of the Greek Emperor, he was destined to fail in his designs. Stephen at once convoked an Assembly of his chieftains, and, encouraged by their support, assumed the offensive against his antagonist. All the strongholds of the Empire along the valley of the Vardar fell into the hands of the Serbs, while

CORONATION-CHURCH OF THE OLD SERVIAN CZARS.

Michael Palcologus, delayed by stress of weather and the state of his own health, was powerless to save his Macedonian possessions. The whole nation was in arms against the Greek Emperor; even Stephen's elder brother, who had abdicated, contributed his services to the common cause. But, before the motley army of many nationalities and creeds which the

Greek Emperor had gathered together could come to close quarters with the Serbs, Michael himself was no more. "God," says the old Servian historian, Archbishop Danilo, "allowed him not so much as to see Servia even from afar." He had only advanced three days' journey from Constantinople when he died, leaving his successor, Andronicus II., to carry on the war. But Andronicus was too much occupied with theological controversies to attend to the less important business of defending his Empire. Stephen continued to pursue his victorious course unchecked, Macedonia lay at his feet, and he penetrated to the shores of the Ægean and set up his standard on the holy mount of Athos, where his great ancestor, Stephen Nemanja, had died. For some years this desultory warfare went on, until at last the Greek Emperor sued for peace. Not desiring to occupy the whole of Macedonia, the Serbs contented themselves with retaining the frontier fortresses as a bulwark of their realm. For the rest of his long reign, Stephen VI. had nothing to fear from the Byzantine rulers. On the contrary, Andronicus was reduced to beg his aid against a new and terrible enemy, who was destined to overthrow both the Greek Empire and the Servian Kingdom by the middle of the following century.

The power of the Turks, of whom we now hear for the first time in connection with Servian history, had grown at the beginning of the fourteenth century to be a standing menace to the Greek Empire. In 1301 Andronicus implored the assistance of his former adversary Stephen, and, after the fashion of the time, proposed to the Servian monarch a matrimonial alliance between the two houses as a precursor of a political union. Stephen was at the moment a widower and had no particular objection to a Byzantine marriage, strenuously though this was resisted by many of his friends. They foresaw that the introduction of a Greek princess into the Servian Court would infallibly lead to those feminine intrigues in which the ladies of the Imperial family were adepts. But Stephen refused to listen to his advisers; and the marriage between himself and the Greek Emperor's daughter Simonis, who was no less than thirty-four years younger than her husband, was celebrated with great pomp at Salonica. Before many years had passed, the Servian sovereign had good cause to rue that day.

He lost no time in performing his promise to his Imperial father-in-law and assisting him against the Turks. A Serb army crossed into Asia Minor, and in 1303 their efforts drove back the Ottoman invaders. Covered with glory, the victorious Serbs returned to their own land. But the danger which menaced the Greek Empire had been only temporarily averted. Twelve years later Andronicus once more applied to Stephen for help. The Servian army entered Thrace and swept the Turks into the sea. Few of the Ottoman soldiers escaped with their lives, none regained their liberty. Twice had Servian arms saved the Byzantine Empire. No less successful was the short campaign against the Bulgarians, who invaded Servia with a body of Tartar allies. The Archbishop called forth the people and led them in person. His efforts prevailed; the Bulgarians were defeated, and compelled by King Stephen, who had now come up, to beg for peace. From this time dates the removal of the archiepiscopal see of Servia from Ušica, on the river Morava, to Ipek, in what is now called Old Servia and no longer part of the Servian Kingdom.

Fortunate in his foreign policy, Stephen VI. was most unhappy in his domestic affairs. His Greek wife, Simonis, intrigued, on behalf of her son Constantine, whom she wished to see as her husband's successor instead of her stepson Stephen, who was the heir-apparent. The Queen was supported by the members of her own family, who wanted a tool of their own as King of Servia ; the claims of Stephen, the rightful heir, found champions among the nobility and priesthood of Servia, who had from the first feared Greek interference. Urged by them, the heir-apparent declared civil war. But the King succeeded in dispersing his eldest son's followers without bloodshed, and the penitent heir returned to the palace and asked forgiveness. But his crafty stepmother, fearing lest he should prevail upon his father to reinstate him in his former position, procured his arrest. This done, she ordered his eyes to be put out, and sent him in chains for safe keeping to her father, who threw him into a Greek monastery. But the orders of the savage queen had been only half executed. After seven years of imprisonment her stepson reappeared in his father's kingdom with eyesight unimpaired. The people believed that a miracle had taken place, and ascribed the marvellous restoration of the prince's sight to the intervention of a saint. But the executioner entrusted with the work of blinding him had only pretended to perform his odious task. He had held the hot plate of metal, which was used for the purpose, at so great a distance from the prisoner's eyes that they had not been injured. The treacherous designs of the Queen had thus been frustrated. The Serb clergy, whose leader, Archbishop Danilo, the chronicler of his times, had procured the release of the heir-apparent, resolved to place their favourite upon the throne. The national party, which had been formed to resist the insidious influence of the Greeks, carried the day, and when the old king died in 1321, the clergy at once proclaimed his eldest son king under the title of Stephen VII., to which he added the surname of Uroš.

His first act was to subdue his half-brother Constantine, who attempted to dispute his right to the throne. But the removal of his rival did not bring peace to the land. The short reign of Stephen VII. is one uninterrupted succession of wars with the King of Hungary, the Bulgarian Czar, and the Greek Emperor, in which the Servian monarch met with invariable success. Instigated by the Bulgarians, the ambitious Hungarian sovereign attacked the Wallachs, who were allies of the Serbs. Stephen VII. crossed the Danube to the relief of his friends, and inflicted an overwhelming defeat upon the Hungarian troops. He then turned his arms against the Bulgarian Czar Michael, who had mortally offended him by divorcing his sister Neda, and sending her and her son Alexander back to Servia. We have described in the second part of the book the terrible disaster which befell the Bulgarian army on the fatal field of Velbužd on the 28th of June, 1330. The Bulgarian Czar fell and his Empire with him. The Serbs did not, indeed, incorporate Bulgaria with their own country, but they took care to keep a tight hold upon its government. Stephen put his sister as regent on the Bulgarian throne for her son Alexander, and for the next generation Bulgaria followed the lead of Servia and recognised the practical supremacy of the Servian kings. Time had, indeed, brought its revenge; the Servian domination over Bulgaria in the fourteenth century was the compensation for the Bulgarian influence over Servia in the tenth and eleventh.

The Hungarian and Bulgarian victories of Stephen Uroš were followed by a successful campaign against the Greek Emperor, which led to the annexation of half Macedonia. But the conqueror committed the mistake of his father and became entangled in the wiles of the Byzantine Court. If any man had had a sad experience of Greek alliances, that man was Stephen 'Uroš. Yet he chose a second wife from among the Byzantine princesses. No sooner had the fair Greek borne him a son than she began to plot against her stepson, Stephen, afterwards known as Dušan, the most famous name in Servian history. The latter took up arms against his father and fortified himself in Montenegro against the Royal troops. The struggle between father and son, which had already been the greatest blot upon the pages of Servian history, once more began. Backed by the nobles, who were jealous of Greek influence, the heir-apparent besieged his sire in his own residence and compelled him to surrender. It is said that he was ready to spare his father's life, but that his partisans urged him to secure the throne by a parricide. The old king was imprisoned in a castle, and there strangled by his son's minions in 1336. With the death rattle in his throat, he cursed his cruel child and all his house. Attempts have been made to extenuate the crime; but nothing can palliate it before the tribunal of posterity. The murderer's horrible deed is branded in letters of blood in the annals of his country, for from that moment he received the surname of *Dušan*, or "the throttler," from the Serb verb *dušiti*, which means to "suffocate." In vain did Dušan endeavour to atone for his crime by building countless churches and convents. His father's curse was fulfilled, not in the days of Dušan but in succeeding generations, and the mighty Empire, which he founded, fell to pieces when its founder was no more.

The first period of Servian history is over. We have seen the gradual development of the Servian monarchy out of a loose federation of chiefs owing nominal obedience to the Greek Emperor. We have traced the struggles of the Servian rulers with their Bulgarian rivals and their Byzantine suzerains. With the accession of Stephen Dušan in 1336 begins the golden age of the old Servian monarchy.

II.

THE ZENITH OF SERVIA UNDER STEPHEN DUŠAN.

(1336—1356.)

THE reign of Stephen Dušan is the apotheosis of the South Slavonic race. Never has the power of Servia been so great or the Servian dominions so vast as under the sway of this mighty ruler, who raised his country to the rank of an Empire, equipped it with a complete code of laws and made it respected and honoured all over Eastern Europe. With excusable pride the Servian patriots of to-day look back to the age of Dušan as the most glorious epoch of their national history, and regard that monarch, with all his faults, as a national hero. The memories of his exploits inspire some ardent enthusiasts with the desire to revive the ancient splendour of his sovereignty, and the "great Servian idea," which from time to time threatens to disturb the peace of the Balkans, is based upon the expansion of Servia under his auspices. When King Milan declared war on Bulgaria in 1885, it was with shouts of "Dušan" that his soldiers set out from Belgrade.

Stephen Dušan was little more than twenty when his father's murder left him in undisturbed possession of the throne. Tall of stature and of a fine presence, he had early proved himself to be a leader of men. When quite a boy he had commanded a wing of the Servian army at the great battle which laid the Bulgarian Empire in the dust, and one account states that he slew the Bulgarian Czar with his own hand. The devotion of his followers to his person was only equalled by the terror of his enemies at his approach. When he once asked his nobles whether he should lead them against the Greeks or the Germans, they at once replied, " Whithersoever thou goest, most glorious prince, we will follow." The Byzantine chroniclers compare his career of conquest to a raging fire or the course of a river in flood. Even the wild Albanians were docile at his command, and rich and cultured communities like Ragusa were proud to own him as their protector. In his double capacity of conqueror and lawgiver, he presents more than one analogy with Napoleon, and his Empire rose and fell with a rapidity which recalls the meteoric flight of the great French Emperor.

Dušan did not commence with any cut-and-dried plan for making himself master of the Eastern world. One of his conquests led to another, until at last he conceived the idea of making Constantinople itself the seat of his government and putting its feeble rulers beneath his feet. His first and most pressing need was an outlet on the Ægean, and the struggle between the Greek Empire and the Turks gave him an opportunity of gaining his object. Entering

Macedonia, he penetrated as far as the Gulf of Volo, and besieged the Emperor Andronicus III. in Salonica. Andronicus obtained peace by the sacrifice of most of the territory which Dušan had conquered. By the treaty of 1340 the Servian monarch obtained such large acquisitions that his dominions stretched from

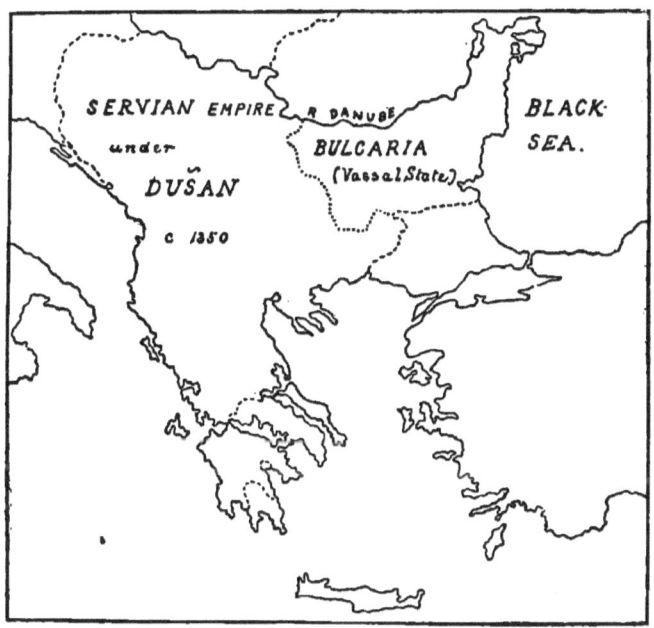

SERVIA UNDER DUŠAN.
c. 1350.

the Danube to the Gulf of Corinth and from the Adriatic to within a short distance of Adrianople. When it is remembered that, in addition to this huge tract of country, Bulgaria was practically under his control, it will be seen by a glance at the map that he was master of the Balkan Peninsula from sea to sea. Here and there a few coast towns, like Salonica and Durazzo, held out against him, but the Byzantine possessions had shrunk to nothing as compared with his mighty realm. Filled with pride, the conqueror comported himself like an Eastern Emperor. He modelled his Court on that at Constantinople, distributed honorary offices to his most distinguished generals, and created an order of merit which he called by the name of St. Stephen. But he had not learnt the great secret of keeping an empire together. He divided his dominions into provinces, each under the government of a powerful chieftain. In this arrangement it is easy to detect the cause of Servia's brief supremacy. So long as there was a strong man like Dušan at the head of this composite state, all went well ; but it needed no gift of prophecy to foresee the inevitable dissensions which would break out whenever his iron hand was withdrawn. When it was attacked later on by an enemy, like the Turks, absolutely united under the authority of one man, the loosely constructed Servian Empire fell.

John Cantacuzene, who had acted as Regent of the Greek Empire during the minority of young John Paleologus, usurped sovereign power in 1341, and, finding no support at Constantinople, retreated to seek the aid of Dušan. Stephen received him in his Court at Pristina with the most elaborate ceremonial and the most profuse hospitality, but declined to assist his distinguished guest except upon his own terms. To his credit it must be said, that the Servian monarch magnanimously rejected the offer of the

Greek Empress Anne, who professed herself willing to divide the Greek Empire with him, on condition that he would rid her and her son of their hated rival. She even sent him the poison for the purpose, and urged him to use it. But Dušan's wife, Helena, pleaded for the life of the guest. Her husband made an alliance with Cantacuzene and assisted him for a time ; but mutual suspicions soon alienated the allies, and Cantacuzene did not hesitate to invoke the aid of the Turks against his former host. At this, Dušan changed sides in the civil war, and joined his arms to those of the Empress Anne and the Bulgarians. In 1346 he for the first time adopted the Imperial title —Imperial power he had long enjoyed—and styled himself " Emperor of the Greeks and Servians." Upon his son he conferred the title of King or *Kral*, which he and his predecessors had borne since the days of Stephen Nemanja. On his head he wore a tiara ; on his coins, minted at Cattaro, we see him seated on a throne, with the orb surmounted by a cross in his hand. In the East the dignity of an Emperor implies as its ecclesiastical counterpart that of a Patriarch. Dušan assembled the clergy of his Empire together with that of Bulgaria in a Synod, and bade them elect an independent Servian Patriarch. Servia was free in things spiritual no less than in things temporal from the Greeks. The first duty of the Patriarch was to crown his sovereign as Emperor at Skopje, in the midst of a brilliant gathering. So great was his fame, that the proud Commonwealth of Venice conferred the title of patrician upon him.

The conclusion of the civil war, which had rent the

Byzantine Empire in twain, checked the successes of Dušan over the Greeks. Cantacuzene won back from him a considerable part of Macedonia, and in 1350 negotiations for peace began. Cantacuzene demanded Thessaly in addition to what he had already recovered. But Dušan refused to be bound by these proposals, which he had at first felt inclined to accept. Once more the rivalry of Cantacuzene and young Palcologus, whose guardian he was, gave the Servian Emperor a chance of recovering his territory. But the arrival of a Turkish army at Adrianople altered the whole condition of affairs, and from that moment to the last year of his reign he engaged in no further campaigns against the Greeks.

On the West, however, he found ample compensation for his later reverses in the East. Louis the Great of Hungary was anxious to avenge the defeat of his father by the Servians under Stephen VII., and was filled with jealousy of Dušan's power. In spite of Venetian intervention—for peace was the greatest interest of the commercial Republic of St. Mark—Louis crossed the Save and took up a position in Bosnia. Dušan suddenly appeared with a large army in front of the Hungarian King, who retreated beyond the Save with considerable loss. In order to keep his dominions secure from a repetition of this attack, Dušan pretended to have qualms of conscience, and sent a royal messenger to the Pope with fulsome promises. But as soon as he found that the King of Hungary was quiet, he threw off the mask and disavowed all intention of becoming a faithful son of Rome. One result of his victory over Louis was the incorporation of Belgrade, previously a part of the Hungarian kingdom, with Servia. Another was his subjugation of Bosnia, which had maintained its independence under rulers of its own, called *Bans*, for many years, and had then fallen under the sway of Hungary. In 1350 it passed to Dušan, together with the sister province of the Herzegovina, which had in early days been Servian, but had been united with Bosnia since 1325. This rounded off the great Empire over which Dušan reigned. The zenith of Servia was attained.

But the Servian Emperor knew that peace had her victories no less than war. Constant as were his campaigns, he yet found time to draw up a complete code of law for his subjects, based upon the national characteristics of the Southern Slavs. This code, promulgated in 1349, is still preserved, and throws a curious light upon the manners and customs of the Serbs at this period. As becomes a " Christian Macedonian Czar"—so the lawgiver styles himself in the preamble—Stephen begins by prescribing for the good government of the Servian Church. " Latin heretics " are to be sent to work in " the deepest mines " or else banished, and any " Latin Priest " found proselytising is sentenced to death. Provision is made for the establishment of an ecclesiastical court, and civil marriages are strictly prohibited. We recognise at once the aristocratic basis of mediæval Servian society in the unequal positions of nobles and peasants in the eye of the law. To kill a peasant is a much slighter offence than to kill a noble ; to pluck a chieftain's beard means the loss of a hand ;

DUŠAN'S CODE.   279

to pluck that of a common man costs nothing more than a small fine. But the Czar was careful to protect the merchants who travelled through his dominions. None of his subjects, however exalted

FORTRESS OF UŠICA.

in station, might detain a trader by force or take his money, and the Czar's officials were bidden to grant every facility for the sale of goods. This was quite in keeping with the enlightened policy which attracted the merchants of Ragusa to the country by mineral concessions, and thus introduced the superior culture of the Dalmatian coast-towns far into the interior of the Peninsula. When a wandering trader arrived in a Servian village at night, it was the bounden duty of the chief man to give him food and lodging in his house or else pay for all that he required outside. And if robbers fell upon him, he could make complaint to the Czar, who would exact punishment from the guardians of the peace. The most stringent enactments for the suppression of brigandage are to be found in the code; the chief inhabitants in each town and village are held personally responsible for the public safety. Drunken assaults were punished with a sound beating, and coiners of false money were burnt alive. Judges were appointed to go on circuit throughout the land, and advocates forbidden to "abuse the plaintiff's attorney." In short, the great Czar had an eye for the smallest as well as the most important affairs of state, and his code, stern though it was, shows that his country was governed according to fixed principles and not by arbitrary rules. The law-book, or *Zakonik*, of 1349 was far superior to the jurisprudence of most Eastern countries of that period.

Dušan was not only a lawgiver, but a patron of literature and learning. He increased the number of schools and welcomed foreign scholars at his court, as well as native historians like Archbishop Danilo, who has painted his portrait in flattering colours. Like his father before him, he encouraged the building of churches and the multiplication of religious books. His finances must have been well managed, for he could afford to have French, German, and Italian mercenaries in his pay, to whom his successes were not a little due.

Meanwhile the Byzantine Empire was tottering before the attacks of the Turks, who had crossed into Europe and were rapidly reducing the Imperial dominions to a single city. Dušan knew the weakness of the Greeks and the strength of the Turks, and conceived the bold idea of ousting the former from their capital and reigning there himself as Eastern Emperor. He believed that no other sovereign could beat back the tide of Ottoman invasion, and he looked with longing eyes on Constantinople, then as now the cynosure of Slavonic aspirations. It was a magnificent scheme, and had it succeeded the whole course of European history would have been changed. New blood would have been infused into the decrepit frame of the Eastern Empire, and a strong and vigorous race might have held the city of Constantine against the Ottoman foe. Dušan made his preparations on a scale commensurate with his great enterprise. He summoned his chieftains together from every part of his vast realm on the feast of St. Michael, 1356. First of all, the holy festival was kept with prayer and praise; then the Czar took the banner of the Servian Empire in his hand and addressed the throng. The utmost enthusiasm greeted his appeal, and an army of 80,000 men was soon at his disposal. Never before had a Servian prince commanded so large a force or started on a campaign with such hopes of success. The feeble Paleologus, who occupied the Byzantine throne, made little attempt at resistance. Thrace with Adrianople fell; the advanced guard of the Serb host reached the outskirts of Constantinople. There was treachery within the gates, for a considerable portion of the garrison was known to side with Dušan. But, just at the moment when the prize was within his grasp, the Servian conqueror succumbed himself. On December 18, 1356, he was suddenly seized with a violent fever at the village of Diavoli, some forty miles from Constantinople, and expired the same night in the arms of his trusty comrades. His sudden death has been attributed to poison, secretly administered by the instructions of Paleologus. There is no direct proof of this theory, but the event certainly benefited the Greek Emperor, and the use of poisons was frequent at the Byzantine Court. Cut off in the full possession of all his powers—for he was not yet fifty—Dušan might, with his vigorous constitution, have had a long and glorious career before him. The expedition, which he had led, came to an end with his death. Constantinople was saved from the Serbs; and instead of following their sovereign in triumph through the gates of the Imperial city, the sorrowing chieftains escorted his dead body to the monastery which he had built at Prisrend. The might of the Servian Empire lay buried with him. The decline of the nation, which he had made so great, had already begun.

III.

THE DECLINE AND FALL OF SERVIA.

(1356—1459.)

BEFORE he died, Dušan had made his generals swear allegiance to his only son, Uroš V., at that time a lad of nineteen. But they did not keep their word for long. Weak in character and pacific by disposition, the young Czar was not the man to keep in order the turbulent grandees whom the strong arm of his father had subordinated to the throne. The system of dividing the Empire into provinces, each under a chief of its own, which Dušan had adopted, lessened the authority of his successor. Domestic quarrels, as usual, were the bane of the Servian Court, and the worst foes of young Uroš were his mother and his uncle. The recent conquests of Dušan had not been thoroughly welded together with the older Servian lands, and were naturally the first to go. Thessaly declared itself independent; the warlike Albanians, who had recognised Dušan as their Prince, broke away from the Serb Empire after his death; the vassal state of Bulgaria recovered its former position; Belgrade, the future capital of Servia, was recaptured by the King of Hungary; Bosnia, under the vigorous sway of Stephen Tvartko, the ablest of all her rulers, severed her connection with the Serbs, and Tvartko assumed the rank and style of royalty. A little later, in 1376, we even find him proclaiming himself "King of Servia, Bosnia, and the sea-coast," and avowing his intention of reviving the glories of Dušan.

Meanwhile, to the foes within there were added the foes without. The Turks had occupied Adrianople in 1360, and to mark the permanent character of their occupation, had transformed the seat of government to that city. They thus became near neighbours of the Serbs, who formed an alliance with their old enemy, Paleologus, against the common danger. The combined Greek and Servian army was defeated under the walls of Adrianople, and the battlefield retains to this day the name of the "Servian rout." This ignominious reverse increased the insubordination of the chieftains. Recognising that their Czar could not protect them, they resolved to protect themselves and each set up for himself in his own province, heedless of the central authority. One of their number, bolder than his fellows and forgetful of the benefits which Dušan had showered upon him, determined to depose his benefactor's son. Voukačin—for such was the usurper's name—wormed his way into the young Czar's confidence, and obtained from him the government of Dalmatia as a reward for his counsels. Uroš refused to believe that a relative and a friend could foster designs against his life and throne, and turned a deaf ear to the warnings of his courtiers. The arrival of Voukačin before his palace at Pristina at the head of an army found him unprepared to resist. The son of Dušan fled almost alone from his capital towards the mountains of Bosnia, but perished on the way by the hand, or at any rate the command, of his rival, in 1367. Such was the inglorious end of the great Serb conqueror's son and heir. Within little more than ten years after Dušan's death his Empire was dismembered and his child a fugitive.

The usurper did not long enjoy the fruits of his crime. The Turks, under the able leadership of Amurath I., one of the greatest generals of his time, continued their career of conquest. Their advance in the direction of Servia aroused Voukačin's fears for the safety of his throne. Summoning the chieftains together, he implored them to forget their dissensions and join him in a campaign against the Turkish conqueror. An army nearly as large as that which had followed Dušan on his last expedition was collected, and Voukačin believed himself to be the leader of a new crusade. At first his efforts were successful, and Amurath received a severe check on the spot, where a few years earlier the Serbs had been routed with such loss. But in the dead of night Amurath surprised the Servian camp and completely destroyed the army of the Christians. The flower of the Serb nobility perished either by the scimitars of the Turks or in the waters of the river Marica. Voukačin, after fighting with desperate courage, fled with a handful of retainers, one of whom murdered him for the sake of the gold chain which he wore. The news of the Servian defeat excited the greatest alarm all over Christendom. The Pope lamented loudly that nothing could withstand the onward march of the Turks. The Servians thought that the sole chance of their safety lay in the election of Lazar, a connection by marriage of Dušan's dynasty, in whose wars he had served with great distinction. Lazar, the last of the Servian Czars, ascended the throne in 1371 under gloomy circumstances. He did not deem it prudent to attack the victorious Turks until he had had time to recruit his scattered forces, and so quietly looked on while Macedonia gradually fell into their hands. But the warlike King of Hungary, instead of assisting his brother of Servia against the Ottoman armies, seized the opportunity of Servia's weakness to attack him. For the second time the Serbs repulsed his attempt; but there was little glory or satisfaction to be won from such a triumph at a time when all the Christian Powers of the East should have been banded together against the Crescent. When in 1386 the Turks invaded Servia and captured Nisch, the key of the whole country, Lazar found himself without allies, and, imitating the craven example of the Greek Emperor, purchased a disgraceful peace by promising to pay an annual tribute and to provide a thousand mercenaries for the Turkish armies. It was, indeed, a change since the days of Dušan.

But at last the Christian states of the Balkans, when too late, discovered that they must unite against the Ottoman power. Tvartko, King of

Bosnia, sent a detachment of soldiers to aid the Serbs; the Bulgarians created a diversion in favour of their neighbours; the Prince of the Zeta joined with the Servian monarch. In the fastnesses of the Black Mountain, where the Turks were in the coming centuries to receive so many fatal reverses, a body of Albanians and Serbs utterly routed the Ottoman force. Amurath I., who was celebrating his marriage in Asia Minor when the news reached him, vowed vengeance. Hurrying back to Europe, he collected an enormous army and marched against the Serbs. The battle, which was to decide for five centuries the fate of the Balkan Peninsula, was fought on the plain of Kossovo, the "field of blackbirds," as it is called in Serb, from the flocks of those creatures which frequent it. Kossovo is at the present day a part of the Turkish Empire, and gives its name to an Ottoman *vilayet* or province. Shut in by a chain of mountains, and of vast extent, the plain seemed intended by nature for an Armageddon of nations. Around this spot, the Waterloo of Balkan freedom, clusters a whole literature of patriotic ballads, from which it is no easy task to discern the true story of that fatal day. "Amurath," says one of the national bards, "had so many men that a horseman could not ride from one wing of his army to the other in a fortnight; the plain of Kossovo was one mass of steel; horse stood against horse, man against man; the spears form a thick forest; the banners obscure the sun, there was no space for a drop of water to fall between them." On the other side Serbs, Bosniaks, and Albanians were banded together in the common cause under Lazar's leadership. On the morning of June 15, 1389, the battle began. Amurath had hesitated at the last moment to attack the allied host, but a dream, in which the angel of victory had appeared to his most trusted counsellor and bade him "conquer the infidels," confirmed his wavering mind. The struggle was furious on both sides, and Lazar held his own against the Ottoman chivalry. But there was treachery in the Servian camp. Vouk Branković, to whom one wing of the Servian army had been entrusted, had long been jealous of his sovereign. It was said that he had already arranged with Amurath to betray his master, and had been promised the crown of Servia as a reward. The Turkish victory was the result of this "great betrayal." At a critical moment, when the future of the day was still undecided, the traitor turned his horse's head and rode off the field, followed by his detachment of 12,000 men. Lazar in vain attempted to sustain the contest against fearful odds. Slowly but surely the Turkish numbers told, and all was confusion in the Servian ranks. Lazar's horse stumbled and fell, and his rider expired beneath the blows of the Turkish soldiers. With him his nine brothers-in-law and the flower of the Servian aristocracy perished. The victory of the Turks would have been complete but for the death of their own sovereign in the hour of his triumph.

Amurath, it is said, was walking over the battlefield after the fight was over, when a wounded Serb, seeing the Sultan approach, crawled to his feet and pretended to make obeisance to him. Suddenly springing up, the man drew a dagger from under his garments and plunged it into the conqueror's breast. The Sultan had received his death wound, and his assassin, Milosh Obilić, after a desperate struggle, was slain by Amurath's guards. Another version of the Sultan's death is given by the Servian bards. According to them, Milosh, taunted with cowardice by the traitor Vouk on the eve of battle, had vowed to prove his loyalty by his conduct next day. Early in the morning he visited the Turkish camp, and prayed to be admitted as a deserter to the Sultan's tent. His request was granted, whereupon he smote the Turkish commander to the heart. To this day his name is held in honour by the national poets, while that of Vouk Branković has been handed down to perpetual infamy. But the assassination of Amurath I. had little practical result; for his son Bajazet I. was proclaimed his successor on the field of battle, and showed by the murder of his brother that there would be no division in the Turkish ranks. As for the traitor Vouk, he was poisoned a few years later by the Sultan's orders.

The battle of Kossovo has never been forgotten in the lands of the Southern Slavs. The most mournful songs of the Servian muse are inspired by the sad memories of that day. Whenever they have risen against the Turk, the cry of "revenge for Kossovo" has been emblazoned on their banners, and the Serbs of Montenegro still wear mourning on their caps for that fatal defeat. The Servian Empire had fallen for ever, though the Turks permitted rulers, or "despots," of Servia to exercise nominal power for seventy years longer. Many noble families fled to the fastnesses of Montenegro, and maintained their faith and freedom from the Ottoman conquerors amid the impenetrable recesses of the Black Mountain. Others migrated to Hungary, and formed those Serb colonies on the banks of the river Theiss from which, much later, succour came to Servia in her struggle for independence. A third body of emigrants found a home in Bosnia, whose rulers had not yet fallen beneath the sway of the all-conquering Turks.

The Sultan Bajazet did not pursue his conquests farther after the battle of Kossovo. His own army had suffered severely, and he permitted Stephen Lazarević, son of the dead Czar, to reign over Servia on condition that he became his vassal. Stephen promised to pay an annual tribute from the Servian silver mines, to relinquish the whole of Macedonia, to put at the service of his suzerain a body of Servian troops under the command of his younger brother Vouk, and to give to Bajazet the hand of his sister Mileva. The vanquished nation had no option but to accept these terms, and Stephen faithfully kept his promise as long as he lived. We find him fighting by the side of the Turks at the great battle of Angora in 1402, where Bajazet became the prisoner of Timour the Tartar. His intervention in favour of his Turkish brother-in-law at a critical moment at the great battle of Nicopolis in 1396 riveted the chains of the Bulgarians; his subjects joined the Turks in their attack upon Miretschea the Old of Wallachia. Thus, such strength as Servia still had was used on the side of her foes. Even more fatal was the marriage of Stephen's sister to Bajazet, for it provided the Turks with a claim, which they afterwards put forward, to the Servian throne. It was a humiliating position for Stephen and his people; but thus only could they retain even a shadow of independence.

The dissensions which broke out between the sons of Bajazet after his death, gave a further respite to Servia and Bosnia. Stephen availed himself of this opportunity to improve the internal condition of his country. Attempts have been made to depict him as the founder of constitutional government in Servia, and he is said to have created two legislative chambers, one composed of chiefs or nobles, the other representative of the people. This is an obvious anachronism; but it is clear that he divided his servants into three classes. The first class formed a sort of cabinet, which conferred with him in an inner room, and discussed the affairs of the realm; the second, in an adjoining department, acted as secretaries, and issued the orders of their superiors to the third class, whose duty it was to carry out those orders at once. It is upon this fact that the theory of a Servian constitution in the early years of the fifteenth century has been based. He secured the restoration of Belgrade by the Hungarians and made it his residence, strengthening it with fortifications and adorning it with fine buildings. Like most rulers of his house, he was a friend of the clergy, and his benevolence and simple life excited the admiration of monastic chroniclers.

But the mutual quarrels of Bajazet's heirs soon tempted the Serbs to intervene. Stephen's younger brother Vouk believed that, by making himself useful to one of the Turkish factions, he could obtain the Servian throne as a reward for himself. But he committed the mistake of choosing the losing side. The victorious faction visited his misdeeds upon his innocent brother, no less than on himself. A new Turkish invasion of Servia under Moussa in 1413 led to the defeat of the Serbs in the plain of Verbica and the loss of more territory on the upper waters of the Morava. But Moussa's rival, Mohammed I., enlisted the Servian "despot" on his side, and the latter assisted him to subdue all the Turkish factions and make himself Sultan. Mindful of the benefits which he had received from Stephen, he restored to the Serbs the territory which Moussa had so recently taken away, and confirmed Stephen in his government. But the tribute continued, and too late the Serbs discovered that by their action in helping Mohammed they had restored unity and strength to the Turkish Empire. In their desire to obtain a temporary advantage, they had permanently injured their own prospects of independence.

This became evident when Amurath II. became Sultan on Mohammed's death. Stephen Lazarević had died in 1427 without heirs, and had named George Branković, son of the traitor of Kossovo, as his successor. But Amurath II. at once claimed a prior right to the Servian throne as the grandson of the Servian princess Mileva, whose marriage with the Sultan Bajazet had been one of the conditions of peace fifty years earlier. The Serbs refused to acknowledged his pretensions, and he replied by invading their country. His success was not, however, so complete as he had expected, and he accordingly offered his protection to Servia and demanded the hand of George Branković's daughter in marriage. But this sacrifice did not secure peace for long. Anxious to conquer the rich kingdom of Hungary, Amurath saw that he must occupy Servia first, more especially as Branković had lately made an alliance with the King of Hungary and had built a strong fortress at Semendria on the Danube for the use of himself and his new ally. Amurath requested that this stronghold should be given up to him; and, when Branković refused, overran the country and placed garrisons in the principal towns. A Turkish mosque was built in Kruševac, the famous residence of many a Servian monarch; Branković, unable to obtain aid from Hungary, which was at that moment distracted by internal dissensions and a terrible epidemic, fled to Ragusa, where an inscription on one of the gates tells to this day how he "came in with all his treasures." Servia in 1440 was entirely in the Turkish power, and Amurath appointed one of his followers to govern it as Pasha in his absence. Yet just at that moment the heroic efforts of a foreign soldier procured a further brief respite for the unhappy Serbs. This was John Hunyad, the celebrated "white knight of Wallachia," whom the Christians of the East looked upon as a deliverer, while the hosts of Islâm believed that he was none other than the evil spirit. At the head of a combined Servian and Hungarian army, Hunyad drove Amurath from the Danube and raised the siege of Belgrade, at that time a Hungarian fortress, which the Turks had besieged for six weary months. The King of Hungary joined in the campaign, and one success after another attended the march of the allies. It was well nigh the last triumph that Servian arms ever won over the Turks till the day of awakening came in our own century. The severe winter, most valuable of all allies in a Balkan campaign, alone prevented the utter annihilation of the Turkish army. Amurath begged for peace, and it was signed at Szegedin in the middle of 1444. Hostilities were to cease for ten years, Servia was evacuated by the Turks and once more governed by its native prince. Never since the defeat of Kossovo had the Serbs enjoyed so much independence.

But it was not for long. In spite of the warnings and entreaties of the Servian ruler, the impetuous King of Hungary tore up the treaty almost as soon as it had been signed, and attacked the Turks. In this brief campaign, which was ended by the overwhelming victory of the Turks at Varna in November, 1444, George Branković took no part; for he foresaw from the first the folly, and deplored the treachery, of this wanton breach of the newly signed peace. But he ultimately suffered even more than the Hungarian people by this defeat, which they had provoked. For Varna speedily completed what Kossovo had begun. The Turks made no difference between Magyars and Serbs when the battle was over. Hunyad once more came to the assistance of the latter, and kept Amurath in check for a time, and Amurath II.'s successor, Mohammed II., made a temporary peace with Servia until he had captured Constantinople. The fall of the Imperial city in 1453 paved the way for the final annexation of the Servian territory to the Turkish dominions. Semendria, the residence of George Branković, was the first object of Mohammed's attack. The Ottoman artillery soon left nothing but a heap of ruins to mark the spot, and the Servian prince was once more a fugitive. Again the heroic Hunyad came forward as the champion of Christendom. Again he saved Belgrade, the "City of the Holy War," as the Turks called it. Serbs and Magyars fought side by side in its defence with the courage of despair, and a brave Franciscan monk, crucifix in hand, urged them to protect the outpost of Christianity. A battle on the Danube gained Hunyad access to the citadel; a successful sally from the walls completed the rout of the Turks. Mohammed II. was wounded, while thousands of Ottoman corpses covered the outskirts of Belgrade. Leaving his baggage and artillery in the hands of the gallant garrison, the Sultan retreated to Adrianople, glad to escape with his life, which he owed to the devotion of his bodyguard. George Branković re-entered into possession of his country, and died shortly afterwards in 1457 at the great age of ninety-one. Servian independence survived him little more than a year, for in 1459 the Turks formally annexed the land, for which a long line of warrior princes had striven so well.

The final blow to Servian freedom was dealt by one of Servia's princes. The old story of domestic dissension repeated itself on the death of George Branković. His widow and three sons, to whom he had conjointly entrusted the government, soon quarrelled. Lazar, the youngest of the three, poisoned his mother and expelled his brothers, in order to reign alone, while he promised to pay an annual tribute of twenty thousand gold pieces to the Sultan. But Mohammed II. was not long content with this partial sovereignty. When Lazar died in 1458, he resolved to incorporate Servia with the Turkish Empire. There was no longer any obstacle to the accomplishment of his plan. Hunyad, who might have prevented it, was now dead; the Serbs had lost all heart, and were ready to purchase peace at any price after the constant struggles of the last seventy years; they had no leader and no enthusiasm. Lazar's widow, Helena, tried to preserve the political independence of her country by offering it as a fief to the Papacy. But the Serbs declared that they would rather be Turkish than Roman Catholic. The same effect was produced in Bosnia by the king's proposal to place his throne under the protection of the Pope, and to form, by a matrimonial alliance with Servia, one united Catholic monarchy out of the two Serb states. There too the people, mindful of the terrible persecutions which they had suffered at the hands of the Popes, welcomed the Turks as deliverers. Thus theological bitterness, alike in Servia and in Bosnia, contributed to the subjugation of both lands beneath the rule of the Sultan. The Serb nobles invited a Turkish magnate, brother of the Grand Vizier, to be their lord, and when Helena put him in prison, threw themselves into the Sultan's arms. Semendria opened its gates to him; city after city followed its example; Helena was allowed to leave the country, and in 1459

Servia had ceased to exist as a separate state. Four years later the last King of Bosnia lost his life and throne, and his dominions, too, became a Turkish province. In Montenegro alone a handful of mountaineers preserved the vestiges of Servian freedom. The people of the old Servian kingdom had either bowed their necks to the conqueror or migrated across the Danube to join the colonies founded in Hungary after the battle of Kossovo, where they maintained in a foreign land their language and customs under a chief of their own.

Thus fell the once mighty Servian state. Lack of unity, alike in politics and religion, was the chief cause of its fall. The feudal system, which allowed the great nobles almost royal power in their own dominions, weakened the central authority and rendered it liable to defeat at the hands of a Turkish autocrat, who took care to remove every rival out of his path. It was only when a strong man, like Dušan, was on the throne, or when, as happened after the death of Bajazet, a civil war broke out among the Turks, that Servia was secure. The mutual jealousies of the Christian rulers of Servia and Hungary hindered, except on rare occasions, a really effective alliance for the common cause. The Serbs, firmly attached to the Greek Church, suspected the Magyars, who came to assist them, of desiring to introduce the Roman Catholic faith. Throughout the history of the Balkans this distinction of creeds proved a real obstacle to a political union. It was so in Servia, it was so in Bosnia, and we shall see it to be the same in Montenegro and Albania. Well organised, strongly united in their devotion to their leader and their religion, the Turks had little difficulty in overthrowing the brave Servian nation, which at one moment had seemed likely to combine all the Balkan lands under a Czar of its own, with Constantinople as its capital.

IV.

SERVIA UNDER THE TURKS.

(1459—1804.)

WITH the subjugation of Servia in 1459, the country entered upon the long period of unbroken Turkish domination. Its geographical situation on the high road to Hungary made it a possession of the utmost importance to the Sultans in their continual wars with the Magyars, and for this reason they kept a much tighter hold upon it than upon Moldavia and Wallachia. In name, as well as in fact, Servia formed an integral part of the Ottoman Empire, and not the faintest traces of independence remained. The peasants were compelled to work on the meadows of the Sultan round Constantinople in summer; the lands of the old nobility were parcelled out among the Turkish *spahi*, to whom the natives had to yield personal services no less than pecuniary payments. No Serb was permitted to wear a weapon —a great hardship to a nation which had always gone about its daily business armed. So strictly was this injunction carried out, that, whenever we hear of a peasant revolt, we find the insurgents equipped with nothing more formidable than long staves. Their horses were all taken from them, and every five years they had to pay a tribute of youths, who went to swell the number of the Janissaries. Thus the strength and rising hope of the nation contributed to the aggrandisement of the Turk. A traveller, who visited the country in the sixteenth century, describes the once haughty Serbs as "poor, miserable captives, none of whom dare lift up his head." And no wonder. Obeying the precept of the Koran, which ordained upon the faithful to "press the unbelievers until they pay poll-tax and humble themselves before thee;" the sultans extorted this hated exaction from the Christian *rayah* on pain of death or imprisonment. Every male from the seventh year upwards was compelled to pay it, and the receipts for payment acquired a double value as tokens of submission and as freepasses. Only when a Serb had paid the capitation-tax was he a free man.

A Turkish pasha presided over the whole Pashalik of Belgrade, as it was now called, which embraced most of the Servian kingdom. But there were still a few Servian districts where, as in Bulgaria and the Herzegovina, Christian chiefs of tried devotion to the Sultan were permitted to exercise hereditary rights of overlordship. These districts enjoyed special privileges. No Turkish horse might enter them—a great benefit, for the proverb says that "where the Turk's horse treads, no grass will ever grow." Elsewhere, however, the Turkish *spahi* received tithes of all the produce of field or vineyard or beehive, and demanded a tax from every married couple, rich or poor, while some villages were the direct property of the Sultan. The pasha had the right of making the villagers work for him on certain days of the year without remuneration, and levied an annual sum from the land. Justice was administered by the *kadi* for Christians and Mussulmans alike, while a Turkish *mollah* had his seat at Belgrade.

As in Bulgaria, so in Servia, the Turks did not attempt to root out Christianity from the country which they had conquered. They long permitted the Serfs to elect their own patriarch, who resided at Ipek; but in the middle of the last century it was considered more politic to have as head of the Serb Church some one who was entirely under Turkish control. The Greek patriarch, who resided at Constantinople, was accordingly entrusted with the office, and from that time forward he managed the ecclesiastical affairs of the Servian Christians and sent Greek bishops to live among them. For Servia this change was a great blow. The one department of public life in which they had retained the right to conduct their own business in their own way, was henceforth in the hands of foreigners, who had more sympathy with the Turks than with their flock. For the bishop owed his appointment to the former, while he had to raise the money to pay for it from the latter. The proceedings of the Phanariote clergy in Bulgaria found their parallel in Servia. The Greek bishops were quite as oppressive to the struggling peasantry as the Turkish officials. Not only did they charge a heavy sum for every priest, whom they inducted, but they levied a chimney-tax on every household. In short, all the worst features of the Turkish administrative system prevailed; the civil, ecclesiastical, and judicial posts were all bought and sold, and the purchase-money ultimately wrung from the unhappy natives. To crown all, no Serb might avenge an insult, committed by a Turk, but when smitten on one cheek, meekly turned the other also. No wonder that the native population avoided the towns, where their oppressors lived, and remained in the country, where Turks rarely came. Distinct and apart, the two nations, conquerors and conquered, lived thus for nearly four centuries, till at last the moment came when Servia awoke from her long sleep and became once more free.

Some efforts were made during this long period to throw off the yoke. There were times when it seemed as if the Serb race was on the point of recovering its lost liberties. But such impulses usually came from without rather than from within. The Serbs, who remained behind in their native country, were too cowed to rise, while if they had had the spirit, they would still have lacked the arms necessary for a successful rising. Occasionally the more daring of them seized weapons from the Turks and took to the mountains, where they became *haiduks* or brigands, and lived by the spoils of Turkish caravans during the spring and summer, seeking refuge in winter among their confederates in the villages. But such attempts as there were to drive out the Turks originated among those Serbs who had migrated over the Danube and settled in Hungary.

The Hungarian Serbs possess a history of their own, which belongs, however, rather to the story of Hungary than to that of Servia. But their expeditions with the Austrian and Magyar armies for the relief of their less fortunate fellow-countrymen deserve mention. The kings of Hungary permitted them to occupy under native chiefs, called "despots," the territory between the rivers Save and Drave and the Banat of Temesvar, and allowed them a measure of independence. The family of Branković continued to furnish them with rulers, with one brief interval, down to the year 1689, when the last of the race was thrown into prison by the Emperor Leopold, and another titular chief with the title of l'oïvode appointed in his place. In 1707, it was thought prudent to deprive the Serb colonists of any leader round whom they could rally, and the Serb Patriarch of Carlovitz, in Lower Austria, was nominated as head of the emigrants. Meanwhile, they had not forgotten their old fatherland. One of their "despots" aided the King of Hungary in his campaign against the Turks in 1475, and the decisive battle of the campaign, which temporarily restored Belgrade to Hungary, was won by a brilliant charge of Serbs. Well had the "despot's" troops earned the title of the "Black Legion." On the death of their conqueror, Mohammed II., in 1481, the Serbs had hopes of recovering their lost country, which a Turkish pretender was willing to restore in return for the support of Hungary against the new Sultan. But the King of Hungary had other schemes in view, and the chance, once offered, never recurred. At the memorable battle of

Mohács in 1526 the " Black Legion " in vain struggled to avert the defeat of the Hungarian arms, and the victory of the Turks led to a further migration of Serbs to Hungary, where they fought strenuously under the brave brothers Bakić against the legions of the Sultan, who had now invaded the Magyar kingdom. A Serb noble commanded the Hungarian cavalry in this war, and lost his life at the siege of Temesvar. About the same time an adventurer named Crinović proclaimed himself " Czar of Servia," and hovered over the Servian frontiers, pillaging and burning every place within his reach. But, in spite of his high-sounding title, Crinović was more of a brigand than a patriot, and his countrymen, oppressed though they were by the Turks, were not sorry when he fell.

No change was effected in the condition of the Serb colonists, when Hungary came into the possession of the House of Austria. They maintained their autonomy under a " despot," as before, and a treaty, concluded in 1577, confirmed their privileges. The Emperor by this document granted them certain districts on condition that they should occupy them as military colonies. After the treaty of Sitvatorlok in 1606, which marked the turning-point in the conquering career of the Turks, the Servian emigrants were definitely merged in the Austrian dominions; they fought for the Emperor in all his wars in Western Europe, but their customs, religion, and complete local autonomy still marked them off as a separate race from the rest of the Empire. They shared in the glory of having saved Vienna from the

Turks in 1683, and the retreat of the enemy inspired the Servian "despot" with the hope of regaining the home of his ancestors. Belgrade and Nisch were won, and at last the Serb legion found itself fighting by the side of Austrian soldiers on the soil of Servia. It looked as if the Serb kingdom were about to revive. But it was no part of the Emperor Leopold's plan to re-establish the independent Servian state; and, fearing lest the Serb "despot" should come to terms with the Turks, he put him under arrest, and invited Arsenius, the Serb Patriarch, to emigrate from Ipek in Old Servia to his dominions. Arsenius came, and 37,000 families with him, to this new home beneath the wings of the Austrian double-eagle. Leopold renewed for the benefit of the new colonists all the privileges enjoyed by the old, and granted them not only religious liberty, but freedom from taxation. But Old Servia has not even yet recovered the effects of that great migration two centuries ago. The fierce Albanians, who have taken the place of the industrious Serbs, have never restored prosperity to that region. For Austria it was of no small political advantage to have the ecclesiastical head of the Serb race under her control. Even their persecution by the Jesuits did not shake the loyalty of the Serbs to the Emperor.

The victories of Prince Eugène, who described the Serbs as his "best scouts, his lightest cavalry, his most trusted garrisons," drove the Turks out of Belgrade once more and gave a considerable portion of Servia to Austria; but the ignominious treaty of Belgrade in 1739 restored all Servia with its capital to the

Ottoman Empire. Again the hopes of the colonists had been dashed to the ground. Despairing of a return to Servia, and deprived by the Empress Maria Theresa of the privileges which they had hitherto enjoyed from the Austrian rulers, many of them emigrated to Russia in 1740, where a large and fertile tract of country was assigned to them on the banks of the Dnieper. No fewer than 100,000 settled in that region, and traces of this Serb colonisation are still to be found. Faithful to the memory of their fatherland, they gave to the towns which they had founded on Russian soil, the names of places which had once formed part of the Servian kingdom.

The Serbs hoped great things from the advent of that philanthropic monarch, Joseph II., to the Austrian throne. Obradović, the poet, implored him "to protect the Servian race, and turn thy face towards a people, dear to thy ancestors, towards unhappy Servia, which suffers miseries without number. Give us back," he cried, "our ancient heroes, our ancient country!" Had Joseph lived longer, the poet's prayer might have been granted. The Emperor made an alliance with Catherine of Russia for the purpose of driving the Turks out of the Balkan Peninsula, and so "avenging," as he phrased it, " humanity on those barbarians." The declaration of war in 1788 was greeted with transports of joy wherever the Servian tongue was spoken. From every side the Serbs flocked to the Imperial standard. Belgrade fell in 1789, Bosnia was in the hands of the Austrians, Albania and Macedonia were rising fast. Colonel Mihaljević, in command of the emigrants, penetrated into the heart of Servia by mountain paths which no army had ever trod before ; Kruševac, the holy city of the Serbs, the residence of the old Prince Lazar, was captured, and its churches, used by the Turks as stables for centuries, were purified, and once again resounded with songs of praise. The hosts of Islâm fled from the land ; it seemed, indeed, as if Servia's hour had come. But the partition of Turkey between Russia and Austria had aroused the usual jealousy of the other Powers, and the untimely death of Joseph II. in 1790, deprived the Christian subjects of Turkey of their protector. The outbreak of the French Revolution turned the thoughts of Austrian statesmen westward; and, in their anxiety to check the movement in Paris, they forgot all about the Balkan races. By the treaty of Sistova, Servia was restored to the Turks, and a Turkish Pasha once more took up his residence at Belgrade.

But the results of the war of 1788 were not altogether lost. Servia had, indeed, been given back to the Turk, but the national spirit had been aroused. The Ottoman officials asked with amazement and alarm, what the Austrians had done to their once humble *rayahs*, whom they scarcely recognised in the disciplined volunteers of the late campaign. The downtrodden peasants, who had cringed before a Turk as he rode along the highway, and lost all sense of manly independence under long years of oppression, had become men and patriots in the storm and stress of the brief Austrian war. Among the valleys and on the mountain peaks roamed the *haiduks;* their hands against the Turks, and the Turks' hands against them, but respected and protected by the people as friends and avengers. Servia had learnt by bitter experience the lesson that "those who would be free themselves must strike the blow." Too often had her hopes been disappointed by Austrian promises of deliverance; too often had the land been won, only to be given back to the Turk. Less fortunate than their Bulgarian neighbours, they found no foreign nation to draw the sword on their behalf. For their restored independence they are indebted not to a Russian autocrat, but to one of their own peasants.

V.

THE STRUGGLE FOR INDEPENDENCE.

(1804—1860.)

AT the beginning of the present century, the Turkish Pasha who governed Servia was Hadji Mustapha, a kind and humane ruler, who enjoyed great popularity with his Christian subjects. Under his beneficent sway the land had peace, trade flourished, and justice was fairly administered to all alike. The grateful people called the governor the "Mother of the Serbs," and it seemed as if his province would be the last to raise the standard of revolt. But the reforms of Selim III., by arousing the anger of the Janissaries against both the Sultan and the Serbs, brought about the insurrection, which ultimately led to the independence of Servia.

The arrogance and insubordination of the Janissaries had long been a danger to the Turkish Empire, and nowhere were they more insubordinate than in Belgrade. Their leaders, or *dahi*, like the Deys of the Barbary states, openly defied the Turkish Pashas who were their nominal superiors; their exactions were more oppressive than the contributions levied by the officials of the Sultan. With a stroke of his pen Selim banished the Janissaries from Servia, confiscated their property, and restored peace and prosperity to the natives. But the Janissaries were only temporarily checked. In conjunction with the notorious brigand-chief, Pasvanoglu of Vidin, they descended upon Servia, and it was with difficulty that Hadji Mustapha and the Serbs repulsed their attack. But the Porte could not reconcile itself to the permanent exile of men who, however unruly, were at any rate true believers. With strange vacillation the Sultan permitted their return. They were not long in resuming their former malpractices, and when Hadji Mustapha enforced the law and protected the peaceful inhabitants, they shut him up in the upper fortress of the city and put him to death. By way of apology they explained to the Porte that "Hadji Mustapha had been untrue to the Turks and a friend of the Christians." Their four chiefs then divided Servia between them, and the new Pasha had to content himself with the mere shadow of power. In vain the people complained to the Sultan. In vain the Sultan threatened the evil-doers with his vengeance. The Janissaries resolved to prevent him from levying a force of Serbs, as Hadji Mustapha had done, and massacred every one whom the people regarded as a leader. Early in 1804 this horrible crime was committed. Every village in Servia flowed with blood, and those who escaped the common butchery fled to the impenetrable forests of Choumadia, a mountainous district situated between the streams of the Western and Lower Morava.

Filled with the desire for vengeance, the survivors met to choose a leader. There was at this time in Servia a certain George Petrović, better known by his Turkish name of Kara, or "Black," George, from his dark raven locks. Kara George is the hero of modern Servian history, just as Stephen Dušan was of the ancient Serb Empire. The son of a peasant, he had taken part in the abortive rising of 1787, and was forced to flee for his life with his old father and his belongings. When they came to the river Save the father refused to go on, and his son, rather than allow him to be seized and tortured to death by the Turks, drew his pistol and shot him dead on the spot. For a while he served as a volunteer in the Austrian army, and when the war was over joined the brigands in the mountains. But under the peaceful sway of Hadji Mustapha he became a breeder of swine—then, as now, the staple industry of his country. He grew rich and respected, though few loved him, for he was silent and morose; and, when he was angry, his temper was terrible. But in battle he towered above his followers, his eyes sparkled, and his foes fled before his maimed right hand. He knew his own weaknesses, and, when his fellow-countrymen asked him to be their leader, he reminded them of his violent character. But they refused to listen to his arguments, and he consented to be their chief. "I am a simple man," he told them; "if you disobey me, I shall not try to enforce my authority by speeches, I shall kill the disobedient." His only brother, whom he dearly loved, was one of the first to incur this punishment. Such was the man to whom modern

Servia owes her independence. To the end he pursued the simplicity of life which had marked his earlier career. At the summit of his power he wore a peasant's garb and pursued a peasant's avocations. He spoilt one of his foreign orders by wearing it when he was mending a cask; and when he exercised princely power, he allowed his daughter to carry up water-cans from the well like a village maiden. He was a great man, though he was innocent of the alphabet and could not sign his own name at the bottom of a State paper.

He soon gathered around him a considerable force. Nobles, like Jacob Nenadović and Milenko, brigands, and even priests came to his assistance. "Every tree," says a patriotic ballad, "became a soldier." At first the Janissaries despised their enemy; a single Mussulman, they boasted, could put fifty Serbs to flight. But Kara George, the "Commandant of Servia," as he styled himself, carried all before him. Belgrade was invested by his army, and the Turkish Government, no friend to the Janissaries, ordered the Pasha of Bosnia to join the Serbs with his forces. Kara George welcomed his unexpected ally with open arms; Belgrade surrendered, and the heads of the four *dahi* adorned the insurgents' camp. The tyranny of the Janissaries was broken, and the object for which Kara George had fought was attained. The Sultan hoped that the Serbs would now return to their old allegiance.

But their successes had inspired the Serb leaders with the idea of emancipating their country from Turkish interference in their internal affairs, no less than from the irregular rule of the Janissaries. As yet they had no desire for complete separation; they only desired local self-government while preserving the external union with Constantinople. Shrewd enough to see that they could not yet stand alone, they sent a deputation to Russia to ask the aid of a country which had lately procured such solid advantages for the Danubian principalities. The Czar promised to support the claims of the Serbs at Constantinople, and the three envoys returned home proud of their powerful patron. But the Napoleonic wars engrossed his attention, and the sole result of his promises was to excite hopes in Servia, which he could not help to fulfil. The Serbs demanded that the fortresses in their land should henceforth be garrisoned by native instead of Turkish troops. The Sultan refused and told off the Pasha of Nisch to disarm the rebels. The Pasha failed in the attempt, the Sultan sent three armies to subdue the Serbs; war between Servia and Turkey had fairly begun. The struggle was severe, for the Sultan's best solders were in the field. But under the leadership of Kara George and his able colleagues, Milenko, Mladen, and Jacob Nenadović, the Serbs held their own against the Turkish armies. The strategical knowledge which many of them had picked up in the Austrian ranks now stood them in good stead. The character of the country made it easy to defend, and thus compensated for their great numerical inferiority. On the 4th of August, 1806, a great victory at Mischar proved decisive for the Servian cause. The flower of the Bosnian chivalry fell, the Seraskier lost many of his solders in the waters of the Drin, Kara George, the "Supreme Chief," as he was now styled, remained master of the day. The Pasha of Skodra, upon the news of his colleague's defeat, proposed a truce, and a Servian embassy was sent to Constantinople to arrange terms. At first the Sultan, terrified at the prospect of an alliance between Servia and Russia, was ready to make almost any concession. He promised the Serbs a government of their own, the possession of all the Turkish fortresses in Servia except Belgrade, where an Ottoman garrison of one hundred and fifty men was still to remain ; and, in lieu of all former taxes, the payment of six hundred thousand gulden a year, in order to provide compensation for the dispossessed Turkish landowners, whose lands would now revert to the natives. But just at this moment there came a turn in the great Napoleonic drama. Believing that Russia would soon be once more at war with the French Emperor and thus have no leisure for Balkan politics, Selim III. revoked his concessions and recommenced hostilities. Kara George lost no time in accepting the challenge. Belgrade once again capitulated to him, but he could not check the fury of his followers against its Turkish inhabitants. For two days the massacre continued ; on the third few survived to tell the tale. It was the revenge of the people for centuries of oppression.

The revolution had overthrown all the existing institutions which the Turks had created, and the first business of Kara George, now that he had freed his country, was to provide it with a government. With the aid of a Hungarian Serb, named Philippović, a Senate, composed of twelve members corresponding to the twelve *nahie*, or districts, of Servia, was established in the capital and entrusted with the tasks of levying taxes for the maintenance of the standing army, organising tribunals and promoting education. Feeling sorely their own literary deficiencies, the leaders of the revolution not only erected elementary schools in every county-town, but started a high school at Belgrade, where history was taught. By the side of the Senate there was an Assembly, or *Skupschtina*, to which the local chieftains came with their retinues every year to decide questions of peace or war and the punishment of great criminals. Kara George exercised, as "Supreme Chief," the executive power, and when the Senate displeased him ordered his soldiers to stick the muzzles of their muskets in at the windows of the hall where it met. "It is easy," he said, "to make laws in a warm chamber; but who will lead against the Turks in the field?"

The dangers which threatened Turkey from every side in 1809 induced Kara George to attack his old enemies. Russia, at peace with Napoleon, had declared war on the new Sultan, Montenegro was in ferment, the Bosnian and Herzegovinian Serbs implored the help of their emancipated brothers. Kara George, with Montenegrin aid, had begun a campaign in the West, and was marching across Novibazar, when the news of a Turkish invasion of Servia on the East recalled him to the defence of his country. But the jealousies of the rival chiefs paralysed his efforts. In his despair he implored the aid of Napoleon, but without success. The Czar was more willing to assist him, and Russian and Servian troops stemmed the tide of invasion. Kara George emerged from the war more powerful than ever, Servia could breathe again, even though the Sultan still declined to recognise her hard-won independence.

But with the disappearance of danger from outside internal dissensions recommenced. Already there were in Servia a Russian and an Austrian party. Kara George had meditated putting the country under the protection of Austria; his own pre-eminence excited the envy of the great military chiefs, who wished to have the Czar as their sovereign. For a time the Russian faction was predominant, but the Treaty of Bucharest in 1812, by which Russia, menaced by Napoleon, sacrificed the Christians of the Balkans, left Servia to her own resources. Turkey at once proclaimed a "holy war" against her revolted subjects; Kara George issued a fiery address in which he prayed God "to put courage into the hearts of Servia's sons." But this time his own heart failed him. He, the hero of a hundred fights with the Turks, lay inactive in the mountains, while the Ottoman armies invaded the land, and, when the critical moment came, he buried his money and retired into Austria. Servia, deprived of her trusted chief, lay at the mercy of the foe. Most of the principal men followed Kara George; after a nine years' successful struggle for independence, the Servian nation had suddenly collapsed.

Among the Serbs who had refused to leave their native land, was a certain Milosh Obrenović, an influential man, who had taken a prominent part in the war. The founder of the present reigning House of Servia, like his great rival Kara George, began life as a humble farm-servant. His father, a peasant named Tescho, had married the widow of one Obren, from whom Milosh derived his patronymic. From his

MILOSH OBRENOVIĆ.

half-brother Milan, who was the son of this Obren, Milosh inherited a considerable fortune ; and the flight of all the native leaders left him the most influential man in the country. Seeing that resistance was hopeless for the present, he left his hiding-place in the mountains and came to terms with the conquerors. Soliman, the new Pasha of Belgrade, received him with every respect and appointed him headman, or *oberknez*, of the three districts where he had influence. His conduct has naturally given rise to very different views of his character. Some regard him as an astute statesman, who saw that the only way to save his country was to worm himself into the confidence of its conquerors, and so moderate the violence of their anger. Others consider him to have been a traitor, who cared for nothing but his own personal advantage. A true hero would hardly have acted like Milosh, for he would have desired that his actions should be above suspicion. But the goodness or badness of his motives, however much they may affect our estimate of his character, does not detract from the importance of his work.

At first he appeared to be a zealous supporter of Turkish rule. When Hadschi Prodan, a patriotic Serb, rose against the conquerors in 1814, he promptly suppressed the revolt, but endeavoured to save the rebels from the results of their acts. But the cruelty of Soliman made him fear for his own safety; his head, he said, was no longer secure. Under a pretext he quitted Belgrade and took to the mountains, where he soon gathered around him a band of malcontents. At Takovo on Palm Sunday, 1815, he was hailed by his comrades as "Supreme Chief" of the Serbs. From every side men flocked to his banner; a guerilla warfare, such as the Serbs love, made terrible havoc with the Turkish troops; even the strong fortress of Passarović fell into his hands. The dread of Russian intervention, which the final conclusion of the Napoleonic struggle in 1815 rendered possible, inclined the Sultan to make terms with the Serbs, who had sent their envoys to seek the aid of the Congress of Vienna. In place of the former Senate, there was established a Court composed, as before, of representatives of the twelve *nahie;* the old *Skupschtina* was allowed to raise the amount of tribute paid to the Turkish Pasha, who continued to occupy Belgrade ; tribunals, presided over by the head-man, assisted by a Mussulman in cases where the litigants belonged to the two races, administered justice in each district ; and, last but not least, the Serbs received permission to carry arms. They had thus regained under Milosh a semi-independence ; internal disputes at once began.

The news of the Turkish defeats reached Kara George in his exile in Bessarabia. The old leader received pressing letters bidding him return, and in 1817 he secretly recrossed the frontier of his native land. To Milosh his return was anything but welcome, for there was no room for two "Supreme Chiefs" in the Servian councils. The two men had never been friends, and Milosh now resolved to rid himself of his rival for ever. He accordingly told the Turkish Pasha of Kara George's arrival, and of the seditious plans which he was forming. The Pasha bade him procure the murder of the rebel ; and Milosh, nothing loth, ordered Vuica, a brigand chief, to send either Black George's head or his own. The order was promptly obeyed. As Kara George slept he was stealthily assassinated, and his head sent to the exultant Pasha. Such was the ignominious end of

Servia's national hero. From that moment began the feud, which is not even yet extinct, between the descendants of Kara George and the house of Obrenović. The history of Servia during the greater part of the present century is one long duel between these rival families.

Milosh was now without a competitor; for he had also secured the execution of the Archbishop of Belgrade and a prominent noble, who had menaced his supremacy. In November, 1817, the head-men of all the districts, together with the ecclesiastical dignitaries of the country, named him Prince of Servia, and declared the title hereditary in his family. The dignity lasted until it was exchanged in 1882 for the title of King. For a long time the Porte refused to recognise him in his new capacity; and, when he sent a deputation to Constantinople, his envoys were imprisoned. But Russia, which had been the first to acknowledge him as a lawful Prince, demanded, in the Convention of Akermann in 1826, the evacuation of Servia by the Turks, and a definite settlement of the relations between the Sultan and the Serbs. When the Porte hesitated to carry out its engagements, the Russian army laid siege to Varna. The attitude of Milosh, who, without actively assisting Russia in the war of 1828, kept the Bosnian and Albanian forces from attacking the Russian troops in the flank, was rewarded by the Czar. In the peace of Adrianople, it was stipulated that Servia should be completely independent of the Porte on payment of an annual tribute, but that the frontier fortresses should be held by Turkish garrisons. A year later, on the last day of November, 1830, the Sultan formally recognised Milosh as hereditary Prince. Milosh had reached the summit of his power; from that moment his influence began to wane.

The Serbs soon found that the government of their own fellow-countryman was not much milder than that of the Turkish Pasha. He collected the taxes with no less stringency; he treated the chiefs with no more respect. The peasants asked themselves whether their desperate struggles with the Turks had profited them much, and whether they had not made all their sacrifices simply for the glorification of one man. Milosh acted as an autocrat. He ceased to assemble the *Skupschtina*, and, in spite of the code which he had introduced for the use of his country, made his own will the highest law. He took what he chose from his subjects at a price fixed by himself, and once ordered a whole suburb of Belgrade to be set on fire, because he wished to build a new custom-house. He handled the people like serfs, and forced them to gather in his hay without payment, like a feudal lord. He enclosed the commons, on which the peasants fed their swine, and aimed at obtaining a monopoly of the staple trade of Servia. The pig has always been an important factor in Servian politics, and this last act of the Prince was most unpopular. Even his own son admitted that Milosh committed great mistakes in his domestic policy. "Am I not the master? can I not do what I will with mine own?" was the father's reply. Simple and genial as he was in his summer home at Passarović or in his winter residence at Kruševac, in the midst of his family, the "peasant-prince" was a tyrant to his people. His refusal to assist the Serbs of Bosnia, who implored his help, was a further ground of complaint. One rising after another broke out, a conspiracy against the Prince's life was discovered, and at last he thought it prudent to grant his people a constitution.

On the 15th of February, 1835, he opened the *Skupschtina* with a speech, in which he promised all the latest inventions of Western politics—the rights of man, ministerial responsibility, and the subordination of the sovereign to the law. A Council of State was called into existence, the Prince reserved for himself the right of supervision alone; by a single stroke of the pen semi-civilised Servia was converted from an Oriental despotism into a constitutional monarchy. The scheme looked beautiful on paper, but events proved that the nation was not ripe for so elaborate a system of government. The constitution of 1835 was unworkable, and Milosh treated it as a dead letter and returned to his old despotic ways. His monopolies of salt and other necessaries were worse than ever, and his subjects felt his exactions all the more because he spent abroad the money which he raised from them. His increasing power had alarmed not only the Sultan, but the Czar, who up to the Treaty of Adrianople had been his friend. The former feared that other Christian races in his Empire might follow the example of the Serbs; the latter was pursuing the time-honoured policy of Russia in the Balkan Peninsula, which consists in allowing the various states to acquire sufficient power to make them independent of Turkey but not sufficient to enable them to stand alone without Russian aid. In order to cripple the strength of Milosh, Russia played the same game as in Bulgaria in 1879, and tried to divide the authority in Servia between Prince and people. The discontented nobles, under Ephrem, the Prince's brother, readily fell in with this scheme. The Czar sent Prince Dolgorouki to Servia with instructions to urge upon Milosh the necessity of a really efficient constitution. Milosh was supported against Russia by the influence of Great Britain, which had lately sent Colonel Hodges as Consul to Belgrade—the first instance of British interest in Servian affairs. The British Government thought that Servia might become a valuable market for Birmingham and Manchester goods, and accordingly desired the maintenance of the commercial autocracy of Milosh. But the Prince reflected that England was, after all, a long way off, and that Servia had no seaboard where British bluejackets could land, if he required their aid. So he yielded to the persuasions of Russia, and by a decree of the 24th of December, 1838, there was established a Senate or Council of seventeen ministers, who were irremovable and enjoyed full legislative powers. Four ministers for different departments were appointed by the Prince, but it was to the new Council that they had to make their reports. The power of Milosh was gone; he had scarcely a friend among his ministers and on the Council; his enemies at once used against him the lever which the new constitution had placed in their hands. In vain his adherents, under his brother Jovan, took up arms against the Council. Milosh found himself deserted, he was told that he must resign in favour of his eldest son Milan. On the 13th of June, 1839, he signed his abdication, and without saying a word, amid the tears of his retinue, he, the second founder of modern Servia, crossed the Save. But his career was not over; twenty years later he was to return and for a brief space once more rule his native land.

Milan Obrenović II., who succeeded his father, died a month later, and his health was so feeble that during that brief period a Regency governed in his stead. Upon his death there broke out disputes as to the succession, which are even now not entirely settled. But the Senate promptly proclaimed Milan's younger brother Prince under the title of Michael Obrenović III., and the Sultan, as suzerain, ratified the decision of the Senate. But, in order to impose a check upon the Prince, the Porte placed Petronievič and Vouičić, two powerful nobles who had acted as Regents for his brother, at his side. Thus, at the very outset of his reign, Michael had two dangerous rivals near his throne, who were certain sooner or later to plot against him. The people were discontented, for, as one of them said, "in the time of Milosh we had only one ditch to fill with money, but now we must fill seventeen, one for each of the senators." They demanded the removal of the seat of government from Belgrade to Kruševac, where it would be more independent, the trial of the

Regents and the recall of Milosh. The Regents fell, and Michael, installed at Kruševac, gained a free hand for his contemplated reforms. But he allowed himself to be carried too far by the zeal of his Minister of Education, an Austrian Serb, who desired to raise Servia all at once to the level of a civilised Western state. The improvement of the education of the clergy, the introduction of written pleadings in courts of law, the collection of statistics, the establishment of an opera and a theatre in Belgrade were excellent things in their way, but they cost money, and it became necessary to increase the taxes in order to obtain it. The peasants, who had been the strongest supporters of the Obrenović family, grumbled and shook their heads over these new-fangled " German " ideas. The return of Petronievic and Vouičić from exile provided the opposition with chiefs, and an open revolt broke out against the Prince. Michael saw himself abandoned by his people as his father had been, Vouičić had seduced his subjects from their allegiance, and there was nothing left for him but to resign. At the end of August, 1842, he withdrew into Austrian territory, and Vouičić formed a triumvirate for the government of the country. But the people demanded a Prince, and the unanimous choice of the seventeen provinces of Servia fell upon the son of the national hero, Kara George, Alexander Karageorgević. Born amid the dangers of the War of Independence in 1806, Black George's son had received an allowance from Milosh, and had served as an officer in Michael's guard. Pleasant and unassuming in manner, he had won the general esteem of his fellow-countrymen, and the great name which he bore made him the only possible successor to an Obrenović on the throne of Servia. The Sultan at once ratified his election, but the Czar Nicholas I., who regarded himself as the "Protector of Servia," insisted upon a new election being held. The fears of Russia that a Karageorgević would prove too independent were, however, idle, for Alexander lacked the spirit of his sire. But, in order to pacify the Czar, the form of another election was gone through, and Alexander once more chosen as Prince, the appointment, however, being only for life. With this concession, and the exile of the two revolutionary chiefs, Vouičić and Petroniević, the Russian autocrat professed himself contented, and for the next few years Servia enjoyed profound peace. Abroad, the Prince abandoned the "great Servian idea" of Milosh, who had dreamed of emancipating all the Serbs outside the principality from the Turkish yoke; at home, he devoted himself to those fiscal and economic reforms which were sorely needed. During his reign the principality made great material progress. Roads opened up the internal commerce of the country, two new codes were promulgated, and great public works undertaken. For a brief space Servia seemed to have reached that happy condition of having no history, to which few states, least of all in the Balkan Peninsula, ever attain.

But the outbreak of the revolution in Hungary in 1848 at once aroused the sympathy of the Serbs of the principality. The Prince preserved official neutrality, but he could not prevent his subjects from volunteering against the Magyars, who showed such slight regard for the claims of other nationalities. The situation was rendered more difficult by the fact, that Milosh and his son Michael openly assisted the Serb revolutionists in Hungary, and thus gained popularity as champions of the Servian race. But a much more awkward problem confronted Karageorgević when Russia entered upon the Crimean War. The Czar, who had been greatly annoyed by the appointment of the Liberal and anti-Russian statesman, Elia Garashanine, as Servian Minister for Foreign Affairs, demanded his dismissal within twenty-four hours. The Prince was on the horns of a dilemma; if he refused to dismiss his minister, he would offend the Czar; if he obeyed the Czar, he would wound the pride of his subjects. He yielded, only to find that Russia was resolved to ask further concessions. But Austria stepped in, and induced Servia to remain strictly neutral in the war of 1854. Nothing loth—for they had no love for their imperious Russian " Protector "—the Serbs confined themselves to preparing an armed resistance to any army, whether Austrian or Russian, which might invade their country. Small as their numbers were, they would have proved most valuable allies to the Czar, and their abstention from all active participation in the war completely altered his plan of campaign. Turkey and the Western Powers remembered this policy of " masterly inactivity " with gratitude at the end of the war. The Treaty of Paris of 1856 provided that Servia should remain under the suzerainty of the Sultan, but that its "rights and privileges should henceforth be placed under the collective guarantee of the Powers," who promised that it should " preserve its independent and national administration, as well as its religious, legislative, and commercial liberty." The Porte retained its right of occupying the frontier fortresses, and continued to receive an annual tribute, but it was specially laid down in the treaty that "no armed intervention could take place in Servia without the previous consent of the Powers." Thus the claim of the Czar to be the " Protector of Servia " was set aside in favour of the joint protection of the European Governments.

But, successful as had been his policy during the Crimean War, Karageorgević soon became very unpopular. His enemies accused him of servility to Austria, and regretted the expulsion of the Obrenović family. The Senate was composed of his opponents, and he accordingly petitioned the Sultan to rescind the existing constitution and substitute for it one much less Liberal. The Senators at once came forward as the friends of the people and sent a counter-petition, to the Porte, asking for a great extension of the national privileges. In the eyes of the masses they appeared as true patriots, while the Prince seemed a reactionary of the worst type. A conspiracy against his life led to the arrest and imprisonment of several popular members of the Senate, and the discontent of the nation increased. Some desired the recall of Milosh and his son ; others the election of Garashanine ; others, again, wished to have Karageorgević's nephew as their Prince. But all were agreed that Alexander must go, and demanded the summoning

THE OLDEST CHURCH IN SERVIA.

of a National Assembly. The Assembly met in December, 1858, and at once demanded the Prince's resignation. Alexander fled to the fortress at Belgrade, and next day old Prince Milosh was restored to the throne. Twenty years after he had quitted his country as an exile, the aged leader returned amidst the acclamations of his fickle people.

Milosh did not long survive his restoration. But before he died he raised the Servian nation to a position which it had never occupied under the feeble rule of his predecessor. Alike to Austria and to the Sultan he quickly demonstrated his determination to allow no foreign interference in the internal affairs of his country. He promptly removed the Turkish guards from the streets of his capital, and demanded the strict execution of the article of the Treaty of Paris which limited the Turkish right of occupation to the frontier-fortresses. When the Porte sent an evasive reply and hesitated to recognise the hereditary claim of the Obrenović family to the throne, he drew up a solemn declaration before the National Assembly, in which he proclaimed the acceptance of both these principles by the Servian people, with or without the consent of the Sultan. In order to ensure the succession beyond all dispute, the Assembly decided that, in default of heirs, the Prince might adopt a Serb of noble birth and belonging to the Greek faith as his successor, and that during a minority a Regency, composed of three ministers, should carry on the government of the country. A month later, in September, 1860, Milosh died. It was well for him that his reign was not extended, for his former experience had not disabused him of his autocratic ideas. He belonged to a past generation, and had learnt nothing, and forgotten nothing during his long exile. His contemporaries, especially the peasants, might look with gratitude upon the great services which he had rendered to his country in days gone by, and pardon his errors of judgment and his despotic ways. But the rising generation, which knew not the Milosh of the struggle for Independence, was rapidly growing restive under his patriarchal rule. No matter was too small, no detail too trivial for his consideration, and he was greedy of power to the last. With his death the heroic age of modern Servia closed; for, with all his faults, Milosh was a hero, not of the ideal sort, but such as are the makers of half-civilised Oriental States. Panegyrists have tried to excuse his complicity in the murder of his great rival, Kara George, which will ever be a stain on his character, and there are as many different interpretations of his conduct in 1813 as there are writers on the period. But, judged according to the standard of Oriental rulers in that age, Milosh was not much their inferior in character and greatly their superior in ability. His name and that of Kara George will ever be remembered in connection with Servia's emancipation from the Turk.

VI.

THE FINAL EMANCIPATION OF SERVIA.

(1860—1878.)

MICHAEL OBRENOVIĆ III., who on the death of his father once again mounted the throne of Servia, inaugurated a new era in the history of his country. If Milosh had contended that "the sovereign's will is the highest law," his son took as his motto the much more modern sentiment that "the law is the highest authority." He had travelled much since his brief and boyish reign eighteen years earlier. His residence in Western capitals had filled him with progressive ideas, and he represented the new spirit which had manifested itself in Servia during his long exile. Michael is the best ruler whom his country has yet had, and his second reign short as it was, has left a permanent mark upon the national life. For he was a moderate reformer, who recognised the great truth that institutions may be excellent in themselves, and yet be quite unsuited to a people which is not sufficiently advanced to appreciate them. He openly avowed his preference for the British constitution, but expressed his conviction that Servia had much to learn before she could understand it. In every department of the State his influence was for good. He began by reforming the Senate of Seventeen, which ever since its creation had been nothing but a Venetian oligarchy, making and unmaking princes at its will, and forming a perpetual hotbed of intrigues. Relying on the assumption that the consent of the Sultan was necessary for their removal, the senators had always set the sovereign at defiance, while they had entirely monopolised legislative power. Michael now adopted a compromise. He left the senators their legislative functions, but made them amenable to the decisions of the law courts, which, without consulting the Sultan, had the right to remove them for misconduct. Having thus curtailed the privileges of the Senate, he proceeded to regulate the authority of the National Assembly, or *Skupschtina*. During the reign of Karageorgević this body had been only twice summoned, the second occasion being the deposition of that prince. The "Assembly of St. Andrew," as it was popularly called from its custom of meeting on the festival of that national saint, had taken that opportunity to assert itself, and, under the influence of a few men of the professional class who had studied abroad, aimed at copying the British House of Commons. But the peasants, with their natural suspicion of those who had acquired more culture than themselves, were not prepared for so democratic a step, and Michael accordingly summoned the Assembly every third year for the discussion of such measures as were laid before it by the ministers. Its duties were to express the wishes of the people on these proposals. It had no power of originating legislation, and it could not touch the budget, which was reserved for the Senate. But as the nation acquired more political education, Michael intended to extend its political rights and even grant it a free press. Another and much more democratic measure he attempted without success. A graduated income-tax is unknown in countries far more advanced than was Servia thirty years ago. But Prince Michael, conscious of the grievous injustice of the existing poll-tax, which had hitherto been levied on rich and poor alike, endeavoured to introduce the principle of payment in proportion to income. The result showed the futility of such a scheme in the then state of public morality, for the returns sent in were constantly falsified. Michael abandoned the scheme, and substituted for it the method of taxing each district at a certain sum, to be collected by the local authorities from those who were best able to pay it. The introduction of the decimal system and the issue for the first time of a distinctive Servian coinage completed his political and economic reforms.

It was to Michael, too, that Servia owed the first attempt at military organisation. Hitherto the Servian armies had been mere conglomerations of individuals, admirably adapted for a guerilla warfare among the mountains, but without discipline, and badly armed. The Prince knew the valour of his subjects, and saw that they only required to be properly drilled and equipped to become efficient soldiers. He accordingly purchased two hundred thousand rifles of the latest pattern, which, in spite of Turkish protests, he smuggled into the country and sold at a very low rate to his people. Conscription at once followed; every Serb above the age of twenty was liable to serve, and a force of cavalry and artillery was raised from the different towns. The effect of this reform was at once felt in the national policy. The Prince found his new army the strongest argument when he spoke in the name of his country and demanded further liberties from the Sultan.

For Michael's foreign policy was as successful as his internal reforms. At the death of his father, Turkish garrisons in the frontier fortresses and an annual tribute still reminded the people of the days of Ottoman domination. Michael resolved to secure the retirement of the last Turkish soldier from his country, and, above all, from the splendid castle which commanded his capital. At the outset he refused to go, as his predecessors had done, to the field before the fortress of Belgrade to hear the Turkish *berat* read, which confirmed his election, but proudly bade its bearer come to his palace. A collision between the garrison and the people in 1862 gave him the opportunity which he sought. The Turkish commandant bombarded the city; the consular body supported the Prince in his protest at Constantinople. The people urged him to join with Montenegro, then at war with the Turks, and he at once resigned his own civil list and offered to devote all his personal property to military purposes. But the Powers suggested a Conference, and the Prince laid before it a demand for the immediate evacuation of every Servian fortress by the Turks. The Conference proposed as an alternative the withdrawal of the Mussulman population from the towns on payment of an indemnity for the property which they left behind, and this the Prince accepted as an instalment. Confident of the support of England, where his wife, Princess Julia, had awakened much sympathy for the Servian cause, he felt that he could afford to wait. It was at this time that Lord Palmerston made his famous pun to the Princess at one of his receptions. As she entered the room her dress caught in the door. "*Princesse*," said the witty Premier, hastening to release her, "*la Porte est sur votre chemin, pour vous empêcher d'avancer.*" The Porte did not block her country's progress much longer. Encouraged by the tremendous enthusiasm which in 1865 hailed the jubilee of his father's rising against the Turks, and relying on the organised army which he now had at his back, the Prince petitioned the Sultan in 1867 for the evacuation or demolition of the fortresses still occupied by Turkish troops. The tactful manner in which the request was made pleased the formalists at the Porte, and the Cretan insurrection made it highly impolitic to offend the Serbs. Austria and England supported the claim, and the Sultan at last withdrew his garrisons with a good grace, merely stipulating that the forts should be kept up by the Serbs, and that on high days and holidays the Crescent should be displayed from one of the battlements. For the first time for centuries Belgrade was entirely free, and the grand old castle, which had braved a hundred sieges, was in the hands of a national garrison. As the last Turkish soldier quitted Servian soil Michael's policy was triumphantly vindicated, for the tribute now alone remained as a relic of the old Turkish days. It was even thought that the Prince would be supported by France and Austria if he added Bosnia to his dominions. Fortune was indeed smiling on the Serbs.

But the hand of the assassin had marked Prince Michael as a victim. From the beginning of his reign there had been a strong opposition against him. His virtues made him unpopular with some, for he rigidly refused to proscribe the adherents of the Karageorgević faction and hand their posts to his adherents. They could not understand the Prince's maxim, that " Servia was so small a country, and had so great a mission, that he could not look at the colour of the men whom he employed in the State service." The Karageorgević party was not in the least appeased by his generosity. The ex-Prince Alexander assumed the part of a Pretender, and his agents represented the fiscal and military reforms of Michael as injurious to the nation. In 1864 the discontented elements in the country united in a conspiracy against the Prince, some desiring the recall of Alexander, others wishing to proclaim a Republic. The plot failed, but the scandal caused by the acquittal of the conspirators, and the subsequent impeachment of the judges who had acquitted them, did no good to the Government. On his way back from the Paris Exhibition the Prince was nearly murdered. But he refused to take precautions, and his carelessness at last cost him his life.

Every visitor to Belgrade is taken to see the beautiful park of Topiderč, which is situated between two low oak-covered hills about two miles and a half away. In this park was the summer residence of the Prince, and it was his usual custom on hot afternoons to walk with his family along a shady path which he had had cut through the woods. All Belgrade knew his favourite walk, and the conspirators had no difficulty in laying their plans accordingly. On the afternoon of the 10th of June, 1868, the Prince set out for the park with his aunt, her daughter and granddaughter, his only retinue consisting of a single aid-de-camp and a groom. As the little party was walking along the narrow path under the trees four men suddenly came round the corner, and, with a respectful salute, stood aside to allow the Prince to pass. Scarcely had he done so than four pistol-shots were heard from behind, and the Prince fell. A few moments after he expired, and his cousin, who was also mortally wounded, died two hours later; her daughter received a severe injury, the aid-de-camp fainted, and the Prince's aunt and his groom alone escaped unhurt. In order to make certain of their victim's death, the assassins drew their knives and plunged them repeatedly into his prostrate body; no fewer than forty wounds were afterwards counted on his corpse. It was owing to this delay and the breakdown of their carriage on the way back to Belgrade that the murderers were baulked of the results which they had confidently anticipated from their horrible deed. Their intention had been to send one of their number at once to the city to proclaim Peter Karageorgević, son of the ex-Prince Alexander, and issue a new constitution in his name. This document was all ready, a list of new ministers had been drawn up, and as soon as the news of Michael's murder arrived those officials who showed any resistance were to be shot. But when their carriage at last reached Belgrade, the tidings had preceded them. The garrison was under arms, the energetic Minister of War, Petrović Blačnavac, the most intimate of the murdered Prince's advisers, was master of the situation, and the chief conspirators were speedily arrested. The four assassins were two brothers Radovanović, one of whom had been convicted of forgery, a wife-murderer named Marić, and a desperado called Rogić. The plot proved to be widespread, and many friends and connections of the Karageorgević family were implicated. Two of the ringleaders were the ex-Prince Alexander's brothers-in-law, another was his lawyer, and Prince Peter himself, at that time an exile in Vienna, was openly accused of being an accomplice. Party feeling ran high. The Conservatives declared the conspiracy to be the work of the *Omladina*, a literary and political society of advanced views, which existed wherever Serbs were found and numbered Prince Peter among its most recent recruits. The National Assembly, which was summoned under these exciting circumstances, unanimously decreed the exclusion of the Karageorgević family from the Servian throne for ever, and to this day the descendants of Black George are exiles. Blood had been requited by blood, and the murder of the Servian Liberator by Milosh Obrenović had been avenged in the next generation by the murder of Milosh's son. The Assembly then proclaimed Michael's nearest relative, his cousin Milan, as hereditary Prince of Servia, under the title of Milan Obrenović IV. As the young Prince was at that time barely fourteen, a Regency of three persons, of whom Petrović Blačnavac was the chief, was appointed to carry on the government till he came of age.

The murder of Michael was indeed a blow for Servia. On his tomb in the cathedral of Belgrade his widow has engraved the words, "Thy memory shall not perish." No epitaph could better have expressed the feelings of the nation towards the best and ablest of all its modern rulers.

The three Regents began their task by securing from the Porte a final recognition of the hereditary rights of the Obrenović family. They then proceeded to draw up a somewhat more liberal constitution than that which had, with some modifications, existed for the last thirty years. Prince Michael in his reforms had only amended the old system of government; the Regents now took the bolder step of abolishing it altogether. The new constitution of 1869 entrusted all power to the Prince and the National Assembly, which was to meet every year and was re-elected every three. This body consisted for ordinary purposes of 120 members, of whom 90 were elected by the people and 30 nominated by the Prince. In order to pacify the jealousy which the Serb peasantry and small farmers felt of the professional class, it was provided that while members of the latter could be nominated by the Prince, no lawyer or official was eligible by the people. On extraordinary occasions a "Great Assembly" of 480 persons, all chosen by the people, replaced the ordinary legislature. The elections were open, and therefore easily manipulated by the Government, and it was found that the Assembly became the tool of the Ministers. This is the constitution which was restored by the *coup d'état* of 1894, when the much more Radical Reform Act of 1888 was abolished by a stroke of the boy King Alexander's pen, and remains in force to the present day.

Prince Milan came of age in 1872, and soon showed his determination to govern in his own way. Educated in Paris, the new ruler had acquired decidedly Parisian tastes, but his abilities proved considerably better than his character. He had a strong will, but his love of pleasure, his reckless extravagance, and his devotion to the gaming-table ruined what might otherwise have been a successful career. A man of fashion rather than a soldier, he found himself compelled to support the agitation of the Serb race against the Turks, and the insurrection which broke out in the Herzegovina in 1875 dragged him, however unwillingly, into war.

During the Regency the idea of a "Great Servia," which should include all the scattered branches of the Serb stock under one ruler, had been sedulously cultivated. M. Ristić, the second Regent and a statesman of marked ability, had been the soul of this policy, which was bound to offend the susceptibilities not only of Turkey, but of Austria-Hungary. It was not clear who was to be the head of this "great Servian kingdom"—Prince Milan of Servia, or Prince Nicholas of Montenegro, a born leader of men, greatly superior in character to the Prince of Servia. Prince Milan was therefore less anxious than Prince Nicholas for a war with Turkey, especially as the latter had declined to acknowledge him as leader of the Servian movement, although he had expressed his willingness to serve under Michael. But the voice of the Servian people prevailed over the hesitation of the ruler, and insisted upon a crusade against the hereditary enemy. Milan yielded, and on the 30th of June, 1876, proclaimed his intention of joining his arms to those of the Bosniaks and Herzegovinians. Montenegro declared war the day after Servia, and a campaign began between the two branches of the Serb race and the descendants of those who had destroyed the old Servian Empire nearly five centuries before.

The Servian army was under the directions of the Russian General Tchernaieff, and consisted, all told, of some 148,000 men. But it soon became clear that the soldiers were not only inferior to the Montenegrins, but were no match for the Turks. At first the superior generalship of their Russian commander enabled them to carry the war into the enemy's country near Ak-palanka. But the Turks soon penetrated into Servia and drove them back. A battle beneath the walls of Alexinac resulted in the complete defeat of Prince Milan's army, and the Porte refused to grant peace except on the most onerous terms. The negotiations begun by England were hindered by the proclamation of the Prince as King of Servia at Deligrad on the 16th of September at the suggestion of General Tchernaieff, and the war went on as before. The capture of Alexinac and Deligrad by the Turks left the road to Belgrade at their mercy, and the Servian troops, with the exception of the artillerymen, became utterly disorganised. An armistice was arranged by the intervention of the Powers, and while Montenegro continued the struggle, Servia made peace with Turkey on the 1st of March, 1877. The war, so far as Prince Milan was concerned, had produced no material result, for the position before it had commenced was maintained. Russia had saved Servia by a timely ultimatum from the consequences of her defeats, and, thanks to the Powers, no loss of territory and no war indemnity were inflicted upon her.

When, in Prince Milan's words, "the defence of the holy cause had passed into stronger hands" and Russia declared war against the Sultan, Servia, from fear of Austria, refrained for some months from taking part in the struggle. She looked on while the Roumanians invested Plevna, and it was not till December that the Prince resumed hostilities. Invoking the names of "the old heroes of Takovo," he crossed the frontier on this second campaign. The result was much more favourable to Servia than that of the first. In spite of severe losses from the ice and snow one detachment won a decisive victory at

Pirot, while another, commanded by the Prince in person, captured the ancient Servian town of Nisch,

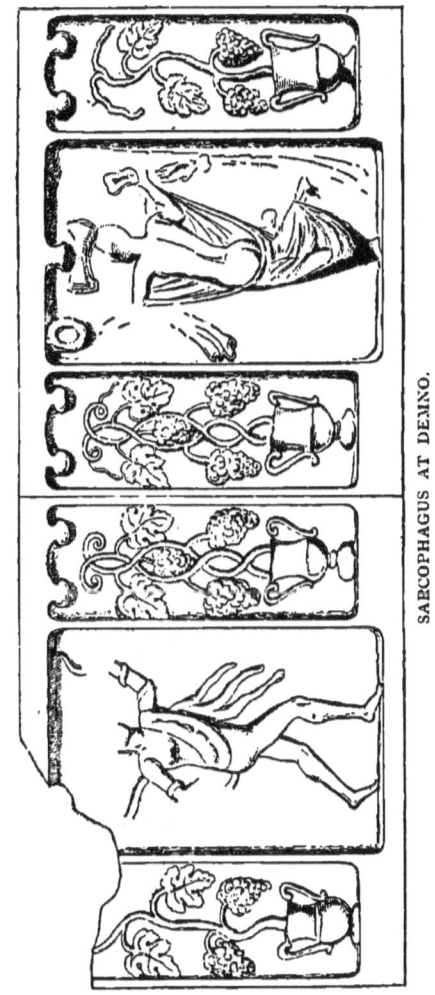

SARCOPHAGUS AT DEMNO.

which since the fatal day of Kossovo, five centuries

before, had been part of the Turkish Empire. Great was the enthusiasm of his people when Prince Milan entered the gates as a conqueror. Nine days later the victory of General Bela Marković (afterwards one of the Regents) at Vranja completed the trio of Servian successes. The armistice and the Treaty of San Stefano cut short the further progress of the campaign.

By that treaty Servia obtained the recognition of her independence, and ceased to be tributary to the Sultan. She was to receive a considerable accession of territory, including the town of Nisch. Still more important, in view of a future union of the Serb race, the south-western frontier of Servia, as drawn at San Stefano, would have gone close by Novibazar, and have thus come very close to that of Montenegro. But the Berlin Treaty of 1878, which replaced the abortive arrangements of San Stefano, provided that Servia should have territorial compensation on the side of Bulgaria rather than in the direction of Montenegro. A wedge was allowed to remain, in the shape of the Sandjak of Novibazar, between the two Serb states, and the right of garrisoning certain places in that region, which was conceded to Austria, has checked the aspirations of the Serbs for reunion quite as effectually as the Austrian "occupation" of Bosnia and the Herzegovina. On the south-east, however, Servia received the Bulgarian-speaking district of Pirot and was allowed to retain Vranja and Nisch, so that the area of the principality was increased by more than one-fourth. She undertook to pay a proportion of the

Ottoman Debt for her new territories, and took over the engagements of the Porte with regard to the railways. Finally her independence, already recognised by the Sultan at San Stefano, was affirmed by the Powers. Thus she was at last free in theory as well as in fact. The practical independence which she had gained when the Turkish garrisons were withdrawn in 1867 was formally completed by the solemn act of Europe in 1878. Four years later, on the 6th of March, 1882, the Prince was proclaimed king under the title of Milan I., and Servia once more ranked as a kingdom.

VII.

THE MODERN KINGDOM OF SERVIA.

(1882—1896.)

THE Berlin Treaty, which was intended as a permanent settlement of the eternal Eastern question, failed to satisfy either Servia or Bulgaria. Each country was jealous of the other; Servia claimed Vidin, Bulgaria desired Nisch and Pirot, and it was not long before an opportunity occurred for the display of their mutual antipathies. On the Bulgarian bank of the river Timok, which forms the boundary between the two states, there is an uninhabited tract of land, called Bregova. No mention was made of it in the Treaty of Berlin, and accordingly the Serbs, who lived on the opposite bank, continued to cross the river for the purpose of tilling this debatable ground, until in the summer of 1884 a Bulgarian regiment drove them out. The high protective tariff, which the principality erected against Servia in the same year, increased the irritation, and when the union of the two Bulgarias was suddenly accomplished in the autumn of 1885, it was impossible to hold back the Servian nation. It must be confessed that there was no adequate motive for war, but all their national susceptibilities were aroused by this unexpected aggrandisement of Bulgaria, and war both king and people would have. M. Garashanine, the Servian Premier, went to war "with a light heart." "*Nous allons piquer une tête,*" he said with a smile, and no one doubted but that Servia would win an easy victory over her embarrassed rival. But, as we have shown in the second part of this volume, the result was far otherwise. Servia, utterly routed at Slivnitza, was only saved by the intervention of an Austrian diplomatist from a Bulgarian occupation, and was fortunate to have escaped, as she had escaped in 1877, without loss of territory or the payment of a war indemnity.

The complete failure of their campaign against Bulgaria caused much discontent among the Serbs. For some time past the Government had been very unpopular, and party feeling had run high. In 1882 King Milan nearly shared the fate of his predecessor at the hand of an officer's widow, who fired at him in the cathedral of Belgrade. Next year the arbitrary measures of the "iron minister," Cristić, led to a peasant insurrection, which was suppressed after considerable bloodshed. The party of the pretender, Prince Peter Karageorgević, son-in-law of the Prince of Montenegro, began once more to raise its head, and a conspiracy was discovered to dethrone King Milan and put him in his place. To crown all came the disastrous Bulgarian war, which emptied the treasury, enormously increased the national debt, and destroyed such military reputation as Servia had gained in the second campaign of 1877. Domestic quarrels in the royal household soon became a public scandal. The king had married a beautiful Russian lady, Natalie Kesckho, daughter of a colonel in the Imperial army, who traced her descent from the old Counts of Baux. From the first the two disagreed, and their opposite political sympathies increased their private differences. The queen was a strong partisan of Russia, the king a friend of Austria; she longed to support the Czar; her husband publicly declared Panslavism to be "the enemy of Servia," and avowed that he would be neutral in any Austro-Russian war. At last he obtained a divorce from his wife, and at once granted a new and much more liberal constitution than that of 1869. The most important article was that which made all classes of the community, and not peasants alone, eligible as deputies, but one-fourth of the National Assembly was still to be nominated by the king. Freedom of the press and the lowering of the suffrage were also points of the new charter, which, in spite of Russian bribes, was accepted by the Assembly early in 1889. The king did not, however, long remain to guide the nation under the new constitution which he had given it. Exhausted with worries, domestic and political, broken in health and prematurely old, he suddenly resigned on the 6th of March of the same year in favour of his son Alexander, a lad of thirteen, and appointed three Regents, the chief of whom was the same M. Ristić, the "Cavour of Servia," who had been Regent during his own minority.

The four years of the Regency were much disturbed by the continual quarrels of the ex-king and his consort, who asserted her right to reside permanently in Servia, where she was very popular. At last, both she and her former husband consented to leave the country, which their presence had greatly agitated. The intrigues of the Pretender and the growth of Republicanism so much alarmed the royal couple that they made up their private differences in

ROSE WINDOW AT KRUŠEVAC.

order to save the throne for their son. That precocious youth showed that he possessed the firm character of the founder of the dynasty by suddenly arresting the three Regents on the night of the 13th of April, 1893, as they sat at dinner with him in the royal *konak*, or palace, at Belgrade, together with all his Ministers. Troops occupied the Government offices, and next morning the young king issued a proclamation, declaring himself to be of age, dissolving the National Assembly and announcing his intention to save the State from disaster. The *coup d'état* of this boy of seventeen was completely successful, and its success encouraged him to another. At midnight on the 21st of May, 1894, he abolished the constitution granted five years before, and restored the old constitution of 1869, in order to destroy the influence of the Radical party. Europe recognised that Servia had a monarch of great determination, who was resolved to govern as well as reign. Whether he will put an end to the deplorable party strife between the three factions of Liberals, Progressists, and Radicals, which is the curse of his country, remains to be seen. But no one can help looking forward with interest to his career. Some have thought that he is destined to revive the Empire of Dušan, and unite once more under a common sceptre the scattered members of the great Servian family. Doubtful though this may be, one thing is certain, that if Servia desires to prosper, she must take to heart her national motto: "Unity alone can save the Servian people."

PART IV.

MONTENEGRO.

> "They rose to where their sovran eagle sails,
>   They kept their faith, their freedom, on the height,
>   Chaste, frugal, savage, armed by day and night
>   Against the Turk ; whose inroad nowhere scales
>   Their headlong passes, but his footstep fails,
>   And red with blood the Crescent reels from fight
>   Before their dauntless hundreds, in prone flight
>   By thousands down the crags and through the vales.
>   O smallest among peoples ! rough rock-throne
>   Of Freedom ! warriors beating back the swarm
>   Of Turkish Islâm for five hundred years,
>   Great Tsernagora ! never since thine own
>   Black ridges drew the cloud and broke the storm
>   Has breathed a race of mightier mountaineers."
>   TENNYSON, *Nineteenth Century*, May, 1877.

"In my deliberate opinion the traditions of Montenegro, now committed to His Highness (Prince Nicholas) as a sacred trust, exceed in glory those of Marathon and Thermopylæ, and *all* the war-traditions of the world."—MR. GLADSTONE, October 18, 1895

I.

FROM THE EARLIEST TIMES TO THE BATTLE OF KOSSOVO.

(1389.)

THE country on the eastern shore of the Adriatic, which we are accustomed to call Montenegro or the "Black Mountain," is usually supposed to derive its name from the black forests of pines which once clothed its grey limestone rocks. From the western half of the country, which composed the original principality, all vestiges of wood have long since disappeared, and the sea of stones, which meets the eye of the traveller in every direction, cannot by any stretch of language be called dark. It has therefore been suggested that the mountain took its title from the "Black Prince," or Crnoiević, who founded a Montenegrin dynasty in the fifteenth century. No trace of the name can be discovered before that period, and it is more rational to suppose that the country was called after its rulers than that the Turks gave it its present designation because of the "black hearts" of its people. But, whatever be the origin of the name "Montenegro"—the Venetian variant of the ordinary word "Monte Nero"—the fact remains that in such different languages as French, Italian, Turkish, Arabic, modern Greek, and Albanian, we find the country described by a name which in each case has the meaning of "Black Mountain." The title of Crnagora, which the natives have bestowed upon their highland home, has the same significance.

The origin of the nation is much less obscure than that of its name. When the Serb kingdom fell on the fatal field of Kossovo in 1389, the mountain-fastnesses between the Adriatic and the valley of the Zeta became the last refuge of those Serb families who preferred freedom in a barren land to a fertile soil and the yoke of the Ottoman invader. The present inhabitants of Montenegro are descended from the aristocracy of ancient Servia, and a believer in the doctrine of heredity may detect in their exquisite manners a proof of their aristocratic lineage. It has been truly said that the Montenegrin is the exact opposite of the Bulgarian. Put both in a drawing-room, and the Montenegrin, who has never bowed his neck to a foreign master, will look and behave like a gentleman, while the Bulgarian, but lately set free from the Turkish bondage, will look and behave like a boor. But put the two upon a waste plot of ground, and the Bulgarian will convert it into a garden of roses, while the Montenegrin will look on. This is the result of the national history. For five centuries the Montenegrins have had to fight for their existence. War has become the great object of their lives, their annals are one long series of heroic struggles for independence, and even now they have not emerged from the military into the industrial state of society. Their history, based as it is in large measure upon oral tradition and the stirring war-songs of the native bards, reminds the reader at every page of the Homeric era of ancient Greece, with its god-like heroes, its hard-fought battles, its raids and forays, its ghastly trophies, and its kings, who, like the *Vladikas* of Montenegro, were "shepherds of the people," its chiefs in council, its judges in peace, its leaders in war.

Although the existence of Montenegro as an independent state dates from the battle of Kossovo, the country had shared the vicissitudes of the Balkan Peninsula for several centuries before that memorable disaster. It was in the earliest times a part of Illyria, called Prævalitana by the Romans, of which Scutari in Albania, or Skodra, as the Turks call it, was the capital. When the Romans first crossed the Adriatic in 229 B.C. to suppress the piracy which crippled their commerce, it was against Teuta, queen of the Illyrians, that they directed their attacks. Teuta at first resisted, but was soon forced to flee, and Rizona, which is mentioned by Polybius as her place of refuge, is the present Podgorica, the largest town in Montenegro and its chief commercial centre. Sixty years later, the prætor Lucius Anicius Paulus defeated Gentius, King of Illyria, and pursued him to Skodra. The country was, however, allowed to remain independent for a time, and formed part of a loose confederation of states. Subsequently administered, like Cisalpine Gaul, direct from Rome, it was not formed into an actual province and finally united to the Roman Empire till the reign of Augustus. Then, as now, it was, in a sense, the meeting-place of the East and West, for Skodra was the dividing-line between the eastern and western dominions of the triumvirs when for the second time they distributed the world between them. Henceforth Roman influence was felt in Montenegro and its borderlands. Roman cities rose at Ascrivium, the modern Cattaro, and at Rhizinium, the modern Risano. The labour of antiquaries has laid bare the remains of Dioclea, an ancient town situated at the junction of the rivers Zeta and Morača, not far from Podgorica, and famous as the birthplace of the Roman Emperor Diocletian. Marble altars and pieces of columns still recall the Roman period, and Prince Nicholas possesses at Cetinje several silver coins, dug up at Dioclea, which bear the image and superscription of the Roman

Cæsars. The numerous inscriptions which have been discovered in the neighbourhood prove that the influence of the Flavian Emperors was powerful even in that remote spot. Dioclea, were it in Italy or Greece, would be the wonder of tourists, the admiration of scholars.

RUINS OF DIOCLEA.
(*From a photo by Mr. C. A. Miller.*)

As might have been expected from its position, Montenegro oscillated between the Eastern and Western Empires. Now it was assigned to the one, and now to the other. At first it was included in the Eastern division, but from the reign of Honorius down to the close of the fifth century after Christ it was transferred to the Western. When that fell, it came back, together with the other districts on the eastern shore of the Adriatic, to the Eastern Empire, whose ecclesiastical supremacy it had already owned. This was a decisive moment in its history, for it was the origin of that firm connection with the Eastern Church which has distinguished Montenegro from the Roman Catholic Albanians along its southern frontier. The inroads of the barbarians now began. Even the bare Montenegrin mountains became a prey to the invaders. In the middle of the sixth century the Slavs entered Illyria, as the western part of the Balkan Peninsula was called, in large numbers, overthrew the armies which met them, and swept over the land. A century later, the Greek Emperor Heraclius, true to the time-honoured policy of casting out one horde of barbarians by another, summoned the Croats and Serbs from the southern slopes of the Carpathians to repel the advance of the terrible Avars. Their efforts were successful. A Serb state, or confederation of seven states, was founded, and of this Montenegro became a member, just as it had in olden time belonged to an Illyrian group. At this period the Montenegrin portion of the confederation took its name from Dioclea, its principal town, and was governed by a governor, or Župan, dependent upon the Grand Župan, who presided over the seven confederate states and was in his turn a vassal of the Emperor at Constantinople. The arrangement was somewhat similar to the Heptarchy in our own early history. The Župan of Dioclea, like his fellows, enjoyed a large measure of independence, and spent a considerable portion of his time in fighting with his fellow-princelings.

Whichever of them became the strongest was recognised by the rest as their head. Presently the slender tie between the Empire and the Serb Heptarchy snapped, and fresh swarms of invaders attacked the confederates. The Župan of Dioclea ruled at this period over a much larger region than the Montenegro of to-day. The village communities of the Herzegovina on the north, and the territory of Albania as far south as Skodra, the coveted coast-strip from Dulcigno to Cattaro and the whole shore of the splendid gulf to which that town gives its name, then obeyed the master of Dioclea. His country became known as the Principality of the Zeta, or Zenta, from the river on which his capital was situated. Gradually the power of the separate confederate chiefs became greater, and the union of the confederation looser. The Župan of Dioclea first assumed the title of his superior lord, and then, under the name of *Ban*, which survives in the Croatia of our own time, declared himself free from all federate control. Obscure as is the history of the old Illyrian province at this era, the importance of the present Montenegro is clear even in those misty centuries. Samuel, the famous Bulgarian Czar, did, indeed, succeed in destroying its capital. But Dioclea rose from its ashes, and in 1050 we find its Prince proclaiming himself King of Servia. The celebrated Pope Hildebrand confirmed his title, and he reigned for thirty years in his Montenegrin capital over the undivided Serb race. His son, Bodin, succeeded him, and even extended his dominion, adding "lofty Bosnia" to his possessions. But discord broke out in his family, his descendants were unable to maintain his position, and the principality sank once more under the Imperial sway.

But it did not long remain an appanage of the Greek Empire. Early in the twelfth century—as narrated in the third part of this book—Stephen Nemanja reunited the Serb states, and made them, including Montenegro, into a substantial kingdom. The Herzegovina and the valley of the Zeta were then separated from the western part of the present principality, and formed three of the nine divisions into which he split up his kingdom. From that date, down to the downfall of the Serb monarchy at Kossovo, the history of Montenegro is part and parcel of that of Servia, which has already been described. A *Župan* or *Ban* continued to reside at Dioclea, but for the next two hundred years he was nothing more than a Serb viceroy. The place continued, however, to have more than local importance. Its situation at the confluence of two rivers, not far from the Lake of Scutari and the coast, combined with its historic traditions to prevent it sinking to the level of a village. It was the seat of an Archbishop, whose jurisdiction extended over the wild mountaineers and lonely shepherds of the region beyond the river; St. Sava, the saint whom every true Serb reveres, dwelt within its walls, and thence issued his orders to the Serb priesthood far and near. From him the first Bishop of Montenegro received consecration, and it was at his call that a council of holy men met at Dioclea to consider the best remedy for the abuses in the Church. Rather more than a century later, the great hero of Serb legend, Stephen Dušan, was

RISE OF BALSHA.

made viceroy of all the old Principality of the Zeta by his father, the King of Servia, and transferred the seat of government to Skodra. Dioclea vanishes from view in the fourteenth century, and is now only a heap of marble ruins.

During the reign of Stephen Dušan there lived in the Principality of Zeta a noble Serb named Balsha, whose family is thought to have come from Baux in Anjou and settled on the eastern coast of the Adriatic a generation earlier. Balsha was a man of some local importance at the death of Dušan, and took advantage of the weakness of the great monarch's successor to seize the fortress of Skodra and make himself master of the lower part of the Zeta as far as the walls of Cattaro. His three sons further extended his conquests; the western half of the present Principality of Montenegro came beneath their sway, and the proud Republic of Ragusa did not disdain their alliance. When Lazar mounted the Servian throne the power of the Balsha family grew in all directions. Their sovereignty stretched as far as Valona in Albania on the one side, and included Trebinje in the Herzegovina on the other. They even made war with ten thousand men against Stephen Tvartko, the redoubtable King of Bosnia. Both combatants found willing allies. The city of Cattaro joined Tvartko, the Republic of Ragusa aided the Balshas, and the latter compelled Cattaro to sue for peace. A little later a much more dangerous foe appeared upon their frontiers. The Turks were advancing through Albania, and the chief of the Balshas at once set out to oppose them. The attempt was useless; Balsha's army was annihilated, and his head carried as a trophy to the Turkish Vizier. George Balsha II., who succeeded him, endeavoured to strengthen his position by a great alliance. He accordingly married the daughter of King Lazar of Servia, who was the widow of Šišman, King of Bulgaria. But his close relationship with the Servian sovereign availed him little. His subjects were ready to hand over the Zeta to Tvartko of Bosnia; the Turks were daily approaching, and had seized Durazzo, Antivari, and Budua in rapid succession. They even traversed the valley of the Zeta, and threatened the heights of Ostrog and the plain of Nikšić, the scenes of many a Turkish defeat in the later annals of Montenegro. George Balsha signed a disastrous peace, by which he surrendered part of Albania to the invaders. But at the time of the battle of Kossovo in 1389 he still ruled over a large tract of territory, stretching from Ragusa to the mouth of the Drin, south of Dulcigno, the south of the Herzegovina and the whole of Western Montenegro, with Skodra as a capital. In that great battle he and his people took no part, for he was on his way to join his father-in-law with all his forces when the fatal news arrived. He returned at once to his own land, determined to defend his mountains to the last gasp against the Turk. Many a noble Serb family sought safety under his protection; Montenegro became the asylum of the Serb race, the house of free men struggling for their liberty. Every Montenegrin looks back to the great disaster of Kossovo with the same keen regret as if it had happened but last year. Every rising of the Serb race is justified by the national bards as revenge for Kossovo, and, more striking still, the headgear of the mountaineers bears even in our own days the traces of the national grief. The crimson pork-pie cap, or *kapa*, which the Montenegrins, female as well as male, wear, has a broad border of black silk as a token of mourning for that defeat; the crimson centre signifies the sea of blood with which the Black Mountain has been washed since then; and the five gold bands, which enclose in one corner the initials of the Prince (" H.I.," or Nicholas I.) in Cyrillic characters, represent the five centuries of Montenegro's stormy history.

II.

FROM THE BATTLE OF KOSSOVO TO THE LAST OF THE BLACK PRINCES.

(1389—1516.)

GEORGE BALSHA was not long allowed to remain unmolested in his mountain retreat. While Durazzo voluntarily surrendered to the growing power of Venice, which had already obtained facilities for her commerce in the Principality of the Zeta, the Prince was compelled to buy the aid of the mighty Republic of St. Mark against the Turks. The price was a high one, but it was paid, for the need was great. Venice received, in 1394, from Balsha, his capital of Skodra in exchange for a petty fortress and an annual subsidy of a thousand gold ducats, the first instance of such an annuity being paid by a foreign state to a Montenegrin Prince. But the assistance of the Republic was less valuable to Balsha than the diversion created by Timour the Tartar's defeat and capture of the Sultan Bajazet in 1402 at the battle of Angora. For a brief space the land had rest from the Turks, and George Balsha's son, the last of the dynasty, who succeeded his father three years later, was bold enough to recapture Skodra and the other places in the Principality occupied by the Venetians. A series of campaigns followed, in which the Montenegrins and Venetians were alternately successful. Mariano Caravella, the Republican commander, reconquered Skodra and most of the lower Zeta. But Balsha, who had fled with his mother, speedily came back and once more drove out the Venetian garrisons. The proud Doge was compelled to seek an intermediary between the valiant mountaineers and himself. A treaty was concluded; Venice gave up most of the territory which she had acquired in the Principality, and agreed to pay to Balsha the subsidy promised to his father. But the peace was soon disregarded. Stephen Crnoievié, the "Black Prince," of whom we now hear for the first time, and whose race played an important part in Montenegrin history, possessed the confidence of Balsha, whose relative he was on the female side. Acting on Stephen's advice, Balsha summoned his forces and attacked Skodra, the great object of contention between Venice and himself. The Venetians were now seriously alarmed. Two of their ablest commanders, Bembo and Dandolo, were unable to retake the town, and, as a last resort, they sent an envoy to Constantinople to ask the aid of the Sultan. But even the assistance of eight thousand Turkish troops availed but little against the stubborn valour of the Montenegrins. A fresh Venetian force under another general was sent, only to be twice defeated, and at last, in 1421, the Republic was compelled to sue for peace. It was no small triumph for these undisciplined bands of Highland warriors to have humbled two such redoubtable foes. Balsha, however, did not long enjoy the fruits of his victories. In the same year he died while on a visit to Servia, and with him his dynasty became extinct.

Balsha had appointed his relative, the "Black Prince," regent during his absence, but an interregnum lasted for some years after his death. Montenegro, at this period, was very far from being a compact state; it consisted of loose agglomerations of territory, varying in size according to the fortunes of war, and inhabited by a migratory population of shepherds and exiles. From every neighbouring land the persecuted or the lawless fled thither for refuge, and a community was thus formed in the fastnesses of the Black Mountain, much in the same way that Rome herself was founded. Every man who had weapons and knew how to use them was welcome there, and when one of the inhabitants fell in battle, another soon filled his place. When not engaged in fighting, the people looked after their flocks of mountain sheep, and the early occupation of these primitive mountaineers has left its mark upon the geography of the country in the name of Katunska, or "shepherds' huts," which is still applied to the *nahia*, or district, in which Cetinje is situated. The Crnoiević dynasty, however, which held sway for the next three generations, consolidated the independence of the Black Mountain. At first, however, Stephen Crnoiević showed no desire to rule over so wild a land. He had retired to Italy on the death of Balsha, and only the entreaties of the people, who needed a leader, brought him back. Meanwhile, the Venetians had renewed hostilities. One after another the fortresses of the lower Zeta fell into their hands. Stephen Lazarević, the King of Servia, intervened as Balsha's next of kin, and in two campaigns inflicted severe defeats upon the Venetian armies. Skodra itself, after a long siege, surrendered to George Branković, his nephew, who was invested by Lazarević with the overlordship of the Zeta. The Venetians recognised him as ruler of the Principality, and promised to pay him the usual annuity of one thousand ducats in exchange for the town of Skodra.

But the people were not disposed to admit the shadowy claims of the phantom King of Servia. That latter country was for all practical purposes dependent on the Turk, and Montenegro has never owned the suzerainty of the Sultan. Accordingly, Stephen Crnoievič was summoned from Italy, and had made himself master of the Zeta before his rival had ever arrived in the Principality. Branković wisely gave way before the superior claims of his popular competitor. He shortly after succeeded to the throne of Servia, and left the "Black Prince" undisturbed. But to mark the complete independence of their land from the fallen monarchy of Servia, the people gave to their new ruler the title of *Voïvode*, or Duke, of the Zeta, a title which is borne to-day by one of the present Prince's sons.

Stephen Crnoievič, at his succession, found himself lord of a large expanse of country. The whole of the present Principality of Montenegro, all the islands in the Lake of Skodra, and the shores of the Bocche di Cattaro, belonged to him; but Skodra itself, which had been regarded by his predecessors as their capital since the decline of Dioclea, was still under the Venetian sway. He accordingly fortified Žabljak, at present a town of one thousand inhabitants, not far from the north-east shore of the Lake of Skodra, and made it his capital. His reign was at first an almost continuous struggle with the Turks. M. Vaçlik, the late secretary of the Prince and an excellent authority on Montenegrin history, estimated that in the twelve years between 1424 and 1436 there were no fewer than sixty-three battles with, and sixty-three victories over, the Ottoman armies. Foreseeing the dangers of a Turkish invasion, the "Black Prince" came to terms with Venice, and on the island of Vranina, in the Lake of Skodra, a solemn league and convention was signed. The Republic promised to pay him a subsidy such as she had paid to the Balshas, and he agreed to assist her in time of war. As soon as he found that the Turks were too much occupied with their enemies in Asia Minor, Servia, and Albania, to farther molest him in his own country, he joined his forces to that of his relative, George Castriotes, or Skanderbeg, who had headed the Albanian tribes against the Ottoman invaders. Skanderbeg is the most remarkable name in the records of Albania. Round his heroic figure all the legendary glories of that strange and incomprehensible race centre. As a boy of nine years of age, he was brought to the court of Murad II., who had him educated in the faith of Islâm, loaded him with favours, and gave him the command of a troop of horse with the title of Bey. It was from this title, corrupted by the Christians into Beg, and joined with Iskander or Skander, the Turkish form of Alexander, that Skanderbeg derived the name by which he still lives in Albanian history. On many a field the young Bey fought under the standard of the Crescent, but the tragic death of his father at the hands of the Turks determined him to become his avenger. At a critical moment, when the fortune of battle was undecided, he deserted to the enemy, proclaimed himself Prince of Albania, and declared war against the unbelievers. From that moment he became the heart and soul of the Christian cause. The national ballads tell how he slew two thousand Turks with his own hand ; and when he died, the Sultan exclaimed with relief that the Christians had " lost their buckler and the arm which protected them." Stephen Crnoiević and his two sons, Ivan and George, fought gallantly by his side, and Mohammed II., the future conqueror of Constantinople, was routed by the Montenegrins in a narrow defile and forced to beat an ignominious retreat into Macedonia. Soliman Pasha, who was sent to ravage the lower Zeta in revenge for this defeat, succeeded in enticing the mountaineers into the open, where their army was almost annihilated. But the siege of Constantinople provided the Turkish forces with other occupation, and Montenegro was spared.

Stephen Crnoiević died about 1466, and was buried in the little monastery on the island of Kom in the Lake of Skodra, which he had founded. His eldest son Ivan, surnamed the Black, succeeded him, and with the new ruler commences a new era in the history of the mountain state. For the reign of Ivan witnessed the downfall of the last of those bulwarks which had hitherto stemmed the tide of Ottoman invasion in its advance upon Montenegro. The Turkish conquest of Servia in 1459, and Bosnia in 1463, was followed in 1476 by the subjugation of the Herzegovina, while the death of Skanderbeg left Albania at the mercy of the Mussulman. Montenegro was henceforth the refuge of fugitives not merely from Servia, but from all the South Slavonic lands; the beach, as Mr. Gladstone has said, upon which all that remained from the wreck of Balkan freedom was cast up by the waves. From this time onwards the Montenegrins fought for their very existence, and at the same time, in saving themselves, they saved others too. It is no exaggeration to say that Italy herself owes a debt of gratitude to this handful of warriors, who acted as her outpost on the farther shore of the Adriatic against the Turk. But neither from Venice nor from any other Italian city did they receive much assistance in their own hour of need. So long as the Venetian possessions were in actual danger, the Republic of St. Mark was glad to accept Ivan's assistance. When Soliman Pasha besieged Scutari in 1474, with an army of seventy thousand men, it was he and his people who raised the siege, and when Mohammed II. renewed the attempt in person four years later, Ivan in vain tried to create a diversion and so save the place. Venice did, indeed, confer upon him and his heirs for ever the title of patrician and his name was inscribed in the Golden Book of the Republic. But when Skodra fell, Ivan had to defend himself and his capital of Žabljak singlehanded. Mohammed II. and his successor resolved to root out the bold allies of Venice, who had dared to resist the Ottoman power. Meanwhile the Republic of St. Mark looked on, heedless of Ivan's appeals for aid, while the Turks came nearer. To assist the Montenegrins would have injured the commerce of Venice with the Levant. Ivan, abandoned by those for whom he had done so much, took the bold resolution of setting fire to Žabljak and seeking a new capital in a safer spot, rather than allow it to fall a prey to the Turks. The year 1484 witnessed this important event. Žabljak was destroyed, and Ivan and his warriors retired to the lofty plateau of Cetinje, four thousand feet above the sea. From that time onwards Cetinje has been the Montenegrin capital. The site is not an ideal one, for the plain, in which the town stands, is often blocked by snow in winter, and the situation is not so central as could be desired. But the recent idea of transferring the seat of government to Nikšić, which has much to recommend it, has been hindered by considerations of expense, and Cetinje, though several times plundered by the Turks, has always risen, phœnix-like, from its ashes. There Ivan built the monastery called after his name, which, after its destruction in 1714, was restored in the form which it still possesses. There, too, he established the see of a bishop, with authority over the Zeta. The lower part of that region now fell under the sway of the Turks and was annexed to the district of which Skodra was the chief town. Deserted by the Venetians, robbed of the most fertile portion of his territory and driven back to the wilderness of rocks which separates the Zeta valley from the sea, Ivan offered his people the alternative of holding out to the last gasp under his command, or of finding another prince, who would make terms for them with the Turks. As for himself, he vowed that he would never surrender. The answer of the Montenegrins was unhesitatingly given. They swore to serve him till death, and promised that, while they would never provoke an attack from the Turks, they would defend themselves, if attacked, with might and main. Every Montenegrin who should be coward enough to leave the battlefield was condemned to an insulting punishment. Deprived of his arms, the craven was to be dressed in woman's garb, a spindle put in his hand, and then the wives and maidens of the Black Mountain would drive him before them over the border with blows as an exile and a renegade. The vow was worthy of the nation which took it, and the Spartan mother, who bade her son return either with his shield or on it, found imitators in Montenegro. As late as the Montenegrin code of the present century we find similar enactments against cowardice, and to-day the same spirit, which animated the subjects of Ivan the Black, breathes in their descendants.

For the rest of his reign he was unmolested, and devoted himself to the erection of a fortress at Obod, near Rjeka, and to the foundation of the first Montenegrin printing-press at the same spot. His son and successor, George Crnoievič, anxious that his country should be no longer dependent upon Venice for its books of devotion, continued his father's work at Obod. Type of extreme beauty was obtained from abroad, and the first volumes ever printed in Cyrillic character were issued from the Montenegrin Press. The earliest of them, published in 1493, or only twenty-two years after Caxton set up his press at Westminster, was a missal, of which a page is still preserved in the monastery at Cetinje, while two years later a psalter and a ritual were produced. Montenegro may well be proud of such an early advancement of learning at a time when even great nations had hardly adopted the new invention. In 1893, the four hundredth anniversary of this Slavonic printing-press was celebrated with much rejoicing, as one of the most memorable events in the history of the nation. Unfortunately, the Turks destroyed the machinery in one of their numerous invasions. It was not till 1832 that the art of printing was reintroduced into the country, and to-day a few pieces of stone in the churchyard are all that remains of the press at Obod.

Ivan the Black died in 1490, while his son George was returning from Venice with the noble Venetian lady whom he had chosen as his bride. The memory of the second Crnoiević Prince lingers even now among the people, whom he prepared so boldly for the dangers which lay before them in the centuries to come. With him the unceasing struggle with the Turks may be said to have begun; under him the fastnesses of Western Montenegro, the kernel of the present State, with Cetinje as capital, became the stronghold of resistance to the Ottoman sway.

His name lingers in the monastery which he founded and where he was buried, in springs of water, in caves, and in many an ancient ruin. And a picturesque ballad represents him as sleeping in a fairy grotto above his castle at Obod, like Kaiser Barbarossa in the German legend, till the hour when the trumpet shall awaken him to lead the Montenegrin nation to the conquest of Albania. The reign of Ivan the Black has also prompted one of the finest poems of the national muse. The story of his elder son Stanicha, or Maximus, and his betrothal to the daughter of the Venetian Doge Mocenigo, doubtless contains much that is of historical value, though the facts have been embellished by the fancy of the bard. "'Listen to me, Doge,' writes Black Ivan to the lord of mighty Venice, 'men say that thou hast in thy house the fairest of roses, and I have in mine the fairest of pinks. Doge, let us unite the rose with the pink.' The Doge of Venice answers in a flattering tone, and Ivan hies him to his court, with three loads of gold, to woo the fair Latin in the name of his son. When he had lavished all his gold, the Latins promised him that the marriage should take place at the next vintage. Ivan, wise though he was, yet uttered foolish words as he departed. 'Friend and Doge,' quoth he, 'soon shalt thou see me return with six hundred chosen comrades; and, if among them all there be one fairer than my son Stanicha, give me neither dower nor bride.' The Doge rejoiced and shook his hand and gave him the golden apple, symbol of wedlock and of beauty. So Ivan returned unto his own people. And as he came near to his castle of Žabljak, his faithful spouse spied him from the turret and rushed forth to meet him, and covered the borders of his cloak with kisses and carried his terrible weapon with her own hands into the tower and placed before the hero a chair of silver. So the winter passed away amid rejoicings. But when spring came, small-pox fell upon Stanicha and marked his face all over. So, when autumn drew near, and the old Prince had gathered his six hundred comrades together, it was, alas! easy for him to find among them a warrior fairer than his son. Then his brow was wrinkled, and the black moustache, which reached even to his shoulders, grew limp. His spouse, aware of his grief, rebuked him for the pride which had led him to seek an alliance with the proud Latins. Ivan, stung by her reproaches, raged like a living fire ; he would hear no more of the nuptials, and bade his comrades depart to their homes. Years passed away ; when, on a sudden, a ship arrives with a message from the Doge. 'When thou enclosest the hedges of a meadow, thou dost mow it or else leave it to another, that the snows of winter may not spoil the grass. When thou askest and dost obtain the hand of a fair maid in marriage, thou must come and fetch her, or else write and set her free from her engagement.'

"Jealous of his word, Ivan decided at last to go to Venice. He assembled all his noble brothers-in-arms from Dulcigno and Antivari, the Drekalović, the Kontchi, the Bratonić, the falcons of Podgorica and the sons of Paul the White, the Vassoiević and all the chivalry as far as the green waters of the Lim. He bade all the warriors come, each in the garb of his tribe, and all in their goodliest array, that the Latins might marvel at the splendour of the Serbs. Many things do they possess, those noble Latins; they can work metals with skill and weave precious stuffs, but what is more enviable still, they lack the

MONTENEGRIN MILITARY INSIGNIA.

lofty brow, the sovereign look, of the sons of the Black Mountain.

"And when the six hundred comrades were assembled, Ivan told them of the rash promise which he had made to the Doge, and the divine punishment which had fallen upon his son, smitten with the small-pox, and added: 'Brothers, let us put one of you in place of Stanicha on the journey, and give him on our return half the presents, offered to him as the real bridegroom.' All the comrades applauded this device, and the young lord of Dulcigno, Obrenovo Djuro, who was recognised as the fairest of them all,

MONTENEGRIN MILITARY INSIGNIA.

was begged to play the part. Long did he refuse, and it needed the richest gifts to make him consent. Then, crowned with flowers, the comrades set sail. The whole artillery of the Black Mountain saluted them at their departure, and the two huge cannons *Kernio* and *Selenko*, which have not their like in the seven Frank kingdoms, nor yet among the Turks.

"Arrived at Venice, they are received at the Doge's Palace. The festivities of the betrothal last a week, and then Ivan cries unto the Doge: 'My friend, our mountains call us home.' Then the Doge rises and calls for the bridegroom Stanicha. All point to Djuro, and the Doge gives him the kiss and the golden apple of wedlock. The Doge's two sons approach, bearing two inlaid muskets worth a thousand ducats. They embrace him as their sister's husband, and give him their presents. After them come the two sisters-in-law of the Doge, each with a robe of the finest linen, woven with gold. Satisfied with the success of their device, Ivan and the men of the Black Mountain return to their own land."

The bride then learnt the trick which had been played upon her. But, according to the legend, she had less objection to give up her handsome Djuro than to relinquish the share of the bridal presents, which he claimed as his due for the part he had played. "'I cannot,' she cried to Stanicha, with tears in her eyes, 'part with this wondrous gold tunic woven by my hands, beneath which I dreamed of caressing my husband. It has well-nigh cost me my two eyes, while I laboured night and day for three years at it. Thou must fight to recover it, even though a thousand splinters of lances should be thy bier, or else I will turn my horse's head and ride down to the seashore. There I will gather an aloe-leaf; with its thorns I will tear my face, and with the blood of my own cheeks I will write a letter, which my falcon will bear swiftly to mighty Venice, whence my faithful Latins will hasten to avenge me.' At these words Stanicha lashed his black charger ; like a tiger it sprang forth till it reached Djuro. Stanicha struck him with his javelin in the middle of the brow, and the fair lord fell at the mountain foot."

The results of this crime were disastrous for Montenegro. The "comrades" of the legend challenged one another to battle; all day long they fought, and in the evening the plain was strewn with the slain. But Stanicha fled on horseback to Žabljak, leaving his wife to go back to Venice. From Žabljak the

MONTENEGRIN MILITAR. INSIGNIA.

murderer went to Constantinople, embraced the faith of Islâm, and offered to reduce his native country under the Sultan's sway. The attempt was unsuccessful. His younger brother George, who had followed Ivan as Prince of the Black Mountain, defeated him at Lieckopolje, and he withdrew first to Skodra, of which he became Pasha, and then to the Albanian village of Bouchati, where his family settled and took the name of Bouchatlia. Three centuries later we shall find Kara Mahmoud, one of Stanicha's descendants, the bitterest foe of Montenegro, and it was only sixty years ago that Moustapha

Bouchatlia, the last of the race, was driven by the Sultan from Albania. But the apostasy of Stanicha had a still more fatal influence upon the future of the Black Mountain. The renegade Montenegrins who had been taken prisoners after Stanicha's defeat were all allowed to remain and practise their new faith in their old country. Ready at all times to join hands with the Turkish invaders, these Mussulman inhabitants became a constant source of danger to the principality. The terrible "Montenegrin Vespers" in the reign of Danilo I. were the result.

George Crnoievič, allied as he was to a noble Venetian lady, and destitute of the martial qualities of his father, soon longed for safety and civilisation, neither of which he could find in his mountain home. It is not certain whether Stanicha invaded the Black Mountain a second time in 1496 and drove him out, or whether he retired of his own accord to Venice in that year, thus setting an example which was followed by the last of his successors. One account of his death says that it occurred in his Venetian palace; another that it took place in Asiatic Turkey, where he is said to have received large domains from the Turks. At any rate, his cousin Stephen succeeded him in 1496 and made good his title over Cetinje and the mountains, where the former inhabitants of Zeta had now finally entrenched themselves. From this time the name of Montenegro became the designation of the principality. But Stephen himself is a mere shadow. It is clear from the letters of Stanicha, which have recently been published, that Stephen and the renegade Pasha of Skodra lived upon good terms, although the latter grandiloquently describes himself as "lord of the Black Mountain." On Stephen's death, in 1515, no opposition was offered to the succession of his son Ivan, who a few months later made way for his son George. This prince, the last of the Crnoiević rulers of Montenegro, remained barely a year in his rough domain. The son of one Venetian lady and the husband of another, himself a patrician of the Republic and long time a resident on her lagoons, he had the utmost distaste for a life of solitude and privation in the monastery at Cetinje. His wife joined her complaints to his own. Without society and amusements, she sighed for the gaiety of her home, and her husband readily agreed to leave Montenegro for ever. He summoned the chiefs and people, told them his intentions, and entrusted them with the weapons which his great ancestors Stephen and Ivan the Black had wielded in defence of their liberties. To the Bishop Babylas, as the next most important personage to himself, he confided the task of governing the country. Thus it came about that Montenegro, like some of the German States in mediæval times, was ruled by an ecclesiastic, who combined the functions of priest, lawyer, and leader in war. This arrangement, commenced in 1516, continued in one form or another down to 1851, and the *Vladikas* or Prince Bishops of the Black Mountain formed a curious exception to the usual class from which sovereigns are selected. The Bishop's selection having been ratified by the assembled chiefs and people, George and his wife, accompanied by not a few Montenegrin nobles, set sail from Cattaro. It was a sad spectacle, this parting of Prince and people. Under the Crnoiević family, the Black Mountain had preserved its liberties from the Turks when every other neighbouring land had been subdued. People wondered if its independence could be maintained in the future.

III.

THE ELECTIVE VLADIKAS.

(1516—1696.)

THE appointment of the Bishop as ruler of Montenegro saved that country from the fate which had befallen Servia and Bosnia. Raised by his ecclesiastical functions above all the chieftains, who would have resented the elevation of one of their own number over their heads, the Bishop was the greatest security against civil war. At the same time a dignitary of the Church was the last person likely to commit an act of apostasy such as that which was so keenly remembered in Montenegro. But it was not the intention of George Crnoievič that the Bishop should have no one to assist him in the work of government. Accordingly, an official, known as the civil governor, was appointed, whose special duty it was to superintend the military defence of the country. The civil governor, invariably chosen from the head-men of the Katunska *nahia* or district, in which Cetinje is situated, was, however, subordinate to the *Vladika*. There was thus no rivalry between them. The civil governor, although the dignity came to be hereditary in certain noble families, while that of the *Vladika* was for long only elective, knew his place, and the only attempt at usurpation in the long history of the office led to its abolition in 1832. The history of Japan furnishes us with an almost exact parallel, for the relations between the Mikado and the Tycoon were until lately almost similar. The only personage to whom the Prince-Bishop owed allegiance was the Serb Patriarch of Ipek, who once in every seven years visited his diocese and consecrated every fresh Montenegrin prelate.

For one hundred and eighty years after their first appointment, the *Vladikas* were elected by the chiefs and people—an arrangement which was ultimately abandoned in favour of the hereditary system. During the greater part of this period the history of the country consisted of little more than one continuous struggle for existence against the Turks, amid which it is difficult to distinguish the shadowy figures of the successive prelates. Babylas himself was allowed to reign in peace, devoting his attention to the printing-press at Obod, which issued books of devotion, still extant, bearing his name on the title-page. His successor, German, was not left unmolested. A pretender, one of the Crnoiević family who had turned Mussulman, invaded the principality just as Stanicha, thirty years before, and with the same result. Voukotić, the civil governor, repulsed the renegade, and such was the zeal of the Montenegrins for the Christian cause, that they marched into Bosnia and raised the siege of Jajce, where the Hungarian garrison was closely hemmed in by the troops of the Sultan. The Turks were too much occupied with the Hungarian war to take revenge, and it was not till 1570 that Montenegro had to face another Ottoman invasion. The next three *Vladikas*, Paul, Nicodin, and Makarios, availed themselves of this long period of repose to increase the publications of the press, and numerous psalters and translations of the Gospels were produced in this small and remote principality. But the Turkish governors of Skodra revived the claims of Stanicha to the Montenegrin throne. Ali, Pasha of that district, defeated in his first attack, renewed it with disastrous results to Montenegro. Pachomije, the Prince-Bishop at that moment, was unable to reach Ipek for the ceremony of consecration, and his authority was therefore weakened in the eyes of his people. The renegades, allowed to settle in the country at the time of Stanicha's defeat, welcomed the Pasha's army with open arms, and, thanks to their treachery, he was able to seize the fortress of Obod and destroy the precious printing-press, which Ivan the Black had established there a century earlier. The national historians are silent upon the subject of the *haratch*, or tribute, which the invaders are said to have exacted from the inhabitants of the free mountain, and which defrayed the cost of the Sultan's slippers. But there can be no doubt that Montenegro suffered greatly from the depredations of Ali. The refusal of its high-spirited people to pay tribute any longer may have been the cause of the Pasha's invasion in 1604 during the reign of Bishop Rufin, when the Turks were driven back with heavy loss

Eight years later the Sultan determined that he would sweep the defiant mountaineers off the face of the earth. An army of twenty-five thousand men was despatched against the principality. The decisive battle took place not far from Podgorica. But the Turkish cavalry was useless in such a country. The small band of Montenegrins held their ground, the enemy threw himself against their rocks in vain, and the flower of the Ottoman chivalry was left dead on the field. Next year a still larger force was collected by Arslan Pasha, and if wars were always decided by mere numbers the fate of Montenegro would have been sealed, for the invaders were twice as numerous as the whole population of the principality. Six months were occupied in skirmishes and ambuscades, and it was not till the 10th of September, 1613, that the two armies met on the spot where Stanicha had been defeated more than a century before. The Montenegrins, although assisted by some neighbouring tribes, were completely outnumbered. But their valour and prowess were out of proportion to their numbers. Seldom have the Turks received so overwhelming a blow. Arslan Pasha was wounded, and the heads of his second-in-command and a hundred other Turkish officers were carried off and stuck on the ramparts of Cetinje. The Ottoman troops fled in disorder; many were drowned in the waters of the Morača, many more fell by the swords of their pursuers. No quarter was given.

Much light is thrown upon the condition of Montenegro at this period and the causes of its invariable success in war even against fearful odds are explained by the accounts of a contemporary writer, Mariano Bolizza. This author, a patrician of Venice, residing at Cattaro in the early part of the seventeenth century, spent a considerable time in the Black Mountain, and published in 1614 a description of the country. At that time the whole male population available for war consisted of 8,027 persons, distributed among the ninety-three villages which Montenegro contained. But these few warriors were continually practising. The rapidity of their manœuvres was extraordinary, and for guerilla warfare they were unrivalled. In battle they always took care to have the advantage of the ground. Their rocks afforded shelter, from which they could aim at their enemies in the open, and they made the most of the smallest cover. The women, accustomed from their infancy to lift heavy burdens, could roll huge masses of rock down upon the heads of an advancing army, and the Turkish cavalry, invincible in a champaign country, was helpless in that sea of limestone. A high military authority, after a visit to the Black Mountain, has recently stated that he perfectly understood the failure of the Turks to capture it.

The condition of the country at this period was naturally unsettled. War was the chief occupation of its inhabitants from sheer necessity, and the arts of peace languished. The printing-press, so active a century earlier, had ceased to exist; the control of the Prince-Bishop over the five *nahic*, or districts, which then composed the principality, was loose; the capital itself was a mere village of a few houses. Still, even then, there was a system of local government. Each *nahia* was divided into tribes, or *plemena*, each presided over by a headman or *kniez*, who acted as a judge in disputes between the tribesmen.

The successes of the Montenegrins gained them notoriety outside the borders of their own country. Accordingly, when Charles de Nevers, the last

A TYPICAL BIT OF MONTENEGRIN SCENERY.
(*From a photo. by Mr. C. A. Miller.*)

descendant of the Paleologi, planned his new crusade against the Sultan with the support of Cardinal Richelieu in 1614, he invited the Montenegrin warriors to assist him. He found them nothing loth, but they declined to move until he began. The accidental destruction of his ships put an end to the crusade, and the whole affair ended in smoke. Another similar attempt, made a little later by a son of Mohammed III., named Jahja, who had embraced Christianity and styled himself Count of Montenegro, was equally futile. This adventurer, whose life was one long romance, laid claim to the throne of Constantinople, and at the head of a body of Montenegrins made a foray into Turkish territory. But the inhabitants of the Black Mountain had soon enough to do to defend themselves. In 1623 Soliman, Pasha of Skodra, with 80,000 men, marched into the country with the intention of finally annexing it. For twenty days the opposing forces were engaged in almost ceaseless conflicts. But the invaders at last drove their enemies back upon Cetinje. The capital was taken, and the monastery of Ivan the Black sacked. A tribute was again imposed upon those who submitted, while the bolder spirits retired to the inaccessible heights of the Lovčen, and thence descended upon the Turkish camp. But nature was once more on the side of the mountaineers. The Pasha realised the truth of the saying that in Montenegro "a small army is beaten, a large one dies of hunger." The bare rocks afforded no subsistence to his host; so, leaving a small army of occupation behind, he returned to the fertile plains of Albania. At once the Montenegrin eagles swooped down from their eyrie upon the Turkish garrisons, while the warlike tribes of the Koutchi and Klementi on the Albanian border fell upon the main body near Podgorica and almost annihilated it. Montenegro was once more free. Had the Albanians of the frontier finally thrown in their lot with their fellow-Christians in Montenegro, the combination would have been irresistible. But the unfortunate division between the Eastern and the Western Church prevented their union. The Koutchi and Klementi had adopted the Roman Catholic faith at the instigation of Italian missionaries, while the Montenegrins have always been devoted to the Greek Church. The effects of this schism have been lasting. Montenegro looked calmly on while the Turks attacked its Catholic neighbours, while the Catholic Albanians usually allowed the Mussulman armies to enter Montenegro with impunity. It was only on rare occasions that the instinct of self-preservation prompted the Albanian chiefs to combine with the warriors of the Greek Church for mutual protection.

For over sixty years no serious attempt was made to conquer the country. But in 1687, the Venetians urged their old allies to assist in a campaign against the Turks, whose power had just received a severe shock at the hands of Sobieski under the walls of Vienna. Forgetful of the selfishness of Venice, and eager to come to blows with their hereditary foes, the Montenegrins consented ; and, aided by the firearms, which now for the first time became general among them, soon dislodged the Turks, who had landed on the shores of the Bocche di Cattaro. But in the following year Venice made peace with the Sultan, who now turned his undivided attention to Montenegro. In vain the *Vladika* Vissarion reminded the Republic that it was for her sake that he had incurred the enmity of the Turks. Not only was he left to his fate, but a Venetian officer, who commanded part of his army, was recalled at a critical moment. Deserted by their allies, the Montenegrins were taken at a disadvantage. Cetinje was once more destroyed, and the monastery of Ivan the Black, with all its precious books and relics, was blown up by the monks, who preferred death to surrender. The loss was irreparable ; and, though Cetinje was speedily rebuilt, the convent lay long in ruins. But the destruction of the capital did not mean the capture of the country. Unable to dislodge the Montenegrins from a strong position which they had occupied, the Turkish commander withdrew, leaving a small garrison at Obod. In spite of the bitter experience which they had had of alliances with the great European Powers, the mountaineers promised to assist the Emperor Leopold I. next year in his campaign against the Turks in Servia and Bosnia. As usual, they were ignored at the peace by their allies. Indeed, the Venetians are accused of having poisoned the *Vladika* Vissarion in order to please the Sultan. But the man was at hand to save the liberties of the Black Mountain. Sava, who succeeded Vissarion, found the Turks too much occupied with the war on the Lower Danube to disturb his brief reign ; and by the time that they were once more at liberty to attack Montenegro, Danilo, first hereditary *Vladika* of the House of Petrović, was ready to defend it.

IV.

THE FIRST THREE HEREDITARY PRINCE-BISHOPS.

(1696—1782.)

THE modern history of Montenegro may be said to have begun on the 29th of July, 1696, with the accession of the present dynasty to the throne. For a period of one hundred and eighty years the destinies of the Black Mountain had been entrusted to the hands of an elective Prince-Bishop, or *Vladika*, who was assisted in temporal matters by a civil governor. But in their constant struggles against the Turks, the mountaineers had learnt by experience the disadvantages which inevitably attend an election to the Crown. They felt that, if they were to hold their own, they must strengthen the position of their ruler by making his office hereditary in one powerful family. As the Prince-Bishop, by virtue of his episcopal station, was forbidden to marry, the Montenegrin ruler had no sons to succeed him. But, in order to secure continuity of government, the *Vladika* was empowered to nominate his successor from his relatives, and the people have never hesitated to ratify his choice. From 1696 onwards, nephew has succeeded uncle in unbroken line. But the separation of the temporal from the ecclesiastical functions of the sovereign by Danilo II. in 1851 has altered the character of the Montenegrin monarchy by permitting the Prince to marry; and, though Danilo II. was followed by his nephew, in future the dignity may be expected to descend from father to son.

Having resolved upon this change in their form of government, the Montenegrins had little doubt whom to choose as the founder of the new dynasty. Every visitor to Cetinje has passed through the village of Njeguš, which lies about half-way between Cattaro and the Montenegrin capital. In the distance the cold grey houses of the hamlet look like a heap of stones, hardly distinguishable from the gaunt limestone rocks which surround it. But no spot in his mountain country is dearer to the Prince than this unpretentious hamlet, for it was the cradle of his race, the impregnable stronghold of Montenegrin independence. The village derives its name from a mountain in the Herzegovina, whose inhabitants had fled for refuge from the Turks to Montenegro a couple of centuries before, and had called their new settlement after their old home. One of the descendants of these Herzegovinian exiles, Danilo Petrović, was a leading man at Njeguš two hundred years ago, and it was upon him that the choice of the people fell. For a long time he declined the proffered honour. He pleaded youth, inexperience, and lack of ambition. He preferred the cloister at Cetinje to the leadership of the nation. But, at last, he yielded to the necessities of his country, and though he was not actually consecrated as *Vladika* till 1700, his accession dates from the 29th of July, 1696. The date will ever be memorable in Montenegro's rough mountain story. This summer Prince Nicholas celebrates the bicentenary of his dynasty by a national festival, or, to use his own phrase, a "rejoicing of his people." Prizes will be awarded for the best history of his family, and a monument is to be erected to the first of its princes.

The long reign of Danilo I. was remarkable for numerous invasions of the Turks, especially during the first few years, and for the first connection between the Principality and the Czar of Russia—a connection which has lasted down to the present day. The ruler found upon his accession that he would have not only to defend his country against the enemy from without, but also to free it from traitors within. Whenever the Turks had invaded the Black Mountain, they had derived great assistance from the Montenegrin subjects who had embraced the Mussulman faith, just as in our own generation the Bosnian converts to Islâm have sometimes been more Turkish in their sympathies than the Turks themselves. Danilo soon had an opportunity of ridding himself of this internal danger, and at the same time of striking a heavy blow at his external foes. We will tell the tale in the words of one of those beautiful *piesmas*, or national ballads, in which much of Montenegrin history is enshrined. This song, called *Sve-Oslobod*, or "Wholly Free," is still sung by the Martinović family, and thus graphically describes the treachery of the Turks, the *Vladika's* sufferings, and his people's vengeance:—

"The Christians of the Zeta, by means of gifts, gained permission from the Pasha of bloody Scutari to build a church. The humble building was completed, and the priest Jove went to the chieftains of the tribes assembled in council and said to them: 'Our church is built, but it will be no place of God until it has been consecrated: let us therefore give money to the Pasha for a safe-conduct for the Bishop of the Black Mountain, that he may come and bless it.' The Pasha granted the pass for the Black Monk [the Turkish name for the *Vladika*, derived from his monkish garb], and the chosen men of the Zeta went in haste to give it to the *Vladika* at Cetinje. Danilo Petrović read the writing and shook his head, and said: 'There is no promise held sacred by the Turks; but for the love of our holy faith I will go, even if I never return.' So he bade saddle his best horse and went with them. But the treacherous Mussulman waited till he had blessed the church, and then seized him and dragged him, with his hands tied behind his back, to Podgorica. At this news, all the men of the Zeta, plain and mountain alike, rose and went to accursed Scutari to implore the Pasha to let the *Vladika* go. But he fixed the ransom at three thousand golden ducats. So the people of the Black Mountain agreed with the tribes of the Zeta, and sold perforce all the holy vessels at Cetinje. The *Vladika* was set free; and when they saw the glorious sunshine of their nation returning, the mountaineers could not restrain their transports of joy. But Danilo, long afflicted by the spiritual successes of the Turks in his land and foreseeing the apostasy of his people from the faith, bade the assembled tribes at once fix a day for the massacre of every Turk throughout the country. At this demand, most of the leaders were silent; the five brothers Martinović alone offered to carry out the plot. Christmas Eve was chosen as the night of the massacre, in memory of the victims who fell at Kossovo. The fatal evening arrived: the brothers Martinović lighted their holy tapers, prayed with fervour to the new-born God, drank each a cup of wine to the glory of Christ, and, seizing their consecrated clubs, rushed off through the darkness. Wherever a Turk was to be found, the five avengers appeared; all who refused baptism were massacred without pity; those who embraced the cross were presented as brothers to the *Vladika*. The people, assembled at Cetinje, greeted the dawn of Christmas with songs of gladness; for the first time since the fatal day of Kossovo, they could cry: 'The Black Mountain is free!'"

These "Montenegrin Vespers," as the massacre of Christmas Eve, 1703, has been called, cleared the land of the Turkish renegades for some time to come. But in 1707 the survivors returned to the attack. The mountaineers not only inflicted upon them an overwhelming defeat, but showed their contempt by demanding a pig as the ransom for every prisoner. Upon this curious incident an eminent British statesman once based an elaborate defence of the Montenegrins against the charge of cruelty. But the nation gained something more important than a herd of swine by this decisive victory. The inhabitants of the seven "mountains," or *Berda*, which now form the eastern portion of the principality, chose that moment for concluding a defensive alliance with the victors, with whom they were formally incorporated eighty years later. In memory of their former independence, the full title of the sovereign is still " Prince and Lord of Montenegro and the Berda " (*kniaz i gospodar slobodne Crnegore i Brdach*).

Scarcely less productive of results was the first appearance of Russia in Montenegrin history. In 1710 Peter the Great, involved in war with the Turks, sought to raise the Christians of the Balkan Peninsula against them. Following the advice of a Herzegovinian noble, he included the Montenegrins in his appeal. One of the national ballads describes the enthusiasm with which the Czar's emissary, Milo Radović, was received at Cetinje. The Emperor's letter, we are told, began with an account of his victories over the Swedes, "Pultava's day," and the treason and death of Mazeppa, and went on to say how, in revenge, the Swedish monarch had urged on the Turks against him. "But," so runs the letter, "I place my trust above all in the stalwart arms of the Montenegrin braves, who assuredly will help me to deliver Christendom, to raise up temples of the true faith and to add splendour to the Slav name. Warriors of the Black Mountain, you are of the same creed, the same language as ourselves; like us, you know no fear. Arise then, heroes worthy of the brave days of old, and remain a nation, which has no peace with the Turks." At these words the excitement was intense. Every warrior demanded to be led at once against the foe. But this enthusiasm was short-lived. The Czar quickly made peace, without taking thought for his plucky allies, who were now abandoned to the vengeance of the Turks. But the courage of the Montenegrins did not desert them. At that time, the whole population of the country did not exceed twenty thousand persons, and as Achmet Pasha was despatched with fifty thousand soldiers against them, the odds seemed enormous. From the plain of Podgorica the Pasha wrote to Danilo: "Send me a small tribute and three braves as hostages. If thou dost not obey, I will set the whole land ablaze from the river Morača to the salt lake [the Adriatic]; I will take thee alive and torture thee to death." The assembled chiefs replied that the fire from their guns would be their only tribute. Three warriors were sent to spy out the enemies' camp, and the *Vladika*, falling upon the Turks as they slept, defeated them with tremendous slaughter. According to the legend, only three hundred Montenegrins fell, while twenty thousand Mussulmans remained dead on the rocks. The victory was the greatest that the Montenegrin arms had won. The date, by a curious coincidence the anniversary of Danilo's accession, is still remembered in the Black Mountain, and the "glorious 29th of July" has thus a double significance for the nation. The battlefield is known to this day as the "felling of the Emperor," or *Tsarevlaz*, because the Sultan's soldiers were cut down like trees. But all danger was not over. Kiuprili, the Governor of Bosnia, collected an army of one hundred and twenty thousand men on the Herzegovinian frontier, and, resolving not to rely on numbers alone, managed, under pretext of negotiations, to obtain possession of thirty-seven Montenegrin chiefs. Kiuprili hung his prisoners, and, having thus deprived Montenegro of its ablest leaders, invaded their helpless country. Once again the Turks occupied Cetinje, and once again its monastery, rebuilt by Danilo after the "Montenegrin Vespers," was razed to the ground. "Not a single altar," says a ballad, "not a single house in all Crnagora was left standing. The young men fled to the mountain fastnesses, the others took refuge on Venetian territory, convinced that the Doge, to whom their long war had been so useful, would not surrender them to the Turks. In vain! The Venetians allowed the Mussulmans to invade their land and put the vanquished to the sword." But the Montenegrins bore no malice against the Doge for his desertion. When the Venetians were blockaded by the Turks in the ports of Dulcigno and Antivari they came to their assistance, and a letter of thanks from the proud "Queen of the Adriatic" was sent to the *Vladika*, whose authority in ecclesiastical matters over the orthodox population of the Bocche di Cattaro was recognised by the Republic. Peter the Great showed his gratitude to his former allies in a more practical way. The year 1715 is remarkable as the first occasion when a Montenegrin ruler visited Russia to seek aid or counsel of its Czar—a journey which every subsequent prince has undertaken. Peter the Great issued two ukases, in which he assured the mountain-folk of his friendship, and sent them ten thousand roubles as well as one hundred and sixty gold pieces. This was the first of many subsidies which Montenegro has received from the Czars.

The Turks, meanwhile, had found it impossible to hold the barren mountains against the guerilla warfare of this indomitable people. Another invasion was less successful; the three Turkish commanders were captured and executed, while seventy Turkish prisoners were sacrificed to the manes of the Montenegrin envoys butchered by Kiuprili. Besides, the Turks had now quite enough to do to defend their own possessions against Prince Eugène. During the next twenty years, Montenegro was only thrice invaded, and thrice were the ranks of Islâm beaten back. One of these battles is said to have lasted for seven days; in another a thousand mountaineers put twenty times their number to flight. But Montenegro had suffered much from this long series of wars. Danilo had, indeed, recovered the district of the Zeta and again restored the monastery at Cetinje. But the losses of the nation may be estimated from the fact that one of the largest tribes had been reduced to forty men. Montenegro had, however, attracted the attention and won the respect of Christendom by its bravery, and when Danilo I. died in 1735 at a ripe old age, he left to his nephew, Sava, a small but honourable inheritance.

Sava, who had performed the ecclesiastical functions of the late *Vladika* for many years past, was suited by nature for the cloister rather than the throne. He is the only one of the seven Petrović

Princes who has lacked character, and a large part of his reign was really a regency, carried on by his nephew Vassili. But his government, if not remarkable for its vigour, is still remembered for the closer connection with Russia which he and his nephew promoted, and for the strange episode of Stephen the Little, one of the most successful impostures in all history.

Weak as was the new ruler, he soon had to exert himself to defend his country from the Turks. The Peace of Belgrade had left them free to devote their undivided attention to Montenegro, and no sooner had it been concluded than they blockaded the Black Mountain. Without either allies or ammunition—for the faithless Venetians had forbidden the traders of Cattaro to sell them arms—the beleaguered warriors were forced to trust to their own exertions and to the weapons which they captured from their enemies' camp. Their triumph was, however, disgraced by a horrible act of revenge. Seventy Turkish officers were shut up in a stable and then burnt alive. Their repulse of the next invasion was a more legitimate source of satisfaction to the mountaineers. "The vizier of Bosnia," in the language of the ballad, "wrote a letter to the Black Monk, Vassili Petrović, saying, 'Black Monk, send me the tribute of the mountain with twelve of thy loveliest maidens, all between twelve and fifteen years, or I swear by the only true God to ravage the country and carry off every male, young and old, into slavery.'" Then the *Vladika* replied as follows: "Renegade, eater of the plums of the Herzegovina, how durst thou ask tribute of the children of the free Mountain? Tribute we will send thee, but it shall be a stone of our rocks, and instead of a dozen virgins, thou shalt have a dozen pigs' tails for thy turban. If thou wilt attack us, come. We trust thou wilt leave thy head with us, and that it will roll down our mountain slopes, already strewn with many a Turkish skull." Infuriated at this reply, the Pasha sent his lieutenant with forty-five thousand men against his scornful foes. For fourteen days the two armies kept up a constant fusillade; then, from lack of ammunition, the Montenegrins had to retire. But an unexpected succour was at hand. Braving the displeasure of the Venetians, a Serb of Cattaro came and sold them in one night many thousands of cartridges. "Like wolves upon a flock of sheep they fell upon the Turkish camp, and pursued the enemy till nightfall over hill and valley." Till the close of Vassili's reign, in 1766, no Turkish soldier set foot again on the rocks of Montenegro.

Meanwhile its rulers had both re-opened relations with Russia. Before he retired into the new monastery which he had built at Stanievié, and resigned all power into the hands of Vassili, Sava visited the Empress Elizabeth at Moscow, paying his respects on his return to Frederick the Great at Berlin. The Empress received him graciously, and, in pursuance of an unfulfilled promise of Peter the Great, allowed his country a sum of three thousand roubles a year as compensation for the losses which it had incurred during the war of 1711. Vassili, in his turn, was made equally welcome. The Empress gave him one thousand ducats for his schools, which had fallen into disuse during the Turkish raids, and, in order to assist him in improving his military organisation, admitted fifteen young Montenegrins to the Military Academy at St. Petersburg. During a third journey to Russia, Vassili died on the 10th of March, 1766, and his remains lie in the church of St. Alexander Nevski at St. Petersburg. Sava, unfitted for the work of government by nearly twenty years of monastic seclusion, was compelled to reassume the reins of power. But he had been little more than a year in office, when a pretender appeared in Montenegro and relieved him of his duties. There is no more curious episode in Balkan history than the successful imposture of this man.

Towards the end of 1767 there arrived in the Bocche di Cattaro a certain Stephen the Little, or Stepan Mali, who gave himself out to be the Czar Peter III. of Russia, believed to have been murdered five years earlier. The impostor acted his part well; under the guise of a doctor, he had paid a previous visit to the Black Mountain, studied carefully the customs of its inhabitants, and convinced himself of their attachment to Russia. Few of them had ever been in that country, fewer still had ever seen the features of the murdered Czar. Marco Tancović, one of the small number of travelled Montenegrins, declared that in the face of Stephen he recognised the Emperor, whom he had met with Vassili at St. Petersburg. The simple people were greatly influenced by what Tancović said. From far and near the chiefs gathered together to see and hear him, and for the moment the dissensions, which had divided them under the feeble sway of Sava, were healed. Stephen told them the story of his life. He said that he had escaped from the daggers of his assassins, and after a long voyage had landed on the eastern shores of the Adriatic. He disclaimed all desire to return to Russia, and said that he asked nothing better than to devote the rest of his days to the cause of Montenegrin independence. The people heard him gladly, thinking that the times demanded a man and not a monk as their ruler; the Serb Patriarch of Ipek, who had delegated to Sava the spiritual jurisdiction hitherto enjoyed by himself and his predecessors, implored his protection from the Turks; even the Serbs inhabiting the picturesque Venetian town of Risano on the Bocche di Cattaro rose in favour of the impostor. Sava was too weak to resist, and was allowed to live on condition that the usurper governed. Whatever his origin, Stephen, at any rate, governed well. He punished crime with the utmost severity; he dared to have two of his subjects shot for theft, and such was the fear which he inspired, that no one ventured to touch a purse and a silver-mounted pistol which he left on the frequented road between Cattaro and Cetinje for several weeks. He established courts of justice, prohibited work on Sunday, ordered a census of all men fit to bear arms, and anticipated the present Prince in his desire to improve the means of communication. But his energy excited the suspicions of his great neighbours. Venice was alarmed for the safety of her Dalmatian possessions; the Turks regarded the usurper as a

Russian agent in disguise. Both declared war against Montenegro. The Venetians encamped near Budua, now the southernmost Austrian outpost in Dalmatia; the Turkish troops, following their usual tactics, attacked Montenegro on three sides at once. The position was critical, all the more so as Stephen showed no desire for fighting, and is even said to have sought safety in flight—a piece of cowardice unheard of in a genuine Montenegrin *Vladika*. But the elements were once more on the side of the mountaineers. After a nine months' struggle, on the 1st of November, says the ballad, a heavy storm of rain, accompanied by thunder and lightning, fell upon the Venetian and the Turkish camps. Next day, the Montenegrins descended and seized the ammunition of their enemies, who fled in terror. The piety of the people saw in this deliverance the hand of Providence, and the bard calls upon his "dear *pobratim*," or brother-in-arms, to "believe in the God from whom the men of Crnagora receive joy, courage, and health." The Russian Government, which had hitherto taken no notice of the pretended Emperor, now sent Prince Dolgorouki to Montenegro with presents and war material in large quantities. Arrived at Cetinje, the Russian envoy assembled the people and read aloud to them two letters of the Empress Catharine II., in the first of which she invited them to join her in war against the Turks, while in the other she denounced Stephen as an impostor, and demanded that he should be deposed. Stephen, confronted with his accuser, admitted the fraud which he had committed. In spite of the entreaties of some of his subjects, who admired his administrative qualities, he was put under arrest, and had it not been for the incapacity of Sava, who was now once more called to the direction of affairs, his career would have been over. But war was impending, the winter was at hand, and as Sava still lingered in his monastic retreat, Prince Dolgorouki resolved upon the bold step of recognising his prisoner as Regent and installing him in office. Another and less probable account of Stephen's restoration to power is that he was rescued from prison by the people, whom he had convinced of his Imperial birth by the fact that he was lodged in a room above the Russian envoy. For five more years he governed Montenegro, and even the loss of one eye from an explosion during the blasting of a new road did not lessen his activity. Borne about his rocky principality on a litter, a gift from the rich citizens of Ragusa, he reigned till 1774, when a Greek servant, said to have been suborned by the Pasha of Scutari, strangled him while he was asleep. By a curious irony of fate, he died like the Emperor whose name he had assumed. Prince Dolgorouki states in his "Memoirs" that he came from Bosnia, and that the Archimandrite Marcović suggested to him the part which he played so successfully. Other writers believe him to have been born in Dalmatia. But upon his abilities as a ruler all are agreed, and Montenegro owes a debt of gratitude to his memory.

Upon his murder, the Pasha of Scutari at once took the field against the Montenegrins. But, though the feeble Sava was now their leader, the valour of his subjects repulsed the Turks with great loss. The victories of Russia had crippled the Ottoman power, and though the victors, as in 1711, did not take the trouble to have their Montenegrin allies included in the treaty of peace, the rest of Sava's reign was free from disturbance. In 1782 he died, after forty-seven years of titular rule, and Vassili's nephew, Peter Petrović, who had held his dying uncle in his arms at St. Petersburg, reigned in his stead.

V.

PETER I.—THE BONAPARTE OF THE BLACK MOUNTAIN.

(1782—1830.)

PETER I. was a man of very different stamp from his predecessor. Energetic and able, bold in war and persuasive in the council-chamber, he was the first Montenegrin ruler who made Europe recognise the growing importance of his small mountain state. Austria, Russia and England did not scorn to accept, and even to solicit, his aid. His rude, untrained forces held the armies of the great Napoleon in check, and he resembled the French Emperor in the efforts which he made to organise his country, to codify its laws and to ensure their enforcement.

He had scarcely returned from the ceremony of consecration at the hands of the Serb Patriarch, who now resided at Carlovitz, when he was compelled to face a Turkish invasion. Kara Mahmoud, Pasha of Scutari, and a descendant of the renegade Montenegrin Prince Stanicha, was ravaging the Black Mountain, and set fire to the monastery at Cetinje, as his predecessors had done. The crafty Venetians, instead of supporting the *Vladika*, were supplying his enemies with provisions; Potemkin, the favourite minister of Catherine II. of Russia, not only refused him assistance, but ordered him to quit St. Petersburg within twenty-four hours. But, when Austria and Russia declared war against Turkey in 1788, they were anxious to use Montenegro as a catspaw. Austria was particularly desirous of a Montenegrin alliance, and offered in return to increase the area of the principality beyond even its present limits. But even the tempting offer of the Herzegovina, which is still the "Naboth's vineyard" of Montenegro, did not gain the active support of the *Vladika*, until Russia had added her request to that of Austria. Meanwhile the latter power, thinking that the redoubtable Kara Mahmoud might be induced to revolt against the Sultan, had sent an envoy to Scutari to treat with him. The treacherous Pasha received the Austrians well, but the escort, which he had sent with them, murdered them on their way back by his orders. The sole survivor of this massacre entreated the *Vladika* to summon the nation to arms, and his entreaties, seconded by those of Russia, prevailed. But Montenegro had to fight, as usual, single-handed; the Austrian soldiers contented themselves with looking on from the top of Mount Lovčen; and as soon as her great allies chose to make peace with the Turks, Montenegro was worse than forgotten. She was, indeed, mentioned in the Treaty of Sistova but only as one of the revolted Turkish provinces! Such a proceeding was to add insult to injury. But the war had incidentally contributed to the consolidation of the principality. The people of Trebinje in the Herzegovina, long noted for their independence and intolerance of Turkish rule, had been driven from their homes by the ravages of the Turks, and sought shelter among the Berda. The four *nahie* of that mountainous district, which had been virtually united to Montenegro under Danilo I., were now formally combined with it into one state, and the eight *nahie* thus formed continued to compose the principality down to the year 1835, when the Koutchi voluntarily joined it. This important accession of territory did not fail to arouse the jealousy of the Turks. Kara Mahmoud resolved to prevent the union, and entered Montenegro at the point where the river Zeta separates it from the Berda. But his efforts were in vain. After a sanguinary engagement near the fortress of Spuž, the Pasha retired wounded from the field, and a subsequent expedition cost him his life. The *Vladika*, posting one half of his forces in one of those mountainous defiles which are so common in his country, and leaving a number of red Montenegrin caps upon the rocks to delude the Turks into the idea that his whole army was in front, surprised them with the other half in the rear. Taken unawares between the two fires, the invaders fell by hundreds; Kara Mahmoud was slain, and when Sir Gardner Wilkinson visited Cetinje, fifty years later, he found the Pasha's skull still stuck, as a grim trophy of victory, on the battlements of the famous "Turks' Tower." The effects of the Turkish defeat were lasting; the union of the Montenegro and the Berda was secure;

the hereditary foes of the Black Mountain ceased for many years from troubling, and the pious mountaineers applied to the battle of Kroussa the verse of the Book of Judges which tells how Midian was subdued before the children of Israel. The Sultan no longer demanded tribute from a nation which knew so well how to defend itself. By a curious coincidence, the victory

THE "TURKS' TOWER," CETINJE,
IN 1848.

took place exactly one hundred years after the selection of Danilo I. as Prince-Bishop.

But with the ensuing year (1797) Montenegro was brought into close contact with even a more formidable neighbour than the Turks. It would be difficult to over-estimate the influence of the Treaty of Campo

Formio upon the fortunes of the mountain-state, for its effects are felt at the present day. That memorable arrangement assigned the Dalmatian possessions of Venice to Austria, and thus made the boundary of Montenegro conterminous with that of the Hapsburgs. The inhabitants of Cattaro, who had long enjoyed the protection of the Venetian Republic, sought the advice of the *Vladika* in their dilemma. They reminded him that when Venice had undertaken to protect them, it was under the express promise that they should recover their independence if ever the Republic failed to fulfil her undertaking. The people of Budua also implored the presence of Peter; in fact, from that moment, the Serbs of the coast came to regard him as their natural head. Even the chiefs of the Herzegovina begged him, as their descendants begged the present Prince, to deliver them from the Turkish yoke. The *Vladika*, with diplomatic tact, advised the citizens of Cattaro to await the course of events. If the power of Venice were restored, they could once more place themselves under the sheltering wings of the Lion of St. Mark; if not, they could come to terms with Austria. Meanwhile, an Austrian army was occupying the Dalmatian towns, and Baron Roukavina, the Austrian admiral, wrote to Peter, asking him to use his influence with the people of the Bocche on behalf of the Power which had assisted him with ammunition in his recent campaign. Peter appears to have adopted the policy of neutrality which was followed by Prince Nicholas during the insurrection at Cattaro in 1869, and the Bocchesi made preparations to submit to their new master.

But scarcely had they admitted the Austrian admiral to their magnificent harbours, when a French fleet arrived off Ragusa and ordered the Austrians to withdraw from the Bocche. In his distress, the Austrian commander applied again to Peter, urging him to join against the common enemy, and even offering to serve under his command. The Czar seconded the request of his ally, and sent a special envoy to Montenegro to enlist the support of its ruler against Napoleon. But before the *Vladika* had taken the field, the peace of Pressburg formally consigned the Bocche to France. The Austrian commissioner at Cattaro announced that in six weeks' time he would hand over the forts.

Great was the indignation of the seafaring population round that beautiful fiord at this second surrender of their liberties. A few welcomed Napoleon as a "father and a mother," but the vast majority resolved to resist. A deputation was sent to Cetinje, where the Russian envoy still was, to ask the aid of the Montenegrins by land and of the Russians by sea. The Russian fleet was summoned from Corfu, and the *Vladika* assembled his chieftains and vowed before them that he would not only close the Bocche to the French, but eject the Austrians as well. At the head of a combined force of Montenegrins and Bocchesi, and aided by a division of the Russian squadron, he laid siege to the fortress of Castelnuovo, at the entrance of the Bocche. The fortress surrendered at once, and having thus turned out the Austrians, Peter was able to devote his attention to the French. He sent an urgent message to the Senate of Ragusa, then an independent Republic, in order to prevent the French from crossing the Republican territory in their march upon Cattaro. But neither the representations of the *Vladika* nor the presence of the Russian admiral prevailed upon the timorous senators. Fearing the wrath of the French Emperor, they opened their gates to his general, Lauriston, whose first act was to suppress their ancient liberties. But the Montenegrins were not so easily daunted by the name of Napoleon. Aided by the Bocchesi and their Russian allies, they defeated the French in a four days' engagement, and drove them back within the walls of Ragusa. The city was surrounded, and would inevitably have fallen into their hands had not orders arrived from the Czar that the Bocche should be surrendered to the Austrians. As usual, the brave mountaineers found that they had been duped. Disgusted at this treatment, the *Vladika* withdrew from the siege. But the guerilla warfare which followed was conducted with the utmost savagery by his subjects and the people of the coast. No quarter was shown on either side. The story that the Montenegrins played bowls with the heads of the French soldiers and remarked how light-headed their enemies were, is probably an invention. But there is no doubt that they decapitated the French general, Delgorgues, who had been made a prisoner. When Marshal Marmont reproached Peter with this horrible custom of his people, the *Vladika* replied that there was nothing surprising in it; what did surprise him was that the French should have beheaded their lawful king. The Montenegrins, he added, might have learnt this barbarous practice from the French, with this difference, that the former only beheaded their oppressors, and not their prince or their fellow-countrymen. In the frequent skirmishes which took place, the French soldiers were no match for the mountain-bands, which harassed them on all sides. Lauriston, who meditated the occupation of Albania and the Herzegovina, tried to win over by promises the highland chief whom he could not crush by force. But Peter was not to be bought by the empty title of Patriarch of Dalmatia. He even warned his old enemies, the Turks, of the danger which threatened them. But when Turkey declared war against Russia at the end of 1806, he did not hesitate to accept the invitation of the Herzegovinian chieftains who sought his aid. But the attempt of the Montenegrins to seize the important fortress of Nikšić failed. It was reserved for Prince Nicholas to capture it seventy years later.

The peace of Tilsit in 1807 gave the Bocche to the French, and for the next six years they remained in almost undisputed possession of the coast. Their Emperor had learned by experience to consider the Montenegrins as dangerous neighbours, whom it was better to have as friends than foes. He accordingly lost no time in making overtures to their warlike ruler. Marmont sought an interview with Peter at the Fort of the Trinity above Cattaro, at which he made him an offer of his Emperor's protection. The *Vladika* coldly replied that that of the Czar was sufficient. But Napoleon did not despair of bringing this wild and independent mountain-folk under his control. He sent Colonel Vialla de Sommières, who was French Governor of Cattaro between 1807 and 1813, to visit their country, and promised to station a consul at Cetinje. De Sommières published some years later an account of his journey, and his book was for many years the standard work on Montenegro. But France gained no hold upon the people. Napoleon's offer to construct a road at his own expense across the principality was declined; for the Montenegrins reflected that where carriages could come up, cannon could come up also. It had always been their settled policy to make access to their country difficult, and not to destroy the natural barriers of rock, to which, like the Swiss, they have owed their independence. "When God made the world, and was distributing stones over the earth"—so runs the quaint saying—"the bag that held them burst and let them all fall upon Montenegro." It is in these stones that the Black Mountain has found its best fortifications—for artificial forts it has none—and it was not till the time of the present Prince that the Napoleonic idea of making a road across the country was ever carried out. Even now it is not by any means certain that this improved means of communication will not be a source of danger in the future. Napoleon was furious at the rejection of his overtures, and vowed that he would lay waste the country with fire and sword, till its name became Monte Rosso instead of Montenegro, the Red Mountain instead of the Black. But his threat was never carried out. He took a mean revenge by depriving the *Vladika* of his spiritual jurisdiction over the

Bocche di Cattaro, but it was not till 1813 that the war was resumed.

The Serbs of Montenegro took no part in the Servian revolution under Kara George in the early years of the century. Peter, indeed, entered into relations with the liberator of Servia, but was unable to assist him. He composed, however, a spirited poem upon the valour and successes of "the brave brother Serbs" and their leader, whose aim it was to form an alliance with Montenegro and drive the Turks out of Bosnia and the Herzegovina. In accordance with this plan, Peter sent a body of his subjects to co-operate with Kara George; but, as no news arrived from the Servian camp, military operations were soon suspended, and the famine, which prevailed throughout Montenegro in 1810, made a second campaign impossible.

When the news of Napoleon's retreat from Moscow became known in Dalmatia, the Montenegrins were not slow to avail themselves of the opportunity. It had always been the desire of Prince and people to obtain the beautiful harbour of Cattaro, which is the principal outlet of their export trade. Even now that they possess two seaports of their own at Dulcigno and Antivari, they regret the old Illyrian town, which in the fourteenth century belonged to the old Serb kingdom and was regarded as an appanage of the Montenegrin princes as late as the reign of Stephen Crnoiević. In 1813, when the principality had no access to the sea, but was cut off from the coast like Servia to-day, the cry for "our old city of Cattaro" went up loud and long. A

British fleet, under Sir William Hoste, proved a valuable ally, and the *Vladika* bade Vouko Radonić, the civil governor, besiege the town, while he himself attacked Budua. Both operations were successful. The Serbs within the walls of Budua joyfully threw open the gates to their protector, and Peter, in the words of a ballad, "mounted on his big horse and light as a grey falcon, entered the town and offered up thanks to God." Cattaro, ably defended by General Gauthier and the French garrison, held out for three months, till on the 27th of December, 1813, it surrendered to the combined British and Montenegrin forces. It was the first time that the name of England had been mentioned in the story of the Black Mountain. But it was not to be the last. Sixty-seven years later, the efforts of the British Government secured to the old allies of 1813 the harbour of Dulcigno, and the good deed has not yet been forgotten in the humble cottages of the mountaineers. They speak still with gratitude of England, and point with pride to the photographs of Mr. Gladstone which hang upon their walls. Were the aged statesman to visit Cetinje—so a Montenegrin once assured the writer—the whole nation would line the road from Cattaro in his honour.

But that "hard-won haven" did not long remain the property of Montenegro. A joint meeting of Montenegrins and Bocchesi had indeed resolved upon the union of the Bocche di Cattaro to the adjoining principality. A solemn document was drawn up on the 29th of October, in the Serb and Italian languages, and signed by the *Vladika* and the civil governor, representing Montenegro and the Berda, and by the chiefs of the coast tribes. A central commission was appointed under the presidency of Peter, and composed of nine Montenegrins and nine Bocchesi, to carry on the present war against the French and secure the future government of the whole country. The union, thus auspiciously inaugurated, did not exist merely upon paper. For the capture of Castelnuovo and Spagnuolo, as well as Cattaro, had placed the whole gulf at the power of the allies. Peter, desirous of the Czar's protection, despatched to Russia a trusty envoy, one of the famous Montenegrin family of Plamenac, whose name, the "flame of fire," is emblematical of its warlike renown. But Russia was indifferent, and Austria, to whom the chiefs of the Bocchesi looked for aid, sought to regain her former Dalmatian possessions. While the *Vladika* was governing his united dominions in anxious expectation of the Czar's approval, Russia and Austria had concluded an agreement by which Cattaro and the coast were to be given up to the latter. On the 2nd of June, the coveted city, which was to have been the capital of a larger Montenegro, opened its gates to an Austrian general, and the Montenegrin day-dream was over, never to return. From that day, Cattaro has nestled beneath the wings of the Austrian double-eagle. The traveller cannot fail to notice the Venetian lions which still adorn the gateway and the ancient houses. But he will be chiefly struck by the frowning Austrian fortresses, which have been erected on every hill, and by the fleet of Austrian ironclads, which he will see lying at anchor in the Bay of Teodo. To Austria, the Bocche di Cattaro have been a valuable addition. From their shores she obtains the hardy seamen who man her ships; in their waters she finds an anchorage, finer than that of Pola, for her men-of-war. But to Montenegro, the loss of the Bocche and the strip along the coast has been irreparable. To be within a cannon's-shot of the sea, and yet to be shut off from it by a narrow piece of foreign territory, is a grievance hard to bear. Peter I. felt it bitterly; he retired from the unequal contest to his mountain-home. Russia and Austria had alike deceived him. No Montenegrin ballad narrates the story of his departure; it was regarded as too sad a subject for song. But Ragusan writers have given us their version of the surrender of Cattaro. The authors were prejudiced against the man who had laid siege to their own city; but they admit that the warriors of the Black Mountain did not evacuate Cattaro until they had fired their last cartridge. Even in their mountains, however, the protection of Russia was denied them. The annual subsidy which the principality had received since the days of the Empress Elizabeth, was stopped in 1814, and it was not till the accession of the Czar Nicholas I. in 1825 that it was renewed. The Black Mountain was under a cloud.

Peter had now time to devote to the internal organisation of his country. With the exception of the Turkish invasion of 1820, when the Pasha of Bosnia was defeated and committed suicide in disgust, the land had peace for sixteen years—an almost unexampled period of repose for its warlike inhabitants. The Montenegrins, indeed, continued to raid the adjacent parts of Albania and the Herzegovina, in quest of food and booty, but the Turkish Government was far too much occupied with the risings in Greece and the Danubian Principalities to organise a war of revenge. But the Montenegrins, demoralised by their constant struggle for existence, and reduced to the greatest extremities by famine, were chiefly engaged in quarrelling among themselves, and so small was the respect which some of the more unruly spirits showed for their ruler, that they accused him of neglecting his ecclesiastical duties. Their complaints reached the ears of the Czar, who despatched an envoy to inquire into the truth of the charge. Peter defended himself in a lengthy document, his accusers repented of the indignity which they had inflicted upon their sovereign, and an understanding was brought about by the good offices of the Russian Consul at Ragusa. The incident is interesting as showing the influence which Russia exerted over the Black Mountain at the beginning of the present century, and the lack of cohesion among the subjects of the *Vladika*. The Montenegrin chiefs still lived, each a law unto himself, and the blood-feud, the border-raid, and other primitive institutions still flourished unchecked. But Peter was fully aware of the need of a strong government. As early as 1796 he had issued a new code of thirty-three articles, to which the chiefs swore to submit. Two years later, judges were appointed to decide disputes, and a general assembly of the people was subsequently summoned, at which the *Vladika* explained the meaning of the new enactments, and insisted upon their prompt execution. Until the Code Danilo replaced them in 1855, the laws of Peter I. continued in force. In 1821 a species of police, known under the Turkish name of *Voulouk*, was introduced all over the country, but even when criminals were brought to justice and tried, it was not always easy to carry out their sentences. The ruler was severe, but public opinion often saw no harm in acts which he regarded as offences. Even to-day the Montenegrin sees nothing wrong in a skirmish with the Albanians on the border, though a stranger in his own land is' sacred in his eyes. Still more difficult was the problem of feeding a population greatly disclined to labour, and unprovided with fertile fields. Famine has always been at once the scourge and the safety of the Black Mountain. The tiny patches of soil, a couple of yards square, scarcely visible among the masses of grey limestone which cover it, barely suffice for the needs of its inhabitants, and are wholly inadequate to support an army of occupation. Wholesale emigration to Servia and Russia was but a partial remedy, and Peter with all his energy could not prevent the frequent recurrence of famine.

Full of years and distinctions, Peter I. was peacefully sitting on the 18th of October, 1830, before the fire in the vast room which was alike the kitchen and the audience-chamber of this primitive sovereign. He was speaking to the assembled company upon the theme which had occupied the last years of his life

—the need of harmony between the different districts of his country. As he spoke, he felt a sudden faintness come on, and begged to be carried to the simple and poorly-furnished apartment where he was wont to sleep without so much as a fire to warm him. That same day he had dictated his will to his secretary, in which he enjoined union upon the chiefs, and begged them, as a token of respect to himself, to keep a truce of God till the festival of St. George in the ensuing year. As his successor, he nominated his nephew Radatamova, a lad of seventeen, who subsequently assumed the name and style of Peter II. The chiefs swore to obey the dying *Vladika's* behests, and with a prayer on his lips he peacefully expired. His body was laid in the chapel of the convent at Cetinje amid the lamentations of his subjects. When, four years afterwards, the coffin was opened the corpse was found intact. The people declared that a miracle had occurred, and the dead Prince-Bishop was canonised as a saint. St. Peter Petrović is still the object of every pious Montenegrin's veneration, and to his open coffin at Cetinje come pilgrims from far and near.

VI.

PETER II. AND DANILO II.

(1830—1860.)

ON the day after Peter I.'s death, the chiefs invested his successor with the ecclesiastical garb—for he had not yet been dedicated to the ministry—placed a bishop's staff in his hand and presented him to his future subjects, who swore on the coffin of the dead *Vladika* to maintain peace and live like brethren one with another. But the new reign did not begin quite smoothly. A slight opposition was manifested to the succession of so young and inexperienced a ruler, and Radatamova himself was by no means ambitious of the onerous distinction. He was fond of solitude, and his poetic nature disinclined him to the duties of government. But his scruples were soon overcome, and the adhesion of Vouko Radonić, the civil governor, and the Archimandrite of Ostrog to his side silenced his opponents. In the chapel of the Madonna on the little island of Kom, in the lake of Scutari, the new ruler was consecrated by the Bishop of Prisrend, whom the friendly Pasha of

Scutari had permitted to perform the ceremony. Three years later he showed his respect for the Czar by journeying to St. Petersburg, where his consecration was confirmed and the dignity of a bishop, under the name of Peter II., was bestowed upon him.

The Turks had ceased to trouble Montenegro since their great defeat in 1820, but the Pasha of Scutari, mindful of the fate which had befallen his father, Kara Mahmoud, earlier in the late reign, had contented himself with the independent position which he enjoyed without encroaching upon the liberties of of his neighbours. But in 1832 Albania was again reduced to subjection by the Sultan, and the old relations between the Turkish governors and the free mountaineers were resumed. But the Turks had not forgotten the bravery of the Montenegrin warriors. They resolved, before attempting to subdue the Black Mountain by force, to try the effect of diplomatic overtures. Following the same policy which had been found successful in Servia, they offered to recognise the hereditary right of the Petrović family to rule over Montenegro, which should receive an accession of territory, provided that Peter II. acknowledged the suzerainty of the Sultan. The offer, repeated in 1856, was indignantly refused. Peter reminded the Sultan that Montenegro had never owned allegiance to his predecessors, while Servia had been for centuries a Turkish province. "As long as my subjects defend me," he said, "I need no Turkish title to my throne; if they desert me, such a title would avail me nothing. His people felt that this indeed was the voice of a true Montenegrin, and at nineteen their ruler could command their devotion to the death. Furious at this refusal, the Grand Vizier despatched an advanced guard of seven thousand men against the haughty bishop. So sudden was the invasion that the Turkish troops had reached Spuž before the Montenegrins knew of their approach. Had it not been for the bravery and the presence of mind of a village priest the invaders might have carried all before them. Near the narrow defile of Martinić, on the same spot where thirty-five years earlier Kara Mahmoud's forces had been routed, the combat took place. The ballad tells us how, in the evening, the wife of the village priest, Radonić by name, dreamed that she saw a dense cloud " coming from bloody Scutari and passing over Podgorica and Spuž. And she heard the thunder burst upon Martinić with a long crash, and the dazzling lightning scorched her eyes and those of her eight sisters-in-law. But from the church upon the mountain-side there came a furious gust of wind, and then another from Joupina, and a third from Slatina, and all three united and drove back the dark clouds into the plain of Spuž. And she awoke and told her dream to her husband, and he arose and loaded his shining gun. And while it was yet dark, the Turks rushed, torches in hand, into the village. The priest Radonić fought at the head of his parishioners till bullet after bullet struck him and laid him dying on the ground. Then he called his two nephews to him and bade them carry off his body lest the Turks should cut off his head, and rouse the Montenegrin braves against the enemy

So the alarm was given and help came." The new Pasha of Scutari fled to the gates of Spuž, and the tide of invasion was driven back. The Grand Vizier prepared to avenge the defeat of his lieutenant in person; but the dangers which threatened the Turkish Empire from Ibrahim Pasha in Syria were so pressing that the expedition was postponed. Hostilities broke out again three years later, when a band of Montenegrins surprised the fortress of Spuž, then in the possession of the Turks, and the tribe of Koutchi, which had just joined the principality, seized Žabljak, the old Montenegrin capital. But Peter II., who had by that time acquired extraordinary authority over his subjects, ordered the evacuation of this place. A pæan of triumph had risen from the Black Mountain at its capture, but the *Vladika*, with the true instinct of a statesman, judged that a good understanding with the Turks was worth more to his country than the possession of a town which was difficult to defend. His people reluctantly obeyed his commands; Žabljak was restored, and an "eternal" peace was concluded with the Turks. But border raids soon commenced between the tribes on either side. The two governments, unable to stop this tribal warfare, agreed to close their eyes to the delinquencies of their respective subjects. It is only quite recently that the shooting of a few Albanians or Montenegrins on the frontier has come to be regarded as an international incident, to be settled by special commissioners. But half a century ago fighting was the sole occupation of the mountaineers, and, rather than allow them to quarrel among themselves, Peter, however unwillingly, permitted them the luxury of an annual foray in the Turkish provinces. Herzegovina has always been the happy hunting-ground of Montenegrin freebooters, and under the direction of a Russian agent, Captain Kovalevski, their tactics were crowned with success. Victory after victory was won for two consecutive years, and in Albania, too, the Turkish towns were continually attacked. Podgorica in particular, to-day the Manchester of Montenegro, but then still in possession of the Turks, was almost daily besieged, and the traveller is shown the famous bridge just outside the town where again and again the Moslem and the Montenegrin warriors fought hand to hand and foot to foot. On one occasion a body of Montenegrins gained access to the place in the guise of deserters, and nearly succeeded in blowing up the fortifications. Forty heads were the ghastly booty of another skirmish, and, in spite of the express prohibition of the *Vladika*, twenty Turkish skulls were still bleaching on the "Turks' Tower" in 1848. The Czar Nicholas I. felt compelled to expostulate with Peter upon the cruelty of his subjects, and disavowed the part which Kovalevski had taken in their raids. For the last ten years of the reign, comparative tranquillity reigned on the Turkish frontiers, broken only by the capture of the Isle of Vranina in the lake of Scutari by the Albanians in time of peace.

Montenegro had, however, begun to recognise that Austria was even a more dangerous enemy than the Turk. The Austrian occupation of the narrow strip of coast between Spica and Cattaro was then, no less than now, a great grief to the people of the mountain behind it. One of the districts annexed along this coast-line was that inhabited by the Pastrović, a race of hardy sailors, who in the old Venetian days had acquired riches, honours, and independence. In the tiny island of St. Stephen, opposite Budua, they had founded their seat of government, where their twelve delegates met in council, and so highly was their assistance esteemed by the proud Republic of St. Mark, that her first families welcomed them as husbands for their daughters. But their fortunes had declined with those of their great ally, and at this time they had been reduced to sell their fertile pasture-lands to their Montenegrin neighbours. In order to put a stop to the frequent quarrels which ensued between the old and new proprietors, the new Austrian Government proposed to eject the Montenegrins, offering them compensation for disturbance. Peter II. gave his consent to the proposal, but the spectacle of the Austrian boundary commissioners at work upon their land was more than the shepherds of the Black Mountain could bear. They flew to arms, and the engineers were forced to beat a hasty retreat. The news spread like wildfire, and on the morrow several thousand men were ready to march against the *Schwabi*, as they called their Austrian foes. For five days active hostilities continued. Repulsed by the disciplined soldiers of Austria, the assailants resorted to the device of putting a woman in the forefront of the battle. No Serb, they knew full well, would dare to fire a shot against an army thus protected. But their opponents had no such scruples. The woman fell, and the Montenegrins rushed in vain against the serried ranks of the enemy. A general conflict followed. The children and the old men of the mountain hurled down rocks upon the heads of the Austrians below, the women brought food and ammunition to their champions in the fight. A native ballad commemorates the bravery of Lieutenant Rossbach, a veteran who had lost an eye at the battle of Aspern, and whom the Montenegrin bard calls "the great one-eyed chief." The struggle between the "intrepid wolves" of Rossbach and the "sons of Ivo Crnoiević" would have gone on much longer, for the blood of the mountaineers was up, and many were the heads of their foes whom they had cut off "with the rapid movement of their sabres." But Peter intervened and forbade any of his subjects to continue the war, under pain of excommunication. The piety of this people prevailed over their angry feelings, and a truce was concluded in 1838, which was converted into a solemn treaty of peace two years later. Austria acquired, by private purchase from the *Vladika*, two of his monasteries, one of which, situated at Stanievič near Budua, had been a favourite residence of his predecessors and had been built by Sava a hundred years earlier. A formal delimitation of territory now took place, all moot points being referred to a Russian official. Peter erected a gibbet on the frontier in full view of Budua, as a warning to his freebooting subjects. But the gallows did not deter them from reprisals, and in 1842 hostilities were renewed and carried on in a desultory fashion. But there has been no regular warfare since then between Montenegro and her dreaded neighbour. Every Montenegrin suspects Austria, and in our own day the *Erzfeind* is more feared in the Black Mountain than that *Erbfeind*, the Turk. For they feel at Cetinje that the wave of Turkish invasion has spent its force, while that of Austrian occupation has been advancing steadily during the century since the Treaty of Campo Formio.

Meanwhile, Peter had effected a most important reform in the internal government of his tiny state. Ever since 1516 the office of civil governor had existed without interruption, and had become hereditary in the family of Radonić, just as that of *Vladika* in the house of Petrović. This system of dual control had worked well on the whole, for the position of the governor had always been inferior to that of the Prince-Bishop, and in the last reign had sunk into comparative insignificance. But Vouko Radonić, who filled the office of *gouvernadour* at the accession of Peter II., was an ambitious man, who fancied he saw the opportunity of asserting his power. He supported the succession of Peter, thinking, no doubt, that with his sixty years' experience he could easily make a puppet of this lad of seventeen. But when the young *Vladika's* firmness of character became apparent, Radonić resolved to overthrow him. Following the usual plan of Balkan statesmen, he sought to make himself the agent of a great foreign power, and entered into communications with Austria. But his intrigues were discovered. Declared a traitor to his country, he was banished with all his family, his old home at Njeguš was burnt to the ground, and his place has from that day remained unfilled. From 1832 there has been no civil governor of the Black Mountain—a change which would perhaps have been less easy to effect had not the hand of an assassin removed the younger and more popular brother of Vouko Radonić. The Austrian Government pensioned the family, and frowned upon the *Vladika* when he visited Vienna.

In 1831 a new element was introduced into the polity of the Black Mountain. It was Peter's aim to check the independent spirit of the chieftains, and control the authority which they exercised over their respective districts. With this object he founded a Senate, or *Soviet*, composed at first of himself as President, and twelve other members elected by the people. But the elective character of this body was soon reduced to a nullity. Danilo II., the next ruler, found that the senators were likely to form the nucleus of a strong opposition. He therefore took the precaution of nominating them himself, and in his capacity of President was able to influence their decisions. The Senate ceased to do anything except register the decrees of the sovereign, and Prince Nicholas, on his accession, was careful to make his father, and subsequently his cousin, President of this docile assembly. Moreover, the creation of a Ministry in 1873 has further diminished its importance, never very great in a country where the Prince is practically absolute. But at first the Senate was entrusted with the double functions of a court of appeal and a legislative body. Its members were paid the modest salary of one hundred florins a year, and the simplicity of its arrangements recalled the primitive days of the Roman conscript fathers. The peasant statesmen sat in a long, low room, separated by a partition from the stable where they had just tethered their mules, and smoking their pipes like the "Tobacco Parliament" of the King of Prussia. In order to save time no adjournment was made for meals, but a sheep was roasted at the ample fire of the Senate-house, and devoured by the hungry legislators in the course of the debate, while the clerk, sitting cross-legged, read aloud official documents, or wrote down on his knees the decisions of the august assembly. Subsequently however, the number of the senators was increased to sixteen, and the indemnities paid to them raised. The President received three thousand five hundred francs, and the Vice-President three thousand; five senators, resident in the capital, were given fifteen hundred francs for their expenses, while the other nine, who were not expected to pass more than three months of the year at Cetinje, were awarded seven hundred and fifty. The refinements of Western legislatures have not yet been introduced, and the senators still sit down to deliberate with their revolvers and yataghans protruding from their sashes. But their power, under the benevolent despotism of the Prince, is zero.

Peter II., like his predecessor, was not only a warrior, but an able reformer and administrator. The revival of learning in Montenegro was due to his efforts. A poet and dramatist himself, partly educated in Russia and fully conversant with the practices of civilised nations, he felt bitterly the dearth of culture in his mountain home. At one time it was even thought that he intended to abdicate, and seek elsewhere that society which he could not find among the shepherds of Cetinje. But he preferred the nobler part of striving to educate his countrymen. At his orders the printing-press, which four centuries

THE VLADIKA, PETER II.,
IN CIVIL DRESS.

ago was the glory of Montenegro, but had been destroyed by the Turks at the siege of Obod, was once again installed in the monastery at Cetinje. The national history was now for the first time committed to print, and a valuable collection of those

ballads, from which we have frequently quoted, was
made. Between 1835 and 1839 Demetrius Milaković,
the Serb historian of Montenegro, published his
" turtle-doves " or *G'rlitze*, containing an abridgment
of the Montenegrin annals down to his own time.
The *Vladika's* own works were an excellent basis for
a national literature, and the quaint historic drama,

THE VLADIKA, PETER II.,
IN HIS PRIESTLY ROBES.

"The Serpent of the Mountain," in which he commemorated the massacre of the Turks by Danilo I.,
is a forcible piece of writing. But the exigencies of
war were unfavourable to the spread of literature.
In the stress of an invasion the Montenegrins melted
down the type of Peter's printing press, and shot
down their enemies with their own ruler's poems.
During the next reign a local almanack, the " Eaglet,"

or *Orlitch*, was the most important publication which came from the Montenegrin press.

Peter II. used his authority to enforce the laws of his predecessor, which were often more honoured in the breach than in the observance. Before this giant of six feet eight inches, who could hit a lemon with a rifle and breakfasted merrily amidst the "music" of Turkish shells and bullets, even the stubborn chiefs of Montenegro felt subdued. Besides, on more than one occasion he proved himself to be literally the pastor of his flock. In the great famine of 1846 he sold his jewels to purchase several shiploads of grain for his starving people. He greatly diminished blood-feuds by ordering that capital punishment should no longer be inflicted by a single executioner, but that the criminal should be shot by a platoon of men chosen from different clans. It was thus impossible for the relatives of the victim to mark out for future retribution the clan which had enforced the law. Fines were exacted for every offence, and the weapons of the offender confiscated until payment was made. A prison was built at Cetinje, and the *Vladika* erected a new palace for himself. This building, now used as Government offices, is known to this day as the "Billiard-table," from the favourite game of its founder. Fifty stalwart Montenegrins were needed to drag the table up the terrible "ladder" of Cattaro to Cetinje, and the feat has never been forgotten. Montenegro owes much of its present reputation for peaceful progress in the path of civilisation to his humanising influence and firm character. He was the last ruler who combined in his own person those triple attributes of primitive kingship, where the sovereign is at the same time a priest, a lawgiver, and a general. When he died on the 31st of October, 1851, at the early age of thirty-nine years, his subjects felt that a great man had gone from among them. His portrait still adorns the capital, and his mausoleum beckons the traveller from the solitary summit of the Lovćen. There, on the spot where he had often communed with nature, far from the habitations of men, he was laid by his own wish. A tiny chapel marks the grave, where, five years after his death, his remains were removed from Cetinje, and frequent pilgrimages to his shrine keep his memory green. Before his death, he had recommended to the chiefs as his successor his nephew Danilo, the son of Stanko Petrović, a young man of twenty-three years of age, at that time absent in Vienna. As in the case of Peter himself, there was considerable opposition to the succession of his nephew. Pero Petrović, another brother of the late *Vladika* and President of the Senate, availed himself of his nephew's absence to push his own claims. But the curse, which the dying Bishop had invoked upon any one who dared to disobey his injunctions, was feared by his people, and Danilo II. was soon recognised as ruler of the country. But he never enjoyed the great popularity of other princes of his house, and his brief reign, though one of the most memorable in Montenegrin history, was marked by discontent, culminating in his assassination.

His first step was to divest himself of those ecclesiastical functions which the rulers of Montenegro had filled since the year 1516, and the head of the Petrović family had performed since 1696. He was moved to adopt this course by various considerations. The compulsory celibacy of the *Vladikas* had always been a disadvantage to their country. Experience had proved that the succession from uncle to nephew was not always smooth. In Danilo's case these reasons of public policy were greatly emphasised by his affection for a young Serb lady, Darinka Kuečić, the daughter of a wealthy merchant at Trieste. It is said that the jests of the Czar Nicholas I. were not without their effect upon the young man, whose natural disinclination to the performance of episcopal duties was well known at St. Petersburg. With few exceptions, the senators acquiesced in the proposed separation of the ecclesiastical and temporal power. Danilo received at the Russian capital the approval of the defender of the Greek Church, and in 1852, not quite a year after his accession, a formal document was drawn up, setting forth the future government of the country. This Great Charter of the Black Mountain consisted of six articles. It began by stating that henceforth Montenegro should be a temporal state, under the hereditary government of a prince; that this prince should be "the illustrious Danilo Petrović of Njeguš," and that after his death the succession should go to his male descendants in order of birth. Provision was then made for the succession in the event of the Petrović line becoming extinct—of which there is no probability. The third article entrusted those episcopal functions which Danilo had abrogated to a bishop or archbishop, chosen by the

Government from among the members of the Petrović or other distinguished families of the country. The remaining clauses of the document confirmed the existing laws and customs of the country, invited Danilo to return as soon as possible from Russia, and appointed commissioners to acquaint him and the Czar with the new state of affairs.

But the transition to the secular power was not accomplished without a struggle against Montenegro's ancient foes. The Turks, who had been comparatively quiet during the last years of the preceding reign, had never recognised the undoubted fact of Montenegrin independence, and regarded this change as a direct infringement of that suzerainty which they claimed for the Sultan. Omar Pasha was ordered to invade the country; but before he had crossed the frontier, a Montenegrin force under George Petrović, one of the Prince's uncles, seized the ancient capital of Žabljak, which had so often been taken and retaken in these border wars. Danilo summoned six thousand men to meet him on the banks of the Zeta, and thus for a time prevented the garrison of Scutari from relieving the captured town. A succession of Montenegrin victories followed, but Žabljak was eventually recaptured, and the Montenegrin frontier closely blockaded. The Turkish fleet arrived off the Albanian coast, Omar Pasha succeeded in entering the country, and Danilo applied for help to St. Petersburg and Vienna. But before his envoy had returned, a great triumph had raised the spirits of his people. On the night of the 20th of January, 1853, the Montenegrins fell upon Omar's camp, captured seventeen standards, and carried off as trophies three hundred and seventeen gory Turkish heads. Omar, nothing daunted, renewed his attack from the Herzegovinian frontier near the plain of Grahovo, while another Ottoman commander penetrated as far as the famous monastery of Ostrog, only to be driven back by Danilo with great loss. Baffled by the prowess of his resolute enemies, Omar now had recourse to promises, and issued a proclamation to all the neighbouring tribes, urging them to lay down their arms. Outside the boundaries of Montenegro his fair words were not without effect, but the blood of the mountain people was up, and for them the Pasha's promises had no attraction. But the diplomatic efforts of Austria and Russia at Constantinople had meanwhile been vigorously exerted on behalf of the principality. The rainy season made the Zeta valley impassable, and the Turkish troops had begun to retire, when orders arrived from the Sultan to stop further hostilities. The campaign had cost the invaders dearly. In three months, four thousand five hundred Turks had fallen in battle more than that number had been disabled, and nine hundred prisoners had been captured by the enemy. Danilo, accompanied by the chief men of his country hastened to Vienna to express his thanks to the Emperor Francis Joseph for his services. Taught by the lessons of the war that the Montenegrins needed better weapons and more discipline than they had had hitherto, Danilo proceeded to reform the military system without delay. Till the year 1853 there had been practically no organisation whatever. As soon as a hostile army appeared, the stentorian voices of the scouts roused the whole male population in a few hours. Each man seized his rifle and rushed to the fray, ready to fight on his own account, without regard to discipline or any preconceived plan of campaign. Peter II. had, indeed, formed a corps of one hundred bodyguards, or *perianiks*, so called from the "tuft of feathers," or *perianica*, which they wore on their caps. His successor instituted a similar body of veterans, and introduced the compulsory registration of all those between the ages of eighteen and fifty. Captains of hundreds and captains of tens were selected, a standard-bearer was appointed for each company, and the outline of the future force was prepared. But there was as yet no attempt to form a standing army; that is not the least achievement of the present Prince. Danilo's soldiers had no compulsory drill, there was no instruction in tactics, no barracks, no army regulations. The warriors were simply told whom they were to follow when the signal for war was given; and, the conflict over, each returned to his cottage. With the exception of powder, the Government provided its soldiers with nothing, and the few cannon which the country possessed had been captured from the Turks.

Montenegro, to the surprise of both Russia and Turkey, and the disgust of many of its own inhabitants, took no official part in the Crimean War. Austria strongly urged a policy of neutrality upon the Prince, and Danilo, so far from deserving the epithets which the English press heaped upon him, did his utmost to restrain his subjects from attacking the Turks. A few skirmishes took place, and there was a strong war-party at Cetinje, headed by Peter Petrović, another of the Prince's uncles and President of the Senate. A plot, in which Peter and his brother George were involved, was discovered, and Danilo's position for a time was precarious. His people, accustomed for generations to indulge in the luxury of border-raids, could not understand the prohibition of their favourite amusement. To attack and harry the Turk at the moment, when he was fully occupied in defending himself against Russia, seemed to them a perfectly natural and legitimate occupation. The nearer the Ottoman forces approached, the louder grew the cry of dissatisfaction with Danilo's pacific injunctions. To sit down calmly when provoked was more than the warriors of Crnagora could endure. For a few weeks in the spring of 1854 war seemed imminent, and even Danilo felt compelled to lodge a protest at Constantinople against the warlike preparations of the Pasha of Mostar, and to make a census of those of his subjects who would be available for military service. Again, in the following year, the threatening attitude of the Montenegrins in the neighbourhood of Antivari endangered the prospects of peace; but once more the combined influence of Austria and their own Prince prevailed over the inclinations of the people. But in the summer of 1855 the temptation proved too strong. In spite of a strongly-worded *firman* from Constantinople, issued with the approval of the allies and the Austrian Government, bands of Montenegrins ravaged the Herzegovina in all directions. Danilo confessed that he could not restrain his subjects from acts of pillage, which he personally disapproved. A revolt was the instant result of this confession. Whole districts of Montenegro rose against the ruler, who refused to lead them against their ancient foes; the warlike tribes of the Piperi and the Koutchi, who had seceded from the principality in 1843 rather than pay taxes, and the inhabitants of the fertile Zeta valley, always the chief sufferers by Turkish raids, proclaimed themselves independent and called upon the rest of the Berda to separate from a Prince who had proved himself so degenerate a descendant of the two Peters. The appeal fell flat; Danilo, at the head of six thousand men, attacked the rebels, who at one time meditated a junction with the Turks. Patriotism alone prevented the execution of this desperate resolve. Rano Bosković, one of the insurgent leaders, set the example of submission to his lawful sovereign, and the revolt was at an end. Danilo confiscated the property of the rebel chiefs as a punishment, and held a strict inquiry into their conduct. But the funds which he had thus acquired were not sufficient. In his dilemma he turned to Vienna, and was even willing to accept an Austrian protectorate in return for a pecuniary consideration. But his offer met with no response, and the new Czar, to whom he then applied, sent him nothing but a formal expression of his thanks for the sympathy which the principality had shown him upon his father's death. At the Congress of Paris in 1856 the Prince found that his grievances met with little heed from the Powers. His vigorous assertion of his country's independence and his claim to an outlet on the sea were alike disregarded, and a subsequent manifesto was equally fruitless. Danilo demanded the formal recognition of Montenegrin independence by the Powers, an increase of territory in both the Albanian and Herzegovinian frontiers, an accurate delimitation of the boundary between Turkey and Montenegro similar to that which had been made in the last reign between Austria and the principality, and the cession of Antivari. The first of these demands was purely a matter of form, for Montenegro had been independent *de facto* ever since the battle of Kossovo in 1389. But Danilo was anxious to have his government recognised in the councils of diplomacy. For a moment it seemed as if the European Areopagus favoured his claims ; conferences were held and notes exchanged upon the subject. But when the Prince visited Paris in 1857 he was informed that if he would recognise the suzerainty of the Sultan, the latter would cede him a piece of territory in the Herzegovina in return for a payment of tithe, would give him a civil list and the Turkish title of *muchir*, and would allow the Montenegrin flag access to all Turkish ports. Peter II. had indignantly refused a similar offer twenty-five years earlier. But his successor was inclined to accept it, and thus close the glorious career of the virgin state by conceding to the Turkish diplomatist what the Turkish armies had never won.

Great was the indignation of the Montenegrins at what they considered an act of cowardice. Danilo's inaction during the Crimean war, his recent refusal to accept the coveted town of Nikšić from its inhabitants for fear of complications with Turkey, the strictness with which he raised the taxes and the sanguinary suppression of another revolt of the Koutchi tribe, had made him very unpopular. During his absence in Paris, his brother Mirko had found that a plot had been concocted by George Petrović and other leading men against him, and the flight of the principal conspirator did not diminish the discontent. The news of this intended surrender to the Sultan was the last straw. Two of his subjects were shot on the charge of attempting his life. The Emperors of Austria and Russia again turned a deaf ear to his requests, and the Turks showed no sign of favour towards him. On the contrary, early in 1858 a Turkish army of seven thousand men under Hussein Pasha appeared on his northern frontier. The French Emperor, who had recently proved his friendly interest by admitting a number of young Montenegrins as pupils to the seminary of Louis-le-Grand, alone took the side of this hard-pressed state. Napoleon III. pledged himself to guarantee the independence of a country which had so boldly withstood the soldiers of his uncle, and a French squadron was sent to Ragusa to watch events.

But it was by their own right hands that the warriors vindicated their threatened liberty. Their army was commanded by Mirko, the Prince's brother, and the most celebrated commander whom even that land of heroes has produced. His exploits gained him the name of the "Sword of Montenegro," and his songs have won him a high place among Balkan poets. He was at once the Lysander and the Tyrtæus of the modern Sparta. His fiery disposition was thought by his countrymen to unfit him for the duties of a ruler, but as a leader in battle he was unrivalled.

The decisive battle took place in the stony plain of Grahovo — a spot which will always be remembered as the Marathon of Montenegro. The Turkish army of seven thousand men lay encamped on the plain, while the Montenegrins lined the narrow rocky defiles which are the sole means of entrance and exit. But before giving the signal for the attack, Mirko made a final effort at conciliation by sending M. Delarue, the Prince's secretary, to see the Turkish commissioner at the fortress of Klobuk, six hours distant. The envoy was arrested on the way, and on the 13th of May the fight began. The Turkish troops, shut up in a basin, like the French at Sédan, were completely at the mercy of their adversaries. Mirko waited until he had surrounded them on all sides, and then gave the order to fire. Volleys of shot fell from the heights upon the helpless Turks, and then, throwing their rifles aside, the Montenegrins drew their yataghans and rushed down like wolves upon the fold. The Turkish artillerymen were cut down at their guns, and the bravery of the Imperial Guard availed nothing against the onward rush of the mountaineers. Flight was impossible, for at the end of the plain a fresh detachment awaited the fugitives. The battle lasted till the following day, and an Austrian gendarme, who visited the fatal spot a few weeks later, counted no less than 2,237 skeletons still lying on the plain. Of the 4,500 Montenegrins only 400 were killed; the losses of the Turks amounted to eight times that number. The marvel was that any escaped. In the arsenal at Cetinje there are carefully preserved a quantity of English medals, awarded to our allies of the Crimea, and captured by the Montenegrins from the Turkish veterans in this battle. But the victory bore other and more valuable fruits. The prowess of the victors spread far and wide; from that time Grahovo has belonged to its conquerors; and though no monument marks the battlefield, the triumph of Mirko is commemorated in one of the finest of the national ballads. Everywhere the *rayahs* looked to Montenegro as their champion, and the hapless Herzegovinians were made to feel the vengeance of the vanquished Turks for the losses which the army of Mirko had inflicted.

Danilo, with his usual caution, hesitated to follow up his victory. He had no wish to assume the offensive, but preferred to await the decision of Europe. In October, 1858, a commission, composed of the Ambassadors of the Great Powers, met at Constantinople. No recognition of Montenegrin independence was made by the Sultan, and the labours of the frontier commissioners, which began next year, were not final. Two more Turkish wars were needed to fix the Turco-Montenegrin boundary.

A scarcely less important event was the promulgation of a new code of laws. The "Code Danilo," as it is called, which came into force in 1855, and remained the law of the land until it was superseded by the recent code of 1888, was printed in both Serb and Italian—a language which is better known than any other foreign tongue in the Black Mountain. The laws of Danilo show a considerable advance upon those of Peter I. But some of the enactments are very curious, and recall a primitive state of society. Whilst one article declares the equality of every citizen before the law, and lays down the democratic principles of the universal ownership of land and the equal right of all to hold office, another allows a man who is struck to kill the striker, provided that he does so at once; but if he delays, the offence is murder. Theft is severely punished, provision is made for the election of judges by the people, and fines are imposed upon any judge who insults a suitor. In short, the "Code Danilo" is the embodiment of that "civil and religious liberty" which the Montenegrin motto declares to be "the reward of valour."

Danilo did not long survive the triumph of his arms over the Turks. In the summer of 1860 he went with the Princess to take a course of baths at the picturesque hamlet of Persano, on the shore of the Bocche di Cattaro. On the 13th of August they had gone for a walk in the cool of the day along the promenade outside the walls of the latter town. As the clock struck ten, the princely couple summoned their boatman for the return journey to their villa at Persano. Danilo was in the act of stepping from the quay into the boat when a bullet struck him and he fell back in the arms of his wife. Tedeschi, his physician, was soon in attendance, but all his efforts were useless. Twenty-four hours later the Prince expired, and the following night his sorrowing widow accompanied his corpse to Cetinje. His assassin, an exiled Montenegrin, Kadić by name, was arrested, tried, and hung without confessing the motive of his act.

VII.

MONTENEGRO UNDER NICHOLAS I.

(1860—1896.)

THE security of the Petrović dynasty on the throne was not affected for a moment by the murder of Danilo II. The late Prince had left no male offspring, for his only child was a daughter; but the succession had been determined five years before his death. His nephew Nicholas, son of Mirko, was then nominated as his heir, and the young Prince was at once proclaimed by the Senate without opposition. His father, Mirko, who, though the elder brother of Danilo, had been passed over in 1851, accepted without a murmur this further disregard of his claims, and in the capacity of President of the Senate was content to serve to the end of his life as the first subject of his son. Together with his wife Stana, who died last year at a ripe old age, he watched with loyal devotion over the young Prince's career.

Nicholas I. was born at Njeguš, the ancestral home of his race, on the 25th of September, 1841, and had therefore not quite completed his nineteenth year when the sudden death of his uncle placed him on the throne. He had been prepared by a Western education for the duties which lay before him. The excellent French which he speaks was acquired at the Academy of Louis-le-Grand in Paris, where he studied after several years spent in learning Serb history and the Italian and German languages under the care of his aunt Darinka's family at Trieste. But the young mountaineer, who had been wisely allowed to run wild as a child in his highland home, felt the atmosphere of the Parisian class-room oppressive and stifling. He took little pleasure in the gaieties of town life, and sighed for the free air of the Black Mountains where his childhood had been spent in manly games. "My country," he once said, "is a wilderness of stones; it is arid, it is poor, but I adore it! And if I were offered the whole of the Balkan Peninsula in exchange, why, I would not hear one word!" His poetic nature, nurtured amidst the grand scenery of his native land, gave early promise of that literary taste to which we owe a volume of Serb poetry and two tragedies, the *Empress of the Balkans* and *Prince Arbanit.* Whenever he could escape from the dull round of his academic studies, he sought fresh air and woods and mountains which reminded him of his own. He learnt to shoot with an accuracy which surprised his countrymen; a fearless rider, he traversed every pass of the mountains on horseback, and imbibed in the nursery those warlike traditions which he was to perpetuate beneath the walls of Nikšić. He seemed to Lady Strangford, when she visited "the eastern shores of the Adriatic" shortly after his accession, "an extraordinarily handsome man, very tall and well made, with hair and eyes nearly black, and a naturally soft, somewhat sad expression of face." When the present writer met him two years ago, he bore his fifty-two years lightly, and his figure was as erect and his eye as keen as when that description was penned. No one can see and converse with him without feeling that he is a born leader of men, who, if he had been Prime Minister of a large state, instead of Prince of a small one, would have made a great mark upon the history of Europe.

Two months after his accession the young Prince married the lady to whom, in accordance with Montenegrin custom, he had been affianced from childhood. Milena Voukotić was the daughter of a Montenegrin *voïvode*, who had been the brother-in-arms of Mirko at the great day of Grahovo. The Princess is still famous for her beauty, and her daughters have won the admiration of the fastidious Russian Court, and are the favourites of Queen Victoria. The nine children, three of them sons, who are the issue of this marriage, have secured the succession to the House of Petrŏvić.

Prince Nicholas had been little more than a year on the throne when war broke out with the Sultan. The Turks were burning to avenge their defeat at Grahavo, while the *rayahs* of the Herzegovina only waited a favourable moment to join hands with their brothers across the border. The insurrection of 1861 in that province excited the utmost enthusiasm in Montenegro. The Prince, at the entreaty of the

Powers, followed at first the neutral policy of his predecessor, and even permitted the Turks to convey provisions across his country to their garrison at Nikšić. But it was again found impossible to check the fervour of the mountaineers. Frontier incidents occurred, and Omar Pasha proclaimed the blockade of the Principality. Early in 1862 he declared war against Montenegro, and his army entered the country in three divisions. Diplomatic protests were in vain, and the Prince's father and father-in-law lost no time in taking the field. The valley of the Zeta, always the weakest point of Montenegro's natural defences, was the principal theatre of the war. Mirko performed prodigies of valour, and his heroic defence of the Upper Monastery of Ostrog with twenty-six men, and his subsequent march to Cetinje with the loss of a single soldier, may be compared with the futile attempts of the Turks to capture that monastic stronghold a century earlier, when thirty men successfully held the shrine of St. Basil and the ledge of rock beneath it, against an army of thirty thousand. No one who has ever visited Ostrog will doubt the possibility of these marvellous feats. The only means of dislodging a well-provisioned garrison is to smoke them out of this hole in the rocks, and the Prince is fond of telling how on this memorable occasion his father came out of it " as black as a coal." In a pitched battle near Rjeka, Mirko, with a mere handful of men, held a large force of Turks at bay, sustaining his strength for a whole day on nothing more substantial than a few pears. Even lads of twelve and thirteen shouldered a rifle, and the Prince's sister followed her father to the war. But the disciplined Ottoman troops, led by the ablest of Turkish commanders, slowly yet steadily drove the gallant defenders back. The rich valley of the Zeta was ravaged by the invaders, and in spite of a temporary advantage gained by the Montenegrins, their enemies advanced steadily upon the capital. Worst of all, the bullet of an assassin had nearly slain the young Prince, on his way to the front with the Dowager Princess and his wife. His attendants were wounded by splinters from the rocks, but he and his family escaped unscathed. His people, dejected by their losses, without provisions, without allies, withdrew from the unequal contest, and even Mirko, after sixty battles, was bound to confess that the game was up. Europe, with the exception of Pius IX., who had forbidden the Albanian Catholics to attack the Montenegrin Christians, had hitherto looked on with indifference. But diplomacy at last intervened; the Prince and the Pasha met at Rjeka, and the Convention of Scutari, dated the 31st of August, ended the war. The terms of the Convention were sufficiently severe. It was expressly stipulated that Mirko should quit his country for ever—a remarkable tribute to his prowess, and the best proof of the fear which he inspired. But this stipulation was never carried out; and the article which gave the Turks power to erect guard-houses along the valley of the Zeta was subsequently abandoned by the Sultan. But no Montenegrin fortifications were to be erected on the Turkish frontiers, no family was to enter the Principality without a Turkish passport, and the importation of war material at the port of Antivari was strictly prohibited. On the other hand, the Turks agreed to allow the export and import of merchandise at that harbour free of duty.

An interval of fourteen years' peace occurred between the first and second Turkish wars of the present reign, and Montenegro sorely needed it. Famine had followed in the trail of the sword. France alone sent corn to the value of 600,000 francs for the relief of the prevailing distress, and Napoleon III. assured Prince Nicholas at the Paris Exhibition of 1867 of his continued good-will toward the warrior-people. But a fresh disaster befell the country. Cholera made its first appearance in the Principality, and the Prince returned just in time to support his dying father in his arms. Mirko has left a great name both as a poet and a warrior, and the rice and coffee plantations which he started show that he was not blind to the uses of agriculture. For a moment it looked as if the Turks would renew their attacks now that their dreaded antagonist was gone. But the alarm passed away, and the Prince was left unmolested to pursue his contemplated reforms.

The first of these was an improved military organisation. The great losses sustained in the late war had convinced him that the measures of his predecessor nine years earlier were inadequate. Arms were the first necessity, and a large number of rifles were purchased in France by means of a lottery; while Napoleon III., the Czar, Prince Michael of Servia, and another Serb provided the funds for further munitions of war. Prince Michael also lent the services of an able gunsmith, who constructed a small arsenal at Obod, on the site of the old printing-press, and of three artillery officers, who started a cannon-foundry near Cetinje. A trumpeter was also sent from Belgrade to teach the Montenegrins the signals in use in the Servian army. Having thus provided his country with modern weapons, Prince Nicholas set about the improvement of his army. In 1870, Captain Wlahović, a Servian officer, and joint author of an excellent work on Montenegro, was entrusted with the task of drawing up a scheme for the better organisation of the Montenegrin forces. The male population between the ages of seventeen and sixty was divided into two divisions, each about ten thousand strong, and subdivided into two brigades of five battalions apiece. Each battalion was formed by eight companies. The staff consisted of the Prince as commander-in-chief, seven *voïvodes*, of whom the first was Elia Plamenac, the present Minister for War, and several aids-de-camp. Every Montenegrin of military age—for the army, as Scharnhorst said of Prussia, was simply " the nation under arms "—received a rifle and a stock of cartridges from the Government. Every one, even in time of peace, always carries a revolver, and carries it loaded, by special command of the Prince. A Montenegrin loves his weapons as his children ; infants are allowed to play with the butt-ends of pistols, and a native proverb says, " You might as well take from me my brother as my rifle." Artillery, which had scarcely existed in the country hitherto, were now made a regular arm of the service, and two mountain batteries formed part of the new military scheme. Cavalry can never be of much use in so mountainous a region; moreover the cost of forage in the western portion of the Principality makes a horse too expensive a luxury for any but a few. In 1894, however, the complete equipment for a squadron of cavalry, together with two instructors, was sent to the Prince by the Sultan. Such was the military organisation of Montenegro till last year, when Prince Nicholas began the experiment of a standing army, drilled by officers who have had a special education in tactics abroad. In August, 1895, a Russian ship arrived at Antivari with a cargo of thirty thousand rifles and a great quantity of cannon, cartridges, and other war material, as a present from the new Czar to his namesake. Russian instructors had already arrived, a military college was established at Podgorica, and barracks for a battalion of soldiers were built at Cetinje. These barracks will be formally opened on the 29th of July of the present year, the bicentenary of the dynasty. Every Montenegrin, except the Mussulman inhabitants of Dulcigno, who are exempt on payment of a capitation tax, will henceforth undergo compulsory military training. But neither last year nor in 1870 was any provision made for a commissariat department. That is the defect of the Montenegrin military system. The wives, daughters, and sisters of the mountaineers still carry their reserves of powder and their food and drink on their backs, and no ambulance corps or intelligence bureau is to be found in the rear of a Montenegrin army.

In the early years of his reign the Prince was

largely under the influence of his aunt, the Dowager Princess Darinka, whose desire was to introduce Western, and especially French, institutions into the Black Mountain. Mirko had acted as a check upon this liberal policy, but shortly after his death a so-called "constitution" was granted. On St. George's Day, 1868, a proclamation announced to the astonished people, accustomed to look upon their *Gospodar* as the incarnation of all authority, that he had voluntarily renounced his uncontrolled rights over the public funds, while reserving the prerogative of pardon and the complete direction of foreign affairs. But neither the "constitution" of 1868, nor the creation of a ministry, with departments for foreign and home affairs, war, justice, and a President of the Council, has in the smallest degree diminished the practical autocracy of Prince Nicholas. He can truly say, like the Grand Monarque, *L'état, c'est moi*. He is practically his own Premier, and both practically and theoretically his own Lord Chancellor and commander-in-chief. Whoever would see benevolent despotism in full working order had better go to Montenegro, whose ruler assured the present writer that thére would be no parliamentary government there for a century. As he once put it in a neat epigram: "A prince ought to be a Liberal, his subjects Conservatives."

All reforms in his country have naturally proceeded from above, and every change which has been effected during his reign has been directly due to his initiative. It was thus, that on the visit which he paid to the courts of Berlin, Vienna, and St. Petersburg, in the winter of 1868-9, he made a powerful appeal to Alexander II. on behalf of Montenegrin education. In spite of the efforts of Danilo II., who gave lessons himself to a few children of the chief families in a room of his palace, and the two small schools founded by his predecessor previous to the year 1869, there was no instruction of any kind to be obtained in the whole country except at a tiny academy for priests, installed in the monastery at Cetinje. The Czar and his family lent a ready ear to the Prince's words. Prince Dolgorouki, one of whose ancestors had visited Montenegro in the days of Stephen the Little a century earlier, was sent on a tour of inspection. Funds were provided for the foundation of a seminary for boys, called the *Bogoslavia*, while a school for the daughters of the best families was established under the auspices of the Russian Empress, and christened the *Jenski Crnogorski Institute*. The success of both has been complete. In a very short time forty pupils of the *Bogoslavia* had qualified as schoolmasters, and scattered throughout the country the seeds of education. The fame of the girls' school has spread abroad. Residents on the Bocche di Cattaro send their daughters to attend it, and foreign diplomatists, accredited to the Montenegrin Court, find there an excellent training for their children. At the present time, primary education is universal in the Black Mountain, and lecturers are appointed by the village councils to explain the advantages of learning. But in time of war, study is apt to be neglected, for instructors of youth eagerly exchange the pen for the sword, and one of the chief inspectors of schools played a prominent part in the rising of the Herzegovina. The highest education is, however, still unobtainable in the Principality. The present Finance Minister, M. Matanović, was educated in Paris, while the Minister of Justice, M. Bogošić, came from Odessa, and many leading men have been at school in Italy. But it is the desire of the Prince that his subjects should be educated in their own country, if possible, in order that they may remain Montenegrins and not imbibe that spirit of discontent which has in some cases been found to be the result of a foreign education. His own sons have accordingly been placed under the care of a resident Swiss tutor.

The insurrection of the people on the shores of the Bocche di Cattaro against the Austrian Government in 1869 was a sore temptation to their neighbours and kinsmen. Touching appeals were made to the Montenegrins by the warlike Krivoscians, who dwelt on the heights between Grahovo and the sea, and had held their mountain fastnesses against every invader for generations. Many of their families fled for refuge over the border, and their fiery war-song bade "the Black Prince" come "at the head of his faithful Montenegrins from the ruins of Obod, whither the good genius of the Dalmatian mountains has flown to awaken him out of his sleep." But although the struggle was so fierce and so near, the Montenegrins remained neutral at the command of their cautious ruler. The Emperor Francis Joseph fully recognised the harm which Prince Nicholas could have inflicted upon him had he chosen, and an Austrian decoration was the outward token of his gratitude.

But when the Herzegovina rose against the Turk in 1875, it was impossible to hold the Montenegrins back. The "Andrassy Note," which had this object, fell flat. From the outset, Montenegrin volunteers took an active part in a rising which began almost at their doors. According to the Turkish version, whole battalions of them fought in the ranks of the insurgents. An army was collected at Skodra to keep them in check; strongly worded remonstrances were addressed by the Porte to the Prince. The reply was a demand for the cession of part of the Herzegovina and the publication of an offensive and defensive alliance with Prince Milan of Servia. On the 2nd of July, 1876, Montenegro followed the example of her brother Serbs, and declared war against her ancient enemy. An army of eleven thousand men, under the command of the Prince, at once invaded the Herzegovina. The old spirit and the new military organisation of the invaders speedily made themselves felt. The Herzegovinians flocked to the Prince's standard, and he soon had twenty thousand men under his control. The first important engagement took place on the 28th, at the village of Vučidol, where Mouktar Pasha, the Turkish commander, was defeated and wounded. A little later, the army of the South, amounting to six thousand men and led by the Prince's cousin, Božo Petrović, the present Montenegrin Premier, twice defeated Mahmoud Pasha at Medun, and, after a four months' siege, that place surrendered. An armistice was concluded in November, and the Prince sent two plenipotentiaries to Constantinople to negotiate a peace. But his proposals were rejected, and in April an eloquent manifesto of their ruler bade the Montenegrins recommence hostilities. They were better armed, thanks to the rifles captured from the Turks, than in the previous campaign, and the knowledge that Russia was about to declare war more than compensated for the defection of Servia. The Prince, who showed himself a master of this mountain warfare, craftily led the Turks on by means of a feigned retreat into the valley of the Zeta. Believing that the enemy had given up the contest, Suleiman Pasha had already telegraphed to Constantinople that the history of Montenegro had closed, and that it was high time to appoint the first Turkish governor. His troops occupied the monastery of Ostrog, the scene of Mirko's heroic feat in the last war. But it was their only success. Surprised and surrounded in the midst of the mountains, they were forced to beat a retreat to Spuž, with a loss of nearly half their strength. Relieved by the diversion which the march of the Russians over the Danube had now created, the Prince laid siege to Nikšić, which, after a four months' siege, fell into his hands. This was the great exploit of the war; loud was the rejoicing at Cetinje, and to this day the Prince recalls with keen delight the "Homeric battles," which he fought beneath the walls of the old Turkish town. The harbours of Antivari and Dulcigno next fell into his hands, and he composed a hymn of triumph to the sea, which, at last, after years of weary waiting, his standards had reached. This was practically the last event of the war. The Prince had summoned Skodra to surrender and was on the point of beginning the siege, when he heard of the armistice between Russia and Turkey. On the last day of January, 1878, he suspended military operations. Sovereign and people had shown

MAP OF MONTENEGRO.

themselves worthy descendants of their warlike ancestors. They had fought with equal courage and success—nearly twenty Turks had fallen for every one of their own warriors—and it was noted as a remarkable fact when a Montenegrin allowed himself to be taken prisoner.

Their efforts had not been in vain. Had, indeed, the Treaty of San Stefano been adopted, Montenegro would have been more than trebled in size and its population doubled, while its eastern boundary would have been almost conterminous with the western frontier of Servia. Thus the two branches of the Serb stock, so long divided, would have been practically reunited, and the restoration of the Serb Empire, which the Prince had told his subjects was his dream, might have been realised. But this did not suit the policy of Austria. The Treaty of Berlin was substituted for that of San Stefano, and the new Montenegrin frontiers, though much larger than those of 1856, were much smaller than those which Russia had tried to procure for her ally. The area of the Principality was more than doubled; its population increased from one hundred and ninety-six thousand to two hundred and eighty thousand. The important places of Podgorica, Spuž, and Žabljak, the old capital of Ivan the Black, were added to it, and Antivari with its harbour was confirmed to the Prince on condition that he should have no ships of war. But he was ordered by the Congress to restore Dulcigno to the Turks, while the village of Spica, which commands the beautiful bay of Antivari, was incorporated with Austria-Hungary. The former of these grievances was soon redressed; the latter still rankles in the breast of Prince Nicholas. The

Albanian towns of Gusinje and Plava were considered an adequate compensation for this bitter disappointment. The Porte now formally recognised the independence of Montenegro, which had practically existed for nearly five centuries, and the Principality took over a portion of the Turkish Debt corresponding to the area of Turkish territory received.

This settlement was not final. Even now, neither the amount of the Debt nor the exact frontier has been determined. The Albanian inhabitants of Plava and Gusinje, notorious for their turbulence, refused to be annexed to Montenegro. An "Albanian League" was formed to resist the cession, and fighting recommenced between the two nationalities. A compromise, suggested by Count Corti, the Italian Ambassador at Constantinople, failed ; but, as a solution of the difficulty, Gusinje and Plava were restored to Turkey, while the district and harbour of Dulcigno were awarded to Montenegro. The Porte refused to consent ; but a naval demonstration of the Powers, held before Dulcigno, at the suggestion of Great Britain, in September, 1880, prevailed upon it to yield. Montenegro at last had gained her coveted access to the sea with a seaboard of thirty miles. A rare example of political gratitude, she has never forgotten the service which England rendered her on this occasion, and the name of Gladstone is held in reverence by every shepherd of her remote mountains.

The fifteen years which have elapsed since then have witnessed the peaceable development of the country under an able and enlightened autocracy

Prince Nicholas has succeeded in making himself a model to despotic rulers all over the world. He has broken down the prejudice of his subjects against highways, and a fine carriage road now connects Cattaro with Cetinje, and Cetinje with Nikšić, by way of Podgorica and Danilograd, while the circle is to be completed by continuing it from Nikšić to the sea at Risano. The fertile valley of the Zeta has thus been opened up, and the roads from Podgorica to the Lake of Skodra, and from Vir Bazar to Antivari, have put it in direct communication with the Montenegrin coast. It is in the eastern part of the Principality, the new Montenegro, that most remains to be done, for the splendid beech-forests which cover that region should, if made accessible by roads, prove a rich source of revenue. The acquisitions of the Berlin Treaty have, in fact, altered the character and must affect the future of the Principality. Montenegro is no longer a barren mountain shut off from the sea, without commerce, without timber, without pasture-lands. Whether its present frontier is as defensible as its old one is a question of opinion; but its material resources are much greater, while the Albanian subjects, whom it acquired at Podgorica and elsewhere, are valuable members of a community which is still indisposed to industrial pursuits. The Prince has done all he can to induce his warriors to follow the arts of peace without forgetting those of war. He has encouraged trade at his two ports by means of bounties, and has sent officials to study commercial life at Marseilles. During a recent journey abroad, he ordered each of his subjects to plant one vine, in order to increase the quantity of the red Montenegrin vintage, which is as yet insufficient for exportation He has cultivated tobacco with success, but even now his land is visited by severe famines. Meanwhile the warriors have not degenerated. The frontier commission, which was appointed to delimitate the Turco-Montenegrin frontier after the Berlin Treaty, gave rise, by its decisions, to a border quarrel between the Montenegrins and Albanians. The blood-feuds thus created—for that practice is not even yet extinct—enabled the mountaineers to "keep their hands in," and frequent encounters took place, which led to diplomatic negotiations with Turkey. At last there was a solemn reconciliation between the combatants. The parties met on the river Lim, and after a religious ceremony the leaders, advancing by couples to the bank with a stone in their hands, flung it into the stream. So the blood-feud was washed away.

With Austria the Prince's relations have been, since 1880, less friendly than with Turkey. He is now hemmed in by Austria on almost every side. An Austrian governor holds Bosnia and the Herzegovina, the cradle of his race; Austrian troops are stationed in the Sandjak of Novibazar, and thus cut him off from Servia; Austrian forts guard the approach from Cattaro, and Austrian diplomacy retains Spica. The enemy of the future is not at Constantinople, but Vienna. Russia has maintained her ancient sympathy with him. Alexander III. gave him a yacht and called him his "only friend"; Nicholas II. has sent him arms and instructors to teach their use, and two matrimonial alliances of his daughters have connected him with the Russian Imperial family. But to regard Montenegro as a mere outpost of Russia is to ignore her whole history and the independent character of her Prince and people.

The last few years have seen the establishment of the first Montenegrin public library and museum, which together with a theatre, where the Prince's plays are performed, occupies a building known as the *Zetski Dom*. In 1888 a new Code, the work of M. Bogošić, of the University of Odessa, which had been projected immediately after the war, was promulgated, and the manner in which the village justices of the Black Mountain interpret it has won the approval of its author. In July, 1893, the Principality celebrated with great rejoicings the four hundredth anniversary of the first Slavonic printing press, the foundation of which we have described, and on the 29th of the same month in the present year it will keep the bicentenary of the reigning dynasty.

The Montenegrins will then be able to look back upon a long and glorious history, while their ruler can justly boast that of the seven princes of the Petrović House he has done the most for his country.

THE END.

INDEX.

A.

Aaron of Moldavia, 52
Actium, battle of, 5
Akermann, convention of, 91
Albania, under Simeon, 138, under Samuel, 152; language and customs, 164; under John Asên II., 175; opposes Montenegro, 465; blood-feuds, 467
Alexander I. of Bulgaria, elected Prince, 219; character, 219; political difficulties, 220; *coup d'état*, 221; "Prince of North and South Bulgaria," 223; his popularity, 224; "hero of Slivnitza," 226; conspiracies against, 227; kidnapped, 227; returns, 230; abdicates, 230; "Count Hartenau," 231
Alexander of Macedon defeats Getæ, 2
Alexander John I. of Roumania, *see* Couza
Alexander I., King of Servia, arrests the Regents, 350; suspends constitution, 351
Alexis, Czar of Russia, 70
Amurath I., defeats Serbs at Kossovo, 288; assassinated, 289
Amurath II., claims Servian throne, 292; defeated by Hunyad, 293
Andrew II. of Hungary, 261
Anne, Empress of Russia, 78

Antoninus Pius, 22
Antony, Mark, 5
Apollodorus, architect of Trajan's bridge, 11; of Trajan's column, 15
Arsenius, Serb Patriarch, migration of, 305
Asên, John I., his revolution, 164; crowned "Czar of the Bulgarians and Greeks," 166; his wars, 168; assassinated, 169
Asên, John II., his prosperous reign, 175; extent of his empire, 175; increase of trade, 177; his capital, 178; refounds National Church, 179; dies, 179
Asên, John III., 182
Asên, Michael, 180
Asên, Peter, 164, 169
Augustus, Roman Emperor, 5
Aurelian evacuates Dacia, 24
Austria, obtains Bucovina, 81; and Dalmatia, 412; her relations with Montenegro, 440, 460, 467
Avars in Roumania, 29

B.

Babylas, Prince-Bishop of Montenegro, 381
Bajazet I., 289
Baldwin of Flanders, 172
Balsha I., 361

INDEX.

Balsha II., 362
Balta-Liman, convention of, 97
Basil, the "Bulgar-Slayer," 33; his campaigns, 155; his cruelty, 156; his conquests, 158
Basil "the Wolf"; his criminal code, 66; his wars, 68; his flight, 68
Bassarab, Matthew, his government of Moldavia, 66; feud with Basil, 68; death, 69
Bassarab, Neagoe, 46
Basta, Italian general, 56
Bathori, Andrew, 54
Bathori, Sigismund, Prince of Transylvania, 53
Belgrade, part of Bulgarian Empire, 138, 154, 170; captured by Hungary, 284; "City of the Holy War," 295; seat of Turkish Government, 301; entirely free, 337
Beltcheff, murder of, 241
Berlin, treaty of, and Roumania, 116; and Bulgaria, 213; and Servia, 345; and Montenegro, 464
Bessarabia devastated by Simeon, 31; annexed by Russia, 85; southern part joined to Moldavia, 101; again Russian, 117; refuge of Bulgarians, 202
Bibescou, George, 95, 96
Bismarck advises Prince Charles, 108; and Prince Alexander, 219
Black George, hero of modern Servia, 311; frees his country, 313; "supreme chief," 315; leaves Servia, 316; murdered, 319
"Black Legion," 303
Bœrebistes, Dacian king, 4
Bogdan, 44
Bogomile heresy, 146, 147; serious results of, 149
Bolizza, Mariano, his account of Montenegro, 387
Boljars, Bulgarian nobles, 157, 158, 192

Boril, Bulgarian Czar, 174
Boris I., converted to Christianity, 131; Roman or Orthodox? 133; retires to a cloister, 134
Boris II., 150, 151, 154
Boris, Baby, his "conversion," 243
Bosnia, united to Servia, 258; conquered by Dušan, 284; independent, 284; Turkish, 297; occupied by Austria, 345
Boyards, Roumanian nobles, their privileges, 47; revolts of, 62; laws relating to, 67; decline of, 77
Brancovano, Constantine, 70
Branković, George, builds Semendria, 293; in Montenegro, 367
Branković, Paul, 254
Branković, Vouk, traitor of Kossovo, 288
Bratiano, John, 96, 111
Brigandage, 199, 225, 302, 307
Bucovina, cession of, 81
Bulgari, their origin, 123; their customs, 125
Bulgarian atrocities, 207, 209; constitution, 216; literature, under Simeon, 141; under John Alexander, 187; revival of, 203

C.

Cæsar, Julius, 4
Cantacuzene, Scherban, 69
Cantacuzene, Stephen, 73
Cantemir, Demetrius, 70
Caracalla, edict of, 21; victory of, 23
"Carmen Sylva," 109
Catherine II. of Russia, her Roumanian policy, 79, 81; writes to Montenegro, 405
Cattaro, Romans at, 356; capture of, 417; revolt at, 460
Česlav, Servian prince, 145, 256
Cetinje, becomes Montenegrin capital, 371; captured by Turks, 389, 391, 399
Charles I., King of Roumania, elected prince, 107; marries,

INDEX. 471

109 ; reforms army, 112 ; at Plevna, 114 ; proclaimed king, 117
Cimpulung, old Wallachian capital, 48
Claudius, Roman Emperor, 24
Clement, Metropolitan, 227
Constantine, Roman Emperor, his bridge, 27
Constantine and Methodius, apostles of the Balkans, 132, 252
Constantine, Bulgarian Czar, 180
Cotiso, 5
Courtea d'Ardges, cathedral of, 46, 69
Couza, Prince of Roumania, 104 ; his rule, 105 ; deposed, 107
Cristić, Servian Minister, 348
Crnoievič, George I., 379, 380
Crnoievič, George II., 381
Crnoievič, Stephen I., 366-9
Crnoievič, Stephen II., 380, 381

D.

Dacia, old name of Roumania, 1
"Dacia Aureliani," 25, 121
Dacians, earliest inhabitants of Roumania, 1 ; first conflict with Romans, 2 ; their exploits, 5 ; subdued by Trajan, 12 ; their characteristics, 16
Dalmatia, union with Servia, 261 ; assigned to Austria, 412
Dandolo, Venetian doge, 172
Danilo, Archbishop, Serb historian, 266, 269, 280
Danilo I. of Montenegro, first hereditary *Vladika*, 391 ; his massacre of the Turks, 396 ; his victory at Tsarevlaz, 398 ; his death, 400
Danilo II., last *Vladika*, divests himself of ecclesiastical power, 438 ; his victories over the Turks, 439 ; his army reforms, 440 ; his unpopularity, 445 ; the "Code Danilo," 447 ; his assassination, 448

Darinka, Princess of Montenegro, 438, 458
Decebalus, Dacian king, his victories over the Romans, 6 ; his defeat, 10 ; his death, 12
Deljan, Peter, revolt of, 161
Desnica, old Serb capital, 254
Despots, Serb, in Hungary, 303
Dioclea residence of Serb rulers, 258 ; Roman remains at, 356
Dobroslav, Serb prince, 257
Dobrudža, The, 2, 116, 124
Domitian, wars with Dacians, 6 ; his road, 9
Dondukoff - Korsakoff, Prince, Russian Commissary in Bulgaria, 215
Dragoche, 35
Dromichætes, Getic king, 3
Dulcigno, demonstration at, 465
Dušan, Czar Stephen, rebels against his father, 270 ; succeeds to throne, 271 ; his vast empire, 274, 278 ; his code, 278 ; marches on Constantinople, 281 ; dies, 282 ; his memory invoked, 225

E.

English influence in Balkans, in the time of Michael the Brave, 54 ; appointment of British Consul at Bucharest, 84 ; Lord Palmerston and Roumania, 98 ; sympathy with Bulgaria, 202 ; Mr. Gladstone and Bulgaria, 209 ; Sir W. White and Bulgaria, 224 ; England and Servia, 323, 336 ; England, ally of Montenegro, 418 ; gratitude of Montenegro, 465

F.

Ferdinand I., Prince of Bulgaria, is offered the throne, 235 ; his accession, 236 ; his character, 236 ; his relations with Stambuloff, 238 ; plots against him, 241 ; his marriage, 242 ; birth

of an heir, 243; dismisses Stambuloff, 244
Flanders, Count of, 107
French Revolution, effect of, on Balkans, 83

G.

Gabriel Roman, Bulgarian Czar, 156
Galitzin, 79
Gepidæ, 28
German, Montenegrin *Vladika*, 384
Getæ, earliest inhabitants of Roumania, 1; attacked by Philip of Macedon, 2; defeat Lysimachus, 3
Ghika, Gregory I., 78
Ghika, Gregory II., 89
Giurgevo, 48, 100
Gladstone, Mr., and Bulgaria, 209; on Montenegro, 353, 370; gratitude of Montenegrins to, 418, 465
Golescou, Constantine, 94
Golescou, General, 106
Goths, invade Roumania, 23; repulsed by Constantine, 27; ravage Bulgaria, 122
Gradina, Trajan's tablet, near, 9
Grahovo, battle of, 446
Greek War of Independence, 86

H.

Hadji Mustapha, "Mother of the Serbs," 309
Hadrian, 22
Helis, 3
Heraclius, defeats Avars, 29, 124; encourages Serbs, 250, 358
Herodotus, on Getæ, 1, 15; on Illyrians, 119
Herzegovina, The, united to Servia, 278; conquered by Turks, 370; insurrection of, 205, 461; occupied by Austria, 345, 467
Hungarians, invade Roumania, 30; invade Bulgaria, 136, 144; wars with Servia, 269, 277; claim Bulgaria, 298

Huns, invade Roumania, 28; their King Attila, 28; invade Bulgaria, 122
Hunyad, John, "White Knight of Wallachia," 293; aids Serbs, 295

I.

Illyrians, old inhabitants of Bulgaria, 119; traces of their language, 125; on Adriatic coast, 250; defeated by Romans, 356
Innocent III., 170
Ivajlo, 181
Ivan the Black, of Montenegro, makes Cetinje his capital, 371; founds printing-press, 372; his letter to the Doge, 374

J.

Jahja, "Count of Montenegro," 389
Janissaries at Belgrade, 309; defeated, 312
Jassy, becomes Moldavian capital, 48; printing-press at, 68; University of, 106
John Alexander, Bulgarian Czar, 185
John "the Terrible," of Moldavia, 49
Joseph II., his scheme for partition of Turkey, 82; helps Serbs, 306
Julia, Princess of Servia, 336
Julianus, 7
Justinian, "Restorer of Dacia," 29
Justinian II. wars with Bulgaria, 126

K.

Kalafat, Russians at, 100; bombarded, 113
Kaliman I., Bulgarian Czar, 180
Kaliman II., Bulgarian Czar, 180
Kalojan, Bulgarian Czar, his correspondence with the Pope, 170; captures Baldwin, 173; his death, 174

INDEX. 473

Kara George, *see* Black George
Karageorgević, Alexander, Prince of Servia, 325; conspiracy against, 328; deposed, 330
Karageorgević, Peter, Servian Pretender, 339, 348
Karakal, 23
Kaulbars, Major-General, 233
Kossovo, battle of, 38, 287, 362
Krum, Bulgarian chief, invades Roumania, 30; captures Sofia, 128; kills Greek emperor, 129; besieges Constantinople, 130
Kumani, invade Roumania, 31; in Bulgaria, 163
Kurt, or Kuvrat, Bulgarian chief, 30, 124

L

azar, Servian Czar, tributary to Turks, 286; killed at Kossovo, 288
Lazarević, Stephen, vassal of Sultan, 290; fortifies Belgrade, 291
Leo, Greek Emperor, 136
Lombards, invasion of, 29
Lysimachus, 3

M.

Macedonia, part of first Bulgarian Empire, 152; in treaty of San Stefano, 211; Bulgarian Bishops in, 240; Serbs in, 270
Marie-Louise, Princess of Bulgaria, 242
Martial, on Dacians, 8
Mavrocordato, Constantine, 77
Mavrocordato, Nicholas, 73, 77
Mavroghéni, Nicholas, 82
Michael, Bulgarian Czar, defeats Serbs, 184, 269
Michael III., Greek Emperor, 132
Michael Obrenović III., Prince of Servia, his first reign, 324; his second reign, 332; his reforms, 334; assassination, 338
Michael the Brave of Wallachia, reign of, 51; annexes Transylvania and Moldavia, 54; collapse of his "big Roumania," 55; his death, 58
Midhat Pasha, 203
Mihnea, Radou, 62
Milan Obrenović II., Prince of Servia, 324
Milan Obrenović IV., Prince of Servia, 340; declares war on Turkey, 342; proclaimed king, 346; attacks Bulgaria, 224, 348; abdicates, 349
Milosh Obrenović I., origin of, 316; "supreme chief," 318; recognised hereditary prince, 321; his autocratic rule, 321; grants constitution, 322; abdicates, 324; returns, 330
Mirko, "sword of Montenegro," 445, 446, 450, 453, 454, 455
Mirtschea the Old, of Wallachia, 36, 38, 39
Mœsia, present Bulgaria, 23, 120
Mohammed I., 292
Mohammed II., 42, 294, 369
Moldavia founded, 36
Montenegrin cap, 363; education, 459; literature, 435, 451; military organisation, 440, 455-457
Montenegro, origin of name, 353; printing-press in, 372, 384, 434, 468; its elective *Vladikas*, 383; its hereditary *Vladikas*, 392

N.

Napoleon I., Balkan policy of, 85; relations with Montenegro, 413-417
Napoleon III., supports Roumania, 102; friendship with Montenegro, 455
Natalie, Queen of Servia, 349
Nemanja, Stephen, unites Bosnia with Servia, 258; his interview with Barbarossa, 260; abdicates, 261
Nicholas I., Prince of Montenegro, his education, 451; his writings, 451; his first Turkish

war, 452; his father's death, 455; his military reforms, 455; his ministers, 458; his second Turkish war, 461; captures Nikšić, 461; builds roads, 466; celebrates bicentenary of his dynasty, 468
Nicopolis, battle of, 38, 189, 290
Novibazar, Austrians in, 345, 467

O.

Obilić, Milosh, 289
Obradović, Serb poet, 306
Obrenović, *see* Michael, Milan, and Milosh
Octavius, *see* Augustus
Oltenitza, 100
Omar Pasha, in Roumania, 100; in Montenegro, 439
Omladina, Servian Society, 339
Omortag, Bulgarian chief, 130
Orsova, Roman road near, 9
Osman Pasha, defends Plevna, 116
Ostrog, Montenegrin monastery, defence of, 453
Ovid, in the Balkans, 5, 17, 121

P.

Panitza, Major, conspiracy of, 241
Paris, Convention of, 103
Paris, Treaty of, 101, 327
Pasvanoglu, of Vidin, brigand chief, 84, 201, 310
Patzinakitai, invade Roumania, 31; and Bulgaria, 145; their settlements, 163
Peace of Adrianople, 91, 320
Peace of Belgrade, 79, 201, 305, 401
Peace, First, of Bucharest (1812), 85, 316
Peace, Second, of Bucharest (1886), 226
Peace of Campo Formio, 412
Peace of Jassy, 83
Peace of Kutchuk-Kaïnardji, 80
Peace of Pressburg, 413

Peace of Tilsit, 85, 201, 415
Peter, Bulgarian Czar, 142
Peter I. of Montenegro, his character, 408; his successes over Turks, 410; his war with the French, 414; rejects Napoleon's overtures, 416; captures Cattaro, 418; his code, 421; his death, 422
Peter II. of Montenegro, his accession, 424; abolishes office of civil governor, 431; establishes senate, 432; restores the press, 434; his writings, 435; his shrine, 437
Peter the Great of Russia, enters Roumania, 72; sends envoy to Montenegro, 397; subsidises Montenegro, 399
Phanariotes, origin of their name, 73; their political influence in Roumania, 73; their luxury, 75; their bad influence, 76; their fall, 89; their ecclesiastical power in Bulgaria, 197; struggle against them, 205
Philip of Macedon, in Roumania, 2; in Bulgaria, 120
Philippopolis, capital of South Bulgaria, outbreak of revolution at, 223
Pius IX. and Montenegro, 454
Plautus, Getic slaves in, 3
Pliny the Elder on Getæ, 1
Pliny the Younger on Dacian war, 11
Podgorica, ceded to Montenegro, 464
Pomaks, Bulgarian Mussulmans, 195
Prêslav, old Bulgarian capital, described, 139
Pristina, old Serb capital, 259, 264

R.

Raeova, battle of, 43
Radou Negrou, founds Wallachia, 35
Radoulescou, John Heliade, Roumanian writer, 94, 98

INDEX. 475

Ragusa, outlet of Balkan trade, 177 ; the "South Slavonic Athens," 195 ; old Illyrian capital, 250; its merchants encouraged by Dusan, 279 ; besieged by Montenegrins, 414
Ristić, Servian Regent, 341, 349
Romans, in Bulgaria, 121 ; in Roumania, 4, 19; traces of their language there, 22 ; they evacuate Roumania, 25
Rosetti, Constantine, 96, 111
Roumanian language, 22 ; literature, 68 ; press, 94
Roumelia, Eastern, under Berlin treaty, 213; its union with Bulgaria, 222 ; called South Bulgaria, 226
Russians, in Bulgaria, 202, 215, 221, 224, 230, 239; in Montenegro, 399, 402, 405, 413, 420, 457, 467; in Roumania, 70, 92, 113
Russo-Turkish wars (of 1711), 70, 72 ; (of 1736), 78 ; (of 1768), 79 ; (of 1787), 82 ; (of 1807), 85 ; (of 1828), 91 ; (of 1854), 99 ; (of 1877), 113, 210, 343

S.

Samuel, Bulgarian Czar, his accession, 151 ; extent of his empire, 152 ; his wars with Basil II., 154 ; destroys Dioclea, 359; his death, 156
San Sefano, treaty of, and Roumania, 116; and Bulgaria, 211 ; and Servia, 345; and Montenegro, 464
Sarmizegethusa, Dacian capital, 7, 11, 17
Sava, Saint, 260
Sava, Vladika of Montenegro, 400 ; visits Russia, 402 ; ousted by Stephen the Little, 403 ; restored, 406 ; dies, 407
Selim III., his treatment of the Janissaries, 309, 310
Simeon, Bulgarian Czar, 134 ; extent of his empire, 138 ;
devastates Servia, 137, 255 ; defeats Hungarians, 31 ; his titles, 139; his palace, 139; patronises learning, 141 ; his death, 142
Šišman, of Trnovo, 145
Šišman, John III., of Vidin, 187
Šišman, Michael, of Vidin, 183
Skanderbeg, Albanian hero, 368
Skodra, or Scutari in Albania, capital of Praevalitana, 355 ; divided West from East of Europe, 356 ; Balsha's capital, 362 ; convention of, 454
Slavs, first mentioned in Bulgaria, 122 ; their origin and character, 123 ; contrasted with old Bulgarians, 125 ; enter Illyria, 358
Slivnitza, battle of, 225, 348
Sofia, captured by Krum, 128 ; conquered by Bulgarians, 168 ; residence of Turkish governor, 195 ; present Bulgarian capital, 247
Stambuloff, Bulgarian statesman, his efforts against Turks, 206 ; Speaker of *Sobranje,* 223 ; appeals to Bulgarians, 229 ; one of the Regents, 231 ; Prime Minister, 237 ; his character, 237 ; his Turkish policy, 239 ; orders execution of Panitza, 241 ; his relations with Prince Ferdinand, 244 ; his dismissal, 245 ; his murder, 246
Stanicha, story of, 374
Stephen the Great of Moldavia, 40
Stephen VI. of Servia, 263
Stephen VII. (Uroš III.), 269 ; overthrows Bulgarian Empire, 184, 270
Stephen the Little, or *Mali,* imposture of, in Montenegro, 403
Stirbeiu Barbe, 99, 103
Stoiloff, M., present Bulgarian Premier, 245
Suceava, old Moldavian capital, 48, 81
Svetslav, Bulgarian Czar, 183

T.

Tacitus, on Dacians, 6
Takovo, 318
Tapæ, battles at, 7, 10
Tartars, 33
Telec, 128
Tennyson on Montenegro, 353
Terence, Getic slaves in, 3
Terterij I., Bulgarian Czar, 182
Terterij II., 183
Tervel, 127
Theodoric, 124
Thrace, 120
Thucydides, on Getæ, 2
Tirgovischtea, Wallachian capital, 48
Trajan, in Dacia, 8; his bridge, 11, 22; his column, 13
Transylvania, Roumanians in, 19, 118; annexed to Hungary, 31; conquered by Michael the Brave, 54; revolts, 56
Trnovo, old Bulgarian capital, "Baldwin's Tower" at, 173; Church of 40 Martyrs, 176; captured by Turks, 188
Tsarevlaz, battle of, 398
Turnu-Severin, Trajan's bridge at, 11
Tvartko, Stephen, King of Bosnia, 284

U.

Ubicini, historian of Roumania, 98
Uroš, Stephen, of Servia, 260
Uroš V., of Servia, 283
Utza, story of, 47

V.

Vacarescou, Roumanian poet, 101
Vassili, Montenegrin Prince-Bishop, 401

Varna, battle of, 199, 294
Velbužd, battle of, 184, 270
Venice, confers title on Dušan, 276; at war with Montenegrins, 365; Venetian marriages of Montenegrin rulers, 375, 380, 381; loses Dalmatia, 412
Vespasian, 6
Vidin, an independent principality, 183; capture of, 262
Vlad "the Impaler," in Wallachia, 40
Vladikas, Montenegrin Prince-Bishops, elective, 383; hereditary, 392; last of, 438
Vladimirescou, Toudor, 87
Voukačin, Servian usurper, 284
Vulković, Dr., assassination of, 242

W.

Waldemar, Prince of Denmark, refuses Bulgarian throne, 234
Wallachia, foundation of, 35
"Wallachian Vespers," 52
Wallachs, origin of, 32

Y.

Ypsilanti, Alexander, 87
Ypsilanti, Demetrius, 88

Z.

Žabljak, old Montenegrin capital, 368; abandoned, 371; seized by the Koutchi, 427; ceded to Montenegro, 464
Zankoff, Bulgarian Liberal politician, 220; Russophil leader, 225, 229
Zeta, principality of, 359
Župans, Servian chiefs, 251, 358

www.ingramcontent.com/pod-product-compliance
Lightning Source LLC
Chambersburg PA
CBHW020831020526
44114CB00040B/561